DANGEROUS PASSAGE

HEALTH, SOCIETY, AND POLICY
a series edited by Sheryl Ruzek and Irving Kenneth Zola

DANGEROUS PASSAGE

The Social Control of Sexuality in Women's Adolescence

CONSTANCE A. NATHANSON

Temple University Press
Philadelphia

Temple University Press, Philadelphia 19122
Copyright © 1991 by Temple University. All rights reserved
Published 1991
Printed in the United States of America

The paper used in this publication meets the minimum
requirements of American National Standard for Information
Sciences—Permanence of Paper for Printed Library Materials,
ANSI Z39.48-1984 ⊗

Library of Congress Cataloging-in-Publication Data
Nathanson, Constance A.
Dangerous passage : the social control of
sexuality in women's adolescence / Constance A. Nathanson.
p.   cm. — (Health, society, and policy)
Includes bibliographical references and index.
ISBN 0-87722-824-8 (alk. paper)
1. Teenage girls—United States—Sexual behavior—History.
2. Sexual ethics—United States—History.   3. Teenage pregnancy—
United States—History.   4. Social control—History.   I. Title.
II. Series.
HQ27.5.N38   1991
306.7'0835'2—dc20   90-20580
                                                        CIP

Chapter 10 is adapted from Constance A. Nathanson,
"Family Planning and Contraceptive Responsibility,"
in Stuart F. Spicker, William B. Bondeson, and H. Tristram Engelhardt, Jr., eds.,
The Contraceptive Ethos: Reproductive Rights and Responsibilities
(Dordrecht, Holland: D. Reidel Publishing Company, 1987), pp. 183–97.
© 1987 by D. Reidel Publishing Company.
Reprinted by permission of Kluwer Academic Publishers.

For Kate, John, and Daniel
GRACEFUL NAVIGATORS

Society [is] a house with rooms and corridors in which passage from one to another is dangerous. Danger lies in transitional states, simply because transition is neither one state nor the next, it is undefinable. The person who must pass from one to another is [herself] in danger and emanates danger to others.
—Mary Douglas, *Purity and Danger*

Contents

Acknowledgments

I HAVE the good fortune to have been a member of the faculty of the Department of Population Dynamics at the Johns Hopkins University School of Hygiene and Public Health since 1973. Although my own research interests initially lay elsewhere, the first half of my tenure at Hopkins coincided with the beginnings of intense interest in adolescent fertility in the United States, fueled to a profound degree by the work of Melvin Zelnik and John F. Kantner, both professors (now retired) in the Department of Population Dynamics. More than I am sure they were aware, the combination of scholarly integrity, skepticism, and humor with which these two men approached their subject both sparked my own interest and suggested to me that there might be more at stake in the issue of adolescent pregnancy than immediately met the eye.

A National Science Foundation Visiting Professorship for Women gave me a year at the Population Studies Center of the University of Pennsylvania largely free of academic duties, and made it possible to get the book under way. I am grateful to NSF, to Frank F. Furstenberg, Jr., and Samuel Preston, who helped to arrange for my sojourn at Penn, and to my colleagues at the Population Studies Center, who contributed in many ways to the productivity as well as the pleasure of my stay in Philadelphia.

Work on this book was also supported in part by NIH Grant LM 04655 from the National Library of Medicine, by NIH Grant P30 HD06268 to the Hopkins Population Center from the National Institute of Child Health and Development, and by the William and Flora Hewlett Foundation.

I owe a very large debt of thanks to all of my colleagues in the Department of Population Dynamics, who put up with my frequent absences of body, as well as of mind, over the five years when this book was being written. They, and most especially my department chair, W. Henry Mosley, provided me with a personally, as well as intellectually, supportive environment. Joy Dryfoos, Jeannie Rosoff, and Richard Lincoln were generous in talking to me about their experiences at the Alan Guttmacher Institute, and I hope they will forgive me for interpreting events in my own way. Nan Astone, Elizabeth Fee, John F. Kantner, Donna Morrison, Dawn Upchurch, and Irving Zola read parts or all of the manuscript and offered both encouragement and valuable comments. I am particularly grateful, in addition, to Kathy Peiss, who commented extensively on the historical portions of my work; I have attended very carefully to her remarks, and the faults that remain are entirely my own. Sheryl Ruzek, one of my series editors at Temple University Press, read several drafts of the manuscript and gave me invaluable conceptual help over many difficult spots. Both she and Janet Francendese have been everything editors should be: patient, supportive, and ready with assistance whenever assistance was needed. Terri Singer, the Hopkins Population Center librarian, together with Tobey Harvey, did a highly professional job of reference checking; and Connie Stewart, my secretary at Johns Hopkins, with eleventh-hour assistance from Ruth Skarda, fought with WordPerfect and triumphed to produce draft after draft of chapter after chapter.

My mother, Elizabeth Linn Murray, who read a very early version of the manuscript and forced me to recognize the true scope of my own intentions, contributed in large part to the shape that this book has finally taken. My children, to whom the book is dedicated, kept me going with a judicious combination of impatience and enthusiasm. And finally, my colleague and friend, Marshall H. Becker, gave me unfailing encouragement and support over the rough places as well as the smooth.

PART ONE *Introduction*

SEXUALITY AND SOCIAL CONTROL
Chapter 1

> One could mention . . . all those social controls, cropping up at the end of the last century, which screened the sexuality of couples, parents and children, dangerous and endangered adolescents—undertaking to protect separate and forewarn, signaling perils everywhere, awakening people's attention, calling for diagnoses, piling up reports, organizing therapies. These sites radiated discourses aimed at sex, intensifying people's awareness of it as a constant danger, and this in turn created a further incentive to talk about it (Foucault, 1978:30–31).

WITH these words Michel Foucault alerts us to the possibility that talk about sex may signal not simply the liberation of modern man and woman from Victorian repression and hypocrisy, but an expansion and diffusion of sexual social controls. The devastating political consequences that now follow from journalistic revelations of sexual "misconduct"—revelations that a few years ago would have been considered not only taboo, but even irrelevant to the evaluation of competence for political office—are only the most obvious examples of the power, as well as the pervasiveness, of sexual discourse in contemporary industrialized societies.

For the past twenty years in the United States, single, adolescent women have been a principal target of sexual knowledge and intervention. During this period, "teenage pregnancy" emerged and gained recognition as a serious public problem.[1] Publicly funded contraceptive services were made available for the first time to unmarried young women. Their rights to contraception and, within limits, abortion without parental consent were upheld by the U.S. Supreme Court. These changes have, however, been accompanied by unremitting controversy around the appropriateness of both contraception and abortion as solutions to the adolescent pregnancy problem, together with mounting advocacy for the alternative of sexual abstinence prior to marriage. Virtually every moral, social, and medical philosophy of adolescent pregnancy's cause

3

and cure has been incorporated into one or more organized programs for its prevention or the amelioration of its consequences: the number of these programs, large and small, defies enumeration. The problem of adolescent pregnancy has demonstrated remarkable staying power in the public-policy arena. However, its social location in the adolescent population (as a generic or a predominantly black problem), its perceived connection with other social problems (school dropout, drugs and alcohol, poverty, welfare dependency, child abuse, AIDS), and the relative emphasis placed on negative personal, as compared with public, consequences of adolescent childbearing have undergone a variety of shifts over time. Finally, there has been, in Foucault's words, a "piling up" of reports, an explosion of popular and professional literature covering every conceivable aspect of adolescent sexuality and reproduction.

What is, and has been, going on here? Are the level and sustained intensity of these activities readily accounted for by a sudden, massive increase in the magnitude of the problem? If not, as I argue, then where is an explanation to be found for the sheer level of attention, for the shifts in problem definition and location, and for the almost exclusive focus on young women? And how new, after all, *are* adolescent sexuality and reproduction as public problems? Women, adolescents, and the control of fertility were, Foucault argues, being consolidated as "privileged objects" of sexual knowledge and intervention early in the nineteenth century (1978:105); adolescent pregnancy would appear to build directly on this legacy, merging these three privileged objects into a single target: the sexually unorthodox and reproductively uncontrolled adolescent woman.

In the existing literature on adolescent pregnancy the foregoing questions are seldom raised.[2] That "children having children" *is* a problem (and that this phraseology appropriately describes the problem) is taken as a given; the questions generated by this framework are the staples of classic social problem analysis: Who does it? Why do they do it? How can we get them to stop? There is no basis within these terms of reference for raising, let alone answering, questions regarding the construction of adolescent pregnancy as a social problem, its historical antecedents, how and why it entered the contemporary public stage, and why the solutions recommended have taken one form rather than another. In this chapter I propose an alternative perspective in which these are the central questions, and I suggest some directions in which the answers may be found.

PREGNANCY makes sex visible; it converts private behavior into public behavior. Adolescent pregnancy is the curiously enigmatic label adopted by late twentieth-century Americans to signal and demand attention to a centuries-old problem: the departure of single young women from age- and gender-based norms of sexual propriety. These norms define adolescent women as children; they define the period between women's puberty and marriage as one of asexuality at best and invisible sexuality at worst; and they define legally sanctioned marriage between members of the opposite sex as the sole approved location for sexual activity, pregnancy, and childbearing. The newspaper headlines, television screens, and magazine covers that bombard us with evidence of how frequently these norms are violated give equal testimony to the liveliness of the norms themselves: "Morality and immorality," as Kai T. Erikson suggests, "meet at the public scaffold (or, nowadays, in the mass media), and it is during this meeting that the line between them is drawn" (1966:12). The "immorality" to which the adolescent pregnancy label draws attention is not primarily reproductive, but sexual. Pregnancy can be terminated by abortion, but there is no action that can eliminate the association of pregnancy with sexual activity: It is its evocation of nonmarital sexuality rather than nonmarital childbearing that gives the adolescent pregnancy label its symbolic force.

In the preface to a new edition of his book *Folk Devils and Moral Panics* Stanley Cohen distinguishes between the study of actors and audiences, of actions and reactions, of devils and of the panics they create (1980:iii). With the exception of Chapter 10, where I describe some results from research on the sexual and reproductive strategies of single young women in Maryland, the focus of this book is on audiences and their reactions: the young women themselves will make but fleeting appearances. There are a number of reasons for this emphasis. First, and perhaps most important, is that the actors—sexually active and pregnant or parenting young women—have in recent years had the stage virtually to themselves. Audience reaction has been treated as unproblematic: "I have never heard an adult argue that adolescents should bear children" (Trussell, 1988:270). The perspective reflected in this statement has generated a body of significant work on the origins of the behavior in question (see, e.g., Hayes, 1987). Nevertheless, it begs the question of why, given the presumption of universal disapprobation, the propriety of adolescents bearing children waxes and wanes so remarkably over time and across cultures as a topic of public interest and a stimulus to public demands for intervention. A second reason for focusing on audiences instead of actors is that sexually unorthodox adolescent women, unlike homosexuals and even prostitutes, have played little conscious role in the creation of their own identity as a sexual category. As James Trussell's remark implies, the contours and characteristics of the adolescent pregnancy problem have been defined by adults. This is hardly surprising. Pregnancy itself is a fleeting identity, few adolescent women have financial or political resources independent of their parents, and there has, at least in the United States up to the present time, been little incentive for either young women or their parents to band together and risk calling more negative public attention to adolescent sexuality than it already receives. Private "cultures of resistance"—for example, the underground exchange of knowledge about birth control and abortion when these actions were illegal or taboo—have existed historically and will spring up whenever the need arises.[3] Their very privacy, however, contributes less to an image of resistance to the norm than to one of acceptance that is accompanied, from an audience perspective, by the gratifying excitement of evasion. Furthermore, private cultures of resistance are, by their very nature, poorly documented. Over the past century and a half, a large body of evidence has accumulated that testifies to the ideologies of and instrumentalities advocated or employed by individuals who concerned themselves with the management and control of young women between puberty and marriage, a task synonymous in the minds of most observers with the management of young women's sexuality. There is, by comparison, relatively little evidence of the sexual strategies adopted by young women themselves.[4] For all of these reasons, the primary focus of this book is on audiences: lay advocates and reformers, politicians, physicians, professors, judges, social workers, and journalists who have pronounced upon and proposed solutions for the problem posed to American society by the sexuality of single adolescent women.

This book departs from current literature on adolescent pregnancy in a second, even more fundamental way: The sexuality of single young women is treated as a problem with a past, a history the details of which may possibly illuminate the present. To paraphrase an anthropologist's comments on the value of the history of science for understanding the cultural origins of current scientific ideas, it is difficult to see how our current ideas about how and why adolescent pregnancy is a problem and what should be done about it are infused by our own cultural assumptions, as well as our own social structural imperatives. It is easier to see how ideas and programs from the past, ideas that now seem wrong and programs that now seem ill-conceived, might have been affected by the cultural assumptions and structural constraints of an earlier time (Martin, 1987:27). The problematic character of female adolescence had been recognized by the mid-nineteenth century, and the essence of the problem was defined as the containment of sex. To gain perspective on our present ideas and actions, it is necessary to see their organic relationship to conceptions that began to emerge at least 150 years ago, conceptions about the fundamental nature of the adolescent girl, about how her problematic sexuality should be managed, and about the threat to public order that her sexuality represented.

However, the uses of history in this book go considerably beyond a search for the roots of the present in the past. Ultimately, this is a work of sociology, not of history. Although it is intended to contribute to the understanding of current policies and policy outcomes in the area of adolescent pregnancy, it has a larger purpose as well: to add to knowledge concerning processes of social control as they have been and are being applied to women's private sexual and reproductive behavior. To achieve this level of generalizability, it is necessary to go beyond the study of a single case. Comparison with historical parallels—the management of "wayward" girls in the late nineteenth and early twentieth centuries, the antiprostitution, anti–venereal disease campaigns of the same period, the "sexual revolution" of the 1920s—has several objectives in addition to the one of providing perspective on current problems and conflicts. First, comparison makes it possible to identify commonalities in conceptions of deviance and in the processes of control that underlie differences between past and present in rhetoric, in substance, and in structural context. Second, study of these differences shows how strategies of control have been adapted to changes over time in social structure and ideology—for example, to the rise of the medical profession as a center of cultural authority over the management of social problems and to changes in socially acceptable roles for women. Finally, comparison may lead to the generation of hypotheses concerning the circumstances—demographic, social, economic—under which individual sexual activities become translated into symbols of social upheaval.

Within the past two decades issues of sexuality and social control have received a marked increase in theoretical attention from a variety of social scientists as well as historians. So far, these lines of scholarship have not converged. Development of a framework within which to address the questions I outlined above requires an effort toward the integration of these two theoretical domains, and it is to that effort that I now turn.

CONCEPTUALIZATIONS OF SEXUALITY

A basic premise on which this work is based is that sexuality is both historically and culturally relative. Biological sexuality represents a "set of potentialities" that take their form and meaning from the social context in which these potentialities are realized (Padgug, 1979:9). In a recent summary of conceptual approaches to sexuality, Jeffrey Weeks (1981) has contrasted the "essentialist" view that has dominated twentieth-century historical (as well as sociological) literature with the challenges to that view presented by the work of such authors as John H. Gagnon and William Simon (1973), Kenneth Plummer (1975), and Foucault.[5] The essentialist framework envisions sex "as an overpowering force in the individual that shapes not only the personal but the social life as well. It is seen as a driving, instinctual force, whose characteristics are built into the biology of the human animal, which shapes human institutions and whose will must force its way out" (1981:2). Set against this overpowering natural force, and keeping it in check, are the countervailing forces of social control, "which exist either in laws and mores or in appropriate internalized repressions learned in early socialization" (Gagnon and Simon, 1973:11). The image these words suggest of an imperative biology pressing continuously against the ramparts of civilization pervades both past and present literature on the management of female adolescence. Nonmarital pregnancy represents, in this context, the ultimate loss of control: by a man driven by his lust, by the girl's mother who failed in her job of supervision, by the young woman who was overcome by passion (or drugs or alcohol or lack of ambition), or by the community in which early sex and childbearing were insufficiently stigmatized.

Against the essentialist perspective are arrayed a variety of critics: sociologists working within a symbolic-interactionist framework (principally Gagnon and Simon); the psychoanalysts Jacques Lacan (1978) and Juliet Mitchell (1975); Foucault; Weeks himself; and a group of anthropologists, represented most recently in two edited volumes by Sherry B. Ortner and Harriet Whitehead (1981) and Jane F. Collier and Sylvia J. Yanagisako (1987). Despite their different theoretical starting points, there is substantial convergence among these critics. Uniformly they reject the idea of sex as an autonomous biological force. There are, however, differences of emphasis. Gagnon and Simon focus on the processes of socialization by which *individuals* learn how to act sexually: the internalization of sexual scripts. Foucault is interested in the historical uses of sexuality as an instrument for the regulation of *societies*. The anthropologists pay attention to culture-specific and, in particular, to gender-specific constructions of sexuality, and are the most radical in their rejection even of a biological substrate of sexual "potentialities."

> Having recognized our model of biological differences [between the sexes] as a particular cultural mode of thinking about relations between people, we should be able to question the "biological facts" of sex themselves. We expect that our questioning of the presumably biological core of gender will eventually lead to the rejection of any dichotomy between sex and gender as biological and cultural facts and will open up the way for an analysis of the symbolic and social processes by which both are constructed in relation to each other (Yanagisako and Collier, 1987:42).

There are, in other words, no "natural" differences between the sexes; all differences, including the biological, are socially constructed.

In addition to their rejection of sexuality as a natural force, what links all of the antiessentialist critics "is a recognition of the social and historical sources of sexual definitions" (Weeks, 1981:4). (There has been far less agreement, or clarity, on what those sources *are*, a point to which I return below.) Historians place the emergence of the "modern" Western concept of sexuality at around the beginning of the nineteenth century (Vicinus notes that the Oxford English Dictionary dates the first use of the word, "sexuality," from 1800) (see, e.g., Foucault, 1978; Padgug, 1979; Vicinus, 1982; Weeks, 1981). Central to this concept is the conversion of more or less disparate biological and behavioral elements into fundamental defining characteristics of the self. "Since the nineteenth century [sex] has been seen as the cause and 'truth' of our being. It defines us socially and morally; its release or proper functioning can be a factor in health, energy, activity; its frustration is a cause of ill-health, social unorthodoxy, even madness" (Weeks, 1981:12).

In particular, recent historical research has suggested that Western cultural constructions of male and female as incommensurate categories, grounded in the "facts" of biological sex, are a product of "the new discourse of the body that dominated the nineteenth century, a discourse that not only attributed a new set of social, political, and cultural meanings to bodies but also placed them at the very center of social, political, and cultural signification" (Gallagher and Laqueur, 1987:vii). The biologization of bodies—and, by extension, of roles and personalities—was especially coercive in its application to women: "Women's reproductive biology, now conceived as a system opposite to men's, is increasingly seen as the key to women's nature" (viii). The operative word in this sentence is reproductive. At the same time that the essence of women became identified with their reproductive functions, their sexuality was being defined out of existence: "The new opposition of male and female turns into an opposition of desire and nondesire" (viii). With relatively little effort this logic was extended to create two further sexual categories: the normal nondesirous woman—the respectable mother, and the abnormal desirous woman—the prostitute. The continuing power of this latter dichotomy is evident not only in its effective use by conservatives of the New Right—the aborting woman, the welfare mother, the promiscuous teenage girl are but the prostitute clothed in modern dress—it is also reflected in the struggle, and failure, of feminists to agree on a positive concept of female sexuality separate from reproduction (see, e.g., Shulman, 1980; Person, 1980; Snitow, Stansell, and Thompson, 1983; Vance, 1984; Rich, 1986; Ehrenreich, 1989).

The critical insight shared by Foucault with the symbolic interactionists was that categorization was not a politically neutral activity. Categories imply the existence of rules by which individuals may be labeled as worthy or unworthy of inclusion. Thus, the possibility of deviance—rule breaking—is inherent in the process of categorization: "The very process of discussing and analyzing sexuality labels it and draws attention to the personal and societal distinctions between the normal and the deviant" (Vicinus, 1982:136). Furthermore, the rules by which categories are defined are themselves the outcome of political activity, activity that Howard S. Becker described as moral enterprise. "Wherever rules are created and applied, we should be alive to the possible presence of an enterprising individual or group. Their activities can properly be called *moral enterprise,* for what they are enterprising about is the creation of a new fragment of the moral constitution of society, its code of right and wrong" (1963:145). Foucault's essential point is that the nineteenth century can best be understood as a period of increasing moral enterprise organized around questions of sex. Physicians, psychiatrists, educators, lawyers, and judges expanded their power over sex not, as has been commonly believed, by suppression, but by incitement and organization. "One had to speak of [sex] as of a thing to be not simply condemned or tolerated but managed, inserted into systems of utility, regulated for the greater good of all, made to function according to an optimum. Sex was not something one simply judged; it was a thing one administered" (1978:24). Knowledge is power, and the production of knowledge about sex became a major instrument in its control. Foucault's recognition that sexual social control may appear in the guise of incitement to discourse as well as denial and censorship should, as Weeks has pointed out, lead us to question not only the idea of Victorian repression, but the assumption of contemporary liberation as well. Rule making about sex—categorizing bodies, classifying practices, labeling "offenders"—is no older than the most recent Supreme Court decision regulating women's access to abortion.

The conceptualization of sexuality in general, and of gender-based definitions of sexuality in particular, as social, historical, and cultural constructs; the identification of what are peculiarly Western cultural elements in these constructs; the dating of their emergence in the late eighteenth and early nineteenth centuries; and the recognition that these constructs may serve quite definite political purposes have been major steps forward in the development of a theoretical framework for understanding sexuality. There has been far less consensus about the forces that have shaped these constructs—patriarchal culture, capitalism, the rising bourgeoisie, and other more or less global concepts have all been invoked—or about whether their principal purpose is to preserve hierarchies of class or gender or both.[6] These questions are central to this book. I return to them often in the chapters that follow, and they are specifically addressed in Chapter 11. What is needed at this point, however, is greater precision in delineating by whom, how, under what circumstances, and to what ends particular constructions of sexuality are likely to be advanced, and how and why these constructions change over time.

If, as Foucault suggests, sexuality in modern societies has become a principal instrument for the exercise of power over "bodies" and "populations," then the agencies that have this power and the means that they employ need to be specified. The power to construct categories of sexual orthodoxy and unorthodoxy and to deploy these categories for purposes of social control is a property of particular individuals and institutions: interested lay and professional persons, the organizations that coalesce around these interests, and representatives of the state. Examination of the processes in contemporary society by which power of this description is acquired and used, and of the shifting composition of interested, or powerful, audiences, has been the province of three interrelated bodies of sociological theory: of deviance and social control, of social movements, and of the emergence and construction of public problems. My framing of the questions addressed in this book, the materials I have consulted, and the interpretations I present are strongly influenced by recent work within these three theoretical domains.

SOCIAL CONTROL, SOCIAL MOVEMENTS, AND SEXUALITY AS A PUBLIC PROBLEM

Cohen defines social control as "the organized ways in which society responds to behavior and people it regards as deviant, problematic, worrying, threatening, troublesome, or undesireable in some way or another" (1985:1). Sometime in the middle of the nineteenth century female adolescence came to be regarded as a time of life that was, sexually, troublesome. There has been a consistent duality in society's organized response. On the one hand, there has been a proliferation of agencies—reform schools, maternity homes, adoption agencies, family planning clinics—for the management of the sexually and reproductively problematic *individual*. On the other hand, there has been a periodic eruption of sexual social movements: movements targeted less at the problematic individuals themselves than at changing the *social norms* by which problematic *categories* of individuals are created, their characteristics defined, and their treatment decided. Both levels of response are "organized" in that the concerns they represent are embodied in formal organizations or have become the domain of socially recognized experts. They are both responses to "public problems," in Joseph R. Gusfield's sense of "something about which 'someone ought to do something'" (1981:5). Thus, questions of problem construction—when and why young women's departures from the path of sexual orthodoxy become a problem demanding public attention, what the "reality" of this problem is conceived to be, and designations of responsibility for causing the problem and for resolving it—are applicable at both the individual and the categorical levels of response. However, given discovery of a problem, these two levels of response are conceptually distinguishable and *roughly* correspond to the traditional domains of, respectively, social control and social movement theory. Individual deviance and the institutionalized apparatus of control are the primary concern of social control theory; social movement theory, by definition, concerns itself with the periodic eruption of movements by which categories are changed and institutions modified or overthrown.

Problems and Solutions

Adolescent pregnancy, together with its predecessors under other names—unwed motherhood, white slavery, ruined or delinquent girls—fall into the category of public problems like drinking and driving, child abuse, and acid rain. Public problems, problems that have made it to the point of demanding public attention, are not "simple mirrors of objective conditions" (Hilgartner and Bosk, 1988:53). They have a history—they are the product of competition with other problems, as well as with alternative constructions of the same problem. And they have a structure—an anatomy that, although its particulars may vary from time to time and from problem to problem, is remarkably consistent in form. This structure—what it is and where it came from—is critical, for how a problem is defined bears a close relationship to how it will be, or fail to be, resolved (Gusfield, 1981:6). Thus, it makes a great deal of difference to the process of problem resolution whether the sexual unorthodoxy of a single young woman is defined as a problem for the medical profession or the church, and whether her behavior is portrayed in terms suggesting seduction, promiscuity, or mere "sexual activity."

Central to the structure of public problems are attributions of responsibility. Gusfield identifies three dimensions of this concept: "ownership," or "the power to define and describe the problem"; causal responsibility, the "assertion about the sequence that factually accounts for the existence of the problem"; and "political responsibility," or the designation of who (an individual, an agency, an organization) is responsible for solving the problem (1981:13–14). This book is, in large part, an account of struggles over these attributions of responsibility. One of the most salient characteristics of young women's sexuality as a public problem has been the inability of any one group to have its claim to the power of definition and description permanently accepted. Ownership has shifted back and forth among moral, medical, and legal authorities; young women are alternatively portrayed as willful sinners or innocent victims; at one time or another responsibility for solving the problem is fixed on the family, the church, the schools, professional experts, or the state. The specific content of these debates and the claims-making power of the various protagonists have, of course, changed over time. However, the structure of the debates and the identity of the protagonists have remained remarkably constant.

The sources of change, as well as continuity, lie outside of the debates themselves, in cognitive beliefs about the intrinsic nature and destiny of unmarried young women; in beliefs about the underlying "causes" of sexual unorthodoxy (genetic, psychological, environmental); and in the demographic, social, legal, and economic structures of society. A central element in cultural constructions of female sexuality arc beliefs about the nature and destiny of young women before marriage. When these beliefs change, for example, from the nineteenth-century presumption of intrinsic innocence to the twentieth-century presumption of intrinsic sexuality, ideas about the management of this troublesome period in young women's lives change correspondingly. Among the structural variables to which I refer are those that have an impact on the situation of young women themselves—their visibility as a social category, their domestic circumstances, their opportunities for school and work—and those that influence the relative power of different groups within the society to affect how young women's situation and its problems are perceived and addressed—the power of "ownership."

Questions of ownership are central to an understanding of how and why strategies for the social control of sexually unorthodox young women have shifted over the past century and a half. I approach these questions within the general framework of what Andrew T. Scull has called "the new sociology of social control" (1988:685). This framework, which owes as much to the work of historians as sociologists, focuses attention on the apparatus of social control—conceived not as an immanent social force but as a congeries of identifiable groups and individuals—and on "the impact of state, economy, and ideology on social control, particularly the ability of these forces to create, redefine, and reorganize our understanding of both the subjects and mechanisms of social control" (687). The value of this framework lies less in its theoretical coherence than in its ability to raise critical questions and give direction to inquiry.

Among the most critical of these questions concerns the benevolence of what have passed in the last century and a half for institutional reforms in the management of deviant behavior—the penitentiary, the psychiatric hospital, the reform school, the juvenile court, the halfway house, the physician's office—and of the philosophies these institutions represent. The hallmarks of this theoretical orientation are skepticism about the meaning of reform and the motives of reformers, rejection of "progress" or "humanitarianism" or "science" as sufficient rationales for changes implemented or proposed, and an underlying consensus that historical change in mechanisms of social control has been in the direction of increasing pervasiveness—"a decline in private space and an increase in public regulation" (Cohen, 1985:124).[7] Our attention is directed to the identity of advocates for change in control mechanisms; to the details of their rhetoric; to the personal, professional, and political interests served by proposed reforms; and to their real-life consequences which, it is argued, often come down neither to amelioration nor reform but to the social control of individual behavior and the depoliticization of social problems. It is with this attitude of skepticism and these questions in mind that I have approached the long record of efforts to manage the sexuality of single young women.

A second central set of questions concerns the relationship of social control processes to the historical, social, and cultural contexts from which they emerge and in which they are deployed. Not only are deviance designations—categories of madness, illness, and sexuality—cultural products but they are also the products of political contest among groups and individuals whose relative power both to impose designations and to propose solutions varies with time and place. In work that clearly has more general application, Joseph W. Schneider and Peter Conrad (1980) have described the political processes by which forms of deviance become designated as medical problems, emphasizing the potential for contest and reversal at every stage and the critical role played by differential access to resources of power and opportunity. Resources acquire their meaning and value only in relation to particular conditions of social structure and ideology: Ownership cannot be understood apart from the conditions in which it arises. It is this premise—in addition to considerations advanced earlier—that has led me to pay far more attention to history than is usual in a work of sociology.

Innovations in the management of sexually unorthodox girls—schools for "wayward" girls, rescue homes, maternity homes, birth control clinics—have invariably been introduced as better ways of "doing good." The theoretical work I have cited suggests a more complex reality—one in which neither intentions nor implementation may be wholly understandable in simple humanitarian terms. Thus, for example, comprehending the failure of nineteenth-century advocates for government-sponsored medical regulation of prostitution as compared with the (relative) success of twentieth-century advocates for medical regulation of adolescent pregnancy through government-sponsored provision of birth control services to teenage women will require less attention to the intrinsic persuasiveness or humanity of the policies proposed than to the historical timeliness of their introduction and the organizational effectiveness and political power of their sponsors. The combination of symbolic resonance with moral ambiguity makes the sexually unorthodox girl both attractive and elusive as an organizational rallying point: The public may be readily convinced there is a "problem," but almost any strategy for its control is vulnerable to attack on the grounds either that it punishes innocence or encourages sin. In these uncertain circumstances, not only the adoption of "reforms" but the readiness of groups and individuals to propose them—to get in the ownership game at all—are especially likely to be influenced by political and ideological considerations that go beyond the reforms' intrinsic merits.

Considerations such as these may account for the curious and uneven course of professionalization in the management of young women's sexual unorthodoxies. It is certainly true, as Cohen and Scull observe, that "social control in the modern era has been increasingly presided over by 'experts' in managing and manipulating an even more carefully differentiated population of deviants" (1983:11). Nevertheless, no single profession has fully established— or has, perhaps, wanted to establish—its claims to the sexually unorthodox girl; moral and professional management prescriptions have often been indistinguishable; and the basic premise of professional jurisdiction has been periodically contested. The most revolutionary strategies—the pill and the federally funded birth control clinic—have been opposed as much for their reliance on professional expertise as for their implicit acceptance of young women's nonmarital sexual activity. In the chapters that follow, I recount the history of these professional ups and downs and attempt to provide some basis for understanding them both in immediate political terms and in terms of the broader social and ideological context that this history reflects. In anticipation, it may be said that professionalization of responsibility for young women's sexual unorthodoxy presents two fundamental problems. First, there is the problem of moral ambiguity to which I have already referred—the bifurcation of female sexuality into dimensions of sin and innocence that we have inherited from the nineteenth century and find difficult to shake. Second, there is the problem—perhaps particularly acute for practitioners of medicine and public health—that sex, unlike smallpox, cannot be stamped out. There is, ultimately, no cure. To accept professional responsibility for the nonpunitive treatment of a problem that one suspects to have been acquired voluntarily and that is also incurable promises little satisfaction, together with considerable vulnerability to criticism when the problem does not, in fact, go away. This problem is acutely felt by nurses who provide contraceptive services to teenage women, as I describe in Chapter 9.

Sexual Social Movements
Unmarried young women's sexuality and its control have been significant concerns in American culture since the early 1800s, sustaining an unbroken record of institutional response. From time to time, however, the nature of these concerns and the character of the response appear to have undergone a profound qualitative as well as quantitative change. From a more or less routine problem of *individual* transgression, quietly consigned to the discreet management of reform schools, maternity homes, and the offices of amenable physicians, young women's sexual unorthodoxies have been transformed into symbols of *social* disorder and change and have become the focus of social movements for sexual control. Studies of adult women and adolescents, of prostitution

and venereal disease, of birth control and abortion, and of the recurrent social movements in which moral concerns have taken on a more or less political form have all impressed their authors with the uses of sexuality not only as a target of individual intervention but as the dominant cultural metaphor for social disorder and social change (e.g., Gordon, 1977; Mohr, 1978; Brandt, 1985; Smith-Rosenberg, 1985). The social conflicts that, in the late nineteenth and early twentieth centuries, were attendant upon urbanization and immigration and, more recently, have accompanied change in the structure of race and gender relationships, have routinely been translated into moral terms. In this moral language, order and stability are represented by the "family" and, more particularly, by the mother "secure in her morality and content in her home" (Fass, 1977:25); whereas disorder is represented by sexuality unsanctioned by legitimate procreational possibility or intent.

Over the past 150 years of U.S. history, there have been two major episodes of sustained public attention to, combined with concerted efforts to make changes in, the management of young women's nonmarital sexuality. The first of these episodes, lasting from about 1885 to 1920, encompassed a series of overlapping campaigns: to raise the "age of consent," to eliminate prostitution, to end "white slavery," and to combat venereal disease. The second episode, the campaign against "adolescent pregnancy," emerged in the early 1970s and is showing some recent signs of tapering off, not because of any decline in public concern with sexual unorthodoxy but due to competition from an even more powerful symbol of sexual disorder: that of AIDS. I believe that these episodes—like the European witchcraze of the fifteenth to seventeenth centuries, the "crime waves" of seventeenth-century Massachusetts Bay, and the political witch-hunts of the McCarthy era in the United States[8]—can be conceptualized as moral boundary crises, events that represent the reassertion of society's moral order against the threat of deviant behavior. At the same time, many aspects of these campaigns fit the definition of social movements as "conscious, collective, organized" attempts to bring about or to resist or reverse social change.[9]

The recurrence of sexual social movements suggests a corresponding recurrence of the social conditions to which these movements respond. A review of recent social movement theory points to three questions with regard to these conditions (e.g., Tilly, Tilly, and Tilly, 1975; McCarthy and Zald, 1977; Zurcher and Snow, 1981; Jenkins, 1983; Walsh and Warland, 1983). First, what is the role of demographic, social, and external political conditions in these movements' emergence, in their persistence, and in their decline? Second, what is the role of the ideologies and beliefs that underlie the movements' sexual reform objectives? Finally, what is the role in these movements' emergence of preexisting organizational capacities, of movement "entrepreneurs," and of temporary social and political interests and opportunities? I address these questions in the body of the book. Here I propose two specific sets of conditions for the emergence of sexual social movements, the first pertaining to ideologies and beliefs and the second pertaining to aspects of the social structure.

Cohen has used the term, "moral panic" to describe those circumstances under which "a condition, episode, person, or group of persons emerges to become defined as a threat to societal values and interests" and evokes a massive, stereotyped, and morally defensive response—a response that may merely reaffirm, or may sometimes change, the society's moral boundaries (1980:9). "Confrontations between deviant offenders and the agents of control," Erikson (1966:12) points out, are fundamental to a community's sense of its social and cultural identity. In interactions that define the limits of permissible behavior, societies (and subgroups within a society) reassert their boundaries, the differences between themselves and "others" beyond the social pale. Moral boundaries are most severely challenged, and response to the challenge is most extreme, when the challenge represents (or is construed to represent) not merely an individual failing but an attack on the basic social norms by which failings are defined (Gusfield, 1967). These arguments suggest the first of the two sets of conditions that I propose: Unorthodox sexual behavior becomes ripe for transformation from an individual failing to a categorical problem and social movements embodying one or another "solution" to the problem are most likely to emerge under conditions where normative violations are compounded by widespread normative conflict over the legitimacy of the norms themselves.

Work within the "resource mobilization" branch of social movement theory suggests, however, that normative violations and normative conflict are seldom the direct causes of problem construction and social movement activity (e.g., McCarthy and Zald, 1977). The structure within which these events become defined is a creation of social movement leaders and spokespersons. The processes of creation itself were described earlier: claims making and attributions of responsibility, which designate the nature of the problem and how and by whom it should be resolved, are an essential phase of social movement activity, as they are of public problem construction generally. However, two structural conditions are necessary for this activity to take place. The first condition is the visibility of normative violations. "It is essential that either the rule-breaking be visible or that the assumption of a transgression becomes public knowledge. Invisible breaches of conduct cannot provoke a public reaction" (Ben-Yehuda, 1985:8). The second structural condition is the presence in society of sufficiently well-organized and powerful groups or individuals to whom the construction and promotion of a boundary crisis around the state of sexual morality appear politically and socially advantageous. Stated more specifically: The elevation of sexuality to the level of a categorical problem and the creation of social movements around this problem are contingent on the presence in society of "entrepreneurial" groups for whom sexual symbols represent an important political resource—a means to power.

My analyses of the recent "adolescent pregnancy" episode (Chapters 2, 3, and 4) and of the earlier sexual social movements of the Progressive Era (Chapter 7) are guided by the propositions outlined above. Chapter 11 summarizes the evidence from these two episodes and draws some general conclusions with respect to conditions for the rise and decline of sexual social movements.

COMMENTARY

The conception of reactions to deviant behavior as a mechanism for maintaining societies' moral boundaries derives from a series of essays by Émile Durkheim (1933, 1938) on the functionality of deviance. Nachman Ben-Yehuda (1985) has called attention to the contradiction inherent in Durkheim's conception. Deviance is, on the one hand, a source of social stability—the "primary and principal function [of societal reactions to crime] is to create respect for . . . beliefs, traditions, and collective practices" (1933:84). On the other hand, it is a source of social change—"Where crime exists, collective sentiments are sufficiently flexible to take on a new form, and crime sometimes helps to determine the form they will take" (1938:71). In a broad sense the two dimensions of response to sexual unorthodoxy that I have identified—strategies of social control targeted to individual deviants and social movements focused on normative boundaries—correspond to these two dimensions of the Durkheimian conception. Periods of normative upheaval and shifting boundaries are preceded and followed by periods of normative consolidation and consensus. The former period both creates and is fueled by the energies of social movement entrepreneurs; the latter calls upon the quieter strengths of "street-level" workers—individuals of various callings who staff the front lines of routine social control (Lipsky, 1980). Periodization, together with the distinction between individual-level deviance that does not challenge social norms and social movements that do, go some way to resolve the Durkheimian contradiction. The critical question that I try to answer concerns the structural and ideological circumstances that account for these broad shifts in societal attention between the problems of stability and change.[10]

All societies construct categories of deviant behavior and devise strategies for its control. However, the substantive concerns around which these activities are organized vary with the social, cultural, and historical settings in which they take place: "Every community has its own characteristic styles of deviant behavior" (Erikson, 1966:19). In the Puritan communities of seventeenth-century New England examined by Erikson in his book *Wayward Puritans*, these concerns were almost exclusively theological. In nineteenth- and twentieth-century Western Europe and America, sexuality in general, and the sexuality of single young women in particular, have "assumed major symbolic importance as a target of social intervention and organization, to a degree that differentiates this period from those preceding it" (Weeks, 1981:11). Drawing on the social control and social movement literature, I have suggested a general framework for conceptualizing these processes of "social intervention and organization." I have not, however, specifically addressed the questions of *why* young women's sexuality became of intense symbolic importance and *why* such a complex apparatus has been, and continues to be, directed at its control. Constraints on female sexuality before marriage are not, of course, unique to recent Western history; it is the quality of attention to this issue—the translation of young women's departures from gender-specific norms of sexual behavior into vehicles for the personalization and moralization of social change—that calls for explanation. Since the explanation itself depends on prior knowledge of the social changes in question and of the structural and ideological contexts in which they have occurred, I defer further consideration of these questions to Chapter 11 when the necessary background will have been presented.

I want, finally, to comment on what may appear as the too relativistic, too cynical, or too deterministic aspects of the conceptual framework I have proposed. Because I have insisted that sexual unorthodoxies—whether they consist in a street-corner flirtation or an untimely pregnancy—are socially constructed does not mean that the consequences of these behaviors are trivial to the individuals concerned. In the early twentieth century, public flirtation could—depending on time and circumstances—end with the young woman in court (Schlossman and Wallach, 1978). In the present social and political climate of the United States, an untimely pregnancy may mean an untimely birth under conditions of wholly inadequate social and economic support. These are severe consequences but they are not inherent consequences of these behaviors; they are the outcome of meanings that are attributed to these behaviors within particular historical settings, settings that shape how those meanings will be understood and the responses that they will evoke.

Second, in conceiving of advocates for this or that management strategy as agents of social control and in searching for the opportunistic interests that advocacy may serve, I am not questioning the sincerity and commitment of reformers. This objection has consistently been raised against recent Marxist and conflict-oriented analyses of social control processes (see, e.g., Cohen and Scull, 1983). Again, history may give some perspective. It is probably easier to accept that late nineteenth-century physicians used the abortion issue as a vehicle to establish their professional authority against a variety of competitors (Mohr, 1978) than that (as I will argue) late twentieth-century birth control advocates used the adolescent pregnancy issue to protect their organizational position in a difficult social and political climate. In neither case is it necessary to question the sincerity of the individuals involved in these issues. But individuals and organizations are limited in their resources, and choices must inevitably be made between many objects equally worthy of attention. Given these constraints, it is hardly surprising that collective class, professional, or organizational interests should enter into the choice equation.

Lastly, there is the question of whether the supposedly "controlled" are controlled in fact. The concept of social control has deterministic implications, particularly when attention is focused almost exclusively on the rhetoric and activities of audiences rather than on the actors to whom their attention is directed. I am sensitive to this issue and have attempted to bring in pertinent data where it exists. In addition, I use a recently-collected set of qualitative data to examine directly the contraceptive- and pregnancy-management strategies of single young women in Maryland. Although these data are limited in time and place, they effectively illustrate the extent to which young women are, in fact, independent agents in the management of their sexual and reproductive fates.

PLAN OF THE BOOK

The plan of the book—specifically, the nonchronological sequence of chapters—reflects its genesis in my desire to make sociological sense of contemporary agitation over the issue of adolescent pregnancy. Thus, Chapters 2, 3, and 4 give the demographic background of this issue, examine in detail the social and political context from which it emerged as a public problem in the mid-1970s, and describe how birth control advocates' initial construction of the issue was contested, and basically transformed, in the 1980s. However, contemporary agitation, as I argued earlier in this chapter, is only partially understandable in its own terms. Concern about the period of female adolescence has grown out of changes that have been taking place since the early nineteenth century in conceptions of young women's "nature" and in the structure of young women's lives. To understand this concern and the strategies it has generated for the management of sexually unorthodox young women, it is necessary to have some knowledge of social changes that have, to a greater or lesser extent, affected all young women living in the United States. Chapter 5 describes these changes for a period from about 1850 to 1960 (i.e., up to the year when I begin the story of adolescent pregnancy). Chapter 6 covers approximately the same time period and examines the shifting strategies of what I earlier called "routine" social control that were deployed prior to the invention of the birth control pill and the legalization of abortion. Chapter 7 is broadly parallel to Chapters 3 and 4. It presents an analysis of public agitation over young women's nonmarital sexuality during the Progressive Era, and provides the empirical basis for a comparison between this and the later adolescent pregnancy episode. Similarly, Chapter 8 is roughly parallel to Chapter 6, and complements Chapters 2, 3, and 4. The latter are focused on the "social movement" dimensions of the adolescent pregnancy issue, while Chapter 8 covers the "routine" social control dimension. This latter theme is continued in Chapter 9, based on an analysis of empirical data from a study of nurses working in Maryland family planning clinics. Chapter 10 is also based on empirical data, this time from a small sample of young women themselves. Finally, in Chapter 11 I weave these various threads together, both to answer the questions with which I began and to comment more broadly on the implications of this work for understanding how Americans think about and manage deviant behavior and social change.

PART TWO *Private Behavior as a Public Problem*

SETTING THE STAGE, 1960–1972
Chapter 2

IN WHAT has become something of a legislative routine, by the end of 1989, thirty-four bills had been introduced in twelve states, and two bills had been introduced in the U.S. Congress addressing the issue of adolescent pregnancy. In the opinion climate of today, this phenomenon caused hardly a ripple. Although there is substantial disagreement on how to deal with the problem— reflected in the rarity with which such bills become law and the blandness of those that do—that it *is* a problem, and a problem that government may properly address, is unquestioned. In the face of this consensus, it may be difficult to recall how recently adolescent pregnancy made its debut upon the public stage.

A few school- and hospital-based programs offering a range of educational, health, and welfare services to poor, predominantly black, "school-age pregnant girls" were quietly inaugurated in the late 1960s, the majority with local community rather than federal support (Howard, 1975; Vinovskis, 1988); and the problem of "illegitimate children [who] are progeny of teenage mothers," evoked occasional outcries from public officials. However, it was not until 1972, with the publication of *Population and the American Future*, the report of the President's Commission on Population Growth and the American Future, that public attention was drawn to "teenagers" as a class requiring the attention of the federal government. In 1972, however, the time for official acknowledgment of an adolescent pregnancy problem was still not ripe. The commission's recommendation that "birth control services and information be made available to teenagers" was singled out for rejection by President Richard Nixon, to whom it was directed: "I also want to make it clear that I do not support the unrestricted distribution of family planning services and devices to minors. Such measures would do nothing to preserve and strengthen close family relations" (*New York Times*, May 6, 1972:1:5). Adolescent pregnancy was not, in fact, officially recognized as a problem by the federal government until 1978, when the first proposed legislation on this topic, the "Adolescent Health, Services, and Pregnancy Prevention and Care Act of 1978," was submitted to Congress by the administration of President Jimmy Carter. My aim in this and the next two chapters is to trace how and why adolescent pregnancy emerged from the relative obscurity of the 1960s to become in the 1980s a major, and highly controversial, public problem.

My approach to this question is guided by the work of Herbert Blumer (1971), Joseph R. Gusfield (1981), Joseph W. Schneider and Peter Conrad (1980), and others. Problems, as these authors emphasize, have histories. They do not emerge full-blown onto the public stage. What we observe at any given moment is the (frequently temporary) resolution of a continuing struggle over the intrinsic "nature" of the problem (e.g., as sin, as crime, as illness), over alternative causal "theories," and over how and by whom the problem should be resolved. It is by paying close attention to these struggles—identifying the protagonists, attending to their words and actions, and learning how the various interested parties will gain or lose by particular outcomes—that we can hope to understand both the emergence and the structure of public problems. The first job of the sociologist interested in a public problem, Gusfield states, is "to account for its status as a matter of public concern rather than accept it as given in the nature of things" (1981:4). It is with the attempt to provide such an account that my investigation of adolescent pregnancy begins.

THE DEMOGRAPHIC BACKGROUND

Logically, the level of public concern may be supposed to increase in proportion to the magnitude of the problem; consequently, the first step in this analysis will be to describe recent trends in adolescent fertility and reproductive behavior.[1] Before doing so, it must be stated that, however seemingly innocent, the very act of description is a mine field: The author must pick her way among demographic "facts," all of which have been or may be used as weapons in the selfsame struggles she is intending to portray. Thus, *how* adolescent fertility is to be described (numbers of births, percentages, rates), over *what* period of time, by *what* maternal characteristics (marital status, race) are political as much as (or often more than) scientific decisions. Even the production of knowledge on which description is based (for example, on the extent of teenage women's "sexual activity") may itself be less a cause than a consequence of newly awakened public concern. Awareness of these pitfalls does not guarantee they will be avoided; it dictates a cautious approach to the data on adolescent reproduction and a heightened sense of the need to place these data in social and historical perspective.

Demographically, adolescent fertility refers to the reproductive behavior patterns of a category defined by age and (almost invariably) sex: women who are age 19 and under. Birth rates (the number of births per 1,000 women) of women aged 15 to 19 are shown in Figure 2.1 for each year from 1920

FIGURE 2.1
BIRTH RATES OF WOMEN 15–19 AND 20–24, UNITED STATES, 1920–1987

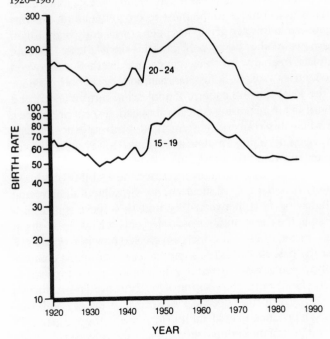

Sources: Robert L. Heuser, *Fertility Tables for Birth Cohorts by Color: United States, 1917–73*, DHEW publication no. (HRA) 76-11152 (Rockville, Md.: National Center for Health Statistics, 1976), Table 3A; National Center for Health Statistics, "Advance Report of Final Natality Statistics, 1987," *Monthly Vital Statistics Report*, vol. 38, no. 3, supplement (Hyattsville, Md.: Public Health Service, 1989), Table 4.

through 1987; to provide some perspective on these rates, parallel data are given for women aged 20 to 24. Birth *rates* for teenage women peaked in 1957, declined rapidly until 1976 and have since plateaued at about the 1976 level. Commenting on these data, Maris A. Vinovskis remarked that, "If the Adolescent Health, Services, and Pregnancy Prevention Act of 1978 is seen mainly as a response to demographic trends among adolescents, it should have been launched during the Eisenhower rather than the Carter administration" (1981:208). Comparison of adolescent birth rates with rates for their 20 to 24 year old contemporaries makes it quite clear, in addition, that the overall fertility experience of adolescent women during this sixty-seven-year time span was in no way unique. Adolescent birth rates are consistently lower than those of older women; however, the pattern of change in rates over time is virtually identical. Social forces that were responsible for the drop in fertility during the depression, for the baby boom between 1950 and 1960, and for the subsequent baby bust acted on both age groups with equal intensity. Finally, although much has been made of high fertility among U.S. adolescent women in comparison with young women from other developed countries (e.g., Jones et al., 1986), neither is this pattern unique to the most recent generations. Fertility among U.S. white women in this age group has been consistently higher than that of their counterparts in other developed countries since at least 1950; the recent trend has, in fact, been toward convergence, not divergence, between the U.S. and other countries' rates (Rindfuss, Morgan, and Swicegood, 1988).

Thus, neither the level nor the pattern of adolescent birth rates can be held directly responsible for increasing concern about adolescent pregnancy; by the mid-1960s, when this concern first emerged, birth rates to teenage women had already been declining for almost a decade. However, birth rates are not the only potentially relevant demographic statistic. During this period two other changes took place that markedly increased the visibility of adolescents as a social category and, more particularly, the visibility of their sexual and reproductive behavior. First, between 1960 and 1970 there was an unprecedented increase in the sheer number of adolescents relative to adults in the U.S. population—in and of itself, this increase created new perceptions of youth. Second, over the past two decades, some rather pronounced changes have taken place in how young women *manage* their reproductive capacities.

Adolescents of the 1960s were the offspring of the short-lived reproductive renaissance of the 1950s. The former decade was, Norman B. Ryder points out, unique in this century. It produced "a 13.8 million increase [in the age group 14 to 24], more than in the rest of the century altogether . . . the relative rise [from the previous decade] was unparalleled" (1974:47). Larger numbers of teenage girls (nearly 10 million as compared with 7 million in 1960) resulted in *more* births to adolescents, even at declining rates, a point to which I return below. However, I believe an equally significant consequence of the sixties "invasion" of youth was sharper public awareness of adolescence as a problematic life stage. By that decade's end, the "rebellion of the young" had already generated an enormous literature; several thoughtful commentaries on the social and political youth movements of the period have been published since (Hodgson, 1976; Matusow, 1984; Siegel, 1984; Caute, 1988). The words of Theodore White will serve to convey, from the perspective of a contemporary observer, a sense of the transformation that had taken place.

> Youth had never been seen as a separate problem group in American history. "Youth" was a family matter, left to parents; left also to schools, which bred patriotism, and to the old loyalties, which furnished "soldier boys" in time of war. Youth was accepted as a glandular episode in the stages of life, which would, without doubt, be cured by the simple passage of time, when "youth" became parents and taxpayers in their turn. But by 1967, "student youth" had become a force in American politics, as it had long been a force in countries overseas (1982:111).

Youth came to be perceived as problematic not only politically, but also culturally and, of special relevance, sexually: Central to the sixties counterculture was "the search . . . for a sexuality of companionship and sensation, divorced from family structure and responsibility—sex now, in short, with no future" (Hodgson, 1976:314; see also Caute, 1988). Absence of sexual restraint was an important dimension in America's image of rebellious youth.[2]

In the 1960s, then, the young emerged as a social category worthy of serious public attention. However, the visibility of teenagers' sexual and reproductive behavior is of more recent vintage, in part the unintended consequence of demographic and social change and in part the intended consequence of deliberate efforts to bring this behavior into the public eye.

The demographic and social changes to which I refer are, first, the bulge in *numbers* of teenage births occasioned by the surplus of adolescent women in the 1960s; second, the relative declines in fertility both of older women and of married adolescents; third, changes in marriage patterns accompanied by an increase in births to single women, particularly single *white* women; fourth, the increasing unpopularity of adoption as a "solution" to unwed parenthood; and, finally, the legalization of abortion. Although I do not believe that these changes were in themselves responsible for the emergence of adolescent pregnancy as a public problem, they have played a major role in public debate on this issue. If only as fuel for the fires of rhetoric, they deserve our careful attention.

In Table 2.1, three different indices of adolescent fertility are compared: the absolute number of births in a given year, the percentage of *total* births represented by births to adolescents, and the birth rate. These data are for selected years between 1960 and 1985 and they are given for three age subcategories as well as for the total population of teenage women under 20.[3] Although the adolescent birth rate reached its highest point in the mid-1950s, the sheer number of births to women in this age group did not peak until a decade and a half later, when the baby-boom teenagers themselves began to have babies. And, because adolescent fertility dropped in the 1970s somewhat more slowly than the fertility of older women, adolescent births were the largest *percentage* of all births in 1975. (It is, perhaps, self-evident from this table that the "magnitude" of the problem represented by adolescent fertility can be exaggerated or minimized depending on whether the observer's attention is drawn to increasing numbers and percentages or to declining rates.)

Historically, public interest has been aroused less by numbers of births, even to women of tender years, than by the *circumstances* under which these births occur. The unwed mother and her child are classic figures in fiction as well as in the sociologist's catalog of unsolved "social problems" (see, for example, Waller, 1936; Davis, 1939; Vincent, 1961; Roberts, 1966). Over the past two and one-half decades changes in sexual intercourse and marriage patterns, as well as changes in adolescent women's *management* of pregnancies conceived outside of marriage have led to increases both in birth *rates* to single adolescent women and to (much larger) increases in the proportion of *total* adolescent births that births to single women represent. Birth rates to single women aged 15 to 19 and (for comparison) aged 20 to 24, by race,

TABLE 2.1

INDICES OF ADOLESCENT FERTILITY, TOTAL AND BY AGE CATEGORY, SELECTED YEARS, 1960–1985

	No. Births	Percent of All Births	Birth Rate
TOTAL[a]			
1960	609,141	14.3	40.7
1970	656,460	17.6	33.4
1975	594,880	18.9	29.2
1980	562,330	15.6	29.1
1985	477,705	12.7	27.4
BY AGE			
10–14			
1960	7,462	.2	.8
1970	11,752	.3	1.2
1975	12,642	.4	1.3
1980	10,169	.3	1.1
1985	10,220	.3	1.3
15–17			
1960	117,904	4.0	42.7
1970	223,590	6.0	38.8
1975	227,270	7.2	36.1
1980	198,222	5.5	32.5
1985	167,789	4.5	31.1
18–19			
1960	423,775	10.0	172.1
1970	421,118	11.3	114.7
1975	354,968	11.3	85.0
1980	353,939	9.8	82.1
1985	299,696	8.0	80.8

[a]Based on births to all women aged 10–19 in years specified.

Sources: The National Center for Health Statistics publishes a yearly series, *Vital Statistics of the United States*, Vol. 1, *Natality*. Volumes for the years 1960, 1970, 1975, 1980, and 1985 were consulted to obtain the number of births by age for each year. Denominators for percentages and rates were obtained from the following sources: U.S. Bureau of the Census, *Current Population Reports*, ser. P-25, no. 519, "Estimates of the Population of the United States, by Age, Color, and Sex, April 1, 1960 to July 1, 1973" (Washington, D.C.: U.S. Government Printing Office, 1974), Table 3; U.S. Bureau of the Census, *Current Population Reports*, ser. P-25, no. 917, "Estimates of the Population of the United States, by Age, Sex, and Race: 1970 to 1981" (Washington, D.C.: U.S. Government Printing Office, 1982), Table 3; U.S. Bureau of the Census, *Current Population Reports*, ser. P-25, no. 1022, "United States Population Estimates by Age, Sex, and Race: 1980 to 1987" (Washington, D.C.: U.S. Government Printing Office, 1988), Table 3.

FIGURE 2.2

NONMARITAL BIRTH RATES BY AGE AND COLOR, 1960–1987

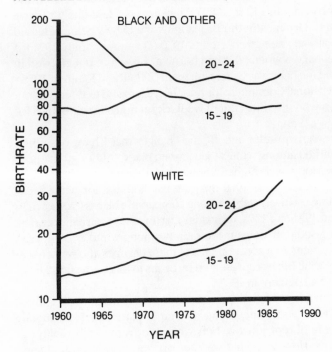

Sources: Alice M. Hetzel and Marlene Capetta, "Teenagers: Marriages, Divorces, Parenthood, and Mortality," *Vital and Health Statistics*, ser. 21, no. 23, DHEW publication no. (HRA) 74-1901 (Rockville, Md.: National Center for Health Statistics, 1973), Table 3; National Center for Health Statistics, "Advance Report of Final Natality Statistics, 1987," *Monthly Vital Statistics Report*, vol. 38, no. 3, supplement (Hyattsville, Md.: Public Health Service, 1989), Table 19.

are shown in Figure 2.2 for the period from 1960 to 1987. Among white 15 to 19 year olds, these rates have increased steadily since 1960; rates for black teenagers increased until 1971, declined from 1972 to 1981, and have risen again slightly from 1983 to 1987. These changes in rates have been relatively gradual; however, the *proportion* of births to single women jumped from 15 percent of total teenage births in 1960 to 31 percent in 1970 and to over 60 percent in 1987. Thus, although recent cohorts of women are *less* likely than women born in the first half of this century to have had a birth by age 20, the births that they do have are *much more* likely to occur while they are still single. This rather remarkable alteration in young women's behavior is a reflection of changes in both sexual activity and marriage patterns: Marriage rates have declined, single women are a good deal more likely now than they were twenty-five years ago to have sexual intercourse prior to marriage, and they are less likely now than they were twenty-five years ago to manage a "premarital" conception by getting married before the baby is born (Hofferth, Kahn, and Baldwin, 1987; Nathanson and Kim, 1989). They are also less likely to have their babies adopted. Declines in the probability of a baby's being released for adoption were already being reported in 1970 (Grow and Smith, 1971). A sample of single teenage women who had borne a child were interviewed in 1976; 93 percent said the baby was living with them (Zelnik and Kantner, 1978). More recently, the National Committee for Adoption estimated that "only about 3 percent of women who give birth out of wedlock relinquish their babies for adoption these days" (Allen, 1989).

Among young women under age 20, the changes that I have described have been more marked among whites than among blacks. Although the non-marital birth rate has long been higher among black than among white young (as well as older) women, since 1970 this rate has doubled for white teen-agers while remaining relatively stable among comparable blacks (as shown in Figure 2.2). Between 1971 and 1979, the odds of having a nonmarital as against a marital birth increased four times more rapidly among white as compared with black young women.[4] As a consequence of these changes, the percentage of all teenage nonmarital births represented by births to blacks declined from 58 percent in 1970 to 45 percent in 1987.

By eschewing marriage and adoption as means of concealment, adoles-cent women in general, and white young women in particular, substantially increased the *visibility* of reproductive behavior patterns in conflict with tra-ditional social norms. However, what was perhaps the most critical change affecting the visibility of teenage women's reproductive behavior came about as a consequence of the legalization of abortion (beginning in the late 1960s with the repeal of antiabortion laws in California and New York and culmi-nating in the 1973 Supreme Court decision making abortion legal throughout the United States). An immediate and highly significant result of legalization was the launching of programs to collect and publish statistics documenting the frequency of abortion by, among other demographic characteristics, age (Tietze and Lewit, 1971; Centers for Disease Control, 1974). Suddenly, not just *births* to teenage women, but *pregnancies* as well had become information in the public domain. Consistently, around 30 percent of the legal abortions reported have been to women under age 20 (Henshaw and O'Reilly, 1983; Henshaw, 1987). These data have been a major source of raw material for the creation of "adolescent pregnancy" as a public problem.

The demographic and social changes in reproductive behavior that I have described are important. However, documentation of these changes in the detail currently available and, by the same token, their dramatic impact on public awareness is a development that had its beginnings in the mid-1970s, initially, I believe, as a result rather than a cause of aroused public concern.[5] In order to understand the origins of this concern, it is necessary to shift our attention from changes in the behavior of adolescents themselves to changes of quite another order—changes that have profoundly affected not only what we "know" about adolescent sexual and reproductive behavior, but how that behavior is perceived, and what we think right to do about it.

OLD WINE IN NEW BOTTLES: 1960–1972

In a single phrase, "adolescent pregnancy" calls our attention to the sexual behavior of two historically "problematic" subjects: children and women (Foucault, 1978). "Adolescent" and "teenager" are, themselves, reassuringly sexless labels—they imply a nondiscriminatory concern with the mistimed reproductive behavior of either sex. Pregnancy, however, is by definition a female problem. Males do not become pregnant. In the course of this book, I hope to show that underlying current controversies around the issue of adolescent pregnancy is a more fundamental concern with social control over the sexual and reproductive autonomy of women. However, societal apprehension about the manner in which women employ, or fail to employ, their reproductive capacities is not a new phenomenon (see, e.g., Gordon, 1977; Mohr, 1978; Weeks, 1981). What requires explanation is the particular form ("adolescent pregnancy") this apprehension has assumed and its translation into a problem requiring concerted public action.

In the past two decades, a very large literature has accumulated describing the negative medical, economic, and social consequences of adolescent childbearing (reviewed in Hofferth and Hayes, 1987). Recent data suggest that the reality behind these descriptions may be somewhat more complex than the simple cause and effect relationship that is ordinarily implied (see, e.g., Strobino, 1987; Upchurch and McCarthy, 1990). However, I call attention to this literature not to discount it, but to emphasize at the outset that, while early childbearing may have consequences disruptive to the individual's life course, there is no evidence that these consequences are more severe now than they were (say) thirty years ago. The production of knowledge about adolescent pregnancy and childbearing has been as much an outcome of public attention as its cause.[6]

Unwed pregnancy, unmarried motherhood, and illegitimate children are problems "as old and unsolved as human existence itself" (Davis, 1939:215); the morals of the young were of as much concern to the ancient Greeks as to ourselves. What was unique in recent history was the "discovery" of a medical solution to these problems and the employment of that solution as the basis for an intense and highly politicized campaign for its adoption as an article of public policy. In the course of that campaign not only were new solutions proposed, but the problems themselves became sharply redefined. I believe that "adolescent pregnancy" became a public problem in the early 1970s with the convergence of two sets of interests. The increasingly open but relatively diffuse concerns of scholars, social workers, and physicians coincided with the need of medical-solution advocates for a new cause on which to focus their campaign. I have selected 1972 as a turning point because it was on May 5 of that year that President Nixon rejected the Population Commission's recommendation that "teenagers" be provided with birth control services. By his action, the president made birth control for teenagers a legitimate issue for public debate if not (yet) for federal action.[7] And I begin with 1960 because on May 9, almost precisely twelve years earlier, the oral contraceptive pill was first approved for public use in the United States.

The period between 1960 and 1972 was one of enormous change in both lay and professional perceptions of sexuality, of the consequences of sexual activity, and of the possibility that those consequences might be controlled. At least four developments contributed to these changes in perception: research and scholarly debate on the "sexual revolution" among college students; parallel, but intellectually largely unrelated, debate on the "problems" of unwed motherhood and the rising welfare costs of illegitimate children; the medical legitimation of birth control that resulted from discovery of the pill; and the politicization of birth control by its (largely lay) advocates. Each of these developments will be described in turn.

The "Sexual Revolution"

In April 1966, the *Journal of Social Issues* published a special number devoted entirely to "the sexual renaissance." Edited by Ira L. Reiss, a leading authority on the changing sexual mores of American teenagers (see, e.g., Reiss, 1967), nine articles explored various aspects of what was clearly perceived to be a major social change. The only question in dispute was whether this change should be described as a "renaissance" or a "revolution." Adopting the more conservative viewpoint, Reiss himself stated that what had changed was not behavior but attitudes: "Evidence from all the available major studies is in strong agreement that although *attitudes* have changed considerably during this period [approximately 1940 to 1965], that many areas of sexual *behavior*, such as premarital coital rates, have not" (1966:126).[8] Attitude change, Reiss held, was in the direction of premarital sexual permissiveness; "permissiveness with affection" was his classic phrase.

The question of change in sexual behavior, the components of change, and the evaluation of change were addressed in virtually every significant article on this topic published between 1965 and 1971 (Broderick, 1966; Smigel and Seiden, 1968; Bell and Chaskes, 1970; Christensen and Gregg, 1970; Cannon and Long, 1971). Although authors disagreed on whether change had been evolutionary or revolutionary, there was remarkable consensus concerning *who* had changed: it was the white, middle-class, college girl.[9] Robert R. Bell and Jay B. Chaskes began their widely cited article as follows: "Over the past twenty-five years it has been generally assumed in the mass media that the premarital sexual experiences of American girls have been steadily increasing. Furthermore, it is frequently assumed that the college girl has been at the forefront in attaining greater sexual experience" (1970:81). The authors went on to assert (based on their data) that there *had* been recent change in college girls' sexual experience. Furthermore, they explicitly associated this change with the 1960s "rebellion of the young."[10] It should not be supposed that preoccupation with the sexual attitudes and behavior of college students was confined to sociologists. Of five *New York Times* surveys on sex-related topics published between 1960 and 1972, four were focused exclusively on college populations.[11]

The literature I have described has several striking characteristics. These characteristics deserve comment for two reasons: first, because I believe that the sexual revolution debate played a significant role in preparing the public for the idea that young people's sexual behavior had become a serious problem;[12] and second, because the contrasts in intellectual concerns and even in language between these writings and more recent work shed light on the ways in which the problem itself has become redefined as new solutions have been proposed.

Among the more remarkable of the characteristics to which I refer is the description of what is supposed by all authorities to be change in the behavior of middle-class white females as a "sexual revolution" (or even a "renaissance"). There was no suggestion in the works I have cited that *male* sexual behavior had changed in any substantial way (a shift from prostitutes to "dates" as sexual objects was mentioned but apparently was not considered revolutionary). The behavior of lower-class white and black women was largely ignored.[13] This selective use of the word "revolution" lends credence to Rosalind P. Petchesky's comment that sexual events "in a white-dominated and bourgeois culture, become visible to that culture, hence definers of 'changing (or deviating) sexual mores,' only when they involve masses of white middle-class young women" (1984:231). What was "revolutionary" was not the sexual behavior itself, but the adoption of this behavior first, by *women* and, second, by *middle-class, white* women.

A second striking characteristic of this 1960s literature on "premarital" sex is a virtually complete absence of attention to the potential *reproductive* consequences of sexual intercourse. It is as if white college girls were too "nice" to do anything so messy as become pregnant, have a baby, or have an abortion. A 1965 report by "a distinguished group of psychiatrists" titled *Sex and the College Student* (cited by Hill and Jaffe, 1966) assumes the ready availability to college students of facilities (contraception, illegal or foreign abortion, easily arranged adoption) for, in fact, rendering these consequences invisible.[14] Thus, the only *relevant* consequences of intercourse were consequences to the individual psyche (guilt, fear) and to the quality of subsequent relationships (see, e.g., Cannon and Long, 1971); insofar as these consequences were minimized by greater social acceptance of intercourse outside of marriage, evidence of greater acceptance was positively evaluated by the authors whose work I have cited. I call attention to these points because they reflect a conception of sexual behavior as a purely personal choice, separate not only from procreation but also from the influence of family and kin, that came, in the 1970s and 1980s, under increasing conservative attack.[15]

Finally, as suggested by their consistent use of the adjective "premarital," 1960s authors treated sex among college students as sex in the context of progress toward marriage. Sexual behavior was described in terms of a stage framework, in which stages of physical intimacy were related to stages in the relationship's progress from acquaintance through dating to engagement. Moral standards were judged by the point on the relationship continuum at which various degrees of intimacy were "approved" by research subjects. Thus, although sexual intercourse "before marriage" was defined as a question of personal choice, it was a choice to be made within the context of conventional morality: women's behavior would, sooner or later, be legitimized by marriage. Among the marked characteristics of more recent literature are changes in terminology that reflect not only the dropping of this latter assumption but a quite different approach to the issues involved in sex outside of marriage.[16]

Unwed Motherhood and the Costs of Welfare

In the fall of 1971, Sen. Russell Long of Louisiana (then chairman of the Senate Finance Committee) gave a speech to the U.S. Senate titled, "The Welfare Mess: A Scandal of Illegitimacy and Desertion" (Long, 1971). The antecedents of this speech and of the line of reasoning it advanced were, first, what Frances Fox Piven and Richard A. Cloward (1971) have described as an "explosion" in welfare rolls during the 1960s and, second, a public perception that this explosion was due to an "alarming rise" in illegitimacy, primarily among black women. This latter perception is amply documented in contemporary newspaper accounts, congressional hearing records, and published literature. Its essence is captured by the following quotation from a government report on *The Negro Family*: "The steady expansion of this welfare program [Aid to Dependent Children] can be taken as a measure of the steady disintegration of the Negro family structure over the past generation in the U.S." (Moynihan, 1965:14). The accuracy of these portrayals, both of increasing "disintegration" (i.e., illegitimacy) and of an association between illegitimacy and increased numbers of families on welfare has been seriously challenged.[17] The issue here, however, is not one of *accuracy* but of *perception,* the perception that public money was being used to "support women living in 'sin' " (Handler, 1972).

The contrast between public response to the "sexual revolution" among college women and to "illegitimacy" among women who were poor and (perceived to be) black was not lost on contemporary observers. In a series of perceptive comments, Adelaide C. Hill and Frederick S. Jaffe called attention to "our society's differential treatment of the issues of sexual morality and of illegitimacy" (1966:212). The behavior of college students, as they pointed out, was addressed in terms of morality and mental health; the question of reproductive consequences was almost never raised. On the other hand:

> In the context of lower-class (and usually non-white) behavior . . . illegitimacy is *always* discussed; it is *never* seen as a different adjustment to the same sexual revolution which has changed the attitudes and practices of all Americans in the last forty years, but rather is presumed to be the outcome of a historic, unchanged, and unchanging lower-class promiscuity that can only be dealt with moralistically and punitively (1966:212).

The social bases for these striking differences in public perception were summarized by Clark E. Vincent:

> As was the case in Orwell's *Animal Farm*, some unwed mothers are more equal than others.... Older, better educated, white unwed mothers who travel to another state to be attended in private practice at no expense to taxpayers and who provide adoptable infants for childless couples are regarded as far less of a problem than, for example, very young, low-income, Negro unwed mothers whose offspring are not in demand for adoption and may be dependent upon taxpayers' support (1966:24).

In the 1960s, single parenthood among white young women was not a "social" and certainly not a "public" problem because it was largely concealed—by marriage before the child was born, by adoption, or by privately arranged abortion. The visibility and (perceived) costliness of poor women's identical reproductive behavior led to its being defined as a "social problem," labeled "illegitimacy," and to a number of proposed "solutions." "Sex and the College Student" made good newspaper copy; however, it was "a rising objection to people who lie about all day making love and producing illegitimate babies" (Russell Long, cited in Moynihan, 1973) that gave single motherhood its initial status as a problem about which the government "ought to do something" (Howard, 1975). Later I argue that the emergence in the 1970s of "adolescent pregnancy" as the dominant metaphor for women's problematic sexual behavior was due in part to the success of birth control advocates in blurring the distinction between the "acceptable" sexual behavior of young women who were white and middle class and the "unacceptable" sexual behavior of women who were poor and black. In recent years, as moral and fiscal conservatives have gained increasing ascendence in domestic policy-making circles, adolescent pregnancy itself has become redefined as a "black" problem. This was not, however, how it was initially portrayed.

Conceptions of a problem are reflected as much in the solutions advanced as in more direct statements of what the problem "is." The recent history of single parenthood has been characterized by a series of struggles among competing "solutions;" no sooner does one approach threaten to become dominant than it is challenged by competing approaches representing competing interests with competing conceptions of the problem's essential nature. This wavelike pattern is a consequence of the fact that any particular "solution" to the "problem" of unwed motherhood reflects not only the unique circumstances of the time in which it is proposed but a much more enduring set of beliefs as well—beliefs about the normative status of women's sexual behavior and about the proper roles in control of that behavior to be played by the individual woman, the professional expert, and the state. In the 1960s, the new visibility of "illegitimacy" generated three types of solutions: punitive, in the form, for example, of limits on the number of children who could be supported under the AFDC program; rehabilitative, in the form of hospital-based programs for the "treatment" of adolescents who were poor, black, and pregnant; and preventive, in the form of government-supported birth control services for low-income women. Much of my remaining account of this period (1960–1972) concerns the emergence and seeming victory of the preventive solution. The other "solutions," however, do not disappear (either in fact or from my account); they represent continuing leitmotifs, temporarily submerged in the contraceptive euphoria of the early 1970s only to reappear later on in slightly altered form.

The Medical "Discovery" of Birth Control

In describing the process by which deviant behavior comes to be defined in medical terms, Schneider and Conrad use the term discovery, "not to suggest that a change in so-called objective conditions is being announced, but rather . . . that the perceptions of such conditions have been reorganized into a new vision" (1980:12). The medical discovery of birth control in 1960 was associated both with a "reorganization" of old facts, the facts of mistimed and "illicit" reproduction, into a medical framework and with the creation of "new" facts, in the form of new classes of "patients," to whom this framework could be applied.

Historically, the perspective of the medical profession on the "artificial" control of reproduction has been one of extreme conservatism (Kennedy, 1970; Gordon, 1977; Reed, 1978, 1979). As late as 1936 (by which time, of course, the U.S. birth rate had reached an all-time low), a committee appointed by the American Medical Association to investigate contraceptive methods reported that: "no type of contraception . . . is reasonably adequate and effective for a large portion of the population. . . . No contraceptive technic other than continence is intrinsically one hundred percent safe" (cited in Kennedy, 1970:214–15). In any case, the only medically acceptable reasons for contraception were to treat or prevent disease. This extreme position was modified in 1937, but the change did not herald any large-scale medical enthusiasm for birth control, primarily, James Reed suggests, due to the limitations of then current contraceptive technology: " 'messy little gadgets . . . pastes, and creams and jellies' were 'an embarrassment to the scientific mind' " (1979:125–26). He cites the finding from a 1957 survey of physicians conducted by the Columbia Bureau of Applied Social Research that "only one doctor in five . . . thought that most married couples got contraceptive advice from medical sources" (1979:125). This is hardly surprising given the additional finding (from the same survey) that, even among non-Catholic doctors, only 29 percent thought "providing contraceptive advice and information should be a standard procedure in the practice of medicine." The remainder would provide this advice only on request (Spivack, 1964). Summarizing the medical position prior to 1960, Reed states: "From the 1830s, when the practice of family limitation first became a subject of broad public debate, until the marketing of the birth control pill in the early 1960s, the majority of doctors viewed the desire for fewer children as a problem rather than as an opportunity to provide a medical service. They associated birth control with threats to the social order that they served and to their profession" (1979:109). Change in this position, Reed suggests, came about as a consequence of two events: the discovery of a "medically respectable" method of contraception and an altered perspective concerning the major source of "threats to the social order."

The oral contraceptive pill was approved by the U.S. Food and Drug Administration (FDA) in May of 1960. It was medically sophisticated—the product of significant developments in the sciences of biology and chemistry; conceptually simple—the analogue in reproductive control to penicillin in the control of infection; and available only by medical prescription: "Suddenly physicians had a much-sought-after service that commanded good fees, lent the prestige of science to the general practitioner, and involved none of the awkwardness of diaphragm fitting" (Reed, 1978:364–65). "From ritual . . . to reason" headlined a 1965 Searle advertisement for Enovid, playing on these themes (*Journal of the American Medical Association* [hereinafter *JAMA*] 194 [13], December 27, 1965:76–77).

Between 1938, when a policy "neither endorsing nor opposing population control" was adopted, and 1964, when birth control was recognized by the AMA's House of Delegates as "a major responsibility" of the medical profession, the issue of fertility control was ignored by American medical officialdom. The explanation publicly advanced for the AMA's change of heart was the compelling nature of the population problem. "An intelligent recognition of the problems that relate to human reproduction, including the need for population control, is more than a matter of responsible parenthood; it is a matter of responsible medical practice" (*JAMA* 190 [12], December 21, 1964:31). In staking claim to this new turf, James Z. Appel, the AMA's president, made clear what was meant by "population control." According to the *New York Times*, "Appel said . . . that the problem of birth control was medical and was not, nor should it be religious. . . . He called for extra efforts to educate the 'lower economic and intellectual levels of society' on birth control. Because of the health hazards resulting from overpopulation, 'birth control is a vital part of preventive medicine and comprehensive health care' " (June 28, 1966:37:2). Both in scientific reports on oral contraception and in more general discussions of fertility control, physicians identified the problem of "excessive breeding" with "the poorest and most illiterate patients." These patients, in turn, were just the ones for whom the solution was "the Pill": "The relatively complex method of oral contraception has been proved to be highly acceptable and successful among welfare patients of very low socioeconomic and educational status who rejected or failed with all previous methods" (AMA Committee on Human Reproduction, 1965:462).

The alacrity with which organized medicine moved to endorse birth control subsequent to the discovery of the pill was due not only to the "effectiveness" of oral contraception (effective and at least equally simple methods have been known and used for hundreds of years) and to its medical respectability, but also to its mode of distribution: Unlike access to condoms or withdrawal, access to the pill was medically controlled. That physician control was a political as much as a medical issue became evident when government concerns about the safety of oral contraception appeared to threaten professional prerogatives. The safety concerns of physicians themselves were a consistent theme in *JAMA* articles during this period. Nevertheless, the House of Delegates and the *Journal* in its editorial pages opposed not only an FDA-required package insert warning women of the pill's potential dangers, but even a brochure directed to patients that was prepared with the participation of the AMA itself: "Imparting information to patients is the physician's prerogative," the editorial stated (*JAMA* 213 [9], August 31, 1970:1481). At the very same time, the AMA's lawyers were warning physicians that "to protect themselves against possible malpractice suits" they should be sure to tell patients about the advantages and disadvantages of *all* contraceptive methods and to remind patients "that the ultimate choice of a method of contraception is their responsibility" (*JAMA* 212 [6], May 11, 1970:959). Choice was the patient's responsibility but control over the information required to make a responsible choice was to be retained by the physician.

The medical position on birth control prior to 1960 was a product of highly traditional attitudes concerning family organization and the roles of women combined with elitist ideas on the eugenic value of different population groups.[18] These ideas did not change with the advent of the pill.[19] In postpill medical literature discussion of birth control was limited almost exclusively to the context of marriage and was advocated as a means of strengthening the family; furthermore, as noted above, one of the major selling points of the pill was its supposed "acceptability" to "patients of very low socioeconomic and educational status." What did change in the postpill era was how the role of medical professionals in implementing these social values was defined. The allure of scientific innovation (not only to physicians, but to many of their patients as well), the ease of medical control, and—probably of most importance, as the next section will show—organized interest group pressure persuaded the profession to reverse its historic position and redefine birth control as in the interests of, rather than as opposed to, traditional concepts of "family welfare" and social stability (see, e.g., Lief, 1966).

Insofar as these concepts were reflected in the pages of *JAMA*, they did not encompass the offering of contraceptive services to unmarried, never-pregnant teenagers. The process by which adolescent pregnancy became defined as a medical problem serves, in fact, as an excellent illustration of physicians' essential conservatism in matters of sexual and reproductive behavior. For a variety of reasons, both social and technological, obstetricians in the late 1950s and early 1960s became increasingly concerned with insuring that women had babies at the "medically correct" time in their reproductive cycles. Beginning in this period, there is an expanding volume of medical literature on the topic of pregnancy and delivery among unmarried adolescent women (Poliakoff, 1958; Aznar and Bennett, 1961; Battaglia, Frazier, and Hellegers, 1963; Hassan and Falls, 1964; Semmens, 1965; Osofsky, 1968). With two exceptions, the reports cited are based on clinic populations of poor, predominantly black, women. The focus of attention in this work was on the identification of pregnancy "risks" peculiar to adolescence; by the mid-1960s, despite what was, in fact, widely conflicting evidence, the presumption that adolescents were a medically "high-risk" obstetrical population was well-established.[20]

The major emphasis in physicians' response to this newly-discovered "'chronic illness' of adolescent girls" (Gordis et al., 1968:855) was not, however, preventive (although medical "treatment" programs described in the literature were all initiated postpill) but ameliorative.[21] Young women (again, all poor and almost all black) are pictured as unable to resolve their problems independently (rendering them appropriate candidates for "treatment" rather than censure), and as requiring intensive medical, social, psychological, and educational services (thereby clearly establishing the "abnormality" of their condition). The one program that did, in this period, offer contraception to "sexually active nulliparous teenagers" did so only under highly circumscribed conditions that the authors were at pains to describe: Birth control was provided only with written consent of "the parents" and "the final decision . . . will be made on the basis of the medical, social, and psychological assessment" (Gordis et al., 1968:852). Quite clearly, responsibility for "the final decision" remained with the professional staff. The program's objective was disease prevention (and, more generally, the control of what the staff defined as deviant sexual and reproductive behavior patterns) not sexual autonomy for teenage women.

That the majority of physicians preferred not to confront the issue of teenage women's sexual behavior or its consequences is apparent in scattered references to the issue in *JAMA*: The physician is urged not to bury "his head in the sand and pretend the problems aren't there;" nevertheless, the "issue of giving contraceptives to unmarried women who have never been pregnant" is acknowledged to be "complicated" and "controversial" (Lief, 1966). How complicated and controversial is indicated by the House of Delegates' rejection in 1970 of a recommendation by its Committee on Maternal and Child Health that a policy statement be adopted "permitting physicians to offer contraceptive advice and methods to teenage girls whose sexual behavior exposes them to possible pregnancy" (*JAMA* 213 [10], September 7, 1970:1554). Ultimately, the "medicalization" of adolescent pregnancy came about less as a consequence of medical entrepreneurship than of lay advocacy, as we shall see.

The Politicization of Birth Control

In 1972, the Social Security Act was amended to require that states provide family planning services to "minors who are sexually active" (P.L. 92–603). Appearances to the contrary notwithstanding, this action was not motivated by an aroused public concern over adolescent pregnancy. The chairman of the Senate Committee on Finance was Russell B. Long; the amendments were an outcome of Senator Long's persuasion that birth control might be the answer to illegitimate babies and expanding welfare rolls.[22] Nevertheless, in order to understand how adolescent pregnancy *did* become a public problem, it is necessary to trace the process by which Long and other makers of public policy became converts to the cause of "family planning."

In the late 1950s, "birth control" was a topic considered barely suitable for public comment, much less political action.[23] In 1958, President Eisenhower, responding to a government-appointed commission's recommendation that there be increased official attention to birth control, stated: "I cannot imagine anything more emphatically a subject that is not a proper political or governmental activity or function or responsibility. . . . This government will not . . . as long as I am here . . . have a positive political doctrine in its program that has to do with this problem of birth control. That is not our business" (cited in Dienes, 1972:266).[24] Nevertheless, as C. Thomas Dienes pointed out, controversy over the government's position (as over its position on birth control for teenagers fourteen years later) moved the issue "from the realm of private morals and theology and into that of public discussion and political action." In the same year that Eisenhower made his famous remarks, a New York City obstetrician working in a tax-supported hospital was advised by city officials not to fit a married woman with a diaphragm on the grounds of opposition from the Catholic church. The test case that resulted was fought and won largely through the behind-the-scenes efforts of the Planned Parenthood Federation of America.[25] In this episode the lines of battle were clearly drawn: between Planned Parenthood's definition of birth control as "a relatively simple and inexpensive medical service" (Jaffe and Polgar, 1968:235) and the church's position that "artificial birth control" was "morally, humanly, psychologically, and politically disastrous" (1959 statement of U.S. Catholic bishops, cited in Littlewood, 1977:24).

During the 1960s Planned Parenthood was largely successful in having *its* definition prevail. "Birth control" was transformed from a political liability to an instrument of public policy.[26] Planned Parenthood gained political acceptance not only for its particular conception of the "subjects" to whom this instrument should be applied but, more important in the long run, acceptance of its overall *authority* to define who those subjects should be. Even at the time of its greatest success the hegemony of Planned Parenthood was by no means complete or uncontested. And, as the decade of the 1970s advanced, advocates of alternative frameworks for "understanding" issues of sexuality, birth control, and reproduction renewed their attack and began, again, to seriously compete with the birth control movement.

To understand the role of Planned Parenthood in the birth control debates of the 1960s (and in the 1970s and 1980s as well) requires some knowledge of its structure and ideology. By 1942, when, on the advice of a public relations firm, the name of the organization was changed from the Birth Control Federation of America to the Planned Parenthood Federation of America, it had long lost its militant character and become a white, middle-class, professionally-led, but largely volunteer movement for social reform through "family planning." Reed ascribes the impetus for the emergence of the birth control movement in the 1920s and 1930s to three motives: "autonomy for women, better marital sex adjustment, and concern over differential fertility" (meaning relatively higher fertility among the poor than the well-to-do) (1978:xi). In the process of seeking social acceptance and respectability, the birth control movement's early emphasis on "autonomy for women" became gradually submerged; relatively greater stress was placed on contraception as a means of promoting "family stability" and of insuring that individuals had no more children than they could "afford."[27] A major dimension of this change was, as Petchesky points out, "the *desexualization* of the birth control issue" (1984:93). Birth control became defined as a health and social planning measure, *not* as a means to the enjoyment of sex separated from procreation.

Among the reasons for this emphasis on the "stabilizing" as opposed to the "liberating" effects of contraceptive use was the central importance to Planned Parenthood (and, earlier, to Margaret Sanger herself) of medical legitimation for the birth control cause. Medical endorsement would enable birth control advocates to appropriate to themselves the power and status of the medical profession and, ultimately, to gain public acceptance for their particular vision of reality. As Barbara Wootton has remarked, "Today the prestige of humane proposals is immensely enhanced if these are expressed in the idiom of medical science" (1959:206). In the longer run, "medicalization" was a strategy for removing the birth control issue from the domain of moral and legal arbiters altogether, a strategy that was intended to change the grounds of debate from questions of "right" and "wrong" to "neutral" medical-technical questions of "safety" and "effectiveness." It is important to keep in mind, however, that this strategy's most active and effective supporters were not representatives of the medical profession but lay advocates "invoking medical values, images and symbols" in aid of their particular cause (Schneider and Conrad, 1980:13). Planned Parenthood's definition of birth control as "an integral and routine part of good medical care" (Jaffe, 1968:69) was, as we have seen, one to which many physicians did not, in fact, subscribe.

Despite Planned Parenthood's efforts to bring the ideology of birth control into conformity with family-oriented values, as well as improvements in its organizational structure, it was, in 1950, "just another voluntary health service organization, with little influence on policy makers," limited in both members and funds (Reed, 1978:269; see also Piotrow, 1973:16). By the mid-1960s a complex set of demographic, social, and political circumstances had created the *opportunity* to convert this position of relative weakness into one of quite remarkable strength.[28] This conversion was *accomplished* by persuading public policy makers that birth control was a cost-effective answer to the problems of poverty, illegitimacy, and the rising costs of welfare. The essence of Planned Parenthood's campaign was caught in Sar A. Levitan's phrase, "fighting poverty with a pill" (1969).

A defining characteristic of the birth control movement is that instead of being centered around a "problem," like alcoholism or child abuse, or around a set of victimized individuals, blacks, women, or gays, it is centered around a "solution." Much like the huckster who sold snake oil off the back of a Conestoga wagon, birth control advocates have chronically found themselves in the position of seeking new "diseases" to cure and new categories of sufferers. Thus, while medical science may have discovered the pill, the discovery of diseases and victims with sufficient political appeal to unlock the coffers of the federal government has been left to the lay entrepreneurs of the birth control movement.[29] And, again like the huckster of old, these entrepreneurs have geared their pitch to the perceived requirements of the audience and of the moment. In the mid-1960s, what the audience required was a "solution" to the twin problems of "illegitimacy" and the costs of welfare, clothed in the rhetoric of President Johnson's War on Poverty. It was within this framework that birth control advocates, in publications, government-commissioned reports, and Congressional hearings, built their case.[30] The central protagonists in this construction of the poverty problem were *Five Million Women* (the title of a Planned Parenthood document published in 1967); this figure was repeated over and over again in the references cited and eventually (perhaps the ultimate endorsement) was used by President Nixon in his 1969 population growth message (reprinted in U.S. Cong., House, Committee on Interstate and Foreign Commerce, 1970). It represents an estimate of the number of poor women "in need" of "family planning" services.[31] Having identified a client population, these documents went on to portray this population as suffering from multiple "unwanted pregnancies," victims both of an indifferent federal bureaucracy and of a medical care system that denied them "access to services providing modern, coitally-independent methods" (Jaffe and Guttmacher, 1968:916). Poverty, in this scenario, was a consequence of large families; large families (as well, quite explicitly, as "illegitimacy" and welfare costs) would be reduced through large-scale government support of family planning services.

The success of the "poverty–family planning" campaign was evident in its results. Between 1967 and 1972, annual federal expenditures on family planning services increased fourteen-fold, from 11 million dollars to 149 million dollars (Rosoff, 1973). Funds were authorized through five different pieces of legislation, enacted, with one exception, in the three-year period between 1967 and 1970, certainly the high point for family planning legislation in the United States. Contemporary newspaper reports, Congressional testimony in support of this legislation, and historical accounts (e.g., Dienes, 1972; Littlewood, 1977) make crystal clear the unique convergence of disparate interests that led to this remarkable success. As Dienes remarked, "The politics of birth control can certainly make strange bedfellows: the dollar-conscious, the anti-Negro, and the humanitarian had found a common cause" (1972:276–77). In the process of achieving this success, Planned Parenthood itself was transformed from "just another voluntary health service organization, with little influence on policy makers" into the nucleus of a highly effective lobbying group with powerful political ties.

I commented earlier that the "poverty–family planning" framework constructed by birth control advocates did not go uncontested. Opposition came from several sources. A few demographers argued against the assumptions underlying family planning programs in general (Davis, 1967) and against the estimate of "five million women" in need of family planning services in particular (Blake, 1969a; Blake and Das Gupta, 1972). Exchanges around this latter issue published in the pages of *Science* (Harkavy, Jaffe, and Wishik, 1969; Blake, 1969b) provide an excellent perspective on the rhetorical purposes served by "scientific" data. A second source of professional opposition was public health physicians (many of whom were located within the federal bureaucracy) committed to "comprehensive" maternal and child health goals and concerned about the competition for resources from single-issue birth control advocates (Jaffe and Polgar, 1968; Wallace, Gold, and Dooley, 1969; Levitan and LaVor, 1969; Piotrow, 1973; Allen, 1974). Finally, opposition came from moral conservatives, represented at this stage primarily by the Catholic church, and from some black leaders who perceived the "poverty–family planning" campaign as politically and racially motivated (Littlewood, 1977). For the time being, however, the framework constructed by birth control advocates dominated public debate.

From the perspective of this analysis, the most significant consequence of the sudden massive increase in federal funds for "family planning services" was the creation of an institutional constituency with a strong investment in the continued existence of these services. Within the rhetorical framework constructed by birth control advocates, family planning services *are* health services, a branch of preventive medicine and, therefore, the responsibility of physicians and health care organizations. "Standards of Care" published in 1972 by the federal funding agency for family planning included medical examination and laboratory tests (Jaffe, Dryfoos, and Corey, 1973). When federal funds became available, they were channeled to hospitals, health departments, Planned Parenthood clinics, and other facilities with the capacity to provide medically-directed services. Between 1968 and 1972, these services expanded enormously. The number of agencies with family planning services increased by 50 percent (from 2,000 to 3,000); clients increased threefold, from about 900,000 to over 2.5 million (Jaffe, Dryfoos, and Corey, 1973). Although I do not have data on changes in numbers of staff or in the proportion of staff paid directly by federal family planning funds, it is reasonable to conclude that these figures also increased. I review these numbers in order to make the point that, in addition to providing services, federal funds were also responsible for creating a network of organizations and individuals whose resources were dependent, at least in part, on those services, and who could be expected to react strongly should those resources be threatened.[32]

Neither the federal government's fiscal support for contraceptive services nor the legislative language authorizing services for "minors who are sexually active" were generated by a perceived "teenage pregnancy" problem. In birth control advocacy literature of that period, the "target" population was defined in terms of poverty, not age, and was referred to as "women" or "families." Throughout the 1960s, marital status and parental status as criteria of "eligibility" for contraception were constant sources of controversy: Use of public funds to provide birth control for unmarried mothers was attacked on the grounds that it would "abet, facilitate and subsidize illicit extramarital relations" (Dienes, 1972:274). No one had the temerity to publicly propose birth control for single women without children. The political sensitivity of the "teenage" issue was clearly reflected in the Congressional testimony of birth control advocates. They never addressed it voluntarily and attempted to skirt it when it was raised by members of Congress: Birth control for adolescents was a question that neither advocates nor politicians found easy to structure in purely "preventive-medical" terms. Given their primary goals at the time, it was a question that advocates apparently preferred to avoid, at least in public.[33] How and why they became less reticent is addressed in Chapter 3.

Summary
Management of reproduction in the interests of family integrity and social stability are relatively constant societal concerns. My purpose in this chapter has been to describe changes that took place between 1960 and 1972 in the ways in which departures from "normative" reproductive behavior were perceived and in the "solutions" that were proposed. The most critical of these changes was the designation of mistimed and socially misplaced (i.e., nonmarital) reproduction as a medical problem: "Illegitimacy," with its implication of moral transgression, became "one of the gravest socio-medical illnesses, unwanted pregnancy" (Alan Guttmacher, cited in Ross, 1970).[34] An essential condition for this designation, I have argued, was the discovery of a medically respectable prophylaxis for socially unorthodox reproduction: "A prospective solution makes possible the existence of the problem by proposing that some obnoxious aspect of life, heretofore thought to be unalterable ('nothing can be done') might be alleviated" (Spector and Kitsuse, 1977:128). Thus, in a very real sense, the definition of unwanted pregnancy as a *medical* (rather than a moral) problem was created by its medical "solution," the oral contraceptive pill. However, the incorporation of this solution into public policies and public programs was not the necessary consequence of the pill's invention nor was it, by and large, the result of medical entrepreneurship; the construction of deviant reproduction as a problem to be solved with public funds was the work of lay birth control advocates.

These changes did not, in any sense, *determine* the emergence of adolescent pregnancy as a public problem. Nevertheless, they set the stage for its emergence, first, by legitimizing the definition of reproductive norm violations as medical problems, properly subject to medical diagnosis and treatment and, second, by creating an organizational network with a substantial investment in the medical model of deviant reproduction *and* with access to the *political* resources for protecting that investment, should protection be required. At the same time, and equally critical, demographic and political events were conspiring to produce what Theodore Roszak (1969) called "the invasion of centaurs," the 1960s discovery of youth as a separate, and potentially threatening, social category. A major component of this threat was, as I have noted, the perception of youth as lacking in sexual restraint.

However, concern about the sexuality of youth was by no means immediately translated into public pressure that "something be done." Deviant *sexuality* was perceived as a white, middle-class problem, essentially divorced from reproduction; deviant *reproduction* was a black, lower-class problem, an appropriate subject for public policy because it affected the public purse. Legislative authority to provide minors with contraceptive services snuck in to the 1972 Social Security Act amendments in the context of an attack on illegitimacy and welfare costs; if, in the climate of that period, this legislative change had been presented as a response to adolescent pregnancy, it almost certainly would have been defeated. How, then, in a period of little more than five years did a problem of unwanted pregnancy among five million poor women become transformed into an "epidemic of adolescent pregnancies" among 11 million teenagers?

MAKING THE REVOLUTION, 1972–1978

Chapter 3

THE gradual displacement of poor women by adolescents both in the rhetoric
of birth control advocates and as the principal occasion for public concern
about what is perceived as deviant sexuality and reproduction can be traced
in a variety of sources: the pages of the *New York Times*, the publications of
the Alan Guttmacher Institute (principally the journal, *Family Planning Perspectives*), and the annals of federal legislation. Between 1967 and 1970, in
a veritable flood of publications, in newspapers, and in Congressional hearings, the victims of unwanted pregnancy had consistently been portrayed as
five million poor women. By 1974, when Planned Parenthood of New York
announced that it would "for the first time" focus "an ambitious birth control
campaign" specifically on teenagers, these five million poor women had virtually disappeared from the public stage. Examination of the *New York Times
Index* under the heading, "pregnancy," shows no references to teenagers, adolescents, minors, or students until 1970 when a single reference occurs. From
then on the number of articles gradually increases, reaching a peak in 1978
of fourteen. This shift in focus is similarly reflected in the pages of *Family
Planning Perspectives*: estimates of the potential client population in "need"
of "family planning services" (a regular feature of the journal) did not include
"teenagers" as a separate category until 1973 (Dryfoos, 1973). By 1976, with the
publication of a special issue on "Teenagers USA," the birth control "needs"
of teenage women had become a dominant theme in family planning rhetoric.
Finally, the "Five-Year Plan for Family Planning Services and Population Research Programs" submitted by the secretary of Health, Education, and Welfare
to the U.S. Senate in 1971 was based on a projection of "need" by the "medically
indigent." Passing reference was made to "the unmarried minor whose family
is not medically indigent," but individuals with these latter characteristics were
not included in the planning estimate. In 1978, legislation was introduced in

Congress specifically addressed to the newly-identified "problem" of adolescent pregnancy, at the same time that the original family planning legislation (authorizing, among other things, the five-year plan) came under increasing governmental attack.

The radical nature of the transformation I have described would be difficult to overemphasize. Excess fertility among the poor had been accepted as a legitimate social problem since Malthus published his famous essay in 1798; the poor but honest (i.e., married) woman struggling to raise too many children on too little income has been a potent symbol of the birth control movement since its inception (see, e.g., Reed, 1978:82). By contrast, as recently as 1945 Planned Parenthood was refusing to mail a pamphlet designed for *premarital* sex education to *unmarried* women (cited in Gordon, 1977:365). Public attention to adolescent pregnancy demanded open acknowledgment of facts the public had always preferred to ignore: that teenage women might have sexual intercourse, that they might become pregnant, and that they might engage in these activities outside the bonds of wedlock (or even of anticipated wedlock). Constructing adolescent pregnancy as a public problem meant not only the redefinition of problematic reproduction on the basis of age rather than socioeconomic status; it also involved the medicalization of sexuality and reproduction among a class of persons to whom these activities were socially proscribed. Before addressing the complex question of *why* these changes occurred, it will be useful to specify more precisely the dimensions of the transformation itself.

THE SOCIAL CONSTRUCTION OF
ADOLESCENT PREGNANCY

"Unintended pregnancy . . . is happening to our young women, not only among the poor and minority groups, but in all socioeconomic groups—if I had a daughter, I would say to 'our' daughters" (U.S. Cong., House, Select Committee on Population, 1978:170–71). These words of the president of the Alan Guttmacher Institute before the House Select Committee on Population sounded a major theme in the construction of the adolescent pregnancy problem: Sexual and reproductive unorthodoxy was redefined from a problem of low-income black women—someone else's problem—to "our" problem, the problem of white, middle-class families, a problem to which even the daughters of Congressional representatives might not be immune. By the mid-1970s, in journalistic accounts as well as in the literature of birth control advocacy, the white, suburban middle-class, high school girl had become the dominant metaphor for deviant sexuality and reproduction. Between 1976 and 1978, the *New York Times* published twenty articles on teenage pregnancy and its management in New York state; in eight of these articles the scope of geographic attention was limited to the Long Island suburbs and Westchester county, bastions of white suburbia. In its influential publication, *11 Million Teenagers*, the Alan Guttmacher Institute included twenty-nine photographs; twenty-seven were of white subjects, over half were middle-class, high-school age girls (twelve) or couples (three).[1] The image of the "at risk" teenager conveyed to the public was not that of a poor, black, inner-city resident. In her place was the girl next door, a rhetorical shift of major proportions that both enlarged the spectrum of persons "in need" of reproductive surveillance and control and substantially altered the meanings attached to their behavior.

With this shift in the principal location of reproductive deviance from poor women to adolescents came a corresponding shift in definition of the "problem" to be solved by reproductive management. In the birth control rhetoric of the 1960s, elimination of unwanted pregnancies was presented as a means to the end of accelerating poor families' "exit from poverty" (Jaffe and Polgar, 1968:228). In the idiom of adolescent pregnancy, the underlying problem became redefined from one of *poverty* to one of *pregnancy* itself. The specter of *adolescent* pregnancy effectively blurred distinctions not only between poor and nonpoor, black and white *women* but also between wanted and unwanted, in-wedlock and out-of-wedlock *pregnancies:* Adolescent pregnancy was described as "tragic," without qualification. A central dimension of this shift in emphasis, one with profound long-range consequences for the management of adolescent fertility, was the designation of sexual and reproductive behavior by adolescent women as a medical rather than a moral problem. The medicalization of adolescent pregnancy (like that of "unwanted" pregnancy generally) was made possible, in part, by the discovery of oral contraception; however, for publicly-funded medical treatment to replace public condemnation of socially-proscribed sexual behavior demanded not only that a treatment exist; it demanded that public perceptions of the behavior itself be radically altered. The shape of this alteration (as proposed by birth control advocates) was anticipated in a 1969 article by Harriet F. Pilpel and Nancy F. Wechsler in which legal advice is offered to physicians wishing to prescribe birth control for "minors."

> The physician would be well advised to defend [against prosecution for treating minors without parental consent] on the ground that the minor had been sexually active, and that in his best professional judgement, he felt that failure to prescribe contraceptives would subject the minor, or the out-of-wedlock children whom she would be likely to bear, to serious health hazards. *An argument could certainly be made that the physician's actions (like most medical treatment) were independent of the "delinquent" conduct of the patient, and were intended and needed to avoid adverse health effects of such conduct* (30; emphasis added).

It would be difficult to find a statement more clearly demonstrating how medicalization was employed to transform traditional conceptions of adolescent pregnancy. In this construction, the moral status of minors' sexual *conduct* remains unchanged; concentration on the consequences of this conduct for the health of mother and child has the combined effects of neutralizing the moral connotations of adolescent sexuality and legitimizing its transfer from parental to professional control.

To bring about the transformation I have described, two principal themes were invoked: the dire biological, personal, and social consequences of pregnancy in adolescence and the preventability of these consequences by means of medically-supervised contraceptive methods.

> Let us suppose there was an illness striking one adolescent in 10 each year, and that this illness had long lasting and sometimes crippling side effects. Suppose, also that it was expensive and difficult to avoid the sequelae once the condition occurred, but that we possessed a reasonably safe and effective means of prevention. Would we emphasize a strategy of prevention or would we try merely to ameliorate the negative effects of the illness after it appeared? Of course, parenthood is not a disease, but when unplanned and unwanted, as it typically is for adolescents, pregnancy in some ways resembles an illness (U.S. Cong., House, Select Committee on Population, 1978:168).

Rhetoric in which the themes of illness and prevention were repeatedly sounded, supported by research conducted within the framework of the medical model, were the major ingredients of a campaign to reorganize public perceptions of pregnancy and childbearing by young single women: from behaviors that were socially reprehensible but biologically normal to behaviors with severe and long-lasting negative consequences for the health of mother and child. In this process of reorganization, emphasis was shifted from the *willful* transgression of moral norms represented by the sexual act of an unmarried woman to the *unwilled* but "inevitable" consequences of that act. As has often been observed, conditions for which the individual is held responsible tend to be treated punitively, while conditions perceived as involuntary are managed with permissive treatment or instruction (Freidson, 1972; Schneider and Conrad, 1980). The designation of adolescent pregnancy as a medical problem was fundamental to the argument that it should be "treated" rather than punished. That the negative health consequences of adolescent pregnancy were not only involuntary but inevitable was used to further argue for treatment by prevention (birth control) rather than cure ("rehabilitation" subsequent to the birth of a child).[2]

The construction of adolescent pregnancy as a preventable illness follows an established pattern in American life in which behaviors formerly designated as "badness"—alcoholism, child abuse, homosexuality, hyperactivity in children, mental illness—have become redefined as "sickness" (Conrad and Schneider, 1980). Medicalization does not alter the negative evaluation of these behaviors; what it does change is how the deviant actors are regarded and the means of behavioral control that are employed. In the case of adolescent pregnancy, preventive "treatment" was justified not on the grounds of its positive contribution to the sexual autonomy and pleasure of teenage women but on its value as a prophylaxis against disease.[3] The proclaimed objective of birth control advocates was not increased adolescent independence but a shift to what was, they argued, a more humane form of social control.

The construction of public problems is a political process. In their struggle to gain a public hearing and to prevail over alternative problem designations, advocates must, if they would be successful, tailor their message to current

social and political realities: nonprocreative sex as a form of adolescent rec-
reation, however desirable in principle, would not prove readily marketable
to members of Congress in charge of disbursing public funds. Nowhere is
this need to fit the message to the audience more evident than in the rhetorical focus of birth control advocates on adolescent *pregnancy* rather than
on adolescent *childbearing*. The consequences invoked to support a disease
model of adolescent pregnancy (infant mortality, prematurity, maternal mortality, blocked educational achievement, welfare dependency, and so on) are,
by and large, consequences of childbirth and childrearing, not of pregnancy;
in principle, these consequences are avoidable by pregnancy termination as
readily as by pregnancy prevention. Nevertheless, however logical the abortion alternative may be, in the United States at the present time its political
sensitivity has rendered abortion essentially unavailable as a salable "solution"
to the problem of untimely childbearing. (Abortion is not, of course, *only*
politically unacceptable; it is socially and/or morally unacceptable to many
young women.) The solutions around which public problems are created must
meet criteria of social and political as well as technological availability. It is in
the light of these requirements that the construction of the adolescent fertility
problem around pregnancy rather than childbearing can best be understood.

TRANSFORMATION OF A PROBLEM:
THE SOCIAL CONTEXT OF CHANGE
In the introduction to his essay on "drinking-driving" Gusfield points out that
"knowledge and law are not shiny marbles lying on the beach and awaiting
only the sharp eyes of skilled men and women to be found. The 'facts' of
alcohol are picked out of a pile, scrubbed, polished, highlighted here and
there, and offered as discoveries in the context of the particular and practical considerations of their finders" (1981:20). Implicit in this image of public
problem construction are both a collection of raw materials waiting to be "discovered" and a creative human agency possessed of sundry "considerations"
on the basis of which these materials are processed for public consumption.
The raw materials of the adolescent pregnancy problem were demographic,
biomedical, and social data and, I believe, a climate of public opinion receptive
to the interpretation of these data in apocalyptic terms; the human agencies
were birth control advocates and, later, advocates of other "solutions," each of
whom employed these data to advance their own particular visions of reality.

Data describing changes in adolescent fertility over the last several decades were presented in Chapter 2. Although birth *rates* to women under
age 20 have been declining since 1957, the baby boom–generated bulge in
numbers of births combined with changes in young women's reproductive
management strategies leading to much higher proportions of births to *single*
(in particular, single white) women were of critical importance in setting the
demographic stage for adolescent pregnancy to emerge as a public problem.
Of equal moment, however, was the publication in the early 1970s of entirely

new types of data, documenting for the first time the sexual intercourse and pregnancy (as opposed to childbearing) experience of young single women in the United States. These data, generated from studies conducted by Melvin Zelnik and John F. Kantner of Johns Hopkins University as well as from the routinely collected program statistics of newly legalized abortion facilities, appeared in *Family Planning Perspectives* almost as soon as they came off the computer and were given widespread attention in the lay press. Data on sexual intercourse were the backbone for estimates of "family planning need" among teenage women; in the absence of abortion data, an advocacy campaign focused on adolescent *pregnancy* could not have been launched (traditionally available vital statistics documented births, not pregnancies).

In the foregoing paragraph, the word "documented" is used advisedly. Without comparable data, it was difficult to estimate the degree to which levels of sexual activity and pregnancy reported by adolescents in 1972 represented departures (up or down) from previous years.[4] The *consequential* changes, therefore, were not changes in adolescent behavior but changes in what we, as a society, were in a position to *know* about that behavior and in the social and political conditions into which that knowledge was introduced. As reflected by the remarks of Pilpel and Wechsler quoted earlier, birth control advocates had been interested in the contraceptive access problems of minors well before the "discovery" of adolescent pregnancy. The new availability of national data offered an opportunity to translate that interest into an active campaign. Opportunities must be seized, however. Data do not speak for themselves. Without the presence in society of groups and organizations prepared to make them publicly and politically visible, data will languish in comfortable silence on library shelves. Documentation of adolescent sexuality became available at a time when organizational, as well as political conditions were favorable for the construction of these data as a major public problem.

The Actors
In the late 1960s, when Zelnik and Kantner's research was initiated, there was relatively little interest among professional demographers in adolescent fertility.[5] The overall contribution of this age group to childbearing in the United States was negligible; medical methods of contraception were expected to diminish its impact even further; and, in any case, major difficulties in conducting research on this topic were anticipated. Zelnik and Kantner were originally interested in both blacks and never-married minors—groups left out of or underrepresented in previous fertility surveys. Their specific focus on teenagers came about through a deal with the funding agency (National Institutes of Health) after their original interest in black fertility was preempted by scholars arriving earlier in the field: Princeton University's Office of Population Research was to conduct another round of its National Fertility Survey in which a large sample of blacks would be included. It was arranged that Zelnik and Kantner would focus on the fertility of adolescent women instead. The Commission on Population Growth and the American Future, appointed by

President Nixon in 1970, then used data from this latter survey as the basis for what turned out to be one of its more controversial recommendations.

Within the period of a few months in early 1972, the U.S. Supreme Court ruled that states could not outlaw the distribution of contraceptives to unmarried persons, the Commission published its recommendation that "birth control information and services be made available to teenagers," and Zelnik and Kantner's initial findings were made public. In the context of the Commission's report, and of President Nixon's specific rejection of its recommendation on teenagers, these findings—among them, that "nearly 50 percent of all unmarried women have had sexual intercourse by the time they are 19 years old"—received substantial public attention. However, while publicity surrounding the report may have forced the topic of adolescent sexuality onto the public stage, the organized efforts of birth control advocates, led by Planned Parenthood's Center for Family Planning Program Development (now the Alan Guttmacher Institute) helped to keep it there. Jeannie I. Rosoff, president of the Alan Guttmacher Institute, has written that Zelnik and Kantner's "findings would have been known only among professionals and some key policy makers without the extensive publicity generated by articles published in AGI's journal, *Family Planning Perspectives*" (Rosoff, 1986:4). This may be overstated. The data were hot property, and Johns Hopkins University itself went to considerable lengths to insure that their importance—and their institutional origins—were publicly appreciated. Nevertheless, it is difficult to underestimate the role of the Alan Guttmacher Institute in insuring that the initial high level of public attention was sustained over a truly remarkable length of time.

The Alan Guttmacher Institute (AGI) came into being in 1968 as the Center for Family Planning Program Development, the "Research and Development Division of the Planned Parenthood Federation of America, Inc." In 1974, the Center was renamed the Alan Guttmacher Institute, but retained its formal divisional status in relation to the Planned Parenthood Federation of America (PPFA). Finally, in 1978, AGI became an independent corporation. However, it continues to have close ties with PPFA: AGI is now described as a "special affiliate" of PPFA; each organization has members on the other's board of directors; and AGI receives regular financial contributions from PPFA. However, the bulk of its support comes from other sources. AGI was initiated with a grant from the Ford Foundation, and continues to be supported primarily by private foundations (Ford, Rockefeller, Mellon, and others).

The founder of AGI, and its president until his death in 1978, was Fred Jaffe, an extraordinarily energetic and committed former journalist who became a single-minded crusader for the cause of fertility control. It was during the period from 1969 to 1972, the glory years of U.S. government support for expansion of family planning services to the poor, that Jaffe and AGI acquired the financial backing, the experience, and the connections in and out of government that made possible not only their rapid expansion into, but their effective dramatization of, the newly discovered problem of fertility control among teenage women. In 1975 and 1976, largely at the instigation of AGI, the National Institute of Child Health and Development's Center for Population Research sponsored two conferences on the consequences and determinants of adolescent pregnancy and childbearing; other public health and medical organizations took up the cause. None, however, approached it with the combined dedication and flair for public relations of AGI. Papers for *Family Planning Perspectives* were actively solicited from individual scholars and at professional meetings; press releases accompanied the journal's every issue; friendly editorial writers were alerted to the need for timely comment. Thus, with all the tricks of the journalist's trade, were the private behaviors of adolescent women converted into public facts.

As the shifts in organizational structure described earlier may have suggested, AGI and PPFA had their differences. From its beginning AGI pursued a course that was not only independent of PPFA, but often more activist than the latter, relatively staid, organization would have preferred. Clearly, AGI's goals of enlarging public access to the means of fertility control were shared by PPFA. However, PPFA viewed AGI's original mission of "developing" family planning services outside of, as well as within, the Planned Parenthood clinic network with some suspicion; and it was occasionally leary of what it saw as AGI's readiness to take on controversial issues. AGI owed much of its influence, nevertheless, not only to its own effectiveness, but to its political base in the largely white, middle-class, and often socially prominent national membership of PPFA.

The Political Moment
"Family planning" had been adopted by the federal government as an instrument of public policy in the late 1960s in the context of the Johnson administration's War on Poverty. In 1972 Richard M. Nixon was elected to a second term by a landslide vote; his victory has been largely attributed to a massive conservative rebellion against the use of government power and government funds to "solve" social problems (see, e.g., Matusow, 1984; Siegel, 1984). Invoking the values of individual initiative, hard work, respect for the family, and moral piety, Nixon suggested in his campaign rhetoric that "the great silent majority of hardworking Americans . . . were shouldering the burden of wasteful and intrusive social programs which rewarded the indolent while taxing the energetic" (Siegel, 1984:251). Observers have accounted for the success of these political themes on both social ("a vast public alienated by rapid racial and cultural change") and economic grounds. Reflecting on the decade of the 1960s and its aftermath, Allen J. Matusow remarks, "Affluence in the 1960s had fostered social optimism and undergirded liberal reform. Recessions in the 1970s fostered social pessimism and expanded the audience for conservative denunciations of Keynesians, civil rights enthusiasts, and advocates of expensive welfare programs" (1984:439). Conservatives in the 1970s were hostile, as W. Norton Grubb and Marvin Lazerson point out, "not to public spending itself, but to public spending that benefits the poor." The poor, in the Nixon bestiary

and in that of many other conservatives, were predominantly (and incorrectly) black (cf., Grubb and Lazerson, 1982:81ff.).

Immediately following his reelection in 1972, Nixon took a series of steps with the objective of dismantling the structure of federally sponsored social programs. Family planning services, enormously expanded under the legislation passed by Congress between 1967 and 1970, were directly affected by these actions. Early in 1973, the administration proposed that family planning programs be absorbed into overall maternal and child health grants to states with the specific allocation of funds to be subject to state control; by 1974, the Office of Economic Opportunity, formerly a major source of family planning program funds, had been abolished. The response of birth control advocates to what they perceived as an about-face by the federal government was unequivocal: "These new and, I believe, ill-advised policies do not just slow but threaten the very survival of a family planning program" (Guttmacher, 1973:175). The so-called "block grant" proposal did not (insofar as it applied to family planning) become law. Nevertheless, by the end of 1972 the growth of federal support for family planning programs had ceased, and the consequences were immediately apparent in program statistics. Annual increases in the number of "patients served" declined from 38 percent in fiscal year 1972 to 11 percent in 1973 (Corey, 1975). In the fall of 1973 *Family Planning Perspectives* complained editorially that "the President's 1969 call for a 'national goal' to provide family planning services to all who want but cannot afford them . . . is apparently regarded today as little more than a curiosity of history" ("In This Issue," 1973: inside cover). The political and fiscal conservatism of the second-term Nixon administration combined with its barely veiled racism seriously undermined the poverty–family planning strategy developed by birth control advocates in the very different political climate of the mid-1960s. However, this strategy was threatened not only by conservatism and racism, but also by changes both in the realities and in the politics of reproductive behavior itself.

The 1960s poverty–family planning campaign was launched in an atmosphere of what might be called "population panic"; the dangers of excess population growth were a consistent, if muted, theme running through the advocacy literature cited earlier in this chapter.[6] In fact, birth rates in the United States had been dropping steadily since 1957. However, it was not until the 1970s that even professional demographers became fully aware of the magnitude and consistency of this drop: the 1950s baby boom had been a historically unique phenomenon; the long-term trend in United States fertility was downward (Westoff, 1978). The implications for their cause of this unforeseen drop in fertility were not lost on birth control advocates. Referring to the problems of obtaining funding for the Alan Guttmacher Institute under these altered circumstances, its president wrote: "Some see little need for [the Institute] now that the U.S. birth rate hovers around 15 and replacement-level cohort fertility seems within reach. Since they believe that the U.S. population problem, as they have defined it, is 'solved,' they would shift attention to other areas deemed more pressing" (Alan Guttmacher Institute, 1975:4).

Not only did the population problem appear to have been "solved"; it had been solved largely as a consequence of changes in the reproductive behavior of older women in family settings. These women, the prime targets of the poverty–family planning strategy, could no longer easily be represented as in urgent need of family planning services. However, organizations do not, as a rule, dissolve because their goals have been achieved. As Peter M. Blau has observed, "The attainment of organizational objectives generates a strain toward finding new objectives. To provide incentives for its members and to justify its existence, an organization has to adopt new goals as its old ones are realized" (1955:243). "Strain toward finding new objectives" was clearly reflected in Jaffe's further comments on the U.S. fertility decline: "Precisely because external events in the U.S. today are not likely to generate a 'crisis' atmosphere in which the necessity for action on family planning and population matters will be self-evident and the support for such action self-generating . . . work in this field becomes even more essential" (Alan Guttmacher Institute, 1975:4).

Older women had become a problematic vehicle for birth control advocacy not only because they appeared to have their fertility under control but also because, increasingly, they were both defining themselves and being defined by medical authorities out of the market for ongoing contraceptive services. The popularity of sterilization over the pill as the "method-of-choice" for women who wanted no more children became clear in the early 1970s. By 1973 "the substantial increase in surgical sterilization during the 1960s" had already effected a decrease in the proportion of poor women estimated by the Alan Guttmacher Institute to be in need of family planning services (Dryfoos, 1973).

The reasons for this change in women's reproductive management strategies are arguable; however, it seems highly likely that fears (among both women *and* their medical advisors) concerning the health hazards of oral contraception, *particularly for older women,* played a significant role (see, e.g., Djerassi, 1979; Petchesky, 1981). Beginning with the 1970 Senate hearings on pill safety sponsored by Sen. Gaylord Nelson, these hazards received intense publicity: The age beyond which women were publicly "urged to adopt other forms of contraception" gradually declined from 40 in 1975 (*New York Times*, August 27:1:2) to 35 in 1977 (and to 30 among smokers) (*New York Times*, October 19:1:3). This advice was reiterated in Food and Drug Administration–mandated patient-package inserts for oral contraceptives. However it may have come about, the move by older women away from oral contraception gave the family planning network an additional reason for reaching out to new categories of clients.

Finally, not only older women but women publicly defined as poor and/or black had become increasingly problematic subjects around which to construct a campaign for family planning. Earlier, I referred to the hostility of conservatives toward government funding of social programs identified with the poor and with blacks. At the opposite end of the political spectrum, fears concerning the eugenic implications of birth control, never far below the surface, were markedly enhanced by a series of involuntary sterilization cases that came to light initially in June of 1973. All of these cases involved poor black women, many of them sterilized through federally funded family planning programs (Littlewood, 1977; Petchesky, 1981). In his decision invalidating a set of proposed federal sterilization guidelines, Judge Gerhard Gesell warned that "the line between family planning and eugenics is murky" (cited in Littlewood, 1977:107); the *New York Times* commented that the political controversy generated by the sterilization cases "threatens to undermine acceptance of birth control programs" (July 11, 1973:16:1). Even in the more favorable climate of the late 1960s, birth control advocates had found it necessary to argue forcefully against the potentially racist and coercive implications of a federally funded campaign against poverty through family planning (see, e.g., Jaffe, 1967). The sterilization controversies created a climate of opinion in which those implications could no longer be avoided.

In the early 1970s, then, birth control advocates found themselves confronting a social, political, and fiscal environment in which issues tied to poverty and to the needs of women publicly defined as over 30 and/or black had been transformed from political assets to political liabilities. This change in the social context in which political and organizational decisions were made played an important role, I believe, in the emergence of adolescent pregnancy as a public problem. Clearly, some activists in the birth control movement had been interested in and concerned about the birth control needs of unmarried young women well before the period when these needs became a cornerstone of their campaigns. Interest was transformed into advocacy at the point when an organizational demand for new objectives coincided with discovery of the data to publicize a new set of clients. In the changed context I have described, these new clients may have appeared attractive on several grounds. "Teenagers" could be (and were) presented as middle class and white. They were medically eligible for oral contraception and socially ineligible for sterilization. Furthermore, because there is in this country widespread normative consensus that adolescent parenthood is undesirable, issues of choice and coercion (insofar as they are raised by *contraception* as opposed to *sterilization*) were less salient. Finally, adolescent women could be shown *not* to have their reproductive capacities under control. It remained but to "scrub, polish, and highlight" the data.

> In almost any other field, these are the sort of data [on adolescent sexuality, pregnancy, and abortion] which would call forth Congressional hearings, Presidential commissions or Departmental task forces to draft programs to *do something* about the problem. Such a program is indeed long overdue, but it has not been formulated by the normal professional, political or philanthropic channels in our society. If it is to be soundly designed and vigorously advocated, active intervention in the natural processes will be required (Alan Guttmacher Institute, 1975:6).

So, with perhaps an unusual consciousness of purpose, was proclaimed the need for construction of a public problem, "something" in Gusfield's words "about which 'someone ought to do something'" (1981:5). From the perspective of the birth control movement, the "something" that should be done was not in question. Pregnancy among adolescent women was described as "epidemic," at once calling attention to its dimensions and locating it firmly within the domain of medicine and public health.[7] The appropriate response to an epidemic was prevention by medical means: Unwanted adolescent pregnancies should be prevented, and prevention should be accomplished, at least in part, through expansion of the federally funded family planning programs established in the late 1960s. As the adolescent pregnancy advocates were quick to discover, however, it was far easier to gain recognition for the importance of the problem than to persuade the federal government that family planning was the appropriate solution. In his analysis of events leading up to the introduction of the Adolescent Health, Services, and Pregnancy Prevention and Care Act of 1978, Maris A. Vinovskis remarks that "Planned Parenthood—through its research and lobbying arm, the Alan Guttmacher Institute—played a major role in convincing the public and our officials of the 'epidemic' of adolescent pregnancy today" (1981:222). In an article published on January 24, 1978 (18:1), the then Secretary of Health, Education and Welfare, Joseph A. Califano, Jr., was described by the *New York Times* as having been "dazzled" by the figures reported in *11 Million Teenagers*, the Institute's 1976 publication in which an "epidemic" of adolescent pregnancy was first publicly proclaimed. Nevertheless, although AGI's "active intervention in the natural processes" played a significant role in convincing the Carter administration that, in Califano's words before a House subcommittee, "something has to be done about that problem," it was less successful in determining how the problem should be solved. As Gilbert Y. Steiner points out, "When it came time to act on Secretary Califano's dictum that 'something has to be done' about the problem of adolescent pregnancy, throwing comprehensive services at pregnant teenagers (as opposed to prevention of the pregnancy or its termination) proved to be the only 'something' compatible with the administration's opposition to abortion and its discomfort with Planned Parenthood's nonconservative approaches to contraception" (1981:78–79).

As it was finally passed, the Adolescent Health, Services, Pregnancy Prevention and Care Act reverted to the "rehabilitative" model of the late 1960s and focused almost exclusively on services to pregnant young women or teenage parents. Neither Nixon in 1972 nor Carter in 1978 was prepared publicly to endorse birth control for unmarried adolescent women. At the same time (late in 1978) Congress amended the Family Planning Services Act (Title X, originally passed in 1970) to add "services for adolescents" to the "methods and services" that federally funded family planning projects were required to offer (without, however, providing any additional funding for this purpose). These equivocal actions accurately reflected an underlying and increasingly public struggle between advocates of the preventive solution to teenage pregnancy and other groups in American society with a very different conception of adolescent sexual and reproductive behavior, which led them to advocate very different solutions.

Representatives of the birth control movement were profoundly dissatisfied with the outcome of their second essay into problem construction. Jaffe described the "policy choice" reflected in the Carter administration's proposals as starving "the one demonstrably successful program (i.e., family planning) in favor of an ambiguous venture into uncharted territory" (i.e., comprehensive programs) (U.S. Cong., House, Select Committee on Population, 1978:174).[8] Nevertheless, as a stage in the social construction of adolescent pregnancy, the addition of family planning "services for adolescents" to the federal mandate was a significant event, an apparent, if perhaps deceptive, victory for the family planning establishment. It put the weight of the federal government behind family planners' conception of adolescent pregnancy as a morally neutral, unfortunate but preventable, accident. It legitimated the medical "treatment" of sexually active adolescents in clinical settings, by implication endorsing the jurisdiction of the medical profession over women in this category and the roles of physicians and nurses in the regulation of their behavior. Perhaps of most importance, by adding the word "adolescents" to federal legislation on family planning Congress transformed the sexual behavior of young and unwed women from shameful acts, privately known but publicly concealed, into public, officially recognized "facts." This dimension of Congressional action would prove to be a double-edged sword. Unrecognized "facts" could be ignored. Officially sanctioned "facts" demanded the attention not only of humanitarian reformers primarily concerned with the untoward health and social consequences of the behavior in question but also of moral conservatives deeply offended by the behavior itself.

Successful command of the public stage requires not only a committed band of claims makers (the term suggested by Spector and Kitsuse, 1977, for problem advocates), but a body politic prepared to believe that the proposed problem is what it is claimed to be, both in substance and in seriousness. Adolescent pregnancy emerged as a public problem in the early 1970s in part because the concerns it aroused drew upon an existing reservoir of moral panic focused on the sexuality of youth, a panic that affected moral conservatives as much as the middle-class liberal reformers of the planned parenthood movement. Jeffrey Weeks's (1981:252) observation about Great Britain that "the problems of youth were dominating themes in the sexual debates of the 1960s" applied with equal force to the United States. Diffuse anxiety about the morality of youth, generated by the countercultural ferment of the late 1960s, created a climate receptive to the 1970s explosion of "knowledge" describing and cataloging in intimate detail the sexual and reproductive behavior of white (as well as black) teenage women. Where there is perceived danger, knowledge of its precise dimensions offers the possibility of control: Demands for control are reinforced and points where control is required are identified (Foucault, 1978). "Adolescent pregnancy" could readily be accepted as a public problem because it fed on as well as fueled preexisting moral concerns. The price of success in constructing the problem, however, turned out to be intense and highly politicized controversy over its solution.

COUNTERMOVEMENTS, 1978–1987
Chapter 4

MORAL CONSERVATISM AND THE NEW RIGHT

A countermovement has been defined as "a conscious, collective, organized attempt to resist or to reverse social change" (Mottl, 1980:620). What Joseph R. Gusfield calls "permissive or legitimizing" movements, movements to redefine behavior from a less to a more positive moral status, are particularly likely to generate strong countermovements (1967:188–89). The 1970s witnessed a powerful movement toward the redefinition of sexual intercourse on the part of young, dependent, single women from a moral to a medical problem, a movement that encompassed not only self-conscious and well-organized advocacy by birth control movement organizations and their allies and the actions of the federal legislature but also a series of Supreme Court decisions substantially enlarging single women's autonomous access to the means of reproductive control. In these decisions the Supreme Court legalized induced abortion (1973), invalidated restrictions on access to contraception by reason of marital status (1972) or age (1976), and limited the state's ability to require parental consent for a minor's abortion (1976, 1979) (cf., Issacs, 1981).[1] Conservatives responded to what they perceived not only as a permissive movement but as a permissive movement sanctioned by the state with an increasingly vocal and politicized countermovement directed to the restoration of traditional conceptions of sexual morality and parental authority. The resulting controversy produced a form of moral "polarization" parallel in many ways to the political polarization of the late 1960s and early 1970s. To understand these developments requires some knowledge of the political and social context in which they occurred.

Opposition to the legitimation of adolescent sexuality that seemed to be implied by the incorporation of "services to adolescents" into federal family planning programs was an integral part of the ideology of a more general conservative backlash "against the social movements and liberal social policies of the 1960s" (Hunter, 1981). The growth of this ideology out of the racial crises of the 1960s, the gradual incorporation of antifeminist and conservative sexual issues, and the development of organizational vehicles (the New Right, the Moral Majority) to convert this ideology into the form of political power have been examined in some detail (Crawford, 1980; Hunter, 1981; FitzGerald, 1981). The centrality of sex and family issues in the agenda of the New Right should, perhaps, have come as no surprise. Seymour Martin Lipset and Earl Raab pointed out that right-wing extremist movements in the United States have characteristically been built on a "sense of status loss" expressed in terms of the loss of moral and "fundamental" values (1970:496–97). Extremist groups "assume the existence of basic American religious or secular verities which are being undermined by conspirators seeking to change the society for the worse" (446). Legalized abortion and contraception for unmarried adolescents threaten those verities because they are perceived as allowing women to violate traditional sexual norms without paying the penalty of pregnancy: The norms themselves are to that degree undermined.[2] In his accusation that federally funded family planning was "a safe-sex program for unmarried adolescents" (quoted in the *Philadelphia Inquirer*, November 3, 1985), Sen. Orrin Hatch captured the essential basis of moral conservative opposition to birth control for teenage women.

With the election in 1981 of a Republican president and a Republican Senate, moral conservatives gained both increased legitimacy for their cause and a platform from which to make their case. Close examination of the ensuing debates, carried on directly in Congressional hearing rooms and indirectly in the publications of conservative authors, make manifest the fundamental social and political cleavages that underlie current conflicts over the management of adolescent pregnancy.[3] A critical factor in these conflicts has been the fact that, during the very period of their greatest visibility, neither adolescent pregnancy and abortion rates nor the adolescent nonmarital birth rate significantly declined. Thus, although the availability of medical contraceptive methods to teenage women increased over the 1970s, along with concomitant increases in contraceptive use, during this same period the birth rate for unmarried adolescent women rose by 21 percent (Zelnik and Kantner, 1980; Torres, Forrest, and Eisman, 1981; Ventura, 1984). And, although more young women were using contraception they also were increasingly likely to seek abortion when contraception failed. These facts provided an entering wedge for groups and individuals wishing to challenge the medical model of adolescent fertility: "Amply warned of the disastrous consequences of giving birth out of wedlock, and *accustomed to seeking medical solutions to their 'reproductive health' needs,* young people dutifully trooped off to the abortion clinic in ever-increasing numbers as the promise of contraceptive protection proved false for them, and they found themselves unintentionally pregnant" (Schwartz and Ford, 1982:155, emphasis added). Indeed, the recent career of the medical model of adolescent pregnancy offers an almost classic example of a process described by Joseph W. Schneider and Peter Conrad in which the failure of medical control of deviance to produce immediate and demonstrable results creates "currents toward demedicalization and either recriminalization or social disapproval" (1980:42).

The social and demographic realities behind the statistics cited above are complex and, indeed, poorly understood. Nevertheless, they have put birth control advocates on the defensive and added considerable apparent force to the claims of their opponents that contraceptive "treatment" of the adolescent pregnancy problem does not work. Thus, changed political realities—a highly conservative federal administration—together with an absence of change in relevant social realities have contributed to current pressures toward a return to more traditional means of social control.

Almost all of the basic themes in the moral conservatives' case against birth control for unmarried adolescent girls were sounded by President Ronald Reagan in an address to the National Association of Evangelicals on March 8, 1983:

> Girls termed "sexually active"—that has replaced the word "promiscuous"—are given ["birth control drugs and devices" by federally subsidized clinics] in order to prevent illegitimate birth or abortion. [In discussions of this issue] no one seems to mention morality as playing a part in the subject of sex. Is all of Judeo-Christian tradition wrong? Are we to believe that something so sacred can be looked upon as a purely physical thing with no potential for emotional and psychological harm? And isn't it the parents' right to give counsel and advice to keep their children from making mistakes that may affect their entire lives? (*New York Times*, March 9, 1983:I,1:18).

In these remarks, the president clearly drew the line between pragmatic "medical" and normative "moral" constructions of adolescent pregnancy. Girls who have sexual intercourse outside of marriage were described in moral ("promiscuous") as opposed to clinical ("sexually active") terms; responsibility for control of their behavior was assigned to parents or, possibly, religious advisors as opposed to "federally subsidized clinics"; and the means of control to be employed were "counsel and advice," as opposed to "birth control drugs and devices."

Central to the debates between moral conservatives and birth control advocates are conflicts over attributions of responsibility: the personal responsibility of teenage women for their sexual behavior and its consequences; the location of societal responsibility for the "management" and control of these activities; political responsibility (or what Gusfield calls "ownership")—the authority to define the problem and to *decide* questions of personal and societal responsibility; and causal responsibility, the determination of why there *is* an adolescent pregnancy problem. These dimensions of responsibility are, of course, highly interdependent. For example, "imputed [personal] responsibility"—whether "the cause of deviant behavior is seen to lie in deliberate choice rather than in accident, inheritance, infection, or witchcraft"—"allows us to predict some of the elements of the way in which deviance will be managed or controlled by others" (Freidson, 1972:334). A principal strategy employed by groups seeking to bring about change in how behavior is *controlled* is to argue for change in the attribution of personal responsibility.

Birth control advocates, as I have noted earlier, prefer to define adolescent pregnancy as a problem in preventive medicine. This construction leads them to focus on the *unwilled* consequences of "premature" childbearing and on the *inevitability* that sexual intercourse, once initiated, will be continued. Both assumptions minimize the role of "deliberate choice" in adolescent sexuality and its outcomes; the latter assumption, in particular, is hotly contested by moral conservatives. "I do not believe that sexual activity is an incurable disease. . . . There are a number of [young persons] who do not continue that. They learn they get burned, they suffer, they do not get happy that way in many cases, and *they can decide* to abstain from further sexual activity until they are married" (U.S. Cong., Senate, Committee on Labor and Human Resources, 1981b:120–21, emphasis added). In these and other comments in the course of a series of congressional family planning "oversight" hearings, conservative senators made very clear their beliefs that sexual activity *was* a deliberate choice, that it did *not* fall in the same category as "accident, inheritance, infection, or witchcraft," and their consequent rejection of a medical model for the control of adolescent sexuality and pregnancy that was perceived to be based on these assumptions.

The notion of social control incorporates both the investment of particular individuals or groups with responsibility for exercising control and the employment of specialized control techniques: punishment for "responsible" deviance; treatment for "nonresponsible" deviance. From the perspective of moral conservatives, to "treat" adolescent sexuality with "contraceptives, with abortion as the backup in the event of contraceptive failure" is to define "moral responsibility . . . as eliminating the inconvenient results of one's own actions" (McGraw, 1980:39). Eliminating the inconvenient results removes both a principal sanction against sexual intercourse by young and unmarried women (the fear of pregnancy) and its principal "punishments" (the fact of pregnancy and the inevitability of childbirth). The value of these sanctions, however, resides at least as much in the visibility they confer on sexually "deviant" behavior as in their physical and social inconvenience. "Invisible" sex is sex that can be neither monitored nor controlled. Thus, successive (so far unsuccessful) efforts at various levels of government to require parental notification when a minor daughter is prescribed contraception by a family planning clinic are clearly intended to render her sexual behavior visible to parents and accessible to parental control, without regard to the convenient or inconvenient results that this action may bring. "Free and riskless sex," sex without visible consequences, had left apostles for a moral construction of adolescent pregnancy with limited means to enforce their conception of sexual morality. Parental notification became the social equivalent of unintended pregnancy, an "inconvenient result" expressly designed to pave the way for the reimposition of traditional moral sanctions.

Questions of *how* and by *whom* deviant behavior should be controlled are, of course, closely allied. "Treatment" is generally defined as the province of professional experts; moral education and punishment, particularly of the young, as the domain of the family. In the litany of moral conservatives few themes have been more consistently invoked than that of the "family" as the repository of fundamental moral values, over against "meddling professionals" and "federal bureaucrats." Tahi L. Mottl's statement that a particularly salient "societal myth" evoked by the Boston antibusing controversy "was the belief that the rights of parents were being abused" (1980:628) applies with equal force to the controversies that have surrounded sex education, school prayer, and birth control for adolescents. Experts, be they educators, social workers, or physicians were seen not as morally neutral advisors, but as crusaders for an alternative morality, profoundly threatening to traditional ways of life: "These [family planning] clinics are promulgating their version of morality in contradiction often to the values of the teenagers' parents and pastors" (U.S. Cong., Senate, Committee on Labor and Human Resources, 1981a:3). It is important to recognize that "morality" in this context refers both to traditional values (e.g., premarital chastity) and to traditional structural forms (parental authority, male dominance) within which those values are to be imposed. At a single stroke, the open sexuality of adolescent women violates *both* hierarchical and gender role norms; it is in this dual violation that its threatening character primarily resides. From the perspective of more extreme conservatives, the stakes in what I define as a conflict between alternative modes of social control were nothing less than the future of American society itself: "The central political question of the coming decade will be which of these two competing moral visions of the family and of humanity will prevail and become the official orthodoxy of our society through the power and authority of the American state" (McGraw, 1980:17).

Insofar as the competition described by McGraw centers on birth control for teenage women, the archenemy of moral conservatives, quintessentially representative of the "secular humanist orthodoxy that rejects God and traditional values," was Planned Parenthood:

> The Federal government has unwittingly given an enormous and unfair advantage to the anti-natalist partisans in this ongoing debate through its continuous funding of family planning programs, which has tremendously enhanced the power, prestige, and influence of Planned Parenthood and other population groups. . . . Planned Parenthood seems to have an inordinate and unwarranted amount of influence in this area of public policy. The national agenda in the area of fertility control is set, essentially, by Planned Parenthood (U.S. Cong., Senate, Committee on Labor and Human Resources, 1981a:104–5).

The cornerstone of the conservative countermovement against legitimation of adolescent sexuality has been a challenge to what is perceived as the political "ownership" of this issue by Planned Parenthood, an ownership sanctioned by the federal government through its funding of family planning programs. In this challenge, political and causal responsibility were merged: Planned

Parenthood, like Socrates in ancient Athens, was cast as the corrupter of innocent youth (and, at least in the passage cited above, of the "unwitting" government itself). The following passages are from testimony by Sen. Jesse Helms
(R-N.C.) before the Senate family planning "oversight" committee and from
the monograph on family policy by Onalee McGraw. With minor variations,
the images of good and evil described in these remarks were repeated over
and over again in the literature of moral conservatism.

> I do not believe the young people of America should be misled and betrayed by
> their elders with a false view of life, a distorted view of human relationships, and a
> destructive set of secular values. That is what title X is all about (U.S. Cong., Senate,
> Committee on Labor and Human Resources, 1984:7).

> The government supported degradation of our young people is being resisted in
> communities across the land. Local pro-family organizations are working to cut off
> the pipeline of government funding which is the lifeblood of Planned Parenthood
> affiliates. . . . Increasing numbers of people see no reason why the humanistic "pro-
> choice" message has to be the only one beamed to our young people (McGraw,
> 1980:63).

The rhetorical step from identification of Planned Parenthood and "family
planning" with the promulgation of (at best) amoral values to holding family
planning programs responsible for adolescent pregnancy itself is a small one
indeed: "We are funding the very problems we set out to eliminate" was
Sen. Jeremiah Denton's succinct evaluation (U.S. Cong., Senate, Committee on
Labor and Human Resources, 1981a:3).[4]

Right-wing extremist ideology in the United States has been characterized
by "moralism," the equation of struggles for political power with contests between ultimate good and ultimate evil ("truth versus error, God versus Satan");
"antistatism," a profound antagonism toward centralized government's "interference" in private affairs; and conspiracy theories, the identification of political opponents with evil conspirators (Lipset and Raab, 1970). All of these
themes are readily discernible in moral conservative rhetoric on the question
of adolescent pregnancy. By an inexorable logic, birth control for adolescents
led to moral decay and the decline of civilization; the Antichrist was represented by the state, who funded these services, and by professional experts
and their allies, who provided them.[5] Although the underlying themes of this
morality play have been relatively constant in American life, it is rare for them
to appear so openly on the political stage. In the process of obtaining the federal government's endorsement of family planning "services for adolescents,"
birth control advocates created an actionable target around which moral conservatives could mobilize their diffuse concerns about sexual permissiveness,
family breakdown, and the decline of traditional values.

The unfolding of the AIDS epidemic in the 1980s not only confirmed
moral conservatives in their conviction of the apocalyptic consequences of
sexual unorthodoxy; it added a powerful new argument to their armamentarium: The only "safe sex" was no sex. In a joint statement on AIDS education

released in January 1987, William J. Bennett, then secretary of education and C. Everett Koop, then surgeon general of the U.S. Public Health Service, said the following: "Young people must be told the truth—that the best way to avoid AIDS is to refrain from sexual activity until as adults they are ready to establish a mutually faithful monogamous relationship. Since sex education courses should in any case teach children why they should refrain from engaging in sexual intercourse, AIDS education should confirm the message that should already be there in the sex education curriculum (Bennett and Koop, 1987). This is by no means an isolated example of the federal government's position; comparable sentiments are reiterated in government documents and by officials at all levels (see, e.g., Bennett, 1987; McDonald, 1987). As Alan Brandt has recently written, "The persistence of such values and attitudes calls into question the received view of the sexual revolution in the midst of which we live. . . . It thus seems naive and wishful to assert that we have conquered the Victorians within ourselves, for underlying tensions in American sexual values persist, tensions that are brought forward in our approach to AIDS as well as other venereal diseases" (1987:202). The same holds true of our approach to adolescent nonmarital sexuality and childbearing.

MOYNIHAN REVISITED

In Chapter 2, I referred to a government report on the "Negro family" released in 1965, calling public attention to disproportionate levels of female-headed families, nonmarital births, and welfare receipt among blacks in the United States.[6] That report, prepared by Daniel Patrick Moynihan (at the time an assistant secretary of labor, currently a U.S. senator from New York), received scathing criticism from black leaders and from many liberal whites for what was perceived as a racist attack (e.g., Rainwater and Yancey, 1967). Indeed, William Julius Wilson attributes what he sees as a relative absence of scholarly attention during the 1970s to the problems of black families directly to the negative reception of Moynihan's report (1987:3–19). Recently, however, there has been a marked revival of attention to these racial disparities and a corresponding reidentification of family "pathology" (Wilson's term) with American blacks. Moynihan's report was prepared prior to the discovery of adolescent pregnancy, and he makes no mention of it. "Teenage pregnancy" is, however, conspicuous among the "social pathologies of American ghetto communities" inventoried in the recent work of Wilson and others (Wilson, 1987:6; see also Murray, 1984; McGhee, 1985; Moynihan, 1986; Moore, Simms, and Betsey, 1986). In this most recent incarnation, the link between family "breakdown" (including teenage pregnancy) and race has been not only accepted but stressed by many black leaders and scholars (e.g., National Urban League, 1985, 1986; Norton, 1985; Wilson, 1987).

Furthermore, just as in the 1960s Moynihan connected the "disintegration of the Negro family structure" with expansion of the welfare rolls, so in the 1980s policy advocates from across the political spectrum make parallel connections between government spending and teenage pregnancy. At one extreme, Charles Murray has proposed that "scrapping the entire federal welfare and income-support structure for working-age persons"—the policy objective he prefers—would (among other things) "drastically reduce births to single teenage girls" (1984:227). Few liberal policy analysts accept the causal relationship this statement implies. Nevertheless, virtually every policy document on adolescent pregnancy issued in recent years informs us (in almost identical phraseology) that, "The nation's major welfare program, Aid to Families with Dependent Children, distributes more than half its payments to women who were teenagers when their first child was born" (Moore and Burt, 1982). This particular citation is from the bookjacket description of a publication by the Urban Institute, a liberal center for social policy analysis.

The framing of adolescent pregnancy as a problem of black teenage women on welfare—I call it the "neo-Moynihan" construction to distinguish it from the medical and moral constructions described earlier—distorts the evidence of both demography and social science. The demographic evidence was presented in Chapter 2: Teenage pregnancy was being redefined from a white to a black problem at a time when both the rates and the numbers of births to single, black teenage women were declining relative to those of whites. Research has consistently refuted the hypothesis—central to Murray's argument—that welfare payments offer an economic incentive for teenage childbearing (Bane, 1986; Wilson and Neckerman, 1986; Corcoran, Duncan, and Hill, 1984; Duncan, 1984; Allen and Pittman, 1986; Bane and Ellwood, 1989; Duncan and Hoffman, 1990). William Julius Wilson and Robert Aponte summarize the results of a "recently completed landmark study of the effects of AFDC on family structure and living arrangements" as follows:

> Using three different methods based on different data sets [Survey of Income and Education, aggregate national data from the census and *Vital Statistics Reports*, aggregate census data by state] to control [for] unmeasured differences [between states] and to provide "a check for consistency across method," Ellwood and Bane found that AFDC has virtually no effect on the fertility of unmarried black and white women (1987:185–86).[7]

Finally, the portrayal of teenage childbearing as a principal drain on the public welfare system is highly misleading. William P. O'Hare points out that in 1984, "AFDC accounted for only 2 percent of the $432 billion in federal outlays for human services" (1985:29). Samuel H. Preston has calculated that the total federal expenditure on *all* major child-oriented programs (including AFDC) was "only 9 percent of per capita expenditure on the elderly" (1984:440). These are only a few of the most salient distortions. A more detailed critique of the linkages that have been forged in recent years between teenage pregnancy, race, family "disorganization," and "welfare dependency" may be found in Tracy Huling (1988). The persistence of the neo-Moynihan construction of adolescent pregnancy in the face of readily available evidence against it suggests that its appeal lies elsewhere than in its correspondence to the facts.

It is ironic that the very same groups from whom Moynihan's critics were drawn—black leaders and white liberals—have been among the contributors to his rehabilitation. However, the ultimate sources of this rediscovery do not lie with blacks and liberals; they can be found in the political and ideological hegemony of right-wing conservativism in the contemporary United States. Right-wing extremism in America has its ideological sources in economic as well as moral conservatism: since the 1920s, government regulation—embodied in the "welfare state"—has been "a staple target for . . . right-wing preservatist politics" (Lipset and Raab, 1970:112). The politically most successful conservative movements—and the movement presided over by Ronald Reagan was surely among the most successful—have appealed to both ideological constituencies.[8] A resurgence of public policy attention to nonmarital childbearing and female-headed families and the indictment of these domestic arrangements as (in circular fashion) both cause and consequence of government-funded welfare programs has been among the legacies of the Reagan era. Constructing adolescent pregnancy in the terms of this indictment appeals simultaneously to conservative "moralism"—belief in the apocalyptic consequences of change in sexual and reproductive norms—and "antistatism"—opposition to what is perceived as government interference in the economy. In the extreme conservative scenario, young women who become nonmaritally pregnant are doubly responsible and, therefore, doubly undeserving—first, for "choosing" sex over chastity, and, second, for "choosing" AFDC over honest work. The legitimacy of these young women's claims on the larger society is further undermined by dramatizing the social marginality of the claimants: Not only do they make babies at public expense; they are also black.

The foregoing themes were clearly stated in the works of George Gilder (1981) and Charles Murray (1984), conservative intellectuals whose ideas had a major impact on the Reagan administration's thinking about domestic programs. The New York Times commented in early 1985 that, "This year's budget-cutting bible seems to be 'Losing Ground,' Charles Murray's book appraising social policy in the last 30 years. . . . In [federal] agency after agency, officials cite the Murray book as a philosophical basis for [cuts in social welfare programs], for it concludes that [these] programs, far from relieving poverty, increase it and should be stopped" (February 3, 1985:IV,20:1). By the early 1980s, the influence of Gilder's and Murray's ideas had begun to appear in the rhetoric and the program agendas of liberal advocates for public attention to the "problem" of adolescent pregnancy. The construction of adolescent pregnancy as a medical/public health problem generic to the teen years—together with the birth control "solution" advocated by proponents of that construction—gradually disappeared from much of the programmatic literature and was supplanted by one version or another of the neo-Moynihan construction—and by "solutions" couched more in economic than in medical terms.

How and why these shifts occurred is a complex question. Since the late 1960s, there has been a sharp, and much publicized, increase in the proportion of female-headed relative to male-headed households in the United States. The relationship of this change to overall variation in poverty rates during this period is a matter of considerable controversy (O'Hare, 1985; Bane, 1986; Ellwood, 1988; Jencks, 1989). It is unarguable, however, that female-headed households are more likely than male-headed households to be both poor and black. As the facts changed, so did the larger intellectual and political climate in which these facts were discussed and their implications evaluated. Two points are important. First, there was a remarkable, and surely unintended, convergence between black intellectuals' discovery of a black "underclass" and of a relationship between black female-headed households and black *male* unemployment (Wilson, 1980, 1987; Norton, 1985) and the equally strong emphasis placed by Gilder and Murray on the negative consequences of AFDC for *male* employment incentives. Both sets of scholars identify "stability" with marriage and the traditional nuclear family, "instability" with nonmarital births and female-headed households. In this value-laden scenario, it is but a short step (one that black scholars avoid but Gilder and Murray take easily) to casting sexually unorthodox women, rather than poverty, as culprits in the production of what these authors define as ghetto "pathology" and social disorder.

The attention given to the black "underclass" family by black scholars has had a profound legitimizing effect, converting "the black family" from a political albatross to a permissible focus of media and programmatic interest by white as well as black individuals and organizations.[9] Construction of adolescent pregnancy as a legitimate black problem has allowed black organizations and individuals to become major players in an important arena of public policy. However (and this is my second point), I believe that this construction, and the corresponding redefinition of adolescent pregnancy not only as a black problem but as a problem of welfare, rather than pregnancy, prevention, is fully understandable only in the context of a very harsh political climate. That is, a climate in which government decisions on the funding of social programs are made (and, even more important, are clearly perceived to be made) by individuals simultaneously hostile to government intervention on behalf of the less fortunate and to medically mediated freedom of sexual and reproductive choice.

PRIVATE BEHAVIOR AS A PUBLIC PROBLEM

My intentions in this and the preceding chapter have been to account both for the emergence of adolescent pregnancy as a public problem in the United States and for the character and intensity of the conflict this problem has generated. The social processes that I have described can be understood (and, indeed, *must* be understood if they are to be fully explained) on two levels: first, as an essentially political struggle for authority to define the "reality" that is represented by women's reproductive behavior and its management; second, as an episode in the history of social control over sexuality and reproduction.

The Contest for Ownership

The stage for political struggle was set in the 1960s: by the designation of socially and temporally mistimed pregnancies as medical problems with medical "solutions"; by the federal government's (apparent) endorsement of the medical framework through its funding of programs for birth control services to poor women; and by the development of a politically powerful organizational network with a strong investment in the medical solution and in the programs by which this solution was implemented. In the early 1970s, a combination of political, social, and demographic events severely threatened this investment. However, these events were a threat primarily to the resources that birth control advocates could command; the medical framework itself was left intact. Building on the newly documented prevalence of sexual intercourse among single, white teenage women, organizations within the birth control movement constructed a clear and present reproductive danger in the form of a new category of clients to whom the medical framework could be transferred. In 1978, the members of this category, adolescent women, were officially recognized by the government as mandated recipients of federally funded birth control services.

The *conditions* for the visibility of adolescent sexuality were provided by demographic and social changes affecting both adolescents themselves and the surrounding social context within which their behavior was evaluated. These changes provided the opportunity but did not create the necessity for adolescent sexuality to attain the level of visibility that it currently enjoys. This visibility is a social product, the outcome both of successful organizational entrepreneurship and of the politicization of adolescent sexuality that success entailed. Gusfield has remarked that "the 'lifting' of a deviant activity to the level of a political, public issue is . . . a sign that its moral status is at stake, that legitimacy is possible" (1967:188). Violation of social norms defining the proper times and circumstances for women's sexuality were not a significant problem for moral conservatives so long as those violations remained socially invisible. In deliberately making them visible and, at the same time, appearing to promote their legitimation through the agency of open federal support for adolescent contraceptive services, the family planning movement presented a direct challenge to the legitimacy of the traditional normative order. The most immediate consequence of that challenge was not an expansion of contraceptive services (indeed, as I have noted, legislative action insuring teenage women's access to medical contraceptive methods largely preceded the emergence of adolescent pregnancy as a public problem) but the mobilization of resistance to expansion, together with a concerted effort to redefine the question of adolescent pregnancy as a moral rather than a medical problem. To understand moral conservatives' attack on the medical model, it is essential to recognize that they were less concerned with the statistical frequency of normative violations than with the normative *status* of those violations. They opposed not only the organizational and political power of birth control advocates, but what they perceived as the morally neutralizing power of the medical framework itself.

Among the most remarkable characteristics of adolescent pregnancy as a public problem have been its staying power on the public agenda and, what is no doubt a closely related characteristic, its protean quality—its adaptability to a variety of constructions depending on individual and organizational needs and the political requirements of the moment. Writing in 1971 about the difference in societal response to white as compared with black young women's nonmarital sexuality and childbearing, Joyce A. Ladner lamented that "institutional racism is so profound, even in the area of motherhood, that the larger society can subjugate, oppress and assign a priority to any behavioral act to suit its best interest, and *change the definition which governs the same behavior* whenever it desires to do so" (239). There is much truth in this statement; however, it is both too limited in its conception of "best interest"—racism has by no means been the only motive for change in definitions of the behavior in question—and too global in its conception of how these changes are brought about. It is not "society" that is responsible, but a series of identifiable groups and organizations—advocates for birth control, for welfare reform, for children, for blacks—all of whom have drawn upon the image of the sexually unorthodox adolescent woman as a symbol of social disorder, but all of whom have fashioned, and refashioned, this image to suit the time, the place, and their particular occasions.

Sexual Social Control and the Medical Solution
Underlying contemporary political struggles over ownership of and responsibility for the "problem" of adolescent pregnancy (and over other reproductive management questions as well) is a more basic and continuing societal concern with the management of sexuality and, in particular, with the management of women's departures from sexual and reproductive norms. The intensity of this concern arises not only from the dual challenge of adolescent sexuality to patriarchal and gender-based definitions of the female role, but also from the threat of penalty-free sexual access to the traditional structure of marriage. In the eyes both of late nineteenth-century feminists and of contemporary moral conservative women, restraints on women's sexual availability protected their bargaining position before marriage and their marriage itself afterwards. Limiting adolescent women's access to birth control is seen as a means to control not only their sexual behavior, but the sexual behavior of males as well.

Departures from sexual and reproductive norms have been matters of public concern since the middle of the nineteenth century. What has changed are the dominant symbols of normative deviation; the designation of deviance as sin, as crime, or as illness; and the principal forms of social control. How the "problem" of adolescent pregnancy as it has been constructed in the late twentieth century fits into this larger picture of social change in the management of young women's sexual and reproductive deviance will be examined in some detail in the next several chapters. Here my analysis is limited to the recent past during which adolescent girls became a dominant symbol for the loss of sexual social control.

The medicalization of adolescent pregnancy and the assignment of responsibility for management of adolescent women's sexuality to medical and health professionals took place in a context of heightened concern about what was perceived as the amoral behavior of white middle-class youth ("the Woodstock nation") and of the gradual lifting of legal sanctions against the sexual expression of minor and unmarried women. These latter changes challenged established forms of social control: the challenge was as much to white middle-class parents' expectations for deferral of present gratification in the interests of future status as to the moral convictions of blue-collar hard hats. Two alternative responses to this challenge emerged; both were intended to regulate and contain the sexually unbridled behavior of the young. One alternative, the alternative preferred by moral conservatives, was repression through the exercise of parental and/or internal controls. The other alternative was represented by medicalization. Within the medical framework, the sexual activity of adolescent women was defined as a health problem to be treated, much like a chronic disease, with long-term medical therapy. The moral status of the activity itself, designated by moral conservatives as the cardinal issue at stake, was regarded, at least in principle, as moot: One does not question the morality of an infectious agent. Medicalization did not, in fact, do away with questions of morality; it merely shifted them to a later stage in the reproductive process. The sexual "morality" of adolescent women was redefined to depend on their contraceptive rather than on their sexual conformity. To paraphrase Irving Zola, though her immoral character was not demonstrated in her having sex it became evident in what she did about it (1975:173). (This process of redefinition is more fully described in Chapter 9.)

Medicalization both "normalized" adolescent women's sexuality, in the sense of situating it within a commonly understood category of adolescent "health" problems, like acne or menstrual cramps, and offered the assurance of professional supervision over behavior with high socially disruptive potential. These were techniques of social control congenial to and calculated to calm the fears of the middle-class constituents to whom the birth control movement has its greatest appeal. Perhaps of most importance, the medical framework, by directing attention to what were defined as the negative health *consequences* of sexual activity, made it possible to actively campaign for the "treatment" of sexual behavior without condoning (or even while condemning) the behavior itself.

At the same time that, on the level of the individual teenage girl, adolescent pregnancy was being defined as a problem to be solved by medical intervention, it was, on the aggregate level, being converted into a vast compendium of "scientific knowledge," leaving few dimensions of the adolescent woman's sexual, contraceptive, and reproductive experience unexamined. Commenting on parallel trends in the eighteenth and nineteenth centuries, Michel Foucault describes these "discourses aimed at sex" as "undertaking to protect, separate, and forewarn, signaling perils everywhere, awakening people's attention, calling for diagnoses, piling up reports, organizing therapies," in summary, "intensifying people's awareness of (sex) as a constant danger" (1978:30–31). Knowledge, besides intensifying awareness, is an essential element in the process of social control. As they awakened public attention, described the "problem," and prescribed "solutions," advocates for adolescent pregnancy as a public problem were simultaneously writing a new chapter in a long history—the history of attempts to control the sexuality of women and adolescents in the light of current conceptions of personal morality and social stability.

PART THREE *American Women's Adolescence in Historical Context*

THE TRANSFORMATION OF WOMEN'S ADOLESCENCE, 1850–1960

Chapter 5

SINGLE young women as symbols of sexual danger were not an invention of the early 1970s; nor have young women always and invariably been such a symbol. The Puritans of New England were more concerned with adultery than with the licentiousness of the young and the single. A shift in this focus—evidenced by public agitation against prostitution and for premarital chastity—began to appear in the United States in the late 1830s and early 1840s; by the mid-1850s concern with the protection and control of single young women had assumed a variety of organized forms. In the same year, 1856, the first supervised boarding home for urban working girls was opened (in New York City) and the first reform school for girls was established (in Lancaster, Massachusetts). In the course of the nineteenth century, women became defined as the keepers of sexual mores. By the same token, their indiscretions were held responsible for the deterioration of morals. As, with industrialization and urbanization, "sexual mores did in fact change, the burden of this transformation came to be placed upon women" (Brandt, 1985:168). By the 1880s, when the image of scarcely adolescent girls recruited into prostitution was effectively employed to raise the "age of consent" for sexual intercourse, young unmarried women had become potent symbols for the dangers of uncontrolled sexuality.

There have been marked changes over time in the perceived social location of sexually unorthodox girls, in the vocabularies by which sexual unorthodoxy is described, and in strategies for its control. The issues that surround the social control of young women's sexuality have, nevertheless, remained remarkably constant: whether the behavior in question is voluntary—a reflection of willful immorality—or involuntary—the result of innocence, force, mental incompetence, or a deprived childhood; whether sexual social control is to be constructed as a moral, a legal, or a public health problem; and whether measures to prevent and/or ameliorate the consequences of sexual unorthodoxy increase, rather than diminish, its extent. Underlying this chapter and the two that follow is the proposition that a careful examination of how processes for the social control of young women's sexuality have been defined and redefined over the past century and a half will contribute to an understanding of the circumstances out of which the current adolescent pregnancy controversy has emerged and of the significance of this controversy for the production of social order and social change.

The data on which this examination is based are the data of American social history during the late nineteenth and twentieth centuries. This was a period of enormous social change, much of it plausibly related to the issues I will address. The most pertinent of these changes will be considered in some detail at later points in the text; here, I limit myself to a brief summary.[1] Between the middle of the nineteenth and the middle of the twentieth centuries the United States changed from a predominantly agricultural society of about 23 million people, in which the majority of the population lived in rural areas and engaged in farming as their principal occupation, to a modern industrial and overwhelmingly urban society of over 150 million. The shift away from agriculture began in the 1850s; by 1920, 73 percent of the employed population were working in nonfarm occupations and, for the first time, the majority were living in cities. Accompanying and contributing to these changes were huge waves of immigration from overseas—between 1902 and 1914 over half a million immigrants, the majority of whom were unattached young men, entered the United States every year—and, within the United States, a vast migration from the country to the city. The latter migration included young women as well as young men, responding to the "lure of the city" and its promise of economic opportunity. In 1900, when the majority of women reported by the census as "gainfully employed" were young and unmarried, only 19 percent worked on farms as compared with 42 percent of employed men. The separation of home and work that characterizes the transition from an agricultural to a modern economy affected adolescents as well as adults: by the mid-1930s, the majority of both sexes were passing large portions of their teenage years outside the family home, at school or at work. Along with these changes came other trappings of modern life—the introduction of the automobile and the telephone, rising divorce rates, declining birth rates—along with changing conceptions of sexuality, of women, and of adolescence itself. Of particular relevance to the *quality* of attention given to adolescence as a problematic period of life have been shifts over time in the proportion of youth relative to the total adult population. This ratio was high in the late nineteenth and early twentieth centuries (between 50 and 70 percent), gradually declined to a low point in 1960 (about 30 percent) and jumped abruptly to about 40 percent in 1970. I argue that shifts in population composition (as well as in its distribution) played a major role in the varying levels of attention given to female adolescence as a *public* problem during the period of this analysis.

Some comment about the sources of historical data on which I have drawn and on my approach to these sources is in order. The level of scholarly attention to women's history generally and to the history of sexuality in particular has increased enormously in the last two decades, and I have been fortunate in being able to make use of a large body of literature focused on these dimensions of American history. In many cases, several books or articles treat the same topic—prostitution in the late nineteenth and early twentieth centuries for example—making it possible to cross-check both facts and interpretations. In addition to historians' accounts of specific topics—prostitution, courtship, temperance, venereal disease, sexuality, juvenile justice, women's work—I have consulted a wide range of more general histories: of women, of childhood and adolescence, of the family, and of the social and political movements that occupied Americans during the approximately one hundred–year period on which these three chapters are focused.

From the present perspective, the most significant gap in this literature is in the history of the adolescent girl. Aspects of American women's adolescence (defined as the period between puberty and marriage) are treated in individual articles or in books devoted primarily to other topics, but no single work examines the full range of nineteenth- and twentieth-century changes in this period of life for women (as the works of Kett, 1977, and Gillis, 1981, have done for men). The reasons for this gap are instructive. It has less to do with an absence of material, I would argue, than with a conception of the nature and conduct of unmarried young women as predetermined by their marital and reproductive futures. Joseph R. Kett suggests that boy's puberty became of interest in the early twentieth century when it was seen to correspond with a period of critical choice between immediate employment and continued education—a period of moral crisis in which life's future prospects would be decided (Kett, 1971, 1977). Insofar as girls' future prospects were decided at birth, a period of struggle with life's purposes was difficult to imagine. The present work makes no claim to the range and detail of historical description and analysis that will be required to fill this gap in women's history. I call attention to it so the reader may be forewarned that it is in my reconstruction and interpretation of changes in the structure of women's lives between puberty and marriage, in the ideology that has surrounded this period, and in strategies proposed for its management that I have had to rely most heavily on my own reading of primary source materials.

A second gap arises from the middle-class and ethnic biases inherent in much of the available data on female adolescence. This is a problem throughout the period under study, but it is particularly serious for the years prior to 1900. For direct information on the experiences of ordinary young women in the nineteenth century, historians are almost wholly dependent on letters and diaries written by the relatively well-educated daughters of native-born, predominantly Yankee parents. A large body of prescriptive literature concerned with molding young women's characters was published in the late nineteenth century, but this too was directed to or clearly assumed a middle-class or upper-middle-class audience. Girls from poor, black, and/or nonnative white families tended to appear only as filtered through the literature of individual or social reform. On the other hand, it was the conceptions of female adolescence held by the dominant social elite, not those of the poor, the black, or the foreign-born, that largely determined strategies of social control on the public, if not the private, level.

My approach to the historical data (both primary and secondary) employed in these three chapters has been selective, both from necessity and in keeping with my particular analytical perspective. I have been less interested in describing and accounting for changes in *behavior* (e.g., changes in actual rates of sexual activity by unmarried young women) than in understanding the quality and quantity of *response* to that behavior as perceived by adults: how young women's sexuality was socially defined and the strategies that were employed or envisioned for its control. Furthermore, in examining these responses I have been (in contrast to the historian) not so much concerned with the detailed description of individual cases as with the discovery of patterns across more than one comparable case (e.g., social movements to raise the "age of consent," to control prostitution and venereal disease, and to promote sex education, considered in Chapter 7).

This book is about strategies for the social control of female adolescence, the social bases of these strategies and, ultimately, their consequences. Since beliefs about the objects of control are among the most important social bases of management strategies, I begin with those beliefs as they stood in the mid-nineteenth century. I then trace changes in those beliefs over the ensuing decades and attempt to account for those changes with reference to larger shifts in the structure of women's lives between puberty and marriage.

PURITY AND PERIL: THE GANTLET OF WOMEN'S
ADOLESCENCE IN THE NINETEENTH CENTURY
Until the seventeenth century, says Philippe Aries, the lives of girls were characterized by "the habits of precocity and a brief childhood" (1962:311). Early training in the work of a wife and mother and early marriage effectively precluded a protracted period of "unsettled" adolescence. Even in the preindustrial economy of New England, when age at marriage was considerably later than Aries's 12 or 14, unmarried girls had a well-defined household role, doing "spinning, weaving, and needlework in their homes and also in the employ of other families" (Cott, 1975:17). Writing in 1904, a Connecticut school principal described these "good old days in New England" in nostalgic terms: "The girl usually remained an inmate of her father's house, and her time and energy were expended for the welfare of the family until her wedding day. In general, a boy was an infant until he became of age, a girl until she married. They were under the influence of home and home training, until they had passed the period of adolescence and were really young men and young women" (Verplanck, 1904, cited in Bremner, ed., 1970:650). As a literal description, this portrait must, of course, be regarded with some skepticism (see, e.g., Hiner, 1975). Nevertheless, it nicely defines the parameters

of a "safe" adolescent passage for girls: from the protection of parents to the protection of husband, with no intervening, and potentially dangerous, gaps. Furthermore, Verplanck's perception of change reflects the consensus of more recent historians. Although they differ on the precise timing, most historians agree that, starting in the late eighteenth century, a combination of economic, social, and ideological changes began to both extend and to complicate young women's transition from girlhood to womanhood. At one and the same time, the roles of unmarried girls became structurally less well defined and normatively more threatened (Cott, 1975; Kessler-Harris, 1982; Weiner, 1985; Demos, 1986; Brumberg, 1988).

In the literature on nineteenth-century childhood and adolescence, three themes predominate: the emergence of a conception of childhood as a separate, and intrinsically valuable, period of life; a belief in the essential goodness, purity, and innocence of young children; and (somewhat in contradiction) an intense concern with the protection of innocence from "pollution by life, and particularly by the sexuality tolerated if not approved of among adults" (Aries, 1962:119).[2] Children "were to stay firmly in Eden, with their hands off the apples and deaf to the serpents" (Plumb, 1975, cited in Weeks, 1981:48). Growing up was viewed with anxiety as a process amounting to nothing less than the corruption of innocence (Degler, 1980:67). Within this framework, the years around puberty appeared "as fraught with peril" (Kett, 1977:113). Incorrect management of this transitional period was associated with fearful consequences in adulthood, particularly for girls. In principle, two alternative modes of coping with this critical period were conceivable: protection through knowledge—the development "of character and reason" (Aries, 1962:119)— or protection through the prolongation of innocence. Although De Tocqueville, writing in 1835, suggested that in the education of young women Americans were taking the former tack, the approach he described was not the one recommended in books of advice appearing later in the century. Prolongation of innocence, grounded in the belief that "a slow and steady regimen in childhood, one that avoided stimulating both sexual curiosity and secular knowledge, would guarantee a noiseless transition from childhood to youth" is described by Kett as the solution to the problems of maturation adopted by American moralists between 1840 and 1880 (Kett, 1977:135–36). Charles E. Rosenberg characterizes the tone of late nineteenth-century medical literature in parallel, if balder, terms as one of "increasing repressiveness . . . sexual activity in youth and adolescence was explicitly and emphatically discountenanced" (1973:134). The discountenancing was most emphatic when the subjects were unmarried young women.

The "invention of the adolescent"—the investment of the years around puberty with distinctive, socially defined, meanings and qualities—has conventionally been dated at the beginning of the twentieth century. Kett has suggested, however, that the adolescent *girl* was "discovered" considerably earlier. Nineteenth-century anxieties about "precocity" (the premature adoption of adult behavior) were, he points out, focused primarily on girls. Furthermore, the dangers to female adolescence were defined almost wholly in sexual terms: "A society which failed to provide a significant social role for women outside of marriage had difficulty envisioning girls passing through a protracted period of adjustment to responsibility (as was required of boys) *but no trouble recognizing the threat to female virtue posed by the sudden onset of sexual maturity*" (1971:295–96, emphasis added). The power of this threat derived not only from the value attached to virtue as an end in itself but also from the conception of virtue as a *condition* for entry into what was regarded as not simply a woman's sole significant adult role, but the only role in which her future security could be reasonably assured; marriage, and marriage alone, "insured a formal, guaranteed, and effective resolution of the difficult transition" from girlhood to womanhood (Brumberg, 1984:189; see also Brumberg, 1988, chapter 5).

In depictions of the late nineteenth-century girl, the central theme was not wordly knowledge but untutored innocence: "Nothing is so suggestive of innocence and purity as the simple beauty of girlhood when seen in its natural freshness," wrote J. H. Kellogg in a widely read book of domestic moral advice published in 1888. Innocence in the lexicon of the nineteenth century meant innocent not only of sexual knowledge but of sexual interest. The "ideology of passionlessness"—the Victorian assumption that women did not share the carnal enthusiasms of men—applied with particular force to the unmarried girl; she was expected and conceived to *be* asexual (see, e.g., Kellogg, 1888; Duffey, 1874; Cott, 1978; Welter, 1978; Meyerowitz, 1988).[3] Properly educated girls, suggested one author, would pass the years before marriage "perfect strangers to any [sexual or amorous] sensations" and would not develop these feelings until a "suitable gentleman proclaimed his intentions" (cited in Haller and Haller, 1974:109). Only the sexual anesthesia of a Sleeping Beauty impervious to all but the kiss of Prince Charming could fully insure the moral safety of the unmarried adolescent girl.

By the same token, evidence of *sexuality* in unmarried girls was greeted with confusion and horror as evidence of innate, probably irredeemable, moral perversity (see, e.g., Mennel, 1973; Brenzel, 1983; Schlossman and Wallach, 1978; Meyerowitz, 1988). The manager of a Philadelphia refuge for wayward children ("waywardness" in girls has almost invariably been defined in sexual terms) spoke for many later generations of moral authorities when he gave his opinion that "the reformation of females 'is a chimera which it is useless to pursue'" (from an 1822 publication cited by Mennel, 1973:17). As these remarks may suggest, boundaries between the girl who was "pure" and the girl who had "fallen" were defined in absolute terms. A girl was either chaste or she was not; there were no shades of grey. Furthermore, although the "pure" might fall, the "fallen" could never again become pure; a girl who compromised her virtue was, in the rhetoric of the time, "ruined." In nineteenth-century moral tales cited by Barbara Welter (1978) death was portrayed as preferable to loss of innocence.[4] The rhetorical association of unchastity with death suggests that to "fall" was to place oneself not only outside the boundaries of acceptable sexual behavior, but of society itself. The identification by nineteenth-century moral authorities of sexuality in unmarried girls with poverty, with prostitution, and with European (as opposed to Yankee) ethnic origins, and the efforts of reform school officials to segregate the chaste from the unchaste "as if loss of chastity was a highly contagious disease, easily caught by mere proximity" (Brenzel, 1983:48) can be similarly interpreted. By these devices, both the limits of moral respectability and the socially outcast status of the morally deviant were clearly affirmed (in addition to Brenzel, see Mennel, 1973; Schlossman, 1977; Schlossman and Wallach, 1978).

At the same time that nineteenth-century writers asserted the categorical nature of moral boundaries, they worried anxiously over their permeability, an anxiety nicely captured by Barbara Brenzel's "contagious disease" metaphor. The flower of innocence was depicted as a fragile one, threatened from within by the storms of puberty and the temptations of masturbation and from without by the assaults of the opposite sex who, "being by nature more sensual," could less readily control their sexual appetites (e.g., Welter, 1978; Smith-Rosenberg, 1985; Clarke, 1873; Kellogg, 1888; Duffey, 1873). John S. Haller and Robin M. Haller note that "the proper training of girls, their personal hygiene, their relations with other children, their reading habits, and the embarrassing problem of masturbation" dominated late nineteenth-century sex manuals (1974:105). The quintessential sexual danger was masturbation: "All through life, 'the penalty of unlawful transgression [would] be visited upon [the offending girl]'" (Haller and Haller, 1974:106). The nineteenth-century obsession with masturbation has been remarked upon by all social historians of this period, although they have tended to focus on it as a male rather than as a female problem (see, e.g., Barker-Benfield, 1978; Weeks, 1981). Reading late nineteenth-century advice books leaves one in no doubt that concern about "secret vice" was as much directed toward girls as toward boys. Perhaps more than any other form of sexual behavior, masturbation exemplifies the difficulties presented by attempts to socially control private sexual behavior. By its nature invisible and autonomous, it defies surveillance: Seemingly "innocent" girls could be masturbating in secret. A central dogma of prescriptive literature on this topic was that, in fact, masturbation *could not* be kept secret; it would show up in disease, sterility, and the like. The association of visibility with social control and of secrecy with sexual autonomy are consistent themes in the history of sexuality.

The dangers of woman's passage from childhood to adulthood were defined simultaneously, and somewhat paradoxically, in terms of threats to her "innocence and purity" and to the proper development of her reproductive system (see, e.g., Clarke, 1873; Duffey, 1873; Kellogg, 1888; Haller and Haller, 1974; Brumberg, 1984; Smith-Rosenberg, 1985). When, in 1900, an American physician wrote that "many a young life is battered and forever crippled in the breakers of puberty" (cited in Smith-Rosenberg, 1985:184), the hazards he had in mind originated not in the corrupt world of adulthood, but in the physiological changes attendant upon the establishment of menstruation. In his essay on the dangers to women of higher education, the Harvard physician Edward H. Clarke stated that the principal responsibility of a conscientious young woman between puberty and marriage was to the construction of her reproductive system.

> The principle or condition peculiar to the female sex is the management of the catamenial function, which, from the age of fourteen to nineteen, includes the building of the reproductive apparatus. This imposes upon women, and especially upon the young woman, a great care, a corresponding duty, and compensating privileges. . . . This lends to her development and to all her work a rhythmical or periodical order, which must be recognized and obeyed (1873:120).

Proper management of this hazardous time of life demanded, most particularly, the avoidance of physical and mental stimulation: "Virtually any interests outside the home during puberty were deplored, as was any kind of sexual forwardness such as flirtations, dances, and party-going. . . . The life style most frequently advocated for the young woman consisted of a routine of domestic tasks, such as bed-making, cooking, cleaning, and child-tending" (Smith-Rosenberg, 1985:187). Within this framework were combined acute awareness of the perils of unmarried adolescence for girls with a social construction of these perils that minimized their sexual and maximized their reproductive connotations. Indeed, the suppression of sexuality was defined, somewhat incongruously, as necessary to the healthy development of young women's reproductive capacities: "To allow herself even a 'partially animal basis' during courtship was to fall prey to the evils of blighted love which weakened not only her modesty but also her most important [bosom and reproductive] organs" (Haller and Haller, 1974:109). Chastity and domesticity during the perilous teenage years were defined as necessary conditions not only for young women's future marital but for their future reproductive success as well.[5]

The "passionless" girl at the mercy of her own passions and those of others is an ironic figure. Protection of her virtue was a responsibility proportionate to its fragility and one for which the young woman herself was held primarily accountable. Her future status and prospects were defined by marriage and motherhood. However, by the beginning of the nineteenth century, the social framework within which her choice of partner was made had already changed to something like its present form. Less and less was either the process of mate selection or the ultimate choice under the control of parents: "In the seventeenth and early eighteenth century, there existed a stable, parental-run marriage system, in the nineteenth century a stable partner-run system" (Smith, 1978:97). The complexities of the sexual encounter under conditions where young women were required to be both innocent and responsible are powerfully reflected in Eliza Duffey's cautionary remarks on the problems of courtship.

> Young girls do not know, but I sometimes think they ought to know, that the passions of men are much stronger and more easily inflamed than their own. A

levity of behavior, thoughtlessly and—inasmuch as she does not know the consequences—innocently pursued by a young girl, has excited the passions of her male companion almost beyond his control, so that, though he has given no evidence of it in her presence, he may have gone from her side directly to the arms of a fallen woman. . . . So let young girls be very careful, and feel that they have not only their own moral safety, but that of their companions of the other sex, in their keeping (1873:97–98).

That these admonitions were taken seriously by at least some middle-class courting couples is strikingly demonstrated in two series of mid-to-late-nineteenth-century letters examined by Ellen Rothman in her recent book on courtship in the United States (1984:128–43). Whatever may have been the *functions* of the ideology of women's passionlessness, these letters provide striking evidence of that ideology's impact on their writers' expectations for and explanations of their sexual behavior.[6] The young woman was expected to gate-keep and to find it relatively easy; the young man was expected to comply and to find it very difficult. That neither partner fully lived up to these expectations (with the possible exception of the very last) was the subject of much discussion between the couples; they rarely questioned the ideology itself. The threat to young women's status represented by sexual arousal was such that, although passionlessness may sometimes have been a burden, it was also a protection and a refuge.

Given that middle-class young couples were both expected to conduct a "self-guided" courtship *and* to conduct it virtuously, the ideology of female passionlessness can be seen as the internalized equivalent of external parental or neighborhood controls. Rothman observes, however, that before the last quarter of the nineteenth century, young Americans "had rarely gone beyond the reach of the informal oversight of family and community" (1984:207). The sheer visibility of young women's behavior in what was still a predominantly rural and small-town society continued to impose some level of deference to familial expectations, at least among the letter writers and diary keepers of the middle class; should ideology fail, a backup mechanism was in place (in addition to Rothman, see Smith-Rosenberg, 1985). Toward the end of the century, whatever may have been the reality of change in young women's behavior (a point to which I will return in the next section of this chapter), there began to emerge a strong perception that this behavior had become increasingly less subject to parental and community constraints. Tighter controls over young women's behavior were advocated; moral authorities expressed anxious concern over the quantity and quality of maternal surveillance and of the moral guidance given by mothers to their daughters (Rothman, 1987:207–8; Kellogg, 1888). Kellogg prefaced the chapter of his popular advice manual devoted to the problems of puberty in girls with the statement that he was induced to write it by "the failure of mothers to do their duty in this respect" (1888:425). No such apologia preceded the corresponding chapter for boys.

Normative conceptions of female adolescence are powerfully shaped by ideas concerning the futures for which young women are being prepared.

In nineteenth-century America, that future was defined in terms of marriage and, more particularly, of motherhood. It was, however, a future less and less taken for granted as the century wore on. These uncertainties were reflected in the perceptions of foreign as well as domestic observers. A French visitor, de Rousiers, writing in 1892, stated the case plainly:

> [In America] it is impossible to know [what] will be the lot of a little girl of ten, and the problem is what sort of training to give her? Americans usually act as if their daughters would never have a husband, and bring them up as they do the boys, letting them have as much liberty as possible, for in this difficulty of telling them what will be the future they prefer to give them the means of making their way in life alone (cited in Bremner, ed., 1970:35).

Evaluation of de Rousiers' impressions must allow for the contrast between French and American mores. However, in much the same vein, the title of a book published in 1882 by the American suffragist, Mary Livermore, asked, *What Shall We Do with Our Daughters?* The gist of the book's message was that young women should be trained to support themselves not only in case they did not find a husband, but to avoid marrying in haste and repenting at leisure (cited in Rothman, 1978:44). This advice directly addressed several critical dimensions of change in the structural positions of unmarried adolescent girls: the decreasing availability of meaningful work within young women's own households; their movement out of unpaid domestic employment at home into the paid work force; and, finally, their movement often with, but sometimes without, their families into the rapidly growing American cities. The long-run consequences of these changes were to increase (certainly in the perceptions of contemporaries and possibly in fact) the exposure and vulnerability of adolescent girls to worldly temptations (symbolized by the alluring but morally corrupt "city") and, by the same token, to create pressures for new institutions to contain and manage young women during the long period between puberty and marriage.

STRUCTURAL AND IDEOLOGICAL
DIMENSIONS OF CHANGE: 1880–1920
The stage for changes in the objective conditions, as well as in the social construction, of female adolescence was set early in the nineteenth century. However, it was not until the last quarter of the century that these changes became clearly visible to, and began to excite comment, concern, and action among, contemporaries. To understand these reactions and how they evolved, it is necessary to begin with a brief description of the demographic and social dimensions of young women's lives in the late nineteenth and early twentieth centuries.

Single young women do not appear as a separate category in the U.S. Census until 1890; *young* women (here defined as between the ages of 15 and 24) are not readily distinguishable until 1870. At the point when they did begin to be separately counted, young women were over a third of the adult

FIGURE 5.1
WOMEN AGED 15–24 AS A PERCENTAGE OF ALL WOMEN AGED 15 AND ABOVE,
UNITED STATES, 1870–1987

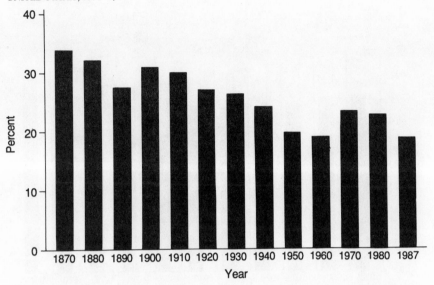

Sources: U.S. Bureau of the Census, *Historical Statistics of the United States, Colonial Times to 1970, Bicentennial Edition, Part 1* (Washington, D.C.: U.S. Government Printing Office, 1975); U.S. Bureau of the Census, "United States Population Estimates by Age, Sex, and Race: 1980 to 1987," *Current Population Reports*, ser. P-25, no. 1022 (Washington, D.C.: U.S. Government Printing Office, 1988).

female population, a proportion that has not been exceeded since, as shown in Figure 5.1. Furthermore, as indicated by the data presented in Figure 5.2, the very large majority of these women were single. In 1890, when the pertinent data first became available, 72 percent of women aged 15 to 24 were unmarried. It was not until the 1980s that this figure again rose above 70 percent. Based on an analysis of marital status by birth cohorts, Irene B. Taeuber and Conrad Taeuber infer that age at marriage was relatively low at the beginning of the nineteenth century and rose gradually, reaching a peak in 1890 from which it again gradually declined (1971:294). (Data on median ages at marriage for males and females for the period from 1890 to 1987 are given in Figure 5.3.) The turn-of-the-century population of young single women was, finally, not uniformly distributed either ethnically or geographically; the highest percentages were found in urban areas, in the Northeast and North Central states, and among women who were white and native-born (Taeuber and Taeuber, 1971:290–304; Kessler-Harris, 1982:98).

The last decades of the nineteenth century were witness not only to the maximum presence in American society of single young women but also to the beginnings of a profound transformation in their daily lives. In historians' discussions of early and mid-nineteenth century girlhood, the increasing prob-

FIGURE 5.2
PERCENT NEVER MARRIED AMONG ALL PERSONS AGED 15–24, BY SEX, UNITED STATES, 1890–1987

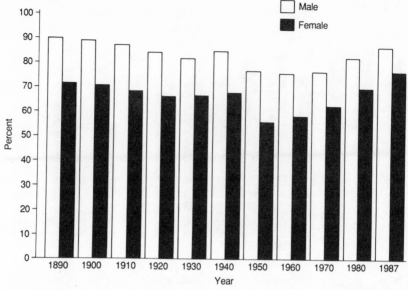

Sources: U.S. Bureau of the Census, *Historical Statistics of the United States, Colonial Times to 1970, Bicentennial Edition, Part 1* (Washington, D.C.: U.S. Government Printing Office, 1975); U.S. Bureau of the Census, "Households, Families, Marital Status, and Living Arrangements: March 1987 (Advance Report)," *Current Population Reports,* ser. P-25, no. 417 (Washington, D.C.: U.S. Government Printing Office, 1987).

lem of finding occupations for young unmarried women is a consistent theme. In the very early days of manufacturing, wage work outside the home—exemplified by the "factory girls" of many New England towns—was considered a respectable alternative for a single young woman, although even then only a tiny proportion were so employed. After about 1840, this option became less acceptable to Yankee young women and their families, due to a combination of low pay with an influx of impoverished immigrant women, and men, into the mills. At the same time, declining birth rates and changes in the technology of housekeeping rendered a daughter's services increasingly dispensible within the home. "Young women suffered even more than young men from a period of life in which they neither went to school nor had a job . . . most young women had little to do for the long period between the time they left school and the time they married" (Katz, 1975:272; see also, Cott, 1975, 1977; Kett, 1977; Lloyd, 1979; Kessler-Harris, 1982). Those young women who "suffered" most were native-born, white, of Protestant stock, and (most probably) middle-class. Michael B. Katz's work and a parallel study by Laurence A. Glasco in Buffalo, New York, indicate that Irish-Catholic and (in Buffalo) German-born girls were very likely to spend a substantial portion of their teenage years

FIGURE 5.3
MEDIAN AGE AT FIRST MARRIAGE, BY SEX, UNITED STATES, 1890–1987

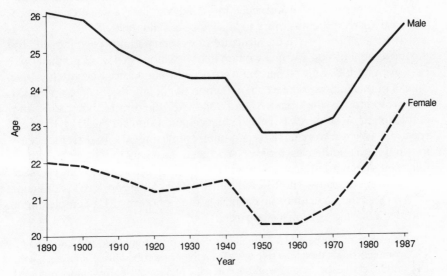

Source: U.S. Bureau of the Census, "Households, Families, Marital Status, and Living Arrangements: March 1987 (Advance Report)," *Current Population Reports*, ser. P-25, no. 417 (Washington, D.C.: U.S. Government Printing Office, 1987).

outside their own homes as live-in domestic servants (Katz, 1975:285; Glasco, 1979; see also Kessler-Harris, 1982).

The congruence between a reality in which genteel young women had little or nothing to do before marriage and an ideology in which home protection and the absence of stimulation were considered essential for a young woman's sexual safety, on the one hand, and the development of her reproductive capacities, on the other, is striking. In the social construction of female adolescence elaborated by Clarke and like-minded moral authorities, idleness during the critical years of puberty was defined as a form of preventive health behavior. Toward the end of the century, however, this behavior pattern (and its supporting ideology) began to change. More and more single young women entered paid nonagricultural employment outside their own homes; the largest *increase* in women wage earners was among the white and native-born.[7]

Between 1870 (when the U.S. Bureau of the Census began to collect data on labor force participation by sex) and 1920, the percentage of women in nonagricultural employment nearly doubled, from 11.8 percent to 21.3 percent. Almost all of that increase took place between 1880 and 1910; it was accounted for by the movement into the labor force of *single* women. In 1900 close to half of *all* employed women were single and between the ages of 16 and 24 (Hill, 1929: Tables 76 and 79); in large cities the percentage was much higher. "The typical woman worker at the turn of the century was unmarried, young," and either a domestic servant or a factory worker (Weiner, 1985:5; Oppenheimer, 1970:Table 5.4). By 1920, she was still unmarried and young, but far less likely to be in domestic service and much more likely to have a white-collar office job, particularly if she was white and native-born (Hill, 1929).

The transformation in the structure of women's adolescence initiated by the movement of single young women into the labor force was a gradual process; even by 1900 only 38 percent were actually employed. Nevertheless, the impact of this unprecedented phenomenon on the minds of contemporaries was profound: "In the decades before and after the turn of the century, the employment of women was a major public issue" (Smuts, 1959:111). The perspectives adopted were anxious and often conflicting. At one extreme, work for single and middle-class girls was advocated as a means by which their virtue might be safeguarded: "congenial and continuous" occupation would protect young women against "ill-directed fancies" (i.e., falling in love) (Rothman, 1978:44).[8] At the same time, the dangers to the "innocent girl" of employment outside her home were all too apparent.

> The labor of "respectable" [in contrast to that of "poor, black, and immigrant"] women brought them one step away from their prescribed place at home, where middle-class expectations would decree a life of domesticity. Even more removed were the rural women who migrated to the cities to find work. Public opinion maintained that these working girls, adrift from any domestic influence, endangered their physical and moral health and the health of future generations (Weiner, 1985:5).

Concern for the moral safety of the working girl was mirrored both by the intense interest displayed by census and labor department statisticians in her "family relationships" (in modern parlance, her living arrangements) and by the emergence of organizations and, ultimately, of legislation for her protection. Data collected in 1890, in 1900, and in 1920 consistently showed that two-thirds or more of single working women lived with their families (the proportion actually increased over time with the decline of domestic service as a principal occupation) (Hill, 1929; Weiner, 1985). Carroll D. Wright, who studied "The Working Girls of Boston" in 1889 commented that the percentage living away from home was "much less than is generally supposed" (cited in Weiner, 1985:18); and, indeed, the image placed before the public throughout this entire period was that of the girl "adrift," living in the city independently of her family (McGovern, 1968; Weiner, 1985; Meyerowitz, 1988). The symbol most often invoked was that of an "innocent country girl" alone and unprotected in the great city. Mark Thomas Connelly suggests that by early in the twentieth century the prodigal son leaving the farm for the city had been supplanted by the prodigal daughter: "The fate of America was the fate of American country girls, and the country girls seemed to be ending 'on the line' or on the streets after they left the country. The response to this situation was a siege mentality regarding the movement of young women away from home and family" (1980:123). Whether or not they lived at home, and even though their eventual goals were marriage and childbearing (see, e.g., Gilman, 1898), paid work beyond immediate family supervision represented a real change in the structure of young women's lives, giving them, however temporarily, an unprecedented degree of autonomy and independence.

This change was translated by many observers into evidence of a clear and present moral danger. Although working girls were not documented by the U.S. Bureau of the Census until 1870, anxiety about their protection from the perils of urban life became evident as early as 1856 when the first boarding home for nondestitute women was founded in New York City. By 1877, twenty such homes existed where young women (principally those who were white and native-born) could live " 'at home,' so their bodies, reputations, and status remained protected" (Weiner, 1985:55). Later, minimum-wage legislation was advocated on the grounds that low salaries threatened public morality by making young women vulnerable to prostitution (Weiner, 1985:74). The proliferation of protective organizations (Traveler's Aid, the YWCA, a variety of "Working Girls" clubs and societies, as well as boarding homes) and the movement for protective legislation coincided with the period of single young women's greatest demographic importance as a percentage of the adult female population and with the mounting evidence of their wholesale departure from nineteenth-century norms of placid homebound domesticity.[9]

A vivid impression of the impact of early twentieth-century young women on the minds of their contemporaries comes from the 1911 report of the Minneapolis Vice Commission.

> One of the most disturbing phases of the present situation . . . and an alarming social symptom is the large number of young girls in the streets at night in the downtown sections. . . . They may be found in numbers loitering about the fruit stores, drug stores and other popular locations, haunting hotel lobbies, crowding into the dance halls, the theaters and other amusement resorts; also in the saloon restaurants and the chop suey places and parading the streets and touring about in automobiles with men (cited in Connelly, 1980:38).

What today would be described as "late adolescent behavior" was regarded by the vice commission as the first steps down the garden path to prostitution.[10] While vice commissions concentrated on the behavior of largely working-class girls, early twentieth-century novels, magazines, and newspapers directed to middle-class audiences commented on her middle-class counterpart, the flapper, in terms that could hardly have contrasted more strongly with Kellogg's vision of fragile and blushing innocence. "Observe, then, this nameless one, this American Flapper. . . . A charming creature! . . . Youth is hers, and hope, and romance, and—Well, well, let us be exact; let us not say innocence. This Flapper, to tell the truth, is far, far, far from a simpleton. . . . Life, indeed, is almost empty of surprises, mysteries, horrors to this Flapper of 1915" (H. L. Mencken, cited in May, 1959:339). Dorothy Dix, writing for the Boston *American* in the early 1900s, left her readers in no doubt as to the consequences of young women's newfound freedom: "Nice girls, good girls, girls in good positions in society—frankly take the initiative in furthering an acquaintance with any man who happens to strike their fancy" (cited in McGovern, 1968:324). Irrespective of the social realities of sexual behavior, fundamental normative change is signaled not by the actions of young women society defines as outsiders— poor, immigrant, black—but by the actions of the "good girls" who occupy the "good positions in society."

Concurrent with change in the structural dimensions of young women's lives were equally profound changes in beliefs about women's sexuality. Rosalind Rosenberg has reviewed three documented surveys of educated married women's sexual attitudes and behavior conducted in 1892, 1910, and 1918 together with the writings of the academic women who conducted these surveys (1982:178–206). She concludes that among "American social scientists and the college-educated Americans they studied . . . a major change [in attitudes toward sex] did take place, and it did so in the first two decades of this century" (179). Women in the 1890s "tended to emphasize the procreative function of sex [while] later subjects argued less often that coitus should be restricted to reproduction, and they were more likely to say that sex was 'physically necessary to the woman as well as to the man for a complete life' " (197).

Ironically, these changes were attributable, in part, to the public preoccupation with sexual morality that stimulated these and other "field" investigations of sexual behavior (see, e.g., Hale, 1971; Strong, 1972; Schlossman and Wallach, 1978; Rosenberg, 1982). The "repeal of reticence" about sexual matters that accompanied Progressive Era campaigns against prostitution and veneral disease legitimated sex as a topic of discussion and markedly increased public awareness of women as sexual beings. A second and equally important source of change were the works of Sigmund Freud and Havelock Ellis. In 1909 Freud gave his famous series of lectures at Clark University in which he introduced psychoanalysis to the United States and shocked some members of his audience by denouncing current sexual taboos. Nathan G. Hale cites the impression of the dean of the University of Toronto that Freud "advocated free love, removal of all restraints, and a relapse into savagery" (1971:22). However, prior to 1920 Ellis's works were far more widely read in the United States, and his attack on "civilized morality" was if anything more explicit than Freud's.[11] He specifically rejected the nineteenth-century ideology of women's passionlessness and of the identity between sexual and reproductive instincts, arguing that women were as capable of sexual feelings as men but untrained to experience them.[12]

The implications of Freud's and Ellis's ideas for the sexuality of women were revolutionary at the time they were announced (Ellis's work was first published in Philadelphia, beginning in 1897); they constituted a fundamental attack on the conception of the innocent and asexual girl that late nineteenth-century moralists had been at such pains to promote. The contemporary audience for these ideas may have been narrow; the evidence for their impact is nonetheless persuasive. Hale reports that between 1910 and 1915 Emma Goldman lectured to groups of college students on the dangers to women's intellectual faculties of sexual repression, basing her arguments on the work of Freud (1971:270). Early twentieth-century writers and political radicals attempted to conduct their frequently rather public personal lives in accord with the new sexual ideology (Kennedy, 1970; Simmons, 1982; Trimberger, 1983). College-educated women, as Rosenberg has documented, shifted to "an unprecedented openness and, in a few instances, even enthusiasm, about sex" (1982:178). By the early 1920s a new profession of adolescent psychologists had already begun the difficult task of incorporating the notion that "girls as well as boys are inheritors of the sexual instinct and tendencies" into a framework within which conventional morality might still be preserved (Davenport, 1924:4).

THE DOMESTICATION OF SEXUALITY, 1920–1960
There is a striking contrast between the single young woman as portrayed in the literature of the 1920s and her post–World War II counterpart.[13] Whether their behavior was deplored as representing the end of American civilization or celebrated as a new beginning, not only sexuality but freedom from social and sexual constraints and autonomy of sexual choice were central characteristics in the portrait of 1920s "bachelor girls" painted by their contemporaries (Fass, 1977; see also, Lindsey, 1925; Calverton, 1928; Lippmann, 1929; Dell, 1930). Traditional morality was overthrown and single young women were seen as the principal agents of its demise. By the end of World War II, this image of the autonomous young woman actively enjoying her sexual freedom had virtually disappeared. Her place was taken by peer-dominated high school and college girls, fearful of their sexual "reputations," their aspirations defined by the "rating and dating complex" (Waller, 1937; see also U.S. Children's Bureau, 1946; Fedder, 1948; Hollingshead, 1949; Burgess and Wallin, 1953; Coleman, 1961).[14] Based on a study published in 1966, Elizabeth Douvan and Joseph Adelson concluded that adolescent girls were decorous, compliant, "(bent) easily to parental regulation," and had little interest in sex (108).[15]

Clearly, these portraits were overdrawn. It is unlikely that young women of the 1940s and 50s were *less* sexually interested (or active) than young women of the 1920s, or that the latter were substantially more free than the former from normative constraints on their behavior.[16] These as well as earlier shifts in the social construction of female adolescence had less to do with changes in young women's actual behavior than with changes in social structure and ideology that affected how that behavior was perceived. Between 1920 and 1960 both structure and ideology conspired to turn the sexually liberated flapper into the socially conforming bobby-soxer. Despite the Jazz Age reputation of the 1920s, by early in that decade a process of accommodation between the new conditions and the old moralities had already begun.

Among the most consistent and striking aspects of scholarly as well as the more hortatory variety of commentary on the young women of the twentieth century is its fascination with the sexual behavior of "nice" girls from "good" families and the identification of meaningful change in sexual mores with change in the social location of overt *female* (not male) sexuality from the nonrespectable to the respectable classes. A historian writing in 1923 described "the changing morality of women"—her contemporaries—as follows: "Girls begin to sow their wild oats.... Girls, from well-bred, respectable middle-class families [have] broken through those invisible chains of custom and asserted their right to a nonchalant, self-sustaining life of their own with a cigarette after every meal and a lover to lend color to life" (cited in Calverton, 1928:91).

Folsom, an early family sociologist, identified the "significant departure" of the 1920s from prior patterns of illicit sexual behavior as residing in "the high social status and non-commercial motive of the *girls* who participated" (1934:401, emphasis added). College students were described as the "advance guard of the younger generation" lending "prestige to mores that are already in the making" (Bromley and Britten, 1938:26). The "illicit" behavior of black, immigrant, and lower-class young women was (and is) discounted; anxiety, fascination, and the fear (or anticipation) of sexual revolution are aroused when the transgressors of moral boundaries are (or are seen to be) daughters of the middle class. By the same token, changes over time both in the dominant social construction of female adolescence and in strategies for managing this dangerous transition have been more powerfully affected by how middle-class Americans have structured, and thought about, this period than by the often very different experiences of groups socially defined as "outside" the mainstream.

The 1920s appeared to contemporaries and, until relatively recently, to many historians as a turning point in the emancipation of women and (a closely related theme) in the liberation of sexual morality from its Victorian restrictions. Although the point is still in some dispute (and seems to depend in large part on how "emancipation" is defined and whether attention is focused on changes in attitudes or in behavior) most historians now believe these changes not only to have begun, but to have had a major impact on public consciousness, considerably earlier (May, 1959; McGovern, 1968; Freedman, 1974; Smith, 1978; Erenberg, 1981).[17] What marked the 1920s was the pervasive adoption of "emancipated" behavior by middle-class youth and the acceptance—rueful or enthusiastic—of this behavior as a fait accompli by the middle-class Americans who observed and commented upon it.

A critical dimension of change was the public assertion of female sexuality. Respectable women proclaimed by their manners, their clothes, their hairstyles, and their use of cosmetics "that they [like prostitutes] were endowed with a sexual personality. They had taken on themselves as potential wives all the characteristics of lovers. The two kinds of women were no longer separate and distinguishable at first glance but one and the same" (Fass, 1977:284). The reasons for this transformation were complex: the new sexual ideologies described earlier, the disruptions of settled life carried in its train by World War I, and the promotion and partial legitimation of women's sexuality by its increasing commercial exploitation. "The first duty of woman," claimed one 1920s advertisement, "was to attract" (cited in D'Emilio and Freedman, 1988:278; see also, Fass, 1977; Bailey, 1988). From the perspective of contemporary observers, among the most powerful forces for change was what might be described as an unprecedented expansion in the sexual opportunity structure. The movement of unmarried young women into the paid labor force and their increasing enrollment in secondary schools and colleges shifted the scene of their transition from puberty to marriage from the back parlor and the front porch to institutional settings outside the home.[18] The automobile, the telephone, and birth control (which, if they were not wholly responsible for altering the conditions of that transition, were often so described) became established necessities of middle-class life during the 1920s and 1930s (Gordon, 1977; Fischer and Carroll, 1988). To contemporary minds, the common denominator of work, school, the automobile, the telephone, and contraception was that they created both new opportunities for sexual encounters and new possibilities for their concealment.[19] Surveillance demands visibility of the behavior in question, and the management of visibility has always been more of a problem for women than for men. Suddenly in the 1920s, not only were single young women discovered to be interested in sex, but they were perceived as being able to act on their interest without fear of discovery.

In a statement that is probably as applicable today as when it was made, Isabel Davenport remarked that "the practical education of the adolescent girl has been at the mercy of several conflicting notions relative to her sexual nature" (1924:2). Confusion in conceptions of female adolescence (as well as inconsistencies in the behavior of young women themselves) arose from the struggle to accommodate recognition of female sexuality into a conventional moral framework in which not only were "adult" forms of sexual behavior to be postponed until after marriage, but indulgence in even the most mild forms of sexual play had been held to permanently unfit the young woman for her ordained family roles. This framework depended heavily for its support on a belief in women's fundamental disinterest in sex and on reproductive intent within marriage as the sole legitimation for sexual activity. Acknowledgment and approval of female sexuality seriously undermined the ideological basis for an asexual female adolescence. Structural change made the monitoring of female sexuality impossible.

Among the first consequences of these changes was to depoliticize the management of young women's sexuality. Late nineteenth- and early twentieth-century movements for the regulation of sexuality by the state (described in detail in Chapter 7) were founded on the construction of "sexually active" single young women as innocent victims of male seduction. Once women were admitted to have sexual interests, this position became impossible to maintain: "What everybody must know is that sexual conduct, whatever it might be, is regulated personally and not publicly in modern society" (Lippmann, 1929:286). In the 1920s two new philosophies concerning the regulation of young women's sexuality emerged. The first was to define the problem away by attributing sexual misconduct to sexual repression; the second (and more widely employed) was what I have labeled domestication: Women's sexuality was accepted and, at the same time, contained by placing it in the service of a new all-encompassing conception of marriage as the sole vehicle for women's satisfaction and self-expression.

Romanticization of youthful sexuality was unique to the 1920s. From this perspective (nicely summarized by Fass, 1977:29–35), what appeared to traditionalists as sexual excess was the outcome of ignorance and repression fostered by Victorian moral cant. Once the weight of this outworn morality was lifted, youth (including female youth) would "naturally" behave in a responsible fashion: "Repression does not repress sexual intercourse, it represses only the sense of sexual responsibility. Repression therefore incidentally promotes premature, accidental, irresponsible and illegitimate parenthood" (Dell, 1930:284). Few observers (then or since) have been willing to rely quite so heavily on the beneficence of natural instincts. However, the "wicked and inexcusable" sexual ignorance of women and girls was denounced even by the less romantic, but in terms that left no doubt as to the underlying intent: Like sexual "precocity" in the previous century, sexual ignorance unfitted the young woman for her "legitimate inheritance of marriage and motherhood" (Davenport, 1924:252ff.; see also Blanchard, 1924; Hollingworth, 1931; Blanchard and Manasses, 1930). Central to the compromise between the new sexuality and the old morality that emerged in the 1920s was the definition of sexual compatibility as a sine qua non for marital happiness (Gordon, 1971). In the terms of this revised moral framework, sexual experimentation (within limits) was legitimized as preparation for marriage and intercourse was sanctified by engagement (see, e.g., Fass, 1977:260–90). In this fashion, the realities of social change were accommodated by redrawing the boundaries of civilized society to include the new, no-longer-innocent behaviors of unmarried young women, but in such a way that their potentially disruptive consequences were neutralized and the old structures and old moralities were preserved.

The New Woman whose flamboyant image dominated the literature of the 1920s had two facets: sexual liberation and economic independence (see, e.g., West, 1955). The accommodation I have described was accomplished by focusing attention on the facet that conflicted least with women's traditional roles: their sexuality. Liberal thinkers of the 1920s and 1930s may have been prepared to acknowledge, even to wax poetic, over youthful female sexuality. However, the possibility that "the flower of American middle-class girlhood" might choose careers over husbands was quite another matter (Davenport, 1924:245). Even among the sexual "progressives" described by Fass there was some reluctance to define women's emancipation as including more fundamental change. Floyd Dell was explicit on this point: "Any theoretical idealization of woman as a wage worker, which is at the same time a depreciation of the importance to her of mating and maternity, [is] the old patriarchal swindle upon human nature. Its aim is to make her a contented wage worker while she is being robbed of her sexual rights" (1930:143).

Ben Lindsey advanced the same idea with highly romanticized accounts of sexually "liberated" young women who, after heart-to-heart talks with the author (in his capacity as judge of the Denver juvenile court) went on to become exemplary wives and mothers (Lindsey, 1925). By the end of the 1920s, economic independence itself was no longer being defined as a road to perdition but as an alternative, even accelerated, route to traditional domesticity.

> When women were still struggling for the right to economic independence there was something of the crusading spirit attached to holding a job. Now that the privilege of self-support is no longer so warmly contested, it has taken a more suitable place, and is conceived as a part of life rather than the whole aim of existence. There is a growing tendency to look upon work as a way of filling in the time before marriage or as a means to early mating without the heart-rending delay which would otherwise be necessary (Blanchard and Manasses, 1930:237).

This sanguine evaluation should be read in the context of two important developments in the evolving structure of single young women's lives. First, by early in the 1920s accelerating secondary-school and college enrollments were making it increasingly clear that the school and not the workplace was destined to become the principal venue for women's adolescent transition. And second, most young women who worked for pay were limiting their labor force participation to the relatively brief interval between school and marriage (Smuts, 1959:142–43).[20]

By the mid-1920s all of the states had passed laws requiring school attendance until (depending on the jurisdiction) age 14, 15, or 16. The biggest expansion in secondary-school enrollments occurred between 1916 and 1940; during this period the number of days attended per pupil increased to nearly their present level (Rothman, 1978; Walters and O'Connell, 1988). From their earliest days, high schools had attracted more girls than boys; the largest recorded disparity was in 1920, when 60 percent of high school graduates were female (Kett, 1977:138; U.S. Bureau of the Census, 1975). In common with work, secondary school offered single young women (in the 1920s and early 1930s, predominantly middle-class young women) an "occupation," as well as removing them for large portions of the day from the immediate supervision of their families. In other respects, the management problems and possibilities presented by these two institutions were defined and evaluated quite differently. Critical to these differences were a number of structural characteristics unique to the school setting.

A central condition for the supposed emancipation of the New Woman was economic independence: "They ['girls and young women'] become conscious of the power that an individual income gives; they choose their pleasures in their own way; they mingle in female masses; they meet more men . . . and they have more alternatives and more kinds of success to allure them" (Coe, 1924:12). By contrast with this scenario, what they saw as the "supervised" and controlled environment of the school appeared to more conservative observers than George A. Coe as one of *relative* moral safety.[21] High school and college were acknowledged to have their moral dangers—the misguidance of peers, the attractions of boyfriends, and the distracting allurements of "the movie, the motor party, and the dance"—but these dangers were ascribed to gaps in surveillance rather than (as in the workplace) to an absence of surveillance altogether (Eggleston, 1923; Goodsell, 1923).

Prolonged education kept single young women in a state of semidependence on adult authority, restraining if not preventing the assertion of sexual autonomy to which (not only in Coe's scenario but in the minds of conservatives as well) they might be led by "the power [of] an individual income." Furthermore (contrary to the apprehensions—or hopes—of an earlier generation), by the 1920s secondary and even college education were no longer offering a serious challenge to traditional conceptions of the futures for which young women were being prepared (Clarke, 1873; Hall, 1905; Wein, 1974; Fass, 1977). While authorities on the management of the adolescent girl might bemoan "the current practice of using the coeducational university as 'a social stalking ground,' where teas, dances, movies, and motor parties easily push into the background the intellectual activities still associated in old-fashioned minds with higher education," they could not at the same time complain that girls who preferred dances to intellectual activities were in much danger of choosing careers over husbands (Goodsell, 1923:267). Based on her detailed study of college youth in the 1920s, Paula Fass observes that "marriage was for the coed what business was in the imagination of her male partner" (1977:366).

The adolescent girl in high school or college appeared neither "alone and adrift," nor yet (in the decades from 1920 to 1960) very likely to eschew marriage and children for a career; her vulnerability, defined almost invariably in sexual terms, was to the influence of peers. Although the adolescent society was, in the 1920s and 1930s, a relatively new phenomenon, its potential power was not lost on contemporary observers. During the young woman's high school years, "perhaps mother does not know one girl with whom her daughter associates day after day. . . . By the time she is a junior . . . she finds herself much interested in both boys and girls. . . . She begins to be careful of her dress. She is interested in making herself attractive to others. She is lonely if she is obliged to be away from the groups of boys and girls" (Eggleston, 1923:62–63). The peer group phenomenon was uniformly acknowledged. However, evaluations of its influence were conflicting. From the perspective of moral conservatives the dangers were clear and present: Not only were boys and girls of sexually vulnerable age being thrown together under conditions of minimum surveillance; "traditional prohibitions upon the approaches of boys and girls to each other's persons," as Robert S. and Helen M. Lynd so delicately put it, were being increasingly relaxed (1929:137). Writers in this vein warned against "sentimental friendships" in high school, emphasized the dangers of petting, and placed responsibility squarely on the girl for keeping sexual encounters under control (e.g., Gibson, 1927; Folsom, 1934:411). These strictures differed very little from Eliza Duffey's admonitions of fifty-four years earlier. In striking contrast were the evaluations of "progressive" educators like Leta S. Hollingworth and Phyllis Blanchard and Carlyn Manasses. Ample opportunity to associate with the opposite sex during adolescence was described as essential to the establishment of heterosexuality and to "normal" mating and marriage (Hollingworth, 1931:118–21); the young woman who petted "may be better prepared for marriage by her playful activities than if she had clung to a passive role of waiting for marriage before giving any expression to her sex impulses" (Blanchard and Manasses, 1930:61). Under the new conditions of sexual opportunity young women's sexuality was to be managed by what I called earlier a process of domestication—sexual competence was redefined by these and other authorities as a necessary precondition for marital success (Gordon, 1971).

If the active expression of sexual impulses was valuable preparation for marriage, then preparation for marriage—or a relationship that could be *defined* as preparation for marriage—justified sex: "Love made sex right" (Fass, 1978:273). Petting, its intimacy carefully graded according to the quality of the relationship, was approved, even enjoined by the peer group; intercourse was taboo except in the context of engagement or, at the very least, romantic love. These, according to the social scientists who documented their attitudes and behavior, were central moral tenets of youth between the two World Wars.[22] The reports of these new commentators on the contemporary social scene began to appear in the late 1920s and 1930s. Based on observation, interviews, and questionnaires (directed, with the major exception of the Lynds's Middletown studies, almost entirely to college students), they recorded the "facts" of "social change in the field of sex," lending to these changes the imprimatur of scientific knowledge. At the same time, these early sociologists came away from their research powerfully impressed with the sexual social controls—the "new code of love mores"—that were emerging from within the peer group itself. By the 1940s and 1950s, the overwhelming influence of peers not only on the rules of sexual conduct, but on every other aspect of high school and college life, had become a dominant theme of research on youth and adolescence (see, e.g., Hollingshead, 1949; Burgess and Wallin, 1953; Coleman, 1961; Havighurst et al., 1962). It was a theme difficult to reconcile with earlier portrayals of the emancipated New Woman eagerly testing her newfound sexual independence.

Sexual social change in the 1920s and 1930s had been identified with change in the attitudes and behavior of unmarried young women. However, as at least one observer of college youth noted even then, it was also young women's behavior that the "new" moral code principally constrained.

A single standard of morality governs men and women as to their overt acts; but a double standard still holds as to attitudes and *motives*. Namely, only romantic love or marital duty excuses or justifies sexual intercourse by a woman, while in a man sex may be more excused or tolerated as an act of physical passion alone . . . sexual aggressiveness is despicable in a woman although pardonable or even admired in a man; and plurality of relationships at any one time is much more condemned in a woman than in a man (Folsom, 1934:408).

Beginning with Willard Waller's classic 1937 paper outlining the "rating and dating complex" on college campuses, there was a distinct shift of emphasis in sociological writing from the dimension of change to the dimension of constraint. No longer depicted as the "vanguard" of a new morality, high school and college girls in the 1940s and 1950s were portrayed as enmeshed in a peer-controlled status system in which their social and sexual "reputations" were constantly at stake. "Popularity" demanded success with the boys; "reputation" demanded that success not be bought at the price of a too-ready sexual acquiescence; the price, if paid, must be concealed: "The peer group itself generally acts to maintain the girl's good behavior, through gossip (and the fear of it) and the high value given to reputation" (Douvan and Adelson, 1966:112).

Thus, in slightly altered form, the "good" girl and the "bad" girl were revived, and "unpopularity" supplanted ruin as the cost of departure from sexual orthodoxy.[23] Furthermore, as dating and petting were legitimized (even a 1946 U.S. Children's Bureau publication acknowledged that "petting . . . is now practiced more generally among those who are considered nice people" [75]) and ideas of "sexual revolution" receded, *unorthodox* female sexuality became, once again, the province of the lower classes. Based on their community studies of high school age populations, Hollingshead and Havighurst reported that sexual intercourse (the new unorthodoxy) among *female* adolescents was confined almost entirely to girls of lower-class origin.[24] The findings of Alfred Kinsey (1948, 1953), Ehrmann (1959) and others supported this view (summarized in Reiss, 1960:89–116).

The 1940s and 1950s were decades of "going steady," early marriage ("young people were moving through the dating system directly—and immediately—into marriage"), and the reaffirmation of traditional domestic and moral values (Zube, 1972; Rothman, 1987; Bailey, 1988). Reflecting this shift away from an emphasis on sexual social change, the tone of counseling manuals for adolescents and their parents, as well as much of the pertinent scholarly literature, was in some ways more reminiscent of the 1890s than of the 1920s and 1930s; the major difference being that the line between respectable and nonrespectable sexual behavior was drawn at intercourse rather than at its preliminaries. The most profound contrast with the 1920s was in the changed portrayal of young women from autonomous pleasure seekers to the passive subjects of masculine caprice.

The cover of a 1946 U.S. Children's Bureau publication, "Guiding the Adolescent," shows a teenage boy and two girls. The central figure, the boy, gazes with evident interest at one of the girls—clearly a new girl in town—while the other, his date, looks on in a frenzy of jealous pique. The message conveyed was not only that "boy-girl relationships"—as these interactions were blandly described—were of paramount importance in adolescence, but that the dominant partner in these relationships was the boy. He was the chooser; the girl must wait to be chosen. Adolescent girls were assumed to be preoccupied with boys but, curiously, not with sex; consequently, since "a girl's body is more slowly aroused physically than a boy's" it was her responsibility to avoid "leading him on" (Fedder, 1948:170). The girl who failed in this responsibility was threatened with being "left out of much that would contribute to her happiness" (U.S. Children's Bureau, 1946:75). The ever-present implication was that to be chosen in the long run she must, in the short run, reject—or at least fend off—the chooser. The contradiction between normative requirements that a girl be *both* successful with the boys *and* (technically) chaste was evident; girls, as a consequence, "engaged in a form of gamesmanship—being (or doing) one thing while appearing to do another" (Douvan and Adelson, 1966:114; see also Hollingshead, 1949:414; Reiss, 1960). Thus the normative structure was upheld, while behavior was adjusted to the realities of adolescent social life.

Whether their behavior was evaluated positively or negatively, in the 1920s and, to a lesser extent, the 1930s, unmarried young women were taken seriously as sexual actors laying the groundwork for new social forms. There was little trace of this serious appraisal in the literature of the 1940s and 1950s. James S. Coleman, for example, was harsh in his comments about adolescent girls' interest in popularity with boys, which was more appropriate, he suggested, to the "life of a model or chorus girl or movie actress or call girl" than to adult realities (1961:55). Alice S. Rossi was equally critical: "Young women seem increasingly uncommitted to anything beyond early marriage, motherhood, and a suburban house" (1964:608). Douvan and Adelson, although their remarks were couched in less evaluative terms, clearly did not regard adolescent girls as straining against the bonds of convention: "The line of moral development in girls moves from a rather passive, childlike acceptance of parental authority to an identification with the point of view of that authority" (1966:109). Not until the late 1960s would the autonomous sexual possibilities of unmarried young women again be taken seriously.[25]

RECOGNITION that girls as well as boys had sexual interests both transformed and enormously complicated the management of women's adolescence. No longer could the state appropriately intervene to protect the "innocent" girl; nor, on the other hand, was there, in the period between 1920 and 1960, any concerted public effort to protect the noninnocent, either in anticipation of or subsequent to her becoming sexually involved. Intellectual acknowlegment of young women's sexuality was one thing—and was reflected in the marked proliferation after 1920 of books and articles on the character and management of "the adolescent girl." "Official" acknowledgment in the form, say, of sex education courses in high schools and colleges, was quite another, particularly if those courses were to include girls (e.g., Davenport, 1924:18).

Although they had varying notions about its content, "sexual enlightenment"—lifting of what was defined as the veil of Victorian secrecy over sexual matters—was the one management strategy on which the commentators of this period were able to agree; not because they believed that adolescent girls no longer required protection but because they had concluded that knowledge was more protective than innocence. By 1946, even the U.S. government lent its stamp of approval to this shift in ideological perspective. "It is now generally recognized that the methods in vogue a half a century back, which attempted to prevent undesireable sex conduct by keeping young people in ignorance and subjecting them to rigid disciplinary measures, were neither wise nor effective and that the results of such methods were more harmful than the indiscretions which they were intended to prevent" (U.S. Children's Bureau, 1946:11).

However, the assignment of responsibility for imparting this knowledge was a constant stumbling block. Whether they based their authority on moral, scientific, or professional grounds, one of the most consistent themes of individuals who chose to write on the management of adolescence has been the inadequacies of parents. Late nineteenth-century mothers were charged with too little surveillance of their daughters' behavior; mothers in the 1920s and 1930s were just as likely to be told that too much, or the wrong kind, of surveillance was responsible for their daughters' going astray (Davenport, 1924; Lindsey, 1925; Dell, 1930; Blanchard and Manasses, 1930). In contrast to the earlier image of the innocent girl, daughters were pictured by some observers as more sexually sophisticated than their mothers. "Grossly ignorant," perversely "picturing sexuality as an emotion utterly incompatible with native refinement of character," inhibited and "mean-minded," mothers were described as ill-prepared and, indeed, reluctant sexual guides and counselors (Blanchard, 1924; Davenport, 1924; Dennett, 1929; Lynd and Lynd, 1937:169–70; Bromley and Britten, 1938). Home instruction was, nevertheless, the sole "accepted means of giving the young sex knowledge or initiating them into the sanctions and prohibitions of the group regarding sex" (Lynd and Lynd, 1929:145). Although widespread participation in "petting parties" was reported by Middletown high school students, the Lynds found that "no formal instruction in sex hygiene is given anywhere in the Middletown schools," nor could information on sex be obtained from the Middletown public library (1929:145; 1937:169). Dorothy Bromley and Florence Britten described what they called the "half-measures" on sex education taken by the nation's colleges: "While men's college heads take it for granted that young men will have learned the facts of life from that well-known school, the gutter, women's college heads assume that what a young woman does not know will not hurt her" (1938:252).[26] These conflicts are, of course, still with us.

Faith in sexual enlightenment and a proper consciousness of the beauties of sex as buffers against premature or wrongly-directed sexual temptation was, in any case, never complete. And although their reading of Freud may have forced the new professionals of youth and adolescence to recognize young women's sexuality, it also offered them a means of reassurance. Though "waves of sexual emotion" might threaten the adolescent girl, they would, under "normal" circumstances, be sublimated into "the emotional outlets of religion and art as a means of satisfaction. . . . There is no surer way to protect the adolescent from temptation" (Blanchard, 1924:133). The U.S. Children's Bureau made the same point in equally hopeful but more prosaic terms: "Happy companionship with a group of young people, engrossing work, intensive study, and service for others will all help to satisfy [the young woman's] growing emotional and physical tension until she is ready to enter into a mature sex relation and assume the responsibilities of wifehood and motherhood" (1946:13). In a shift of emphasis consistent with the changes I described earlier, experts of the 1940s and 1950s were far less likely than their immediate predecessors to portray young women's sexuality in positive terms and far more likely to represent the girl with too much sexual interest as pathological: "frigid," "immature," and "emotionally starved" (U.S. Children's Bureau, 1946; Douvan and Adelson, 1966). Parents were urged by the U.S. Children's Bureau to treat sexual overindulgence, like overeating, as a "health" problem, although the consequences of which they warned were social rather than medical. "The girl who permits promiscuous petting with unlimited privileges gets the reputation of being 'easy' and 'common.' As a social asset, she is less valuable" (1946:76). Should all else fail, at least one leading authority advocated "the . . . desirability of an early marriage" (Havighurst et al., 1962:130; see also Bailey, 1988:46).

The 1946 U.S. Children's Bureau publication I have cited, "Guiding the Adolescent," did not, of course, mention birth control.[27] Even among the most "progressive" thinkers of the 1920s and 1930s, there was no consensus on the subject of contraception for unmarried young women. There were those who believed that knowledge of contraception was widespread among the young, and was a principal condition for what they defined as a "revolution" in female sexual morality: "Girls and women today . . . can disdain virtue because its absence does not induce ruin" (Calverton, 1928:142; Lippmann, 1929; Folsom, 1934:422). "Cold-blooded contraceptive preparedness for miscellaneous sex-encounters" by adolescent girls was, on the other hand, rejected by Dell as a "myth," and, incidentally, inconsistent with his philosophy of youth's "instinctive" sexual shyness once freed from the trammels of Victorian morality (1930:167, 299, and *passim*). Conservative observers were, like Calverton, inclined to see birth control as itself an engine of change, but not, of course, in a direction they applauded. "Added to these dangerous suggestions [from 'salacious literature'] is the knowledge that devices of contraception, purchasable at any corner drug store, have brought about in women a change in attitude toward extramarital sexual relations" (Smithies, 1933:260).[28]

The sexuality of the "modern" girl was, in the period between 1920 and 1960 (and, indeed, until 1970, as I described in Chapter 2), a sexuality singularly divorced from problems of pregnancy and birth. In the minds of conservatives, and of some liberals as well, to be "modern" was to be contraceptively knowledgeable almost by definition: The sophisticated girl avoided pregnancy or got an abortion; the unsophisticated avoided sex or got married. In either case the inconvenient consequences of sexual activity were rendered invisible. Bromley and Britten devoted the penultimate chapter of their 1938 book, *Youth and Sex*, to what they called "paying the piper," college girls' experiences of abortion. By the 1940s and 1950s, not only abortion but pregnancy and birth control as well had disappeared from the indexes, and practically from the texts of books on "normal" (nondelinquent) youth and adolescence.

GLEN H. ELDER has argued that their depression experiences played a major role in causing young women who grew up in the 1930s to value the security of marriage and family life over possible alternative futures, and that World War II experiences of father absence and maternal power and responsibility may have had similar consequences for the 1940s generation of adolescent girls (1974:202–39). To these conditions should be added the difficulties placed in the way of even a limited period of autonomous sexual life by the structure and ideology of sexual encounters. Young women's sexuality was privately acknowledged, and the structural conditions of adolescent and young adult life placed her in constant male company with very little in the way of surveillance. *Public* acknowledgment of unmarried female sexuality in the form of open access to birth control and abortion services was not, however, forthcoming until the early 1970s, nonmarital births continued to be highly disapproved, and there was, in any case, no acceptable framework for childrearing except in the context of marriage. Finally, sexual activity on the part of unmarried young women was ideologically *defined* as the prelude to marriage. This combination of conditions seems likely to have played a significant role in the pressures experienced by young women in the 1940s and 1950s toward an early marriage and a future of domestic sexuality.

RESCUE WORK TO SOCIAL WORK: MANAGEMENT OF THE SEXUALLY UNORTHODOX GIRL

Chapter 6

THE discovery of unsupervised young womanhood as a reservoir of potential danger to the social order was made in the middle of the nineteenth century, as I have described in the preceding chapter. A range of institutional responses to this danger was quick to follow. "Reformatories, mental hospitals, public schools, orphanages, and various urban missions" formed, as noted by Barbara Brenzel, "a web of institutions that would mediate between older values and the consequences of unchecked economic and technological change" (1983:8). The first institution in the United States specifically designated for the protection and rehabilitation of "wayward" girls was the State Industrial School for Girls in Lancaster, Massachusetts, founded in 1856. In 1883 the first Florence Crittenton Mission was opened "for the rescue of outcast women and girls" (Wilson, 1933:1); and in 1886 the Salvation Army heralded the opening in Brooklyn of a "Rescue Home for Fallen and Homeless Girls" (McKinley, 1980:54). By 1910 levels of governmental as well as private philanthropic attention to female delinquency (defined almost wholly in sexual terms) had markedly increased (Schlossman and Wallach, 1978); among the first activities of the U.S. Children's Bureau, founded in 1912, was to issue a series of reports on "illegitimacy as a child welfare problem" (U.S. Children's Bureau, 1920, 1921, 1924). In 1920 a paper titled, "The Child-Mother as a Delinquency Problem," was published by the principal author of these reports: The Bureau defined "child-welfare" to include not only the illegitimate baby but its sexually unorthodox mother as well (Lundberg, 1920).

The subjects with whom these institutions were specifically concerned varied (from the girl who was only in "danger" to the girl who had already given birth), as did their objectives and modes of operation. These unique characteristics are important for what they reveal about change over time in the social construction of women's sexual deviance and in what have been considered appropriate forms of regulation and control. The description of these characteristics will occupy us below. First, however, attention should be called to what these institutions had in common—the assumptions they shared about the vulnerabilities of female adolescence, about the meanings of chastity and sexuality for unmarried girls, and about the requirements for "reform" of young women who departed from the path of sexual orthodoxy.[1]

In the opening remarks of her address to the 45th Annual Conference of Florence Crittenton Homes, held in 1928, one of the home superintendents commented that there is "no new problem involved in the questions of social sin, the unmarried mother and the delinquent girl. They have existed from the earliest times, but are constantly reappearing in different forms" (National Florence Crittenton Mission, 1928:34). While sexuality and motherhood outside of orthodox familial boundaries are as constant as those boundaries themselves, the meanings attributed to these behaviors and the strategies advocated and implemented for their management have varied with the social and cultural setting in which the behaviors were found. From the mid-nineteenth century, when, in the United States, the period between puberty and marriage began to receive public recognition as particularly dangerous for women, strategies for the management of this period have taken three principal forms: protection of the unmarried girl from loss of sexual status; restoration of that status if it should, after all, be lost; and finally, if restoration was deemed impossible or impractical, the placement of the girl, literally or figuratively, outside the social pale.[2] Underlying these strategies has been a set of relatively constant assumptions about the nature of the problem presented by unmarried young women's sexuality and motherhood.

Writing in 1939, Kingsley Davis remarked about unwed pregnancy that "in scarcely any other way can a woman lose status so completely" (227). The threshold for attribution of irretrievable loss has shifted over time from unchastity to pregnancy to parenthood. Nevertheless there is substantial continuity between the opinions expressed by a Philadelphia Refuge official in the 1830s that the reformation of females "is a chimera which it is useless to pursue" (cited in Mennel, 1973), by a writer on delinquency in 1905 that the boy who gets into trouble can start over while the delinquent (read sexually active) girl's "chance to retrieve herself . . . is very small" (cited in Schlossman and Wallach, 1978), and by Arthur Campbell in 1968 that the girl with an illegitimate child "suddenly has 90 percent of her life's script written for her" (238). Before the early part of the nineteenth century, "a woman convicted of even a sexual offense might repent, accept her punishment, and return to society" (Freedman, 1981:14). Since that time, unmarried young women's sexual and/or reproductive unorthodoxy, much like the occurrence of sexual acts between men, has been seen not as incidental behavior but as definitive of the actors' present identity and future prospects.

A second continuing thread has been the responsibility of parents, and more particularly of mothers, for their daughters' unorthodox behavior: During the critical transition from puberty to marriage, parental guardianship had obviously failed. Boys' delinquencies, note Steven L. Schlossman and Stephanie Wallach, were far less likely to be blamed on their parents (1978:84). The language in which these attributions were couched changed over time from moral to eugenic to social scientific to psychiatric. "Disorderly," "disreputable," and "sorely lacking moral instruction and example" were among the terms used by Lancaster's administrators to describe the homes of its young female inmates. "Obviously," Barbara M. Brenzel remarks, conditions such as these "could be blamed only upon the mother" (1980:118). By the early 1920s, "broken homes" had become a popular catchphrase, carrying the implications both of bad parental example and of inadequate supervision, making "it necessary for the girl to shift for herself" (Lundberg, 1920:167).[3] A 1946 U.S. Children's Bureau publication, after insisting on the complex and "deep-rooted" causes of illegitimate birth, goes on to identify the first of these causes as an absence of "love and security in [the young women's] own home . . . through companionable relations with their parents" (Morlock and Campbell, 1946:11). Finally, not only were parents held responsible for their daughter's misconduct, should they become aware of her behavior the expected consequences were family disgrace and parental rejection (see, e.g., Barrett, 1897; Johnson, 1926; Reed, 1934; National Florence Crittenton Mission, 1948).[4]

In the late nineteenth century and much of the twentieth century, agencies for the management of "wayward" girls and unwed mothers defined their tasks within the framework of the assumptions I have described. Restoration to respectable sexual status was assumed to require a second identity transformation, virtually a conversion experience in which the young woman repented her past actions and accepted the version of her behavior advanced by the agency as well as her need for the specialized services it had to offer. Essential to this experience was physical removal from the "risk-creating environment" in which her misbehavior had been spawned. The confidence with which conversion was anticipated varied with characteristics of the girl herself (her age, experience, and the enthusiasm of her conversion) and with shifts over time in the dominance of more or less deterministic causal theories of sexual misbehavior. On the other hand, the consequence of failure have uniformly been portrayed as inevitable and disastrous: a continued plunge down the slippery slope to sexual ruin.

Who was to manage the sexually or reproductively unorthodox girl, how she was to be managed, what the essence of her problem was conceived to be, and how it should be explained are closely interrelated questions. During the precontraceptive era, managerial responsibility shifted back and forth, and was often shared, among religious (or religiously motivated) bodies, courts and legal authorities, and public and private welfare and social-work organizations. With the exception of psychiatrists, the medical profession had little direct impact either on formulations of the problem or on proposed solutions.[5] It is to the portrayal of these formulations and solutions that I now turn.

THE SEXUALLY UNORTHODOX GIRL

Before the modernization of sexual ideology wrought by Ellis and Freud had begun to take full effect, the "normal" adolescent girl was *defined* as sexually innocent and without sexual interests. Consequently, girls who "embraced immorality" willingly were a source of confusion and consternation, demanding explanation and differential treatment. Running through the early literature of reformatories and rescue homes is a distinction between the "innocent" girl forced into sexual knowledge against her will for whom, although she was morally tainted, redemption might be possible and the "promiscuous" girl for whom there was not only little hope of personal redemption but who was regarded as a potential danger to others. Thus, in an article appearing in an 1897 publication of the National Florence Crittenton Mission an "innocent girl," betrayed by false promises, who "fell" out of "hunger and want," and was filled with remorse and regret was contrasted with a girl in whose nature "sin was strongly imbedded"; the latter, unrepentant, was told to leave the home as "her influence was deleterious to the welfare of others, who desired to be saved" (Prindle, 1897:44).

Whatever the means of redemption to be employed, the distinction between young women likely to prove amenable to reform and those who were perceived as irredeemable has been a constant theme in the literature of agencies for the management of sexually unorthodox girls and has formed one of the major bases on which girls were selected into one or another management strategy. From the perspective of the evangelically oriented reformers who founded the first of these agencies, the reform schools and the rescue homes of the late nineteenth and early twentieth centuries, "innocence" was the essential criterion for redeemability. Thus, as Brenzel points out, the major question they faced was, "When was a young girl too sexually experienced so as to no longer qualify as an innocent child to be redeemed?" (1983:48).

Although the precise criteria for "too much" sexual experience varied widely, a central dimension was whether the experience was *voluntary* (see, e.g., Brenzel, 1983:48; Schlossman and Wallach, 1978:75; Lunbeck, 1987:521). On this basis, some reformers found it easier to attribute innocence to the girl whose sexuality did not become visible until she was "caught" by a pregnancy than to the (perhaps no more experienced) girl who "courted" disaster by flirting openly in public and/or who successfully avoided pregnancy or terminated it by abortion. This perspective was reflected in Florence Crittenton Home reports throughout this institution's existence. As late as 1968, the director of one such home was quoted as saying, "These are your loving, trusting girls in here. Your other girl who is probably doing the same thing doesn't get caught because she is too smart" (cited in Rains, 1970:219). By being "smart," the girl who did not get caught failed the test of innocence.

Underlying the evangelical perspective was an explanatory framework in which autonomous sexual interest by an unmarried young women could only result from "original sin." On the other hand, the innocent girl who had fallen might continue in her downward path not from innate perversity but because, rejected by family and friends, she saw starvation as her only alternative. To "rescue" young women from the lives of prostitution to which they were otherwise (as these reformers saw it) inevitably consigned was a principal aim of early reform institutions. "Moral rescue in the form of an officially expressed definition of their clients as essentially respectable," aided by policies through which clients were selected who fit this definition, has remained the aim of religiously inspired, traditional maternity homes throughout their history (Rains, 1970:220; see also National Florence Crittenton Mission, 1928, 1938, 1948; Wilson, 1933; Verner, 1976; McKinley, 1980).[6]

However, maternity homes were by no means the only agencies with an interest in the sexually unorthodox girl. The courts, correctional institutions, and, with the establishment of the U.S. Children's Bureau in 1912, an increasingly professionalized child-welfare bureaucracy all laid claim to the problems "of social sin, the unmarried mother and the delinquent girl."

The term "delinquency," as applied to females in the early years of the twentieth century, *meant* overt sexuality: "When we speak of the delinquent girl we usually have in mind the sex offender. . . . We do not think of the problem of the delinquent boy as primarily related to sex as we do in the case of the girl" (Johnson, 1926:385). During the nineteenth and for much of the twentieth century, offenses against sexual morality, a rubric that covered a wide range of behaviors from staying out late at night to pregnancy, were the principal reasons for which unmarried young women were prosecuted in court and committed to reformatories (Tappan, 1947; Schlossman and Wallach, 1978; Freedman, 1981; Brenzel, 1983; Rafter, 1983; Hobson, 1987). Concerns about questions of innocence, volition, and redemption occupied secular as much as religious agencies of reform. However, by the late nineteenth century, representatives of secular institutions had begun to search for "scientific" rather than religious bases on which to make the pertinent distinctions.

Scientific theories to explain overt sexuality in unmarried young women shifted over the first decades of the twentieth century from hereditarianism ("vicious parents, especially mothers") to mental retardation ("the weakness of the feeble-minded girl") to mental illness ("immorality is not 'original sin,' but psychological sickness").[7] These theories had as their common denominator the assumption (an assumption they shared with the theory of "betrayed innocence") that the sexual young woman could not be held fully responsible for her conduct. However, unlike the evangelicals, the first "scientific" reformers based this assumption not on intrinsic innocence but (in circular fashion) on a conception of sexuality as, in and of itself, evidence of psychopathology (Lunbeck, 1987) or mental incapacity (e.g., Falconer, 1918; Lundberg, 1920; U.S. Children's Bureau, 1924; see also, Hobson, 1987: Chapter 8).

Theories of sexual misconduct founded on the presupposition of "normal" young women's sexual disinterest were self-evidently difficult to reconcile with the ideas of Freud and Havelock Ellis. A motivational psychology in which the sexual instincts were the prime movers spelled the downfall of the ideology of the innocent girl. By the late teens and early twenties a budding child-welfare profession had begun to claim the problems of "sex delinquency" and the unwed mother. Psychogenic theories were adopted with enthusiasm by many in this rather disparate collection of social scientists, physicians, and lawyers (many of whom were women). However, relatively few of his contemporaries shared Ben Lindsey's reading of psychoanalysis as confirming the "naturalness" and, therefore, the essential innocence of youthful sexuality (1925:17,155).[8] Rather, to most child-welfare workers these theories suggested that *all* young women who became sexually involved were at some level collaborators in their own fate; inside every unmarried mother there lurked a "mental condition that made unmarried motherhood possible for her" (National Florence Crittenton Mission, 1928:48). By the 1940s, psychiatrically trained caseworkers had supplanted the evangelicals' presumption of innocence with a presumption of responsibility: "Often . . . there is a conscious or unconscious blotting out by the girl of any responsibility for her act. She will tell you she was drugged, or the situation was one over which she had no control" (National Florence Crittenton Mission, 1948:17).[9] Earlier in the century, the girl who participated voluntarily in a sexual act was regarded as the least promising candidate for redemption; under the influence of psychoanalysis, this position came to be occupied by the girl who failed to acknowledge her participation. However, the acknowledgment required was not of autonomous sexual interest, but of underlying psychological problems: "All unmarried mothers, with the exception of those coming from cultural backgrounds where illegitimacy is not severely disapproved, have emotional problems in varying degrees of acuteness. Many of these girls need psychiatric treatment" (Young, 1954:201).[10] In the circular fashion characteristic of such theories, sexuality itself was treated as sufficient evidence for the diagnosis of emotional problems.

"Explanations" of young women's departures from sexual orthodoxy, whether those explanations were couched in the language of theology, biology, or psychiatry, acted to preserve the normative status quo by treating departures from it as aberrations to be explained. From the perspective of those who would "reform" her, the most disturbing case was the girl whose behavior could not readily be accommodated by whichever of these theories was currently fashionable. Emma Lundberg, the Children's Bureau's first expert on illegitimacy, proposed a four fold typology of "girls and women who become mothers out of wedlock." The first three types fit the stereotype of the essentially "good" girl, victimized through mental deficiency, weakness of character, or male brutality. The fourth type, "the *really* delinquent girl or woman" is she who "*knowingly* chooses antisocial conduct, her illegitimate maternity being only an incidental evidence of repeated immorality" (1921:205, emphasis added). Similarly, unwed mothers whom tests proved to be "normally intelligent" (U.S. Children's Bureau, 1924:232), in whose appearance "there was nothing to indicate sensuality, hardness, or instability" (Johnson, 1926:391), or, more recently, who "were not upset by their situation and . . . not in some way asking for help" (Rains, 1970:227) were described in the literature of reform with puzzlement and often with suspicion. Knowing, intelligent, stable young women who were not asking for help not only violated normative conceptions of the unwed mother; they were, in addition, unlikely to be responsive to efforts for their redemption.

Underlying changing conceptions of the sexually unorthodox girl—as "innocent" or as steeped in "original sin," as mentally deficient or "really delinquent," or, finally, as emotionally disturbed—was the larger problem of coming to terms with women's sexuality, particularly the sexuality of women who were young and unmarried. By displaying their sexuality openly, "delinquent" girls and girls who became unwed mothers were perceived as making a claim to adult status and, at the same time, as symbolically asserting their independence from adult expectations and adult control.[11] Insofar as they could be portrayed as innocents betrayed, as mentally ill or incompetent, or as prepared to acknowledge psychic complicity, those claims were muted, adult authority was reestablished, and social order was seen to be restored. On the other hand, sexually unorthodox girls who behaved as autonomous adults rather than as innocent or incompetent children were doubly unacceptable: first, in the implied claim to adult status inherent in their precocious sexuality itself and second, in their failure to mute or withdraw that claim by an "appropriate" presentation of self.

MANAGEMENT STRATEGIES

I have argued that nineteenth-century changes in the structure of female adolescence played a major role in drawing reformers' attention to (what they saw as) the potential dangers of this period for young women and to the need for new mechanisms of protection and, if necessary, rehabilitation. The form that these mechanisms would take was largely determined, first, by what I have described as rather constant assumptions about the nature of the problem presented by young women's unorthodox sexuality, second, by the shifting explanatory frameworks discussed above, third, by changing conceptions of the futures for which young women were being prepared and, finally, by broader social changes in how American society saw fit to manage its problems. The regulation of private behavior became defined as a public responsibility and embodied in formally organized institutions and agencies.

The institutionalization of strategies for the care, protection, rehabilitation, and control of sexually unorthodox girls, in the form of specialized agencies as well as special legislation, was part of the same movement that resulted in the development of the juvenile court, in agitation for child-labor laws, and in protective labor legislation for women. Pressure for these reforms sprang from the conviction that, in an increasingly urban and industrialized society, individual families could no longer be trusted to safeguard the well-being of their dependent members and from the equally strong and closely related belief that "society had the right—indeed the duty—to intervene at *any* point where the well-being of its members was threatened" (Boyer, 1978:197).

These convictions developed gradually over the course of the nineteenth century; however, it was during the Progressive Era that their influence reached its peak.

Age-of-consent legislation and its various legislative successors, sex education, the establishment of "homes" for working girls in the cities, the U.S. War Department's Committee on Protective Work for Girls, and even the movement for more "wholesome" city recreational opportunities were all rationalized in part as "protection" of the innocent girl, reflecting at one and the same time continued adherence to the ideology of innocence and a growing conviction that innocence was threatened under conditions of modern life. The shifting ideological, cultural, and organizational frameworks within which young women's sexuality was managed are most clearly revealed by the activities and beliefs of individuals—evangelists, judges, physicians, social workers—and agencies—maternity homes, courts, reformatories, the Children's Bureau—who assumed direct responsibility for girls who were actual or who were seen as potential violators of the moral code.

Schlossman and Wallach note that early twentieth-century writers on female delinquency saw all mothers, regardless of economic circumstances, as "obliged to keep their girls at home, when not in school or church, and to transform homes into refuges for protecting female virtue" (1978:84). Reform schools and maternity homes defined their tasks in similar terms: They supplied an institutional alternative when mothers, schools, and churches all had failed. Their objectives, however, went beyond protection; they included reformation and, to a greater or lesser degree, retribution.

Among the most striking characteristics of these institutions as they were originally designed was their emphasis on the physical removal of nubile young women from their home surroundings for extended periods of time—often until they reached marriageable age. This point is well documented in research on the policies of correctional authorities in the late nineteenth and early twentieth centuries (Brenzel, 1983:82,121; Schlossman and Wallach, 1978:67,75; Freedman, 1981:148; Rafter, 1983:307). Paul Tappan commented on the "high frequency of rather long indeterminate sentences" imposed on girls who came before the Wayward Minor Court of New York City in the early 1940s (1947:90).[12] Long stays also characterized the traditional maternity home. The Florence Crittenton charter specified "a stay of at least six months after the birth of the child" (Wilson, 1933:41). However, the actual length of stay may often have been longer. "We find six months a reasonable time for the older girl and those coming from the better class homes, but it is usually advisable for the girls of school age to stay from one to two years, with continued supervision after they leave the Home until they are out of high school" (National Florence Crittenton Mission, 1928:44). Photographs of mothers with children well past babyhood, which were included in many early reports, suggest that actual practice frequently conformed to what was "usually advisable."

Segregated institutions for sexually unorthodox girls reinforced normative sexual boundaries by physically placing girls who had transgressed those boundaries outside the pale of ordinary social life. The "voluntary" acknowledgment of societal norms by the pregnant single young woman who sought concealment in a maternity home was in this respect no different than the forced confrontation with those norms of the openly sexual girl committed to a reform school or (as also happened in the early twentieth century) to an institution for the "feeble-minded." In addition to their normative function, segregated institutions provided a setting in which transforming influences (to be described below) could be brought to bear free from extraneous distractions. Finally, and less obviously, the character of these institutions and the uses to which they were put reflected prevailing (and culturally quite distinctive) conceptions of female development, of female sexuality, and of the futures for which young women were destined and should be prepared.[13]

Summarizing the substantial body of literature on delinquent girls published in the first three decades of the twentieth century, Schlossman and Wallach note that "adolescent girls were considered much less malleable than adolescent boys. . . . Most writers assumed that by the time girls had reached puberty the most promising time for shaping their character had long since passed" (1978:83). Girls were inherently less redeemable than boys; more particularly, their sexuality, once aroused, could not easily be restrained: "After one sex experience it becomes harder for them to resist temptation" (Yarros, 1920:223; see also Mangold, 1921:185–86). These ideas, combined with authorities' conviction of maternal responsibility for daughters' delinquency, led to the perceived necessity for institutional segregation of "sexual" girls both for their own protection and for that of the community.

In the nineteenth century the emphasis of institutional philosophy was on protection of the girl herself: wayward girls were in "need of protection or firmer, more loving supervision" (Brenzel, 1980:207). This emphasis continued to dominate traditional maternity homes well into the twentieth century (see, e.g., Rains, 1970:224). However, among the new professionals in social welfare and corrections it was increasingly supplanted by a philosophy that stressed control of the girl and protection of society (see, e.g., Freedman, 1981:147). Among the more extreme statements of this latter view was that of a social scientist, G. B. Mangold, who viewed the "feeble-minded" as a "prolific source of illegitimacy." He goes on to state that "a program of moral education and sex instruction will not solve the problem, unless [these women] can live in a practically perfect environment in which immoral suggestion will never tempt. Such a hope is visionary; consequently a policy of segregation and institutional care must be adopted" (1921:185–86). To implement this policy, Mangold recommended "colonies composed of women of this type," whom, he suggested, "can be made almost entirely self-supporting" (187). Lest this example appear farfetched, Schlossman and Wallach cite the efforts of female reformatory sponsors in California to insure their inmates' isolation from the opposite sex. They concluded that "the mile separating the male from the female institution was inadequate. A new facility far removed from males was essential to eliminate 'the influences that mysteriously emanate from the proximity of the sexes'" (1978:75–76). Her innocence lost, the sexually aroused, parentally unsupervised, unmarried young woman was regarded as the moral equivalent of a loose cannon, a danger to herself and to all around her.[14]

To remove that danger required not only that the young woman be placed out of harm's way; given the assumption of sexual unorthodoxy as character *defining*, it required a fundamental character transformation: "We begin by assuming that every girl is in dire need of a Saviour to deliver her from the power of the Evil One and that without that power all of our efforts in her behalf will be in vain. *Regeneration, not merely reformation, is our aim*" (National Florence Crittenton Mission, 1928:58, emphasis added). Within the evangelical framework of Florence Crittenton philosophy religious conversion was a principal means by which transformation was to be effected. However, although the means of conversion were different, the *aim* of the psychiatrically oriented maternity home studied by Prudence Moss Rains in the late 1960s was not.

> The professional staff at Hawthorne House shared a view of their clients which included these presuppositions: illegitimate pregnancy is psychologically motivated, psychologically caused: without some understanding and alteration of the psychological situation which led to pregnancy, girls are likely to get pregnant again; therefore, *the central purpose of the time girls spend at Hawthorne House should be to work out some understanding of the "reasons they were there"* (1971:60, emphasis added).

Rains called the "working out" process "conversion to a psychiatric view of the past." Entrance into a maternity home was, of course, voluntary and its purposes benevolent. There is, nevertheless, a distinct resemblance to what W. I. Thomas in describing reformatories called "a society of the bad, which corresponds to the theological purgatory from which there is a chance to return to a society of the good." In the reformatory, "the punishment is supposed to atone for the offense and effect the reformation" (1923 [1967]:171). In the maternity home, the same results were to be produced by religious or psychiatric conversion.[15] In return for concealment, young women were expected to atone by accepting the agency's version of the past and embracing the means that it offered for redemption.

Precisely how redemption is defined reflects, as Brenzel has observed, the notions of gender and class current at a given historical period: The meaning of redemption varies with the futures for which young women are being prepared (1983:166). Describing the Lancaster reform school in the late nineteenth century, Brenzel goes on to state:

> At that time the nature of women was presumed to be domestic. Lancaster was designed to address this stereotype. Therefore it offered what was "natural" for the reformation of poor girls, that is, a program of domestication. The theories of the causes of wayward behavior were to change. . . . Lancaster's job, however, continued to be the domestication of girls so that they would be better able to fulfill their "natural" roles (166).

Training in "household duties" continued to be a programmatic mainstay of maternity homes as well as reformatories during the early twentieth century (National Florence Crittenton Mission, 1928:36, 40, 63; Schlossman and Wallach, 1978:77; Rafter, 1983:297). As late as 1948, a Florence Crittenton Home report described its occupational therapy program as including "hand work" and "homemaking" (National Florence Crittenton Mission, 1948:16).

Reading of this literature suggests that the perceived redemptive effects of domestication went beyond simply preparing young women for their "natural" roles (whether in their own home or an employer's). Schlossman and Wallach assert that correctional administrators regarded insufficient reverence for domestic pursuits as itself among the causes of wayward behavior (1978:77). Instillation of reverence for these pursuits was, by the same token, among the cures. Much like other forms of salvation, the "rigorous pursuit of domesticity" would both atone for past immoralities and transform errant young women into docile—that is, sexually controlled—representatives of their sex (see also Rafter, 1983; Hobson, 1987:195).

Among the most explicit expressions of domestic ideology was the requirement, written into the 1883 constitution of the National Florence Crittenton Mission, that "everything possible shall be done to keep mother and child together" (Wilson, 1933:41). The basis for this requirement was clearly enunciated by one of the organization's founders.

> The rewards of motherhood are the most blessed hopes in every woman's life . . . and why should not the poor girl who has nothing else to live for at least have that sweet consolation. . . . The influence of the nursery in the progress of right living *is not the training the child gets there so much as it is the training the mother gets there.* [We have seen] the wonderful regenerating influence that has come to a girl through motherhood (Barrett, 1897:13, emphasis added).

Until at least the 1930s the dominant philosophy, not only among Florence Crittenton workers but in the child-welfare literature generally, was against adoption (Lundberg, 1920; Mangold, 1921; U.S. Children's Bureau, 1924:5,235; Johnson, 1926). Motherhood was defined both as redemptive—fostering responsibility and decreasing the likelihood of subsequent illegitimacy—and as retributive—preventing immoral young women from living "a lie before the world" (Mangold, 1921:103). The Children's Bureau advocated the policy of keeping mother and baby together "at least during the nursing period" as a means of reducing infant mortality (1924:5).

The first Florence Crittenton Mission was opened in New York City in 1883. In 1930, a carefully conducted survey in the same city identified no less than eighty-seven social agencies claiming to offer some form of service to "illegitimate families" (the mother, the baby, and, rarely, the father). This number amounted to an agency for every twenty-one recorded illegitimate births! (Reed, 1934). This proliferation of agencies arose less from an increase in illegitimacy than from changes in the social organization of "charitable" activity (Chambers, 1963; Trattner, 1974; Gettleman, 1975).[16] Over the first three decades of the twentieth century, the "benevolent impulse" that had activated the wealthy businessman-turned-evangelist, Charles Crittenton, became rationalized and bureaucratized, its expression increasingly dominated both structurally and ideologically by the new profession of social work. By means of the juvenile court, with its emphasis on social "diagnosis and treatment" of offenders, social work's claim was extended beyond the unmarried mother to the "delinquent" girl as well (Tappan, 1947; Schlossman, 1977).

The bureaucratization of sexual unorthodoxy and the hegemony of social-work theory and practice over its management did not go uncontested. The conflicting claims of older evangelical and moral perspectives, medical impatience with social work's "comprehensive" approach, and differences of philosophy among agencies with different objectives and different client commitments are clearly evident in Ruth Reed's account of New York City's social-service structure in 1930, in Tappan's study, a decade later, of the city's Wayward Minor Court, and in the annual reports of the National Florence Crittenton Mission between 1928 and 1948. The somewhat plaintive remarks of the latter organization's general superintendent published in its 1938 report give a flavor of the Florence Crittenton perspective.

> I have a feeling that some of our Homes have discarded some of their cherished, traditional rules on the recommendation of some agencies and before much time has elapsed will find their discarded rules brought to them in the guise of new theories. . . . I am the first to acknowledge our debt to cooperating agencies, but surely after fifty years we are justified in having a voice when the welfare of the unmarried mother is under discussion (National Florence Crittenton Mission, 1938:4).

Among the cherished traditional rules under heaviest attack was the requirement that "everything possible" be done to keep mother and baby together. Reed's account of New York City's social agencies in the early 1930s gives a vivid picture of conflict between the perspectives of agencies that "because of their traditions and direction which has been given to the work by their founders" emphasized respecting the "natural tie between mother and child" and those that "are almost as much interested in finding a baby for a couple wishing to secure a child, as they are in aiding the unmarried mother" (1934:75–76). Florence Crittenton fought a valiant rearguard action (introducing medical arguments for what had once been a policy based wholly on moral principles); however, the 1948 report reflected near total capitulation (the president alone defended the old rule), both to the policy of adoption and to its psychiatric rationale:

> It is usually the emotionally mature girl who places her child for adoption; while the girl who is immature emotionally holds fast to her baby because her emotional needs are great. She frequently has been a very deprived person (17). . . . The girl who places her baby for adoption in 99 cases out of a hundred is the one who has a deep love for her baby, and feels that the baby should have a real home with a father and mother (16).

The reasons behind this shift in policy were complex. In part, it reflected the increasing ascendancy of psychiatric over moral "explanations" of unwed motherhood. Advocates of adoption defended it on grounds of the psychosocial well-being of both mother and child; the traditional Florence Crittenton approach had never considered the child's welfare independently from that of the mother: The mother's moral welfare was best served by keeping the child. However, there were, in addition, powerful structural reasons for the increasing emphasis on adoption. The first of these was the expanding adoption market. Zelizer cites a 1927 *New York Times* report that "the new problem in adoption 'has become one of finding enough children for childless homes rather than that of finding enough homes for homeless children'" (1985:190). Reed also referred to the influence of demand on agency policy—one agency reported ten times the number of suitable homes as babies (1934:90). Equally important, I believe, were ideological as well as structural changes that affected the futures for which young women were being prepared: marital futures in which companionship and sexuality rather than motherhood had become the central focus, and (somewhat later) educational and occupational futures in which motherhood was perceived as a hindrance rather than as a principal agent of reformation (Fass, 1977:82–83, 336; Zimring, 1982:21).[17]

The conflicting claims of alternative strategies for management of the sexually unorthodox girl emerged with perhaps the greatest clarity from Tappan's sociological study of the Wayward Minor Court of New York, "an experimental tribunal for adolescent girls," established in 1936. Tappan described the court's principal objective as "to control the sex behavior of the unmarried [female] pre-adult" (1947:36). However, the means by which that objective was to be accomplished were less clear: "One finds a struggle among philosophies of moralistic judgement and punitive treatment against a violation of the social mores, of a nonmoralistic and clinical effort to cure disease and protect society, and of a reformative attempt to produce a better adjustment to the community and its standards" (1947:88). Ideologically, Tappan maintained, the court's philosophy was reformative and even preventive; its practice was retributive (as reflected in its high rates of adjudication and commitment): "Though the wayward adolescent is often spared serious penalties today, the adolescent sexual delinquent [by definition, a female] continues to feel the sting of a traditional reproach and repression" (1947:87). The conflicts among moral, preventive, and rehabilitative philosophies described by Tappan in the 1940s were still alive and still unresolved at the end of the 1980s.

In principle, management of the sexually unorthodox girl might have included some attention to her male companion(s). In practice the responsible agencies found many reasons not to offer that attention. In traditional evangelical ideology, the counterpart of the innocent girl was the scheming and brutal man who loved and left. He played no part in maternity-home plans for reformation. Reed's data documented the persistence of this attitude in the 1930s. Certain agencies, she remarked, believed that "the care of the illegitimate family did not require that cognizance be taken of the existence or of the responsibility of the unmarried father." "Our policy," said one social worker, "is to help the mother to forget a disagreeable experience. Therefore we ask no questions about the father. He is of no importance in the situation" (1934:157). Although what data are available suggest that girls did sometimes bring paternity suits for support from the putative father, this option was viewed with distaste not only by young women but by many authorities as well. The burden of proof was on the girl to prove she was not "promiscuous"; the very secrecy that many agencies considered themselves in business to protect was violated; and the financial gains to be set against these losses were very small: "The courts discourage vigorous action against the male and fail to attain results" (Davis, 1939:226; see also Mangold, 1921:48; Johnson, 1926:391; Lundberg, 1933; Reed, 1934:187–90). Thus, the double standard prescribing female responsibility for sexual and reproductive unorthodoxy was upheld by the structure as well as by the "science" of sexual social control.

SOCIAL LOCATION AND THE PROCESS OF SELECTION
The management strategies I have described did not select at random from the population of sexually unorthodox young women. Girls were sorted into different moral careers on the basis of social location and of perceived redeemability. The poverty and immigrant origins of girls brought to court and reformschool attention have been well documented (Seagrave, 1926:529; Schlossman and Wallach, 1978:71; Brenzel, 1980:203, 1983:81; Freedman, 1981; Lunbeck, 1987). Mabel Seagrave, a physician, commented on this selectivity: "The fact that comparatively so few sex delinquents of American parentage have come to the organized agencies for handling these cases perhaps merely shows that American parents handle [them] privately" (1926:527). Tappan suggested that the courts saw "merely those individuals among the sexually active who are so inept in their expression as to be 'trapped' by parent, police officer, or nature" (1947:35). Juvenile court practice, by including the social background of the accused as a basis for adjudication, increased the likelihood that young women with less "socially desirable" characteristics would be placed in a correctional institution rather than released on probation (Platt, 1977; Schlossman, 1977; Schlossman and Wallach, 1978; Tappan, 1947:107ff.).

The judicial system selected for those sexually unorthodox young women without the social or personal resources necessary for avoiding exposure. Middle-class nonethnic girls found their way or were directed to maternity homes or child-placement agencies, institutions specializing in concealment (Reed, 1934; Vincent, 1961; Rains, 1971).[18] A medical social worker interviewed by Reed made her basis of selection quite plain: " 'I send them to an agency [for casework] only if they are low-class and ignorant. I would not dream of mentioning an agency to a nice girl. She wouldn't stand for it. If a nice girl wants to give up her baby I send her to ———, where they make the least fuss about taking babies' " (Reed, 1934:130). "Fuss" was defined as intrusive social investigation that might compromise the "nice" young woman's wish to conceal her "illegitimate" condition.

Young women were selected into different management strategies not only on the basis of socioeconomic characteristics but also on the basis of perceived redeemability. Reformers throughout the period of my analysis and irrespective of institutional affiliation preferred younger girls without a previous sexual history (Brenzel, 1983:48, 208; Wilson, 1933:8; Rains, 1970:221). Gradations of "innocence" were defined on the basis of "promiscuity," prior pregnancy, and/or the presence or absence of venereal disease and employed as bases of selection by reform schools, social agencies, and maternity homes. Brenzel describes nineteenth-century reform school authorities as advising exclusion of girls they described as promiscuous: "Promiscuity, because perceived as voluntary, was considered both undeserving of pity and untreatable" (1983:48). By the early twentieth century, on the other hand, "promiscuity, real or suspected" had become a principal basis for commitment to a reform school. "The judge refused to consider sending girls who were not virgins to foster families or orphanages. Only the reformatory would accept them" (Schlossman, 1977:179). Similarly, whether or not a paternity case would be taken to court often hinged on agencies' perception of the mother's "promiscuity." "But," asserted Lundberg who studied this question, "the word seemed to be used rather loosely" (1933:94). Maternity homes frequently "have the rule that they will never take a girl for her second confinement. They feel that they are justified in this on the ground of taking only first offenders" (Falconer, 1918:255). These examples make the point that whatever a young woman's ultimate disposition may have been, her sexuality, as filtered through the normative preconceptions of the authorities she encountered, played a central role in deciding her fate.

By the late 1940s, under the influence of psychiatric conceptions of sexual unorthodoxy, maternity home workers had begun to couch their selection criteria in psychiatric rather than moral terms. Intake was based on "the ability of the individual to form a casework relationship; the capacity of the individual to change" (National Florence Crittenton Mission, 1948:15). However, Rains's study of these homes in the 1960s indicated that underlying the changed vocabulary were very similar criteria to those employed in the earlier, more frankly moralistic, period. "Maternity homes tend to recruit girls who are suitable to the transformation from 'sexually promiscuous girl' to girl-in-trouble, and tend not to recruit girls who would threaten such a transformation. Maternity homes recruit relatively young girls . . . who have never been married and who are pregnant for the first time" (Rains, 1970:221).

Between the two World Wars, the sorting processes that I have described were instrumental in preserving an appearance that traditional boundaries between "respectable" and unorthodox sexuality were being maintained. The sexuality of young women who were poor and of foreign or (later on) of black parentage was selectively made visible by courts, reformatories, and social agencies. The newly acknowledged sexuality of Yankee, white, middle-class girls was accommodated by privately obtained contraception and abortion, by marriage, and by the maternity home and, thereby, decently concealed. Furthermore, whether their stock-in-trade was retribution or accommodation, visibility or concealment, the management institutions I have described uniformly upheld and reinforced the legitimacy of traditional norms of gender and sexuality; individuals might transgress but the standards by which transgression was publicly defined remained firm.

SOCIAL MOVEMENTS FOR SEXUAL CONTROL, 1885–1920

Chapter 7

> Societies appear to be subject every now and then to periods of moral panic. A condition, episode, person or group of persons emerges to become defined as a threat to societal values and interests; its nature is presented in a stylized and stereotypical fashion by the mass media; the moral barricades are manned by editors, bishops and politicians and other right-thinking people; socially accredited experts pronounce their diagnoses and solutions; ways of coping are evolved, or (more often) resorted to; the condition then disappears, submerges or deteriorates (Cohen, 1980:9).

IN MY introductory chapter I suggested that since the mid-nineteenth century the United States has experienced two major periods of "moral panic," in which the principal focus of attention and anxiety has been what was perceived as the sexual unorthodoxy of unmarried young women. The first of these episodes began almost one hundred years ago, with the mounting of a national campaign to raise the "age of consent." It took the form of a series of interrelated social movements for the regulation of nonmarital sexuality, and it lasted until about 1920. My purpose in the present chapter is to describe these social movements, to offer an interpretation of their emergence, and to lay the groundwork for a comparison between this earlier panic and the adolescent pregnancy anxieties of the more recent past.

THE RISE AND DECLINE OF TURN-OF-THE-CENTURY
SEXUAL SOCIAL MOVEMENTS

The "age of consent" is that age above which a young woman may legally consent to sexual intercourse. Whether or not she, in fact, consents, intercourse with a girl under the age of consent is a crime punishable by law. Between 1885 and 1895 all but eleven of the forty-eight states and territories raised their age of consent, from a median of 10 years of age to a median of age 14; by 1895 the age of consent was defined as 16 or over in twenty-two states. Legislation to raise the age in places under federal jurisdiction (e.g., military bases, Indian reservations) was passed by Congress in 1887 (increasing it to age 16) and in 1899 (again raising it to an all-time high of age 21) (Pivar, 1973:140–43).

Overlapping these legislative actions were a series of changes in federal law designed to tighten the regulation of international and interstate travel "for the purpose of prostitution or debauchery, or for any other immoral purpose." A 1907 law, greatly expanding earlier efforts in this direction, was struck down by the Supreme Court as too sweeping in its provisions. In response, Congress passed the White Slave Traffic Act of 1910 (now more popularly known as the Mann Act). Under the act, a person guilty of transporting girls or women for the purposes described was liable to fine (up to five thousand dollars) or imprisonment (up to five years). Penalties were doubled if the woman was under age 18. Judicial interpretation made clear that the Mann Act covered voluntary as well as involuntary travel and that "other immoral purposes" meant nonmarital sexual activity irrespective of whether money had changed hands (Wunsch, 1976:134–37; Connelly, 1980:128).

During this same period, states and municipalities took a variety of actions directed explicitly against prostitution. Red-light districts had been an accepted feature of the nineteenth-century American city. Between 1912 and 1916 these districts were closed in some two hundred cities. Legislative changes were made as well: "In 1910 twenty-two states and territories had legislation pertaining to pandering; the comparable figure for 1921 was forty-eight. During those same years most states enacted injunction and abatement laws—by which private citizens could restrain the operation of bordellos" (Lubove, 1962:328). These actions on the part of government—age-of-consent laws, the Mann Act, the closing of brothels—were in direct response to a remarkable upsurge in the late nineteenth and early twentieth centuries of organized social movements for the control of unorthodox sexuality—in particular sexual intercourse between unmarried partners. Physicians, women's groups from the most conservative to the most militant, and politicians of every stripe took part in a series of interrelated actions and debates lasting for a period of over thirty-five years. The rhetoric of these movements strongly suggests that a central underlying concern was the sexuality of what we would now describe as "adolescent" females.[1] Historians are agreed on the character of these activities as social movements—"the antiprostitution drive . . . assumed the characteristics of a national crusade"—and on their timing—they emerged in the late Victorian era; by 1920, they had virtually disappeared (Boyer, 1978:195). There is much less agreement on their interpretation. I address the latter question following a more detailed description of the movements themselves.

It is impossible to comprehend the sexual social movements of the late nineteenth and early twentieth centuries without reference to the Victorian code of "civilized morality" espoused by the movements' adherents. In the terms of this code, which "remained the dominant ideal of the middle and upper classes until about 1912 and of the men and women who became America's intellectual and political leaders in the Progressive era," any sexual activity outside the bonds of wedlock was simultaneously a cause and a symbol of moral degeneration. Included among its tenets were both the ideology of female innocence and adamant opposition to the double standard: A single standard of chastity before marriage and virtuous monogamy thereafter was applied to both sexes (although it was expected that men would experience greater difficulty in living up to it). Underlying these ideas was the further belief that "civilization and progress depended directly on the control of sexuality and on the stable monogamous family." Upon adherence to the code of civilized morality rested not just the welfare of individuals, but of the entire society. Ideals of sexual purity have found fertile soil in the United States; the latter part of the nineteenth and early twentieth centuries was the period of their greatest public and political hegemony.[2]

Age-of-consent laws, the White Slave Traffic Act, and the other state actions to which I have referred aimed to give to the code of civilized morality the force of law. Young women below the stated age of consent were *legally,* not just ideally, defined as innocent (a point that gave considerable pause to some legislators considering bills setting the age as high as age 18 or 21).[3] These actions reflected the conviction of reformers that in an increasingly urbanized society something more than strength of moral character was required for the protection of virtue. That "something more" was the power of the state to define moral transgressions as criminal acts. Writing in 1912, Jane Addams called attention to the novelty of this approach: "A new form of social control is slowly establishing itself on the principle, so widespread in contemporary government, that the state has a responsibility for conditions which determine the health and welfare of its own members; that it is in the interests of social progress itself that hard-won liberties must be restrained by the demonstrable needs of society" (206). "The effort to obtain legal protection for purity marks a new era in the history of the development of our race," wrote a female lawyer in 1887, at the very outset of age-of-consent agitation in the United States (Mark, 1887:1). Thus, the sexual social movements I describe emerged in the context of an ideology in which society's future was portrayed as dependent upon individuals' adherence to a draconian moral code, and of an increasing belief that state power was an efficient and appropriate means by which adherence to this code might be insured.[4]

The groundwork for these social movements was prepared in the period before the Civil War.[5] As early as 1834, the New York Female Moral Reform Society was founded "to convert New York's prostitutes to evangelical Protestantism and close forever the city's numerous brothels" (Smith-Rosenberg, 1985:109). The roots of this activity lay in the Protestant revival movement of the early nineteenth century. Prior to the war, much of the energy released by this movement went into abolitionism. After the war, many abolitionists, continuing, as they saw it, their work toward societal perfection, became involved in movements for "social purity." The backbone of these early efforts, David J.

Pivar argues, were women: William Lloyd Garrison's "unrealized dreams were assumed by the woman's movement. Feminists undertook the social mission of transforming older institutions and constructing new ones to humanize social life" (1973:36).

The central focus of the social purity movement in its earliest post–Civil War incarnation was opposition to government "regulation" of prostitution (by medical inspection of prostitutes and their confinement to specified sections of the city).[6] By 1885 organized efforts to bring about regulation in the United States had effectively been repulsed. In the process of combating regulation, however, a network of organized groups—women's clubs, societies for moral education, vigilance committees, the Women's Christian Temperance Union (WCTU), suffragists—had been drawn into or, in some cases, been created by, activities against prostitution. These groups were ready recruits for a new social-purity campaign—this time on a truly national scale—a campaign to raise the age of consent.

The Age of Consent
The spark that ignited public agitation for change in the age of consent in the United States as well as in Great Britain was a sensational exposé of child prostitution by William Stead that appeared in the London press in the summer of 1885.[7] Pivar states that purity-reform leaders "seized upon the interest in age of consent to initiate a public campaign . . . [and] riding the popularity of the Stead exposé . . . brought the first phase of American age of consent lobbying to a rapid climax" (1973:140, 144; see also Wunsch, 1976:124).

The level of public interest in this issue, particularly on the part of women, was described as intense. In 1888, legislation was introduced in Congress raising the age of consent to 18. Its wording had been drafted by the WCTU, and its submission was accompanied by petitions from the National WCTU and from chapters in at least twelve separate states and territories (U.S. Cong., House, 1888:1326; U.S. Cong., Senate, 1888:1432). In an 1895 article, Frances Willard (the WCTU president) recounted that pledges to work for raising the age of consent were circulated "by hundreds and thousands of copies, the demand for these being greater than for the literature of the temperance movement" (199). A series of articles in the journal, *The Arena*, gave detailed state-by-state reports by local observers of activity on this issue. In Michigan, for example, "no legislation ever attempted . . . created so much interest or was so generally discussed" (*The Arena*, October 1895:214).[8] Michigan was not unique. As Pivar points out, "age of consent legislation served admirably for purity reform as a vehicle into mass politics" (1973:119). Senator Blair introduced his bill to raise the age of consent to 18 into the first session of the 50th Congress (February 20, 1888) with the statement that "today the traffic in girls and young women in this country, especially in our large cities, has come to be more disgraceful and worse than ever was that in the girls of Circassia. . . . There are developments in one of our great cities which show how grievously girlhood and young womanhood are in absolute need of the protection of law" (U.S. Cong., Senate, 1888:1326).

The "criminals" under age-of-consent legislation were male. Nevertheless in the rhetoric surrounding this legislation males were shadowy figures.[9]
At center stage were the "innocent" victims, routinely described as "girl-
children," "infants," and "baby girls."[10] The period of life that reformers were
most concerned to protect was, however, the period that we would define as
adolescence: "Thousands of immature girls, just passing through the transition
period that divides childhood from womanhood, are being dragged down
from a state of purity to one of pollution" (*The Arena*, November 1895:405).
"The maiden will be allowed to develop into the woman. . . . These three
or four added years of comparative safety will be an incalculable blessing"
(*The Arena*, January 1895:207). Furthermore, their rhetoric supports the conclusion that age-of-consent agitators (like their counterparts in Great Britain)
were particularly fearful of the dangers to poor girls obliged (as the reformers
saw it) to work away from the family protection afforded by "comfortable,"
"Christian" homes: "Ye citizens of Iowa who dwell in comfortable homes, ye
who have surrounded your children with the protective environment of the
Christian home, will you not hearken to an appeal for legal protection for
the girls of the poor, for the girls who have lost a mother's watchful eye and
protecting care" (*The Arena*, July 1895:218). "In that struggle [with poverty]
girls of young and tender years, as pure and innocent as yours and mine, will
have to work in the factories, in the stores, in the hotels and boarding houses,
coming in contact with all sorts of people, some, alas! watching for victims to
indulge their brutal lusts. The state should throw every safeguard around them
possible" (*The Arena*, November 1895:405).

There is a very fine line between "protection" and control. Age-of-consent
legislation, as Deborah Gorham points out, "is explicitly designed to deny to
a girl the right to make decisions about her sexuality if she is younger than
the stated age" (1978:365). The very possibility of autonomous sexual decision
making is removed by *defining* young women as innocent children, "themselves entitled to protection, if need be, from even their own ignorance or
desire in this matter" (*The Arena*, August 1895:356). Reformers believed that if
mothers could no longer be counted on to protect and control their daughters
during the perilous transition from childhood to adulthood, this deficiency—
one which they identified with cities and with the lower classes—would have
to be remedied by a beneficent state.

White Slavery, Prostitution, and Venereal Disease

In his notorious series of articles, "The Maiden Tribute of Modern Babylon,"
William Stead "revealed" the existence of an organized commercial traffic in
English girls—"the daughters of the people"—for purposes of prostitution.
Although it made an occasional appearance, this conception of an organized
"white slave traffic" played a relatively minor role in U.S. agitation for sexual
control prior to 1900. By the end of the twentieth century's first decade, however, "indignation and concern over white slavery" in the United States had become "intense, widespread, and often hysterical" (Connelly, 1980:115). From
a variety of perspectives—the rhetoric employed, the individuals and groups

who became involved, the solutions proposed—the age-of-consent debates appear as a species of rehearsal for the considerably broader and more highly politicized public outcry over white slavery.

Jane Addams ascribed the emergence of white slavery as a public problem in the United States to an "international agreement for the repression of the trade in white women" signed in 1904 by thirteen European governments and subscribed to by the U.S. Senate in 1905: "The discussion of the international [white slave] treaty brought the subject before the entire country as a matter for immediate legislation and for executive action" (1912:23). Recent historians have dated its emergence from the 1909 publication in a well-known muckraking journal of an article titled, "The Daughters of the Poor," by George Kibbe Turner (e.g., Wagner, 1971; Wunsch, 1976; Connelly, 1980; Filene, 1986). Peter G. Filene has summarized the events that ensued.

> A torrent of books, articles, plays, and movies dramatized the operations of an international syndicate that seized innocent girls and sent them into the hands of pimps and madams. Women's clubs, civic leagues, ministerial associations, and WCTU chapters united to lobby for bills closing the red-light districts. Reformers organized local and national committees to publicize the commerce in female bodies, while mayors in dozens of cities established vice commissions to investigate prostitution and find remedies (1986:87).

The white slavery threat drew upon and, at the same time, exacerbated preexisting concerns about prostitution and venereal disease, primarily, I believe, because it located the threat within the precincts of the American home ("65,000 daughters of American homes each year conscripted into the great army of prostitutes") rather than in the alien world of brothels and red-light districts (U.S. Cong., House, 1910a:821).[11] Much as in the earlier age-of-consent debates, the principal focus of Progressive Era reformers' rhetorical attention was not the professional prostitute nor (even less so) her customers, but the unmarried young woman in the city. Congressional debate on the White Slave Traffic Act identified the young women at risk as "inexperienced country girls, lured to the cities by promises of good positions; heedless impulsive girls, trapped into runaway fake marriages; trustful city girls, who visit ice-cream parlors and unsuspectingly eat or drink that which has been 'fixed' for their ruin" (U.S. Cong., House, 1910a:821).

The heroines of the white-slave tracts were almost invariably innocent girls from the country who left home for "the great city" in search of employment and excitement and who, once there, were readily duped by white slavers, usually of foreign extraction (Connelly, 1980:114–35). The central figures in Jane Addams's A New Conscience and an Ancient Evil, credited with a major role in arousing the public against prostitution, were not prostitutes but "the phenomenal number of young girls who are utilized by modern industry" (1912:55). Allan M. Brandt notes that doctors were especially concerned about the threat to young women "of the wage-earning class" who might be led by "such harmless pleasures as dancing" to engage in premarital sex (1985:29). As these latter comments indicate, the behavior that most frightened reformers was not prostitution in the narrow sense of sexual intercourse for pay, but "any premarital or non-monogamous female sexual activity." The Chicago Vice Commission, for example,

> regularly turned its attention to aspects of urban social life that only the most ecumenical definition of prostitution could include: dance halls where young working women met men, assignation houses where married individuals conducted extramarital affairs, lake boats where adolescents congregated unchaperoned, unsupervised picnics, summer amusement resorts, saloons, and vaudeville halls. . . . Thus, in the moral world of [the Commission's report], potentially all sexual activity unsanctioned by marriage could be characterized as prostitution (Connelly, 1980:17–18).

Progressive Era reformers routinely condemned the double standard, advocated chastity for men, and painted lurid portraits of the male white slaver. Nevertheless, it was the sexuality of women, and particularly that of women whom we would describe as "sexually active" adolescent girls, that attracted their most avid attention and concern. To reconcile that concern with the ideology of innocence and, at the same time, justify the need for new mechanisms of control, reformers defined adolescent girls as "children" and their sexual behavior as involuntary.

In Progressive Era literature as well as art, the principal victims of white slavery were portrayed as asexual children. "There is something literally heartbreaking in the thought of these little children who are ensnared and debauched when they are still young enough to have every right to protection and care" (Addams, 1912:136). Mark Thomas Connelly vividly describes a sculpture, *The White Slave*, executed in 1913 by the American artist, Abastensia St. Leger Eberle, in which the subject is portrayed as "a barely pubescent child-woman." "The persistent tendency to characterize white slaves in juvenile terms, as ruined children or childish victims" was, he remarks, "the most curious aspect" of this theme (1980:126). Not only did this characterization deny the sexuality of adolescent women; it insisted upon their subordinate status *as a social category* and legitimatized their subjection to adult control.

Slavery is, by definition, involuntary. However, it was just this aspect that congressional supporters of the White Slave Traffic Act most particularly insisted upon: "The characteristic which distinguishes 'the white-slave trade' from immorality in general is that *the women who are the victims of the traffic are unwillingly forced to practice prostitution*. . . . Its victims are those women and girls who, if given a fair chance, would, in all human probability, have been good wives and mothers and useful citizens" (U.S. Cong., House, 1910b:11). Justification for state "protection" (rather than punishment) of sexually unorthodox females demanded that their actions be defined as "involuntary." By constructing young women's behavior in this fashion, legislators preserved the ideology of female innocence and need for protection and, at the same time, gave recognition to the potential sexuality of "thousands of women and girls." Innocence was threatened, but the threat was external and alien to the girl herself. In reality, as James Wunsch has described in some detail, the White Slave

Traffic Act was most often employed as a means of control rather than protection, denying the sexual autonomy of willing young women by threatening their partners with prosecution (1976).

The highly sensationalized portrayals of white slavery both drew upon and, simultaneously, renewed and revitalized not only the same ideological concerns but also many of the same organizations that had been behind the antiregulation and age-of-consent debates. There were some important differences, however. The evangelical flavor of the earlier movements was supplemented (and ultimately replaced) by an aura of science and objectivity and by a passion for publication of the "facts" about prostitution and venereal disease. And a far broader range of participants were enlisted—not only women and the clergy, but politicians and, perhaps of the greatest long-run significance, physicians. In this process, the movement itself became professionalized and institutionalized to a far greater degree than had occurred during the agitations of the late nineteenth century.

The rise and fall between 1890 and 1919 of public attention to "prostitution" is documented by an analysis of *Readers' Guide* listings for this period. Of the 206 entries recorded, 70 percent were from the period from 1910 to 1914, 18 percent from 1890 to 1909, and 12 percent from 1915 to 1919 (Wagner, 1971:153). The drop-off in public interest was as rapid as its rise. In 1919, Dr. O. Edward Janney, a physician who had been prominent in all of the purity movements from age-of-consent to white slavery to prostitution, proclaimed that the "organized traffic in women—a fixed system in 1906 was completely destroyed by 1916 and it is now so much a thing of the past that it is hard to make men believe that such an evil existed in our land" (cited in Wunsch, 1976:138). "The white slavery agitation, the growing influence of sex hygiene, temperance, and women's rights movements, coupled with pleas from press and pulpit" were, according to Wunsch, "sufficient to force the police to close brothels formerly tolerated" (1976:152). Whether because the problem of prostitution was believed to have been solved, or for other reasons, the public by 1919 had lost interest in the "social evil" and its attendant problems: "One of the more familiar chapters in American social history recounts how the nation in the 1920s turned away from the moral control obsessions that had loomed so large a few years before" (Boyer, 1978:218).

THE MEANING OF TURN-OF-THE-CENTURY
SEXUAL SOCIAL MOVEMENTS
Historians' interpretations of the late nineteenth-century and early twentieth-century moral-reform movements I have described can be roughly divided into two categories. To the first category belong several major studies of the period as a whole (i.e., Hofstadter, 1955; May, 1959; Wiebe, 1967; Boyer, 1978) as well as works more narrowly focused on aspects of the reform movements themselves (Connelly, 1980; Filene, 1986; Schlossman and Wallach, 1978). Moral reform is interpreted by these scholars as an aspect of America's re-

sponse to the personal and social upheavals associated with the transition from a predominantly agrarian to a predominantly urban and industrial society. Connelly, Filene, and Schlossman and Wallach go further and identify the most important dimension of those upheavals (from the perspective of its part in engendering and sustaining the reform movements) as change in the social and sexual roles of young women. By contrast, the second category of historians (a category that includes Degler, 1980; Smith, 1973; and most feminist historians) have interpreted these movements as "efforts to overturn women's subordinate status" by constraining the sexuality of *men* (Freedman, 1982:209). These are very different interpretations of essentially the same phenomenon and any new approach must take them both into account. However, for reasons that I will briefly describe, my own interpretation draws more heavily on the first category of historical research than on the second.

Work from the feminist perspective appropriately raises the question of whose "interests" were served by the ideology of social purity. However, much of this work fails to distinguish between the interests of young unmarried women as compared with older married women or of middle-class as compared with lower-class women.[12] Furthermore, interests are defined solely in terms of the sexual power-structure without taking into consideration broader political interests that the purity ideology might have served. I also believe that this interpretation gives insufficient attention to the content of participants' own accounts of their motives and objectives. Finally, although the question of why so many women participated in these morally repressive movements is an important one, I believe an adequate interpretation requires that the participation of other groups in society be taken into account as well.

I suggested in Chapter 1 that understanding of the rise and decline of sexual social movements would come from the answers to three sets of questions regarding, first, demographic and social conditions external to the movements themselves; second, the movements' underlying ideologies and beliefs; and third, preexisting organizational capacities and interests. The demographic and social conditions most relevant to the emergence of these movements in the late nineteenth century were described in Chapter 5. Here, I will briefly recall the most important of these conditions, and then turn to a more detailed consideration of the movements' ideological and organizational dimensions.

The Demographic and Social Context
Urbanization, industrialization, a massive influx of "new immigrants" from eastern and southern Europe, robber barons, city bosses, and the closing of the Western frontier are the conventional historical landmarks of late nineteenth-century America. Less frequently observed, but equally important from the present perspective, were the marked changes during this period in the structure of young women's lives. The population of the United States in the late nineteenth century was marked by an exceedingly high proportion of single young women and the concentration of these young women in cities and

in the Northeast and North Central states, where they substantially outnumbered young men. Close to one-quarter of the adult female population living in 1890 were single and between the ages of 15 and 24; even in 1972, when baby-boom babies were in the flower of their youth and marriage rates were already on the way down, the comparable figure did not go above 18 percent. As early as 1869 the *New York Times* estimated that "about a quarter of a million young women in the eastern seaboard states could never look forward to any matrimonial alliance" (cited in Kessler-Harris, 1982:98). An expert witness testifying in 1883 before a congressional committee stated that, "since one-third of all women over twenty-one were not married, marriage was 'no longer a career for women, nor a means of support for them'" (cited in Kessler-Harris, 1982:98). The second major—and closely related—social change affecting young women was their increased participation in the paid labor force. Not only were young women in the late nineteenth century unlikely to move quickly from puberty into marriage, they were also less likely, and less able, to find adequate occupation at home in the period before they married. Out of necessity—because their families could no longer support them at home or needed their wages to survive—or out of inclination, single young women looked for work in the cities and towns of the East and the Midwest. Work, however, was not always easy to find and the wages paid to women workers were often extremely low. Curiously, as Alice Kessler-Harris observes, despite "endless government statistics demonstrating financial need, the feeling prevailed that women brought their low pay on themselves" (1982:100): they "'work for small pay, needing money only for dress or pleasure'" (cited in Kessler-Harris, 1982:100). The reality of a large and highly visible floating population of young women who were both single and poor, combined with the perception of these young women as actively in search of the pleasures that money can buy, played directly into the moral anxieties of late nineteenth-century middle-class men and women: "The deepest fear was that wage-earning women would slip into the ultimate disgrace of prostitution" (Kessler-Harris, 1982:103).

The high proportion of young women in the population, their concentration in cities, and their marital and employment behavior are demonstrable facts. The realities of prostitution and venereal disease in the late nineteenth and early twentieth centuries are far more difficult to determine. Even some contemporaries questioned the scenarios of syndicated seduction and betrayal and the staggering prostitution and venereal disease statistics cited by moral-reform advocates. Investigations of reported white-slave "syndicates" in Philadelphia and St. Louis found evidence for the protection of prostitution by police and politicians, but no large-scale "traffic" in female bodies (Wunsch, 1976:125–26). Walter Reckless concluded from his retrospective study (published in 1933) of Chicago court records that there was "no evidence ... of the existence of gangs of white slavers . . . [and] very little evidence to support the charge that men were purposely and consciously sent out to trap girls by the managers of a resort or syndicate of resorts" (1933:42). Studies conducted at the time suggested that the majority of prostitutes were not "girls" in any case, but women over age 20 (Connelly, 1980:127). Based on her recent detailed investigation of prostitution in the nineteenth and early twentieth centuries, Barbara Meil Hobson argues that vice commissioners' image of "a highly organized prostitution empire in the hands of a few vice moguls" netting profits in the millions was undoubtedly incorrect. However, there were increases between the late nineteenth and early twentieth centuries in the market for prostitution, in opportunities for women to become prostitutes, and in prostitution's level of organization: "The economy of prostitution had become more organized and rationalized" (1987:140).

Reformers may have exaggerated the dimensions as well as the power and profits of vice. Richard Cabot, a Boston physician who studied venereal statistics, charged that the huge rates of infection cited by Prince Morrow, a leading medical warrior against venereal disease, were "wild guesses published for campaign purposes" (cited in Brandt, 1985:13). Claims as to the number of prostitutes in New York City ranged from 15,000 to 100,000 (or one prostitute for every seventeen males over the age of 14) (Wunsch, 1976:154). The demographic and social realities of urban life at the turn of the century—"low wages paid to women, local government and police corruption from sex commerce, and the spread of venereal disease [in an age when no safe cure existed]"—were sufficiently visible, as well as serious, to provide ample grist for the reformers' mill (Hobson, 1987:140). Nevertheless, at a period characterized by profound belief in the compelling quality of "facts," the statistics and the seduction scenarios were intended not just as descriptions of social reality, but as red flags to arouse the professional and public constituencies to whom these portrayals were addressed. Furthermore, compelling although they may have been, the "facts" would not have had the desired effect had not those constituencies been fully prepared to feed upon them with, as Filene puts it, "horrified zeal" (1986:87).

The Threats of Social and Sexual Change

Until very recently, historians of the nineteenth and early twentieth centuries were consistent in portraying the moral-reform movements of this period (among which they include temperance as well as social-purity movements) as aspects of a reaction by Anglo-Saxon Protestant middle-class Americans, typically rural or small-town in origin, to the rapid urbanization and industrialization of American society. Robert Wiebe depicts this process as the breaking down of stable, "usually homogeneous, usually Protestant" local communities. "Men of breeding" whose ideas were formed within "a decent world where their word mattered, where their standards were honored and their families secure [were, as the century turned, confronted by] foes of extraordinary raw strength—huge, devouring monopolies, swarms of sexually potent immigrants, and the like. . . . Accustomed to a steady ripple of attacks, these men . . . now saw a tidal wave that might sweep away all of legitimate society" (1967:51–52). Hofstadter points out that from the perspective of native-born rural migrants, the city "seemed not merely a new social form or way of life but a strange threat to civilization itself" (1955:176). Old values and old ways of life were perceived as no longer able to command either deference or respect. Moral reform movements, then, represented "a determined effort to reassert [the old social and moral order] through force of law" (Boyer, 1978:216).

Sociologists who have studied this period have conceptualized late nineteenth-century and early twentieth-century moral crusades in similar fashion, as symbolic political protests against a sense of lost status and power (e.g., Gusfield, 1963; Lipset and Raab, 1970). This perspective has much in common with Kai T. Erikson's (1966) thesis regarding the uses of confrontations over deviant behavior as means by which a community "draws a symbolic set of parentheses" around its own behavior, thereby locating and asserting its moral boundaries and defining the outer limits of its toleration for departures from group norms. Indeed, it extends this thesis by suggesting that among the circumstances most likely to precipitate such confrontations are a dominant group's perception that its prestige and status are threatened. However, neither the historical nor the sociological analyses I have cited explain why, in the period under study, sexuality became a pivotal issue around which these confrontations were organized. Nor are these analyses entirely consistent with the evidence that at least some participants appear to have become involved in sexual social movements primarily for what they could gain rather than to protest what they had lost. Finally, any argument that relies too heavily on "social change" as a social movement catalyst runs into the problem that even rapid social change is fairly gradual and that, as John D. McCarthy and Mayer N. Zald have observed, societies sustain a more or less constant reservoir of discontent (1977:1215). To account for the rise and fall of sexual social movements we must take into account *both* the specific normative conflicts that these movements embodied *and* the social and political interests that exploitation of these conflicts may have served.[13] Before advancing such an interpretation, however, it is necessary to specifically address the question of whether it was with male or with female sexuality that the turn-of-the-century sexual social movements were primarily concerned.

As I observed earlier, there is a substantial body of historical work interpreting late nineteenth-century and early twentieth-century sexual social movements as promoting the freedom and autonomy of women "inside and outside the family" and as "primarily concerned with controlling the sexuality of men" (Degler, 1980:291). This argument is based on the premise that these movements' repressive sexual ideology acted to increase women's power, first, by limiting male access to sexual gratification except on women's terms (i.e., within marriage) and, second, by enabling women to exercise control over reproduction in an era when artificial birth control was morally suspect. However, insofar as this argument has validity, it is restricted to the "freedom and autonomy" of women within or immediately prior to marriage. It entirely overlooks the emphasis of moral-reform movement literature (ranging from Helen Gardener's 1895 articles in *The Arena* to Jane Addams's *A New Conscience and an Ancient Evil*) on the threats to and temptations confronted by *unmarried* young women as well as what I have described as the "shadowy" presence in this literature of men. The central problem in the age-of-consent debates, in the white-slavery tracts, and in the vice commission reports on prostitution was not male sexuality or the dangers to married women but the sexuality of adolescent girls.[14]

The argument that change in the social and sexual roles of young women was critical to the emergence of these sexual social movements is supported by the work of several historians (e.g., Gorham, 1978; Schlossman and Wallach, 1978; Connelly, 1980; Filene, 1986). The evidence of these changes underlies the first portion of my interpretive argument. I believe that a principal condition for the emergence of sexual social movements in the late nineteenth and early twentieth centuries was the perception by reformers that previously accepted boundaries between orthodox and unorthodox (or "respectable" and "deviant") sexual behavior were being breached by large numbers of unmarried young women.[15]

In the nineteenth century female sexuality was identified with immigrants, women of the lower class, and prostitutes—in other words, with categories of persons outside the boundaries of respectable society. In the early twentieth century, the complex array of demographic, economic, social, and ideological changes that I have described began to dim the clarity of this demarcation. The "pure" girl and the "fallen" could no longer be so easily distinguished. The nineteenth-century image of the innocent girl was challenged by vice investigators' reports of flirtatious working girls; by the currency given in newspapers, magazines, and works of fiction to the manners and morals of the "flapper"; and by structural changes that increased both the visibility and the perceived vulnerability of adolescent women as individuals and of female adolescence as a period of life.

Not only the boundaries of gender-appropriate sexual behavior were obscured; more subtle distinctions of age and class were blurred as well. Young women between puberty and marriage, socially defined as still under the protection of their parents, were seen as threatening to assume adult sexual prerogatives. Reformers' insistence not only on rhetorically portraying the objects of their concern as "little children" but on the incorporation of this definition into legal statutes can be read as an affirmation of traditional status boundaries between adults and children, and an assertion of the former's rights of dominance and control over the latter. In the late nineteenth century, the female "children" for whom reformers invoked the protection of the state were also predominantly working class. By extending to them the same "protection" already enjoyed by the daughters of the middle class, it was hoped that their behavior could be assimilated to middle-class norms of sexual morality. With the emergence of the middle- and upper-class flapper early in the twentieth century, assimilation appeared to be moving in precisely the opposite direction: Even the innocence of girls from "comfortable Christian homes" could no longer be assumed.

Reflecting on these changes from the perspective of 1923, W. I. Thomas wrote:

> Fifty years ago we recognized, roughly speaking, two types of women, the one completely good and the other completely bad,—what we now call the old-fashioned girl and the girl who had sinned and been outlawed. At present we have several intermediate types—the occasional prostitute, the charity girl, the demi-virgin, the equivocal flapper . . . no one of these girls, neither the orderly nor the disorderly, is conforming with the behavior norms of her grandmother (230–31).

By enlisting the state on the side of innocence, by defining adolescent girls as "children" and their sexual behavior as involuntary, by (almost in the same breath) lumping together all sexual activity by unmarried young women as prostitution, by agitating to protect working girls against evil men rather than to insulate them from temptation by raising the minimum wage, and by promoting repressive sex education, moral crusaders sought to reaffirm the boundaries between innocence and sin flaunted so blatantly by Thomas's "intermediate types." The solutions of these reformers to the problems presented by the newly recognized stage of female adolescence were simultaneously to deny its reality and to invent new forms of social control.

Placing the rise of sexual social movements in the context of change in the pattern of young women's transition from childhood to adulthood also suggests one reason for these movements' decline. Reformers' concern about how to manage this dangerous period in young women's lives may have been partially assuaged by what I called in Chapter 5 the "domestication of female sexuality." In the early 1920s sex, as well as work, before marriage became redefined as valuable preliminaries to a lifetime career of domestic bliss. Sexual experimentation (within limits) was legitimized as preparation for marriage, intercourse was sanctified by engagement, and paid work became a means to accelerate the day of the wedding. In this fashion, the realities of social change in women's lives were accommodated by redrawing the boundaries of civilized society to include the new no-longer-innocent behaviors of unmarried young women.

A SECOND condition for the emergence as well as the persistence over some thirty-five years of the sexual social movements I have described was the perception by reformers that sexual behavior formerly designated as deviant was in danger of becoming legitimized. "What appeared most disturbing to reformers," Hobson observes regarding the response to prostitution, "was not the increasing numbers of prostitutes or the visibility of sex commerce, but the tendency toward institutionalized and state-sanctioned prostitution" (1987:147). Widespread *behavioral* violation of traditional sexual norms was bad enough; the possibility of a shift in the norms themselves, converting deviant into acceptable behavior, was even worse.[16] During the period in question, state regulation of prostitution, the prospect of a medical cure for venereal disease, the new sexual ideologies of Freud and Havelock Ellis, and even the public attention to matters of sex generated, in part, by these movements themselves were all symbolic of the threat that formerly unorthodox sexuality would become legitimized.

In the late nineteenth century, the threat of legitimation was epitomized by state regulation of prostitution. In the venereal epidemiology of the period, as Brandt has observed, while "an 'innocent' woman could only get venereal disease from a 'sinful' man . . . the man could only get venereal disease from a 'fallen' woman" (1985:32). From this perspective, the problems of prostitution and venereal disease were one and the same: control of venereal disease demanded the control of prostitution. "Regulationists" would accomplish this objective by the state-supervised medical inspection and treatment of prostitutes. In the eyes of its opponents, regulation was tantamount to public legitimation of nonmarital, nonprocreative sex; only the complete suppression of prostitution was morally acceptable as a solution to the problem of venereal disease. The threat of regulation was instrumental in bringing the late nineteenth-century social-purity movement into being. It continued to galvanize the movement's activities long after regulation itself had ceased to be formally proposed, due in part to reformers' perceptions that, while de jure regulation had been defeated, de facto regulation persisted:

> When the first New York committee investigating vice made its pioneering investigation of urban prostitution in 1902, it listed thirty-two cities where police admitted that a "system of regulation" was in effect, and thirty-three cities where special areas in which prostitution was permitted had been established. Police and courts in many American cities had a de facto regulation system of prostitution through fines, segregated zones, and venereal medical certificates, regulation in all but name and statutory code. It seemed that the American cities were only a small step away from a formal system of state control (Hobson, 1987:147).

State control of prostitution amounted—in reformers' eyes—to officially sanctioned repudiation of traditional moral values. From the perspective of moral reformers (including some physicians prominent in the social-hygiene movement), the prospect that venereal disease might be prevented or cured was scarcely less frightening than the specter of regulation. Individuals might sin without fear of the consequences. Immorality would go unpunished. The value of disease as a form of social control was pointed out in no uncertain terms by a prominent turn-of-the-century Johns Hopkins gynecologist: "I believe that if we could in an instant eradicate the diseases, we would also forget at once the moral side of the question, and would then, in one short generation, fall wholly under the domination of the animal passions, becoming grossly and universally immoral" (Dr. Howard Kelly, cited in Brandt, 1985:46). Condoms were being advertised for the prevention of venereal disease (as well as conception) as early as 1870; in 1909, Salvarsan, the first effective treatment for syphillis, was discovered. Although physicians prescribed Salvarsan privately, moral crusaders' opposition to anything that might appear as "official" endorsement of sin played a role in slowing the growth of public health efforts against venereal disease (Brandt, 1985:46).[17] Not until the late 1920s, when the Progressive Era sexual social movements had disappeared, did physicians become willing to admit openly that condoms were protective against venereal infection.

Condoms and Salvarsan threatened to make sexual sin "safe." The writings of Freud and Havelock Ellis threatened to do away with the concept of sexual sin altogether. Several historians have argued that the intellectual "demystification" of sex these authors initiated, combined with "a widespread revulsion against the growing frequency and legitimacy of sex as an everyday topic of discussion" played a significant part in the early twentieth-century resurgence of sexual social movements (Schlossman and Wallach, 1978:86; Hale, 1971; Strong, 1972; Connelly, 1980). *How* significant is difficult to evaluate since reformers were in some measure responsible for the changes to which they are portrayed as responding. Pivar describes the age-of-consent agitation as having "initiated a mass public debate on sex" (1973:146); it was, remarks another historian, "the progressive crusades that repealed reticence [about sexual matters] on a national scale" (Hale, 1971:254). Sexual imagery served moral crusaders as a valuable resource in mobilizing popular support for repressive public actions. The sense of having let loose a beast that they could not, in fact, fully control may have added to their repressive zeal.

The Political Moment

A perceived blurring of sexual boundaries and the threat posed by the prospective legitimation of sexual unorthodoxy may have been necessary but were probably not sufficient conditions for the emergence of sexual social movements in the late nineteenth century and their persistence and reinvigoration in the early twentieth century. A third, critical, condition was the presence in American society of groups that could be mobilized around these concerns and for whom they represented a means to social and political power. At least three such groups are clearly identifiable from the literature on this period. They are (roughly in the order of their appearance on the stage of movement activities) women, reform-minded politicians and business elites, and physicians.

WOMEN

By the late nineteenth century questions of sexual morality had become a major vehicle for the organization and politicization of women. The effectiveness of sexual issues in mobilizing support was openly acknowledged by Francis Willard, president of the WCTU, largest and most powerful women's organization of the period. The WCTU established a department for the suppression of prostitution as early as 1883, and WCTU chapters were responsible for bringing the age-of-consent issue to congressional attention. The positive effects on sexual morality of women's political participation was, in addition, a central argument of the woman suffrage movement, and this argument became particularly important in the early twentieth century as the movement attempted to broaden its base of support (Kraditor, 1965; Buechler, 1986).

From the perspective of the middle-class women who participated in early twentieth-century reform movements, prostitution was a quintessentially "woman's issue," a direct attack on motherhood and the sanctity of the home. "Women," wrote Mary Beard in 1916, "will be found today in the United States as leaders in the crusade against the social evil" (97). Even the conservative Congress of Mothers argued for a variety of reforms directed toward the social and moral uplift of the "unskilled classes" on the basis of the protection they would afford against immorality (Beard, 1916:100). Jane Addams gave explicit recognition to the value of moral issues in activating women and bringing them into the political system: "As the first organized Women's Rights movement was inaugurated by the women who were refused seats in the world's Anti-Slavery convention held in London in 1840 . . . so it is quite possible that an equally energetic attempt to abolish white slavery will bring many women into the Equal Suffrage movement" (1912:197). With rare exceptions, Progressive Era women who spoke out on the "social evil" were uniform in their adherence to the Victorian code of "civilized morality." They did not, however, speak with one voice on the question of how the problem of prostitution should be prevented or resolved. Protection of the sexually innocent girl (as well as the civil rights of the non innocent) vied with control of the sexually unorthodox; raising the minimum wage as a means to remove women's *need* to engage in prostitution vied with the prosecution of pimps and the closing of brothels.

The increased social conservatism of the woman suffrage movement over this period has been fully documented; parallel changes were evident even within the initially much more conservative movement for sexual reform (Kraditor, 1965; Wunsch, 1976; Buechler, 1986). Steven M. Buechler has linked the increasing conservatism of women's movements to the emergence in the United States of a more differentiated social class structure. As middle-class women began to define their interests on the basis of class rather than gender, they became more committed to the preservation of the existing social order. A second source of conservatism may have been women's assumption of responsible roles in an increasingly professionalized and bureaucratized social-service system. Describing consequences of the shift from prison reformer to prison administrator, Estelle B. Freedman observes that, "because they perceived women as a sexual class, separate from men, nineteenth-century reformers crossed the boundary between themselves and fallen women. Once they took charge of prisons, however, sex was no longer the determinant of power. A new hierarchy placed the keepers above the inmates, in part because of the privileges they had enjoyed as middle-class women, but also because of the nature of institutional relationships" (1981:105). Increased class- as well as institution-based commitments were reflected in the ascendancy by the end of the Progressive Era of repressive as compared with more socially or economically radical solutions to the problem of women's socially threatening sexuality. "If Progressivism had two spirits, one of uplift and one of social control, it was the latter that lived on" (Freedman, 1981:146).[18]

The political value to women's organizations of sexual morality issues was (at least) two fold. First, these issues offered an avenue of access to the public

arena in an area where women were already held to be authorities by virtue
of their sex and of their position in late-Victorian society as guardians of home
and family. Expertise based on ascribed characteristics maximized the number of potential movement recruits. Second, politicization around "moral"
home and family issues defused opposition in a period when public political
activity by women was itself morally suspect (e.g., Buechler, 1986:8). These
strategic considerations played a significant role, I believe, in persuading the
leadership of late nineteenth-century and early twentieth-century women's
organizations to keep sexual morality issues alive. These considerations became less important following the passage of the Nineteenth Amendment in
1919 giving women the right to vote; this latter event was one of several factors
contributing to the sexual social movement's decline.

POLITICIANS AND BUSINESSMEN

Perhaps the most telling evidence of the public's preoccupation with illicit
sexuality in the early twentieth century was the adoption of this issue by politicians, either on their own initiative or in response to the force of public
opinion. The alleged "protection of vice" by police and political machines
"helped carry [a Missouri District Attorney] to the Governor's mansion and
twice in 1894 and 1901 helped bring Tammany to defeat in New York. Similarly
exposés in Minneapolis in 1902 and Philadelphia in 1904 led to reform vic-
tories" (Wunsch, 1976:87). The politics of turn-of-the-century vice crusading
are described in detail by Roland Richard Wagner (1971) and James Wunsch
(1976). Wagner observes that George Kibbe Turner's famous exposé of white
slavery "made prostitution an issue in the New York City elections of 1901"
(128), and, although it did not prevent the reelection of the Tammany mayor, it
did lead to the defeat of Tammany candidates for borough presidencies and for
the City Council. Wagner suggests that, in fact, the major purpose of Turner's
article was political. S. S. McClure, publisher of *McClure's Magazine*, where the
article appeared, believed that "the traffic in vice" would have a more powerful
impact on public opinion than complaints about financial waste in government (McClure, *My Autobiography*, cited in Wagner, 1971:123). He was proven
correct. Two months after the New York City elections "a Tammany judge re-
luctantly created a grand jury to investigate white slavery" (Wunsch, 1976:87).
Between 1910 and 1916, fully twenty-seven municipal governments carried out
parallel investigations. The massive and statistically detailed reports that resulted (Chicago's report, *The Social Evil in the City*, was four hundred pages
long, with seven chapters and eighty-five pages of appendices) have been
portrayed as evidence of Progressive Era reformers' "conviction that once an
evil was made public and exposed, 'society' would spring to eliminate it"
(Connelly, 1980:23). However, the evidence suggests that "vice investigations,"
launched by political machines themselves as well as by reformers, were also
examples of a classic political alternative to defeat at the polls. By very early
in the twentieth century it had been amply demonstrated that "vice crusading

could be excellent politics" (Wunsch, 1976:85). Clearly, the message did not fall on politically deaf ears.

To head his grand jury investigation of New York City vice, the "reluctant" Tammany judge appointed John D. Rockefeller, suggesting something of the complex relationships between business, politics, and moral reform in the early twentieth century. Beginning in the mid-1890s and lasting almost until World War I, a series of "committees" composed of and/or financially supported by New York's wealthiest business elite—bankers, industrialists, railroad magnates, department store owners—publicized prostitution, white slavery, and police corruption in the City and agitated for moral reform. Among the practical meanings of "reform" appears to have been the replacement of Tammany by a city government more amenable to business control: What New York required to insure the purity of family life, stated the wealthy chair of an early committee, was a "strong levelheaded business man at its head" (cited in Wagner, 1971:94). However, these men's participation in moral-reform movements was more than a simple bid for political power. The cause of purity held the promise of protecting their reputations, their fortunes, and the social order on which their wealth depended.[19]

The period of moral-reform activity at the turn of the century coincided with events on the larger political and social stage of American life that may have appeared particularly threatening to the millionaires newly created by the enormous industrial expansion of the late nineteenth century. Driven in part by popular hostility to the concentration of economic power in the hands of Rockefellers, Morgans, Carnegies, and their ilk, Congress in 1890 passed the Sherman Antitrust Act; in 1903, President Theodore Roosevelt "staggered Wall Street" by invoking the act against a company organized by Morgan, among others. At about the same time an exposé of Rockefeller's ruthless business practices appeared in the popular press. It has been suggested that "Rockefeller's major philanthropic acts had distinct chronological juxtaposition with Rockefeller's major business troubles and public embarrassments" (Goulden, 1971:123). For Rockefeller and his fellow millionaires, public enlistment on the side of virtue may have represented a form of insurance against public assault—not only on their characters, but on their fortunes as well.

Threats to big-business hegemony came not just from the "trustbusting" activities of Theodore Roosevelt but also from the potential for social disorder—as these men saw it—generated by the process of industrialization itself. The last quarter of the nineteenth century has been described as a period of "unparalleled industrial violence": strikes were frequent and often bloody. It was the period when the social and economic evils attendant on rapid urbanization—poverty, slums, and disease—were first brought home to Americans through the efforts of muckraking journalists. These evils were associated, furthermore, not just with industrialization but with an enormous influx of European immigrants into American cities—an influx with political consequences that threatened the traditional influence in city government of Yankee business elites (Hammack, 1982; Beisel, 1990). Finally, it was the period when solutions to social problems that would have required fundamental change in the economic structure of society achieved their greatest popularity among American voters. The Socialist Party of America was founded in 1901. In 1904 and 1912 its presidential candidate received 6 percent of the vote; by 1912 more than fifty cities had elected Socialist mayors. To counter fundamental social change from below—socialism drew its major support from organized labor—business leaders espoused moral reform from above: "Wall Street . . . has undertaken to purify the Bowery" (cited in Wagner, 1971:104). These male reformers equated prostitution not only with poverty but also with "the lack of a moral civic life, a type of 'anarchy' that threatened society." Suppression of prostitution created the appearance of order without disturbing the fundamental social and economic relationships on which the prosperity of these turn-of-the-century industrialists was based.

The access of the newly emerging, largely masculine, entrepreneurs of municipal reform—ambitious district attorneys, muckraking journalists, and businessmen seeking leverage against machine politicians—to resources for calling public attention to the evils of prostitution and white slavery—through articles in the popular press, through the formation of citizen's committees and the instigation of vice investigations, and through the publication of reports—was far beyond that possessed by the women's groups who had first promoted these issues. Their objectives were, nevertheless, much the same: to mobilize a receptive constituency and to ride that constituency into a larger share of social influence and political power. The political success of municipal reformers' efforts was sporadic; however, their success in organization building was considerable. By 1909, the American Vigilance Association, an amalgam of earlier and smaller social-purity groups, had become a national organization with the president of Stanford University at its head and board members drawn from all over the country (Wunsch, 1976:142).

PHYSICIANS

The medicalization of sexuality and gender in the nineteenth century has become a familiar theme in American social history.[20] However, it was not until the early twentieth century that American physicians became actively involved in organized (as contrasted with individual) efforts for the management of sexual unorthodoxy.[21] From a nineteenth-century position advocating the medical inspection of prostitutes as a simple matter of public health, physicians had, by the beginning of the twentieth century, moved to a position where the only behavior they allowed to be compatible with health (for either sex) was chastity prior to marriage and monogamy thereafter. Regulation of prostitution was supplanted by a highly repressive "sex education" as the medical prescription against venereal disease. These ideological shifts took place simultaneously with the increasingly organized and institutionalized expression of medical opinion on questions of sexual behavior.

In the late nineteenth century, purity reformers undertook the conversion of organized medicine and public health to the antiregulationist position because, Pivar suggests, they "appreciated the authority of the medical profession on sex issues" (1973:87).[22] During the 1890s the leadership of both the social-purity department of the WCTU and the American Purity Alliance was passed from lay temperance reformers and former abolitionists to physicians. In 1900, the New York County Medical Society formed a Committee on the Social Evil and, in 1905, Prince Morrow, the physician probably most responsible for developing and articulating a medical rationale for the Victorian code of civilized morality, founded the American Society for Sanitary and Moral Prophylaxis (ASSMP). Connelly notes that "in its first five years the ASSMP grew impressively, both in size and in influence. . . . Within a year of its founding, Morrow could claim that because of its activities, more attention had been focused on prostitution and venereal disease 'within the last ten months than in the previous twenty years' " (1980:15). Finally, in 1913, the ASSMP merged with the American Vigilance Association to form the American Social Hygiene Association. This was an act with profound symbolic importance: the absorption of the last organization representing the old lay evangelical school of moral reform by the medically dominated organization of professionals created by Prince Morrow. Not only did this merger provide the earlier social movements with a secure institutional foundation but by converting sexual morality into "social hygiene" and the achievement of social purity into a problem for professional experts, it permanently changed these movements' character.

Physicians' takeover of the social-purity movement was an aspect of what Paul Starr has called "the consolidation of professional authority" that took place between 1850 and 1930 (1982:79–144). In a series of campaigns, first, in the latter half of the nineteenth century, against abortion; second, in the early twentieth century, for a medicalized sexual morality; and third, later in the twentieth century, for medically supervised birth control, physicians successfully established themselves as the principal guardians, and arbiters, of traditional moral values. In part, as several historians have suggested, the articulation of medical justifications for "civilized morality" reflected physicians' need for public support to consolidate and defend their rising professional status (e.g., Reed, 1979; Brandt, 1985). At the same time, a close look at these three campaigns indicates that physicians played a very active role in reshaping moral ends, as well as organizational means, to suit their own professional purposes.

The similarities and differences between the social-hygiene campaign and the antiabortion and birth control actions that preceded and followed it respectively, are instructive.[23] The abortion issue was constructed essentially out of whole cloth by mid-nineteenth-century "regular" physicians; they became outspoken against abortion not in deference to popular morality but in furtherance of professional dominance: to drive out competitors, to police the behavior of their colleagues, and to establish their position as moral authorities. By contrast, the two later events both involved physicians moving in and redefining issues and problems originally constructed by lay reformers.

In both cases the process of medicalization was immediately preceded by a period of professional agitation over the invasion of "moralists," "radicals," and other nonmedical persons into what was claimed as medical territory, and, simultaneously, by a courtship of medical endorsement on the part of lay reformers themselves.

The interrelationship between moral values, professional interests, and medical constructions of reality is strikingly illustrated by the social-hygiene campaign, and by the shift in physicians' posture toward prostitution and venereal disease that this campaign reflected. Nineteenth-century physicians were no less conservative in their sexual ideologies than their early twentieth-century counterparts.[24] They justified the regulation of prostitution as medically necessary to protect the moral purity of the home by providing a safe alternative outlet for imperious male passion. The code of "civilized morality," however, demanded a single, chaste, sexual standard for men as well as women and by the late nineteenth century pressure on organized medicine and public health from the then equally well-organized advocates of moral reform became overwhelming. Both medical groups retreated from their support of regulation, leaving something of a policy vacuum. The vacuum was, however, very quickly filled, as I have described, by the recasting of *anti*regulationist moral arguments into medical terms. This strategy was highly successful in retrieving physicians' position as arbiters of sexual morality. It placed them squarely in the moral camp of the Progressive Era social and business elites on whom they depended for financial and institutional support and led ultimately to the medicalization of the moral-reform movement itself.[25] Once social purity had been defined as the province of experts, its fate as a social movement was sealed.

Recapitulation

Theories of the rise and decline of social movements suggest that their explanation requires attention to both the ideologies and beliefs that these movements embody and the social structural conditions under which they appear. I have proposed two sets of beliefs underlying turn-of-the-century sexual social movements: the perception, first, that traditional moral boundaries between the sexual behaviors of males and females, of youth and adults, and of the lower and upper classes were being breached by large numbers of young women; and second, that social and economic forces were conspiring to legitimize sexual behaviors formerly defined as deviant. I have suggested that these beliefs were fueled in part by structural realities: the existence in the United States at the turn of the century of an unusually large population of single young women made highly visible by their geographic distribution and by certain of their social and behavioral characteristics. Finally, perhaps the most critical condition for social-movement emergence was the presence of identifiable groups of enterprising individuals—newly politicized women, ambitious politicians and businessmen, and professionalizing physicians—anxious to establish their moral and political authority in the society of their time. It was the organized activities of these groups that transformed what were real changes in the pattern of young women's lives into the targets of a moral crusade.

A major purpose of this chapter, as I noted earlier, has been to provide the basis for a comparison between the characteristics of turn-of-the-century sexual social movements and the more recent crusade against adolescent pregnancy. I defer that comparison to the book's concluding chapter so that contemporary strategies for the *management* of young women's sexuality, described in the three chapters that follow, may be taken more fully into account.

PART FOUR *Aspects of the Contemporary Scene*

CONTEMPORARY MODELS OF SEXUAL AND REPRODUCTIVE CONTROL

Chapter 8

CONFLICT AND CONSENSUS

In a book on the role of the state in family policy, Gilbert Steiner remarked that "the hardest family problems for government to deal with are those that involve choices between incompatible goals or values each of which has merit, each of which commands responsible and consequential support" (1981:49). Steiner described adolescent pregnancy as "among the most intractable of these problems." In an earlier chapter I attributed the emergence of adolescent pregnancy as a public problem in large part to the activities of birth control advocates, and indicated how, in the late 1970s, their ownership of the problem was challenged: by moral conservatives, by economic conservatives, and by blacks. The struggle between medical, moral, and economic constructions of this problem has, in subsequent years, neither diminished nor been resolved; indeed, it has been further complicated (and, to some degree, overshadowed) by the more recently discovered sexual threat of AIDS. These struggles have profoundly affected the types of management strategies proposed. In the sense Steiner intended, that of fundamental conflict over the moral acceptability of alternative "solutions" between groups with relatively equal power (or lack of power) to finally capture the problem and impose their own unitary construction upon it, adolescent pregnancy has remained intractable. As a consequence, even the most progressive of current government programs (the program recently adopted by New York State, for example) represent an uneasy compromise between radically different conceptions of cause and cure.

In this chapter I examine the principal strategies currently advocated or employed for the management of unmarried young women's sexual and reproductive behavior, with particular attention to the social and ideological premises on which these strategies are based. Joseph R. Gusfield has observed that "modes of conceiving of the reality of a phenomenon are closely related to the activities of resolution" (1981:6). In the case of adolescent pregnancy, powerful ideological and/or political commitments for or against particular "activities of resolution" (abortion, birth control, nonmarital childbearing) are inextricably linked to widely disparate constructions of the nature of the problem to be solved, the social location of the problem, what has caused the problem, and who should be responsible for its solution. Illustrations of these differences abound.

In 1986 the U.S. House of Representatives Select Committee on Children, Youth, and Families published a report entitled, *Teen Pregnancy: What Is Being Done? A State-by-State Look.* Appended to this essentially bland report in which, the introduction observes, states were deliberately allowed to "speak for themselves," are three sets of "Additional and Minority Views" in which the varying perspectives of committee members are made explicit. At one extreme, two members of the committee define the problem of adolescent *pregnancy* largely in terms of the impact of early *childbearing* on women's future alternatives: "Strategies which have only recently begun to direct girls into higher-paying, nontraditional fields will be lost on a generation of mothers who, lacking an education, may become dependent on public assistance for long periods of time. Far too many young women are narrowing their options in their teen years" (369). At the other extreme, this conception of the problem is openly rejected. There is, states the minority, "a fundamental disagreement among Committee Members as to what the real problem is. . . . This lack of definition manifests itself in a general failure to distinguish between married and unmarried teens and in a far greater emphasis on birth rates than on pregnancy rates" (375).

From the minority's perspective, it is the present moral status of the young woman who becomes pregnant, not the impact of the pregnancy on her future options that is at issue: Among other things, a definition of the teenage pregnancy problem centered on its consequences too obviously raises the question of whether or not those consequences are avoidable. Individuals are unlikely to define *problems* in terms that invite *solutions* they find unacceptable. Abortion to prevent birth and birth control to prevent pregnancy are logical but, to the minority, unacceptable means by which young women may avert the consequences of their sexual activity. Consequently, they prefer to define the problem not as the *consequences* of sexual activity but as sexual activity itself: "Very little effort has been made to prevent teens from becoming sexually active. . . . And this increase in sexual activity has led to a proportionate increase in pregnancies to unmarried teens" (378).

In its "Additional Views" the committee majority argues for according programmatic priority to pregnancy prevention; by prevention, the context makes clear, the majority means contraception. Particular emphasis is placed on school-based clinics "that have already shown enormous potential."[1] This approach is characterized by the minority as leading "further from the family, towards schools as the provider of guidance" as contrasted with the "family path," which "leads back to the family and acknowledgement of parental responsibility" (379). School-based clinics are equated with replacement of "real guidance with medical technology" as the solution to teenage pregnancy: "Progressively over the past 25 years we have, as a nation, decided that it is easier to give children pills than to teach them respect for sex and marriage" (386). Given these fundamentally conflicting ideologies (and, at least as much to the point, the political realities they represent) it is hardly surprising that the committee was unable to come up with the "guidance" that, according to the two members cited earlier, "should be the role of a Congressional Oversight Committee" (370).

Underlying the committee's debate are, in the first place, a set of familiar ideological conflicts: conflicts over the normative status of adolescent female sexuality; over the meaning of sexual unorthodoxy—as a product of personal or social pathology requiring compassionate treatment to avert its largely unintended consequences, or of willful immorality for which the consequences are well deserved; and over the location of responsibility for sexual social control in individuals, families, professional experts, or the state. A less familiar aspect of the current debate is the unprecedented degree of uncertainty it reflects over the futures for which young women are being prepared. Past strategies for the management of young women between puberty and marriage were (whatever the young woman's present moral status) almost invariably based on the assumption of an exclusively domestic future. That assumption as a basis for public policy is currently under attack not only because it is inconsistent with the reality of many women's lives, but because it is equally unacceptable (for very different reasons) to individuals with otherwise highly conflicting positions on the "moral" dimension of adolescent pregnancy. Having agreed to disagree on the latter question, policy makers have found common ground on the former, predicating their management strategies on a future for young women of economic rather than domestic bliss.

Conceptions of the adolescent pregnancy "problem" have, as I have suggested, distinctive programmatic implications. These implications, their translation into specific strategies of intervention, and the controversies these interventions have generated are described in the following section. I will then examine in greater detail, first, the changed assumptions about young women's lives on which intervention proposals are currently based; and second, the processes by which young women with different social and ethnic characteristics are selected into different intervention strategies. Finally, I will consider the causal models of adolescent pregnancy that underlie most contemporary management strategies.

CONTEMPORARY MANAGEMENT STRATEGIES:
A SELECTIVE REVIEW
Programmatic efforts to address the "problem" of adolescent pregnancy have become a minor industry in the United States. A 1985 survey for the National

Governor's Association identified nine states with "coordinated initiatives" (leadership or strong support from the governor and/or state legislature; broad agency and community involvement; comprehensive service provision), an additional thirteen states with formally established task forces on adolescent pregnancy (most of which had been recently formed or had recently issued reports), and nineteen states where a single agency (usually either health or education) had implemented specific policies focused on "at-risk, pregnant, and parenting" teens (Kimmich, 1985). Only ten states were described as lacking a "systematic focus on the adolescent pregnancy problem." At the federal level, the Office of Adolescent Pregnancy Programs currently funds eighty-five "Adolescent Family Life Demonstration Projects." Forty-eight of these projects provide "comprehensive services to pregnant adolescents, adolescent parents and their families"; twenty-eight provide "services to promote abstinence from adolescent premarital sexual relations"; and nine combine both care and "preventive" services (U.S. Office of Population Affairs, 1987).

These efforts share certain premises in common: adolescent pregnancy—almost by definition—is a problem primarily of women, not men;[2] there is a sexually and reproductively orthodox path that young women are expected to follow; departures from that path tend to be treated as individual-level problems (the "choices" of willful, misguided, or improperly socialized young women) rather than as products of social structural constraints or as signals of larger social change; negative outcomes associated with adolescent childbearing are attributed directly to early and/or nonmarital parenthood rather than to the circumstances in which parenthood takes place or (even less) to the absence of societal supports for unconventional childbearing schedules or for alternative patterns of transition from girlhood to womanhood. Beyond these shared premises, agreement among program advocates ends. The questions under debate—whether young women's departures from the path of sexual orthodoxy are to be designated as a moral problem, a problem in preventive medicine and public health, or a problem in welfare economics—are essentially political; they revolve around the allocation of power in the arena of social policy. How they are answered determines in whose turf the adolescent pregnancy problem will lie—who will be the "official" agents of social control for this particular form of deviant behavior. It is with respect to these questions of deviance designation and social control responsibility that struggles in the adolescent pregnancy arena are most intense.[3]

Contemporary policy and programmatic literature divides strategies for the management of adolescent pregnancy and parenthood into the two categories of prevention and amelioration (Moore and Wertheimer, 1984; Hofferth, 1987a). Prevention is currently used to include both prevention of sexual activity (i.e., through "abstinence education") and prevention of pregnancy among the sexually active (through contraceptive use). Amelioration refers to health and social programs designed for "pregnant and parenting" teenage women who plan to keep their babies, to adoption, and (more recently) to government-funded welfare programs (principally, Aid to Families with

Dependent Children). For reasons that have more to do with ideology and politics than with logic, abortion (the management strategy chosen by close to half of pregnant teenage women) is categorized sometimes as prevention, sometimes as amelioration, and sometimes as part of the problem. Numerous books and articles reviewing the content and outcomes of these programs and policies have appeared in recent years (Moore, 1981; Zellman, 1981; Stuart and Wells, 1982; McAnarney, 1983; Burt et al., 1984; Weatherley et al., 1985; Hofferth, 1987a; Vinovskis, 1988; Trussell, 1988). I do not propose to duplicate these reviews but, rather, to examine the underlying constructions of the adolescent pregnancy problem on which major programmatic efforts directed toward its solution are based.

At least three identifiable constructions are presently in competition for command of the adolescent pregnancy turf: the public health–preventive medicine construction; the moral construction; and the economic or "neo-Moynihan" construction. These constructions were initially described in Chapters 3 and 4 in the context of my account of the emergence and transformation of adolescent pregnancy as a public problem. They represent, of course, abstractions from a much more complex reality. Depending on the larger political climate as well as on the particular occasion, adherents of one construction readily borrow from the rhetoric of another: moral constructionists would like adolescents to be told that premarital sexual activity is dangerous to their health; public health–preventive medicine constructionists are quite prepared to advocate birth control on the grounds of keeping young women off the welfare rolls. There is, nevertheless, a fundamental conflict between the formers' rejection of sexual activity outside of what are defined as the morally correct circumstances and the "scientific management" approach to the same behavior adopted by the latter. This unresolved conflict—as well as the relative power of both moral and economic constructionists in the United States at the present time—is directly reflected in the content and objectives of contemporary adolescent pregnancy programs.

In 1984, the National Academy of Sciences established a panel on adolescent pregnancy and childbearing, chaired by a dean of the Harvard Medical School. In addition to medicine, the disciplines represented included public health, sociology, psychology, economics, law, and history. Most panel members were recognized experts in the field of adolescent pregnancy; several had been directly involved (as birth control advocates) in the initial construction of adolescent pregnancy as a public problem. The panel's final report was released late in 1986; its recommendations were unequivocal.

> The primary goal of policy makers, professionals, parents, and teenagers themselves should be a reduction in the rate and incidence of unintended pregnancies among adolescents. . . . [Furthermore] the panel believes that the major strategy for reducing early unintended pregnancy must be the encouragement of *diligent contraceptive use* by all sexually active teenagers. . . . The panel concludes that *the contraceptive pill* is the safest and most effective means of birth control for sexually active adolescents (Hayes, 1987:6–8; emphases added).

In keeping with its heavy emphasis on contraceptive *access,* the panel specifi-cally endorsed "comprehensive school-based clinic models" for the provision of contraceptive services to adolescents. It went on to recommend that abor-tion should be available to adolescent women without mandatory parental consent and under conditions that preserve "dignity, confidentiality, kindness, and excellence of health care" for young women who choose to terminate a pregnancy.

There is ample evidence (recently reviewed by Hofferth, 1987a) that contraception is the most efficient means of preventing teenage pregnancy; and abortion is an efficient means of preventing birth, once a pregnancy has occurred. Local availability of family planning and abortion-clinic services are associated with lower rates of adolescent childbearing. Hard evidence for the effectiveness of other approaches to prevention of either first or higher order adolescent births is relatively weak (Hofferth, 1987a; Vinovskis, 1988; Weather-ley et al., 1985; Perlman, 1984). From the perspective of moral conservatives, however, adolescent pregnancy is a problem not of unintended pregnancy but of precocious sexual activity. Contraception and abortion strategies—however effective—are regarded as, at best, irrelevant and, at worst, as contributing to the problem they are intended to solve.[4] Particularly offensive are policies that would introduce into the public school—traditionally regarded as guardian and protector as well as shaper of moral character—not only sex education— of which more below—but birth control prescriptions as well.

The National Academy of Sciences report is but the latest in a long history of attempts to define female sexual unorthodoxy as a public health problem and to place it under medical control. In particular, it represented a major effort to regain for birth control advocates the authority over the adolescent pregnancy turf that had been seriously eroded during the years of Reagan conservatism. The long-term success of that effort remains to be seen. How-ever, much as the moral reformers of the late nineteenth-century opposed the medical regulation of prostitution, so contemporary moral conservatives op-pose the medical management of adolescent pregnancy and childbearing: The immediate reaction of federal officials to the Academy report was decidedly negative. Reagan's secretary of education, William Bennett, remarked that "it was not the first time a prestigious sounding group has advocated a dumb policy."

There is, however, a considerable difference between what a socially con-servative government's spokespersons are prepared to acknowledge and advo-cate as public policy and what that government is actually doing as reflected in how federal dollars are being spent. The major Reagan administration ini-tiative in the area of adolescent pregnancy, known colloquially as the Chastity Bill, created the Adolescent Family Life Demonstration Projects, programs to encourage sexual abstinence or to provide comprehensive care for pregnant adolescents (contraception for the young woman who was neither pregnant nor abstinent was specifically excluded). The total budget for these projects in 1983 was $10,251,106 (Office of Adolescent Pregnancy Programs, personal communication); since then this figure has fluctuated up and down within a very small range. By contrast, the federal expenditure for contraceptive services in 1983 under Title X alone was $117,112,000 (Gold and Nestor, 1985).[5] About one-third of family planning clinic clients are adolescent women; however, even when this latter figure is reduced proportionately, the government was spending a minimum of four times the amount of money on contraception for adolescents as it was on the more conservative programs the administration advocated publicly.[6] This apparent contradiction (which has not altered under the Bush administration) reflects both the influence of Congress on federal spending and, in recent years, the care taken by birth control advocates regarding where, how, and to whom they make their case.

The currently problematic character of a contraception/abortion strategy as the solution for adolescent pregnancy is clearly reflected in recent programmatic literature. At a news conference announcing a new "adolescent pregnancy initiative," New York State officials described it as marking "a basic shift in dealing with teenage pregnancy." "The emphasis . . . has largely been on birth-control information and devices or counseling women on alternatives after they become pregnant. [The new initiative is] 'a preventive type of program where you won't even be talking about that' " (*New York Times*, April 6, 1984 II, 2:1). Until very recently it was possible to assume that "prevention" of adolescent pregnancy *meant* contraception. In a shift that reflects not only the underlying struggle for ownership of this issue, but also the increased power of more conservative constructions, this meaning is blurred in recent policy documents: Prevention is now used to mean prevention of sexual activity as well as of pregnancy (U.S. Cong., House, Select Committee on Children, Youth, and Families, 1986; New York Governor's Task Force on Adolescent Pregnancy, 1987). In her report to the National Governor's Association on state-level adolescent pregnancy programs, Madeleine Kimmich described family planning (i.e., birth control) as a "traditional" solution to adolescent pregnancy; the "new" solution (according to the report) is comprehensive services. Clearly, rhetorical shifts in the meaning of prevention as well as statements of what is "old" and what is "new" are intended to advance particular programmatic claims, not to be accurate representations of reality.

Under the rubric of preventive medicine–public health are included two (historically, but not necessarily) competing approaches to the "scientific management" of adolescent pregnancy: the preventive approach, encompassing contraception and induced abortion; and the ameliorative approach ("comprehensive services"), originating in the 1960s medical discovery of pregnant adolescents as a high-risk obstetrical population. The majority of physicians and policy makers have been more comfortable with the latter than with the former. Nonmarital sexuality unsoftened by the prospect of motherhood has historically been met with condemnation and even punishment rather than with protection or treatment. Strategies aimed at ameliorating the *consequences* of sexual unorthodoxy have been easier to defend as services to mothers and innocent babies that are designed to avert future more serious, and largely nonsexual, problems—problems for which the victims themselves could be portrayed as not immediately responsible (for examples of this rhetoric in a contemporary context, see Zellman, 1981; Weatherley et al., 1985). Furthermore, from the physician's perspective, soon-to-be-delivered teenage women represented an identifiable and, hence, far more manageable medical problem than their elusive sisters who were merely "sexually active."

When, in 1978, the federal government first gave official recognition to "adolescent pregnancy" as a public problem about which something should be done, "throwing comprehensive services at pregnant teenagers," as opposed to prevention of the pregnancy or its termination, was, as I have indicated earlier, the only "something" on which policy makers could agree (Steiner, 1981:78–79). "Comprehensive services"—medical, social, and educational services for those unmarried pregnant girls who choose to keep their babies and, to a lesser extent, for new mothers—have continued to be the least controversial response to the problem of adolescent pregnancy and parenting. The basic elements of the comprehensive services model were already present in the programs for pregnant school girls developed in the 1960s under medical auspices. Indeed, in its emphasis on services such as counseling and "relevant" learning (budgeting, child development), this model had many parallels with the traditional maternity home.[7] However, its underlying rationale was medical rather than moral or psychiatric. Pregnancy and motherhood were represented as "diseases to be contained and cured," demanding the intervention of medical experts, rather than as evidence of moral or mental deficiency. Domestic training, the classic strategy for reform of "wayward" girls, was justified in the interests of maternal and child health rather than as a means of spiritual transformation.

In part this shift merely exemplified the twentieth-century ascendancy of medical over moral or legal paradigms of social control. Defining teenage "pregnancy and parenthood" as medical problems legitimized the humanitarian treatment of young women who, unlike the maternity-home residents of a previous era, failed to acknowledge their wrongdoing by decently concealing it. However, not only did the medical imprimatur effectively defuse controversy; the relative decline in birth rates of older women gave health agencies and medical professionals an institutional incentive to serve this population that other agencies (e.g., public schools and local governments) notably lacked.

With one exception—the disappearance of abortion counseling—the *content* of "comprehensive service" programs has changed very little since the mid-1970s. However, in striking illustration of the preventive medicine–public health construction's recent eclipse and the ascendancy of the neo-Moynihan construction, "economic self-sufficiency" has begun to displace "health of mothers and babies" as the principal *rationale* for the comprehensive services model. Project Redirection, a demonstration program funded by both government and private foundation sources, offers a clear example of this shift in emphasis. After detailing the negative economic consequences of teenage parenthood and noting that these consequences "have attracted particular concern in this era of fiscal restraint because the economic burden is borne by the public as well as by the teens themselves," the project's final report goes on to state that its "overall goal . . . is to redirect the lives of young mothers and mothers-to-be onto a path of long-term economic self-sufficiency" (Polit, Kahn, and Stevens, 1985:2–3). In keeping with this aim, Project Redirection placed substantially more *emphasis* on educational and employment-related services than had earlier comprehensive programs. Nevertheless, the services that young women were most likely to *receive* through Project Redirection were, as in earlier programs, health related: medical care for themselves and their babies and birth control counseling (Polit, Kahn, and Stevens, 1985:59). This disparity suggests the continuing importance of the difference, referred to in the preceding paragraph, between health-related and other agencies in *institutional* incentives to provide special services for teenage women.

Individual comprehensive services programs have contributed to the positive pregnancy outcomes of individual young women. The recently published, five-year follow-up of Project Redirection participants demonstrates positive project impacts on young women's employment, on their parenting skills, and on their child's cognitive development (but not on education or subsequent childbearing) (Polit, Quint, and Riccio, 1988). Overall, however, there is little evidence that even the most carefully designed of these programs have more than limited and short-term effects on young women's sexual, reproductive, or economic futures (Weatherley et al., 1985; Hofferth, 1987a; Vinovskis, 1988). Based on a detailed study of comprehensive programs located in ten communities across four states, Richard A. Weatherley and his colleagues conclude as follows:

> As public policy, the comprehensive services model is perhaps better suited to political compromise and symbolism than effective problem solving. The model is based on faulty assumptions: that the appropriate services exist and need only be administratively linked together; that localities have the capability and resources to mount such programs with minimal state and federal assistance; and that the problematic aspects of adolescent pregnancy and parenthood are best addressed through services. *A national policy that seeks to address the problems associated with unintended adolescent pregnancies by encouraging the development of some or even many such comprehensive programs will necessarily have limited effect* (1985:259).

The continued popularity of comprehensive services programs does not depend on their effectiveness, however—indeed, they are rarely evaluated—but on their correspondence to a long-standing cultural preference for the rescue of girls who have "fallen" over preventive measures likely to be portrayed as the condoning of sin. In terms of the models I outlined earlier, these programs are public health–preventive medicine's compromise with the moral construction of adolescent pregnancy.

The competition between birth control and comprehensive services advocates is, in large measure, a competition among professionals for local, state, and federal health-program resources. The balance of power between adherents of these two approaches has been profoundly affected by the legitimacy currently accorded to moral and economic constructionists; nevertheless, theirs is a relatively polite, largely intraprofessional conflict. There are other battlegrounds, however, where preventive medicine–public health and moral constructionists confront one another more directly, and where the terms of battle have proved far less amenable to control in professional terms. Among the most important of these battlegrounds are public schools. Schools have recently emerged as the favored venue for a whole range of adolescent pregnancy related programs; at least one of these programs, however, has been the focus of intense debate since the beginning of this century.

As a strategy for the management of adolescent sexuality, sex education has a history almost as venerable as (although far more controversial than) that of the maternity home. In one form or another, it has been taught in at least *some* public schools since the early 1920s (Usilton and Edson, 1929). However, sex education with the specific goal of preventing adolescent pregnancies has come into vogue only relatively recently, corresponding both with the emergence of adolescent pregnancy as a public problem and with a substantially increased level of public controversy surrounding *what* should be taught, *where* it should be taught, and *who* should teach it (Hottois and Milner, 1975; Scales, 1980, 1981, 1986; Richardson and Cranston, 1981; Dunn, 1982; Muraskin, 1986; Bennett, 1987; MacDonald, 1987).

What is currently being taught in American public schools under the "sex education" (or, more delicately, "family life education") label is difficult to evaluate. Recent curriculum surveys vary rather markedly in their results depending on the population surveyed (school principals, other school personnel, students) and on how sex education is defined. Based on a 1977 national survey of high school *principals,* Margaret Terry Orr (1982) reports that 36 percent of U.S. public high schools offered a sex education course (compared with a 1922 figure of 47 percent, cited by Allan M. Brandt, 1985:30). In 1982, Freya L. Sonenstein and Karen J. Pittman (1984) conducted a survey of "the appropriate" respondents in each of 179 school districts in cities over 100,000. They report that sex education, "in some form" is provided by 80 percent of these districts. However, only 25 percent are judged to offer "in-depth" discussion of contraception and in only 11 percent is the topic introduced before the ninth grade. Finally, based on a 1984 national survey of young adults, William Marsiglio and Frank L. Mott report that "sixty percent of women and 52 percent of men now in their 20s took a sex education course by age 19" (1986:151). Forty-nine percent of women and 47 percent of men reported learning about types of contraception; 38 percent of both groups said they learned where contraception could be obtained. These results should not be surprising. Fear of controversy, combined with the traditional autonomy of local school districts, virtually guarantees an absence of consistency in whether and how "sex education" will be taught in American public schools.

Sex education in the United States may always have been controversial, but the contours of the debate surrounding it have changed substantially over time. In the early twentieth century the central point at issue was whether traditional moral values were best preserved by keeping children and young adults in ignorance of sexual matters as long as possible (preferably until marriage) or by a repressive sex education leading (according to its proponents) to sexual impulse control through fear of disease and/or "ruin." The latter was the position advocated by that era's counterparts of the public health experts of today.[8] By the late 1960s, when sex education again became a controversial public issue, the "expert" position was no longer predicated on the *repression* of sexual impulses but on their *management* based on factual information (including contraceptive information) and on training in "responsible" sexual decision making (meaning, among other things, contraceptive use if pregnancy was not intended). As a consequence, advocates of formal sex education in the schools became identified not only as a threat to parental authority (as they had been in the past), but as a threat to traditional moral values as well. From the perspective of sex education's opponents, "outside" professional experts were the very personification of these threats (National Education Association, 1975). In the most recent permutation of the sex education debate, traditional morality has again assumed the mantle of public health, the central issue has become not so much the desirability of sex education as its content, and professional experts are ranged on both sides (e.g., Marks and Cates, 1986; MacDonald, 1987; Bennett, 1987).[9]

The new conservative prescription—"abstinence education"—is virtually identical to the position of turn-of-the-century Progressive physicians. The assumption—attributed to "well meaning health professionals"—that teenage sex is inevitable is rejected. As in the early twentieth century, sexual control is to be accomplished largely through fear of its negative consequences. Sexual activity prior to marriage is to be presented to adolescents in much the same terms as drugs or alcohol (the analogy is often made) as dangerous to their present and future mental, physical, social, and economic health. This approach has acquired considerable recent legitimacy even among traditional opponents of sex education. Formal curricula presenting the "abstinence" message in the context of public health have been developed (e.g., the "Sex Respect" curriculum developed by Coleen Mast under a federal government grant); several states have enacted or are considering legislation requiring that sex education courses emphasize premarital abstinence (Alan Guttmacher Institute, 1988); abstinence education has been endorsed by public health and educational spokespersons for the federal government (Bennett, 1987; Bennett and Koop, 1987). The new legitimacy of chastity as a medical prescription can largely be explained by the impact of the AIDS epidemic on both public and professional consciousness: Departures from sexual orthodoxy now carry the ultimate threat of death (see, e.g., Brandt, 1987). In addition, however, the current public-policy emphasis on *individual* life-style modification as the principal means to disease prevention and health promotion has made it easier, I believe, for some health experts to analogize sex with drugs and alcohol as simply another personal "risk factor" that individuals are better off without.

Conflicts between moral and medical designations of deviant behavior and between the management strategies that these constructions imply are not unusual in recent history (Conrad and Schneider, 1980). Rarely, however, has a problem—once discovered—proved as resistant to capture by any single set of claims-makers, or as readily redefined to conform with current social and political realities, as has the problem of adolescent pregnancy. In the 1980s, both medical and moral constructions of this problem were eclipsed—in greater or less degree—by the neo-Moynihan construction: the designation of adolescent pregnancy as a problem of black teenage mothers on welfare. As exemplified by Project Redirection, the chief programmatic impact of this construction has been to redefine the objectives of adolescent pregnancy management strategies from pregnancy prevention and the health of mothers and babies to the production of economic self-sufficiency.[10] This shift incorporates some quite novel assumptions about the structure of young women's lives.

THE CONTESTED STRUCTURE
OF YOUNG WOMEN'S LIVES
The construction of adolescent pregnancy as a problem of teenage mothers on welfare has been the single most powerful force in shaping public-policy approaches to the management of sexually unorthodox young women in the 1980s. It is in the context of this construction, I will argue, that policy analysts have embraced a redefinition of female adolescence as preparation for the world of work outside, rather than inside, the home and have clothed their strategies for the management of adolescent pregnancy in the rhetoric of fiscal conservatism (e.g., Moore, Simms, and Betsey, 1986; Polit, Kahn, and Stevens, 1985; New York Governor's Task Force on Adolescent Pregnancy, 1986).

Strategies for the social control of female adolescents are predicated on a set of normative assumptions about the futures for which young women are being prepared. Until very recently, the dominant construction of this period was as a prelude to marriage and motherhood (although, as I have described in earlier chapters, the relative centrality in this construction of the future *maternal* as compared with the future *spousal* component underwent a considerable shift over time). Management strategies were designed to prepare young women for their domestic futures and to insure that their access to these futures was protected or (if necessary) restored. This construction has not disappeared (as evidenced by comments cited earlier from the more conservative members of the House Select Committee on Children, Youth, and Families). However, it is now in competition with a powerful alternative construction in which young women's futures, like men's, are defined in terms of occupational attainment and "economic self-sufficiency." Common to both scenarios are an essentially deterministic conception of young women's moral careers,[11] in which future prospects are regarded as preordained on the basis of present sexual or reproductive behavior, and an assumption of inherent conflict between women's traditional private-domestic roles and the nondomestic-public roles of student and wageworker. The difference is that in the new scenario it is young women's economic rather than marital prospects that their sexually unorthodox behavior places in jeopardy; education and wage work are no longer portrayed as, at best, temporary distractions along the path to traditional domesticity but as ends in themselves; untimely childbearing (and sometimes even marriage as well) have become the distractions.

With the emergence of adolescent pregnancy as a public problem in the 1970s came a major expansion of academic research on the social and economic, as well as the biomedical, consequences of early childbearing (recently reviewed in Hayes, 1987; Hofferth and Hayes, 1987). A substantial body of evidence has accumulated demonstrating that associations found between adolescent childbearing and infant mortality, as well as other negative pregnancy outcomes, are due to social processes of selection into early parenthood: Early childbearers are more likely to live in socially and economically deprived circumstances; it is these circumstances, not biological age, that account for the biomedical problems that have been associated with adolescent pregnancy and birth (Strobino, 1987; Geronimus, 1987). The dominant interpretation of parallel negative associations between early childbearing and educational/occupational attainment has been to attribute low levels of attainment among early childbearers directly to the facts of ill-timed pregnancy and birth (McLaughlin, 1977; Card and Wise, 1978; Moore et al., 1978; Haggstrom et al., 1986; Hofferth, 1987a). Recently, however, this interpretation has been challenged by a number of scholars. Studies have raised, first, the question of whether it is early childbearing or educational attainment that should be given causal priority in accounting for the relationship between these two variables and, second, the question of whether off-timed childbearing must, inevitably, be disruptive of future status attainment (Mott and Shaw, 1978; Rindfuss, Bumpass, and St. John, 1980; Rindfuss and St. John, 1983; Furstenberg, Brooks-Gunn, and Morgan, 1987; Rindfuss, Swicegood, and Rosenfeld, 1987; Upchurch and McCarthy, 1990).

Conflict between childbearing and attainment in the public worlds of school and work has been a consistent theme of writers about female adolescence since the latter part of the nineteenth century. However, the recent literature I have cited reflects a striking change in the direction of these writers' concern. Whereas turn-of-the-century scholars like Edward Clarke and G. Stanley Hall saw attainment in the public sphere (education, in particular) as interfering with young women's *reproductive* potential, in the work of many present-day scholars reproduction is interpreted as interfering with attainment. Underlying scholarly (as well as interventionist) rhetoric is a set of beliefs—made explicit in the use of phrases such as "off-time" events, "accelerated role transitions," "normative schedules"—as to the *correct* timing and sequencing of events in young women's transition from puberty to adulthood, a timing and sequencing pattern that young women disregard at their peril. A 1985 report by the New York Governor's Task Force on Adolescent Pregnancy leaves no doubt as to the correct pattern: "Teenage parenthood interrupts the normal [sic] transition to adulthood during which adolescents complete school, find jobs, and eventually establish their own families. As a result, adolescents who become pregnant are at risk of severe problems which may impede their opportunities to lead fulfilling adult lives" (n.p.).

"Normality" is defined not only in prudent, middle-class terms, but in terms of what was, until recently, the normatively approved child-to-adult transition pattern for *males*. Earlier in this century, sexual unorthodoxy was attributed by reformers to young women's insufficient attachment to *domestic* roles; in this, most recent, construction it is attributed to their imperfect attachment to the *nondomestic* roles of student and paid worker. If early childbearing inhibits young women's educational and occupational attainment, then, it is argued, educational and occupational attainment—expanding young women's "life options"—will prevent early childbearing (e.g., Dryfoos, 1984; Moore, Simms, and Betsey, 1986).[12] This hypothesis was embraced with enthusiasm by the New York Task Force: "Youth must be given hope for the future and realizable options and opportunities if they are not to become parents by default" (1986:33). Embedded in this statement are both of the normative presuppositions I identified above: the traditional assumption of inherent conflict between domestic and public roles; and a quite nontraditional assignment of priority in the management of women's adolescence to preparation for the *public* sphere.

There is a clear relationship, as Tracy Huling has pointed out, between this new application of equal-opportunity ideology and the longstanding position of liberal policy analysts that "young people with limited educational and employment opportunities will turn to less socially acceptable pursuits to create identities which afford them some control over and meaning in their lives" (1988:48). And since this new scenario is specifically focused on expanding the educational and employment opportunities of young *women* it is doubly appealing to feminist liberal policy analysts (and social scientists). However, I would argue that the adoption by action-oriented bodies (e.g., the New York Governor's Task Force) of the "life options" approach to adolescent pregnancy owes as much or more to its appeal, for very different reasons, to social and fiscal conservatives: expanding "life options" readily translates into a set of policies not only for preventing early childbearing but also for protecting the public purse. "A lack of education leads to a deficiency in vocational skills, hence employment opportunities, thus resulting in a greater risk of poverty and economic dependency. . . . Women who delay pregnancy until their twenties have an earning capacity which is twice as high as that of their teenage counterparts" (New York State Temporary Commission, 1983:17–18).

Among the most striking implications of management strategies generated by the construction of adolescent pregnancy and single parenthood as a welfare problem is the extent to which these strategies denigrate motherhood as a socially valued activity:

At the same time that federal welfare and labor policy denies the value of women as wageworkers, it also denies the value of the homemaking and childcare work that women have traditionally done. This denial is effectuated primarily through the wagework requirements which force AFDC mothers to seek work when their youngest child reaches the age of six. The government in effect conveys the message that homemaking and childcare are not important or socially desirable pursuits and will not be affirmatively fostered (Law, 1983:1318).

Recent federal welfare legislation has reduced the youngest child's *maximum* age (the point at which his or her mother must seek outside work as a condition of benefit receipt) to three.

These work requirements cannot, of course, be understood apart from the larger social climate in which they were enacted: the fact of vastly increased labor-force participation by women, including mothers of young children, and the reflection of this change in increasing ideological acceptance of working mothers (Thornton and Freedman, 1983; Bianchi and Spain, 1986). David T. Ellwood has pointed out, however, that single mothers can become self-supporting only if they work full time, and full year and, he argues, it is unreasonable to expect them to do so: fewer than one-fourth of *wives* with children under 6 are fully employed (1986). Based on computer simulations, Kristin A. Moore and Richard F. Wertheimer found that preventing high-school drop out would reduce the number of adolescent childbearers receiving welfare payments at age 20 to 24 by only 6 percent, primarily because of "the relatively low earnings of women—even when they are high school graduates" (1984:285). Social policies aimed at changing the work behavior of individuals are unlikely to have much effect on such structural sources of poverty as "the relatively low earnings of women."

Policy makers' verbal professions of support for traditional family values— in particular the value of mothers caring for their small children at home— clearly do not extend to financial support for the realization of these values among the poor. Increasingly, as Kathleen Gerson has pointed out, "traditional patterns of female domesticity are becoming . . . the luxury of the more affluent pockets of the middle class" (1985:217). The redefinition of female adolescence as a period of preparation for future economic self-sufficiency may be consistent with liberal feminist ideology, as well as (in a restricted sense) with current social reality. However, it is in the context of the American public's highly selective enthusiasm for childrearing as an occupation—enthusiasm that rapidly disappears when the rearer threatens to become a charge upon the state—that the popularity among *conservative* policy makers of a construction of female adolescence in traditionally masculine terms can most readily be understood.

SOCIAL LOCATION AND STRATEGIES OF CONTROL

A dimension of the adolescent pregnancy debate largely muted in official reports but with nonetheless profound consequences for the public and political acceptability of alternative "solutions" concerns the social location of the problem: *who* in society becomes, or rather is perceived to become pregnant and to give birth out of wedlock. Birth control advocates had been at pains to define adolescent pregnancy as a problem generic to the teenage years, not as a problem specific to low-income black adolescents; indeed, their emphasis on its universality played an important role in bringing the issue to public attention, as I have pointed out. By the mid-1980s, however, the notion that teenage pregnancy and parenthood were black problems had been so "deeply imprinted in the public mind" that the National Academy of Sciences report on adolescent pregnancy in the United States was described by the *Wall Street Journal* as a "study of sex and pregnancy among *black* teenagers" (cited in Furstenberg, 1987:382). Understanding of contemporary strategies for the management of adolescent pregnancy requires that the social location of this behavior—not only as it is but also as it is perceived—be taken into account.

I described recent changes in patterns of adolescent fertility in the United States in Chapter 2. Here I propose to reemphasize, and briefly elaborate, three points. First, delayed marriage combined with a much increased propensity toward sexual intercourse prior to marriage have in recent decades created a uniquely large pool of young women vulnerable to the experience of nonmarital pregnancy; second, these underlying behavioral changes have been more pronounced among whites than among blacks; third, persistent race and socioeconomic status differences in the *management* of nonmarital intercourse and its consequences have meant that, given sexual intercourse and pregnancy, the probability of nonmarital *childbearing* has continued to be substantially higher among young women who are poor and/or black than among other subgroups in the U.S. population. In 1985, 54 percent of all adolescent nonmarital births were to white young women, compared with 42 percent in 1970. However, the *proportion* of nonmarital relative to total births among black adolescents is still about twice the proportion among whites (in 1985, the figures were 90 percent and 45 percent). Furthermore (largely because the socioeconomic status *distribution* among blacks is highly skewed toward the lower end of the scale), a higher proportion of black as compared with white nonmarital births are to young women who are poor (Hofferth and Hayes, 1987:Table 6.12, p. 480).

Race and socioeconomic status differences in reproductive outcome result from selective processes that operate at each stage in the progression from nonmarital intercourse to nonmarital birth. Graphic evidence of these processes is presented in Table 8.1. The data presented in this table were calculated directly from original data collected by Melvin Zelnik and John F. Kantner (Zelnik and Kantner, 1980; Zelnik, Kantner, and Ford, 1981). Following the practice of these investigators, the index of socioeconomic status (SES) employed is an average of the education completed by individuals who "raised" the young woman (usually the biological parents or parent). The label "parents' education" rather than "raisers' education" is used in the table.

In Table 8.1, percentages of young women at each SES level who reported

TABLE 8.1

NONMARITAL INTERCOURSE, PREGNANCY, AND BIRTH BY SOCIOECONOMIC STATUS AND RACE, 1971 AND 1979

Parents' Education	1971			1979		
	Inter-course %	Preg-nancy %	Non-marital Birth %	Inter-course %	Preg-nancy %	Non-marital Birth %
WHITE						
Less than high school graduation	28.7	23.9	24.0	53.3	35.4	35.7
	(728)	(209)	(50)	(371)	(198)	(70)
High school graduation	25.7	26.1	10.0	42.8	30.4	29.3
	(448)	(115)	(30)	(315)	(135)	(41)
Some college or above	22.3	12.0	21.4	42.6	20.5	13.3
	(525)	(117)	(14)	(342)	(146)	(30)
BLACK						
Less than high school graduation	55.7	50.7	69.4	68.5	54.8	62.2
	(601)	(335)	(170)	(359)	(246)	(135)
High school graduation	48.9	36.6	50.0	66.5	34.1	63.6
	(190)	(93)	(34)	(194)	(129)	(44)
Some college or above	40.7	27.3	66.7	62.4	31.5	56.5
	(135)	(55)	(15)	(117)	(73)	(23)

Source: Calculated directly from data collected in 1971 and 1979 National Surveys of Young Women. For a complete description of survey methodology, see Zelnik and Kantner (1980) and Zelnik, Kantner, and Ford (1981).

Note: Numbers in parentheses are the N's on which each percentage is based. Thus, looking at the first row of figures, in the 1971 sample there were 728 young women who were white and whose mothers had not graduated from high school. Of these 728, 28.7 percent (or 209) had sexual intercourse and were, therefore, at risk of pregnancy. Fifty (or 23.9 percent of the 209) became pregnant and, of those 50 who became pregnant, 24 percent went on to have a nonmarital birth. The remaining calculations were carried out in an identical fashion.

having had sexual intercourse, having been pregnant (given intercourse), and having had a nonmarital birth (given pregnancy) are shown by race for the years 1971 and 1979. Within each race and time period, variation by SES in the probability of nonmarital intercourse is relatively small; however, lower SES is uniformly associated with a higher probability of pregnancy. Effects of SES on the likelihood of a nonmarital live birth are less consistent and are overwhelmed at all SES levels and in both time periods by the effects of race. Irrespective of their socioeconomic status, black young women were far more likely than white young women to resolve a nonmarital pregnancy with a nonmarital birth.

Underlying the variations in reproductive outcome shown in Table 8.1

are marked differences in management strategies: higher SES young women are more likely to use contraception, particularly at first intercourse (Hogan et al., 1985; Mosher and Bachrach, 1987); and they are more likely to resolve a nonmarital pregnancy by abortion (Powell-Griner and Trent, 1987) or by marriage before the birth of the child. Similarly, white young women are more likely than black young women to use contraception (although the size of this difference varies across studies and depends on how contraceptive use is measured); unmarried white young women who become pregnant are more likely than unmarried black young women to obtain an abortion, and white young women are much more likely to marry before giving birth.[13]

The reasons for persistent race and socioeconomic status differences in reproductive management are matters of debate; the question is as much political as it is scientific. However, the outcome of these differences is clear. The particular sexual and reproductive management strategies young women select (or are selected into) vary with their social location and the social and economic power at their command. Although recent changes in sexual behavior and patterns of family formation have been most marked among young women who are white, these young women are least likely to employ strategies of reproductive management that bring their behavior to public attention, particularly if they are from families relatively high in socioeconomic status. The clients of strategies that select on the basis of *visible* sexual unorthodoxy— nonmarital pregnancy (in its later stages) and nonmarital childbearing—are predominantly poor and of minority status. This was true of the earliest school- and hospital-based programs for single pregnant young women and new mothers developed in the 1960s and early 1970s[14] and, despite the marked changes in patterns of reproductive management that I have described, it is true in the 1980s. In the period from 1982 to 1983, 48 percent of the clients entering the twenty-eight comprehensive services projects funded by the federal Office of Adolescent Pregnancy Programs were black, 8 percent were from other minorities; close to half received some form of welfare assistance (Burt et al., 1984). Project Redirection, the major innovative comprehensive program of the 1980s, was even more selective: 91 percent of its clients were black or Hispanic; all, by design, were from low-income households (Polit et al., 1985).[15] This is, of course, a self-reinforcing process: the selection of poor and minority young women into formal programs for pregnant adolescents further contributes to perceptions of the public and policy makers that the problem of adolescent pregnancy *is* a problem of poor and minority adolescents.

How this selection process operates in practice has been vividly described by Gail L. Zellman (1981) and, more recently, by Richard A. Weatherley and his colleagues (Weatherley et al., 1985; Perlman, 1984). In response to Title IX of the 1972 Education Amendments prohibiting schools from barring pregnant and parenting students, many school districts established separate educational programs, away from regular school sites.

> In several cases, the special program site had been a minority school, before it had been reassigned to the pregnancy program; the "minority" label stuck, and few

nonminority students would enroll. In one Local Education Authority (LEA), the racial stereotype of the program is so strong that LEA staff actually have different informal policies for minority and nonminority students who become pregnant. Minority students from anywhere in the LEA are expected to transfer to the program; nonminority high school students are expected to drop out of school, while nonminority junior high school students are encouraged to get physician approval to remain out of school until after delivery (Zellman, 1981:30).

Based on their systematic observations of a range of program efforts, these scholars agree (in the words of Weatherley et al.) that "a powerful stigma is attached by many to adolescent sexuality, pregnancy, and parenthood. *This stigma extends to services designed to prevent pregnancy or to assist teenage parents and their children*" (1985:213–14; emphasis added). The latter stigma in particular has multiple consequences, all of which reinforce the selective processes I have described. First, families with sufficient resources will be highly motivated to select their daughters *out of* stigmatized services (and, indeed, are encouraged to do so, as Zellman's account demonstrates). Second, school and other administrators sensitive to community feelings are motivated to reduce the visibility of *programs* (as well as individual pregnant students) by locating them where they will be invisible to dominant groups in the community, often in minority neighborhoods (see, e.g., Zellman, 1981:7; Weatherley et al., 1985:214; Nash and Dunkle, 1989). Finally, historical evidence as well as the more recent work I have cited indicate that formal preventive and ameliorative medical and social-service programs *predicated on* prior sexual unorthodoxy are relatively more acceptable to the community at large when they are directed at poor and minority young women (for recent evidence, see Weatherley et al., 1985:220).[16] Women with these status characteristics carry a stigma that overrides their sexual unorthodoxy; they are already outside the social pale. Providing adolescent women who are poor and black with humanitarian assistance not only does not establish or legitimize new sexual norms; it calls attention to and reinforces the traditional sexual values of the dominant community.

MODELS OF CAUSE AND CURE
"White slavery" and "prostitution" were employed in the early twentieth century as generic labels to identify and call public attention to the sexually unorthodox behavior of single young women; much the same purpose is served in contemporary American society by the label "adolescent pregnancy." The negative consequences of adolescent pregnancy described in policy and programmatic literature are, literally, consequences of parenthood, not of pregnancy. Adolescent pregnancy has become a generic term for the sexual unorthodoxy of young women, not just because the ideological and political inadmissability of abortion dictates that—at least in public discourse— the consequences of pregnancy and childbirth shall be indistinguishable, but also because the pregnant young woman carries, so to speak, her unorthodoxy on her sleeve. She visibly symbolizes the breakdown of both moral and

medical forms of social control. Corresponding to the different constructions of the adolescent pregnancy problem I have described are equally different conceptions of *why* this breakdown has occurred.

The causal models of adolescent pregnancy espoused by contemporary policy makers and program advocates may be divided into three categories: (1) adolescent pregnancy is the outcome of social, political, and health-care system barriers limiting teenagers' access to contraception and abortion services; (2) adolescent pregnancy is the outcome of the state's legitimation of sexual permissiveness (through its subsidization of family planning services), and/or its legitimation of welfare dependency (through its subsidization of single parenthood); (3) adolescent pregnancy is the outcome of deep-rooted cultural-motivational forces (frequently identified with poverty and minority group status). The first and second of these models are emphasized by preventive medicine–public health and moral/economic constructionists, respectively; however, cultural-motivational forces are invoked by all parties to the adolescent pregnancy debate—by medical model adherents to account for adolescents' failure to make what they define as appropriate use of *available* reproductive health-care services; by moral/economic conservatives to argue that these same services are not only counterproductive (because they legitimate sexual activity) but irrelevant to the fundamental causes of adolescent pregnancy. A recent publication of the federal Office of Adolescent Pregnancy Programs (a bastion of moral conservatism) put the latter argument succinctly: "The roots of the problem of adolescent pregnancy are deeply embedded in social, cultural, and religious norms and in family structure and functioning. Increasingly, there is a recognition that *mere provision of more sex education and easier access to contraception* is not a sufficient solution" (U.S. Office of Population Affairs, 1986; emphasis added).

In the late 1960s, birth control advocates mounted a powerful attack on what they termed the "culture of poverty" approach to unwanted pregnancy, describing it as "the New Cop-Out" (Jaffe and Polgar, 1968). In today's very different political climate, this same approach has been adopted by some of the strongest birth control advocates. Over half of a recent book by Moore, Simms, and Betsey on "racial differences in adolescent sexuality and fertility," is focused on cultural-motivational differences in aspirations, opportunities, and family structures between black and white young *women,* hypothesizing that fundamental deficits in these characteristics among black women are the "cause" of their unorthodox sexual behavior (including early sexual activity *and* nonuse of contraception) (1986). Despite its *programmatic* emphasis on contraceptive and abortion services, a very similar behavioral model underlies much of the National Academy of Sciences report on teenage pregnancy: adolescent pregnancy and childbearing are conceptualized as pathological (and pathogenic) conditions with identifiable causes and cures. Although the report includes frequent references to social and cultural variation, the dominant causal framework (not only of the report but, it must be said in fairness, of most of the literature it reviews) is psychological. Teenage women's sexuality and reproduction are described in voluntaristic terms, as "choices," whose origins lie within the deviant individual, rather than in economic and social structures that differentially reward and support more or less conventional transitions to female adulthood. Ironically, the passing of the nineteenth-century ideology of the innocent girl combined with medicalization of the means of protection have made it increasingly difficult for even the most humanitarian of contemporary middle-class reformers to define the sexually unorthodox girl who gets "caught" by a pregnancy as other than personally responsible for her fate. No longer the innocent victim of an evil man, or even the unconscious victim of her own neuroses, she is, at best, the victim of faulty socialization that failed to train her for sexually "responsible" decision making (i.e., decision making in accord with middle-class values). Thus, at the same time that young women in the United States continue to be denied the conditions for a truly autonomous sexuality, they are increasingly likely to be held responsible for failures to act autonomously.

Causal models of sexually unorthodox behavior are powerfully affected by the social location attributed to its perpetrators. Insofar as departures from traditional sexual morality have been linked with "outsiders"—immigrants, slumdwellers, minorities, and the poor—responsibility for these departures has been attributed to characteristics seen as peculiar to the occupants of these marginal social categories. In modern parlance, these are "culture of poverty" theories—arguing that "the poor have different values, aspirations and psychological characteristics than the rest of us," and that it is the social and psychological deficits inherent in these differences that are responsible for early pregnancy and childbearing (Huling, 1988:50). Within this causal framework, nonmarital pregnancy, and allied forms of sexual unorthodoxy, are interpreted as pathological conditions of women (rather than, for example, as the outcome of unplanned and, hence, unprotected intercourse by two normal persons of the opposite sex). As the perceived social location of sexual unorthodoxy has shifted over time, theories of its origin in a pathogenic social and/or cultural environment have been periodically rediscovered; they had a substantial vogue in the early part of this century and again in the 1950s and 1960s. The examples cited earlier reflect their most recent revival as the conceptual basis for contemporary strategies aimed at managing adolescent pregnancy by altering the values and aspirations of young women who are poor to correspond more closely with those of the middle class.[17]

There is a striking resemblance between the perspectives of contemporary "adolescent pregnancy" reformers and those of their forerunners in the late nineteenth-century movement for social purity. The former, like the latter, are largely middle-class and predominantly women (Weatherley et al., 1985). Describing the basis for social-purity reformers' approach to what they defined as the problem of "juvenile prostitution," Deborah Gorham remarks: "Whereas their own daughters were—in theory, at any rate—both protected and controlled, in the eyes of the reformers poor girls of the same age experienced neither the benefits of protection nor the constrictions of control. The perceived independence of girls of the 'outcast' class was particularly upsetting to middle-class observers" (1978:374). The assumption of adult sexual and reproductive roles by young women socially defined in contemporary American society as "children" has continued to profoundly upset middle-class reformers and politicians. The means by which middle-class girls are "protected" from disruption of an increasingly prolonged period of adolescent semidependence have, of course, markedly changed, from carefully guarded "innocence" to birth control pills and, if necessary, abortion. Lower-class girls are far more likely to experience "disruption," in part because they lack access to middle-class resources for reproductive control, but also because the "conditions conducive to adolescence"—conceived as an extended period of preparation for adulthood—are unevenly divided not only by class (as Gillis pointed out in his study of adolescence in Western Europe) but also by race and gender (Gillis, 1981:134; see also Geronimus, 1987; Burton, 1990).

Virtually all contemporary strategies for sexual and reproductive control share two assumptions: first, that there is a single "correct" path for women from puberty to adulthood; and, second, that the sources of departures from that path—of behavior that deviates from sexual and reproductive orthodoxy (however orthodoxy may be defined)—lie within the individual, in personal failures of moral, medical, or social control. In keeping with this model, the most popular solutions—whatever may be their specific terms—have been couched at the level of individual behavioral control or change. Lorraine V. Klerman and James F. Jekel introduced their study of programs for "school-age mothers" conducted between 1967 and 1973 by outlining several institutional-level strategies for the management of adolescent childbearing, including "the alleviation of poverty and the provision of institutional supports for alternative life-styles." They went on to comment that "none of these seems fully acceptable at this time. . . . The most prevalent strategy in contemporary American society is to provide services to the pregnant girl in such a way as to minimize the deviant aspects of her situation" (1973:8). Ten years later, these authors repeated the same point coupled with the same sense of resignation to the dictates of American society (Klerman, Jekel, and Chilman, 1983:180). This position was recently restated by Weatherley and his colleagues in forceful terms: "Services are designed to change and control individual behavior; the social conditions that underlie such behavior and its consequences are largely ignored. The problem is defined as residing within the individual, in this instance, the 'bad girl'" (1985:259). To date, these expressions by recognized social welfare experts of fundamental disagreement with the social control paradigm on which current adolescent pregnancy programs are based have had no noticeable effect on public policy.

THE LIMITS OF PROFESSIONAL POWER: MEDICINE AS AN AGENCY OF MORAL REFORM

Chapter 9

IN RECENT YEARS, birth control advocates have found it necessary to share the adolescent pregnancy turf with a variety of other claimants offering other—often competing—solutions. Nevertheless, and despite the public controversy surrounding it, birth control for teenage women has continued to be the management strategy most heavily subsidized by public funds (Gold and Guardado, 1988). Family planning clinics serving unmarried adolescent clients—virtually all of whom are women—have become a fixture of the sexual scene in this country: these clinics receive a million and a half visits every year from adolescent women seeking birth control. In this chapter and Chapter 10, I shift from what has been a relatively abstract analysis to a direct focus on experiences with the birth control strategies of health-care providers and of young women themselves.

Birth control for the majority of teenage women in the United States is a medically mediated service. Of the nearly one-third of single women aged 15 to 19 who use contraception, 69 percent obtain their method by medical prescription: 6 percent use a diaphragm, the remaining 63 percent—i.e., 20 percent of the teenage female population in this country—use the pill.[1] Pills and other prescriptions require entry into the health-care system and interaction with (usually several) medical and allied personnel. Medicalization—the construction of adolescent pregnancy as a medical problem and the fixing of responsibility for its solution on the health professions and their various representatives—is inherent in contemporary birth control strategies. In this and the following chapter I explore the meaning and consequences of medicalization for women who provide these services—the nursing staff of health department family planning clinics—and for those who receive them—the clinics' teenage clients.

The data on which this exploration is based were collected as part of a much larger study of contraceptive use among adolescent women attending county health department family planning clinics in Maryland. Just over half of young women in the United States get their birth control prescriptions from a clinic (the rest go to private physicians); the majority of these clinics—58 percent in 1983—are run by health departments (Torres and Forrest, 1985). From the present perspective the most important distinguishing features of the health department setting are its goals—teenagers are provided with preventive medical care at little or no cost—and its staffing patterns—the dominant professionals in this setting are nurses. Health department clinics, like hospital clinics and private physicians' offices, are fundamentally health-care institutions.[2] Expectations for behavior in these medical settings tend to be structured in terms of the traditional doctor-patient relationship: the client is exempted from responsibility for her condition and is, in turn, expected to trust the provider and to comply with her or his advice (Parsons, 1951). Interviews with health department nurses clearly reflect the problems they confront in applying this model to their encounters with teenage contraceptive clients.

The state of Maryland includes the suburbs of two large cities plus geographically extensive but (relatively) sparsely populated rural areas. Outside of the two cities (which were not included in the study), the state has twenty-three counties; at the time of this study (1981–1984) four counties were predominantly suburban, the rest more or less rural. The study itself covered twenty-one of the twenty-three counties (two very small counties refused participation); these twenty-one counties had a total of seventy-eight physically distinct family planning clinics. The research was designed to examine influences on young women's contraceptive use arising from the clinic itself—its structure and the attitudes and perspectives of its staff—as well as from the background and attitudes that young women brought with them to the clinic (this latter phase of the study will be further described in Chapter 10). Consequently (in addition to the collection of quantitative data required by the project's principal objectives), I observed clinic activities—both casually and, in the case of seven clinics, deliberately over a period of several days each—and carried out lengthy qualitative interviews with ten family planning nurses scattered throughout the state. Less extensive qualitative data probing nurses' perspectives were obtained from another 375 nurses, and 338 (86 percent of the 393 nurses working in these clinics at the time of the study) responded to a mail questionnaire. My analysis in this chapter draws primarily on the observational and qualitative data, supplemented by quantitative information where appropriate.

I quoted from remarks made by President Ronald Reagan in 1983 before the National Association of Evangelicals in the context of controversy over the question of whether parental consent should be required for birth control services. "Girls termed 'sexually active,' "—that term, he said, "has replaced the word 'promiscuous'—are given birth control drugs and devices by federally subsidized clinics in order to prevent illegitimate birth or abortion. . . . Isn't it the parents' right to give counsel and advice to keep their children from making mistakes that may affect entire lives? . . . The rights of parents and the rights of family take precedence over those of Washington-based bureaucrats and social engineers" (*New York Times*, March 9, 1983 I, 1:18). Whatever the role of "Washington-based bureaucrats and social engineers" in federally subsidized family planning clinics may be, it is not one of providing "counsel and advice" to young women in danger of making a mistake. Within the framework of the current system for services provision, that responsibility devolves upon the health professions—in the clinics under study, upon family planning nurses. And for these women—Reagan's comments notwithstanding—that responsibility represents a considerable source of discomfort. To identify the sources of their discomfort is to shed light on some basic dilemmas raised by the availability of effective contraceptive methods to single teenage women.

THE CLINIC SETTING
Picture a one-story red brick building, surrounded by a small plot of poorly tended grass, and a large expanse of asphalt populated by no-longer-new government issue sedans in unobtrusive colors. Walk up the few steps into a large, open waiting room where benches are aligned in meetinghouse fashion as if waiting for the service to begin. On the walls are posters, often handmade, extolling the virtues of good nutrition (with vivid, if inexpert, illustrations of apples and cheese), the evils of cigarettes and alcohol, or, one of my favorites, displaying baby pictures from the clinic's former maternity patients. On a typical morning in a busy family planning clinic, the waiting room pews are fully occupied by lank-haired young women, and a few men, all identically attired in blue jeans, sitting in rows to face the invisible minister. The silence of the waiting patients is broken by the yelling of babies, the shushing of tired and impatient mothers ("I'm going to whip you!" muttered under the breath), and, like a baseball commentator announcing the batting order, the periodic appearance from somewhere backstage of a clinic nurse, neatly clad in inevitable blue, calling the next patient.

Although the foregoing description is reasonably typical, clinics can vary tremendously in atmosphere, from rushed, harassed and harassing to cheerful and relaxed, depending on the size of the premises, the number of patients waiting to be seen, the number of staff available to see them, and on the manner in which that staff goes about its business. The basic elements of clinic procedure are, however, remarkably unvarying across the seventy-eight clinics we studied; these procedures are based on guidelines established by the Maryland State Health Department Family Planning Division. From an analytic perspective, the most important component of these procedures are the contraceptive education and counseling sessions. These sessions are always conducted by a clinic nurse; they are the vehicle nurses use to convey the clinic's contraceptive philosophy to its clients.

In the context of health department family planning clinics, birth control pills (and other contraceptive methods, although pills are far and away the most popular method in these clinics) are not a morally neutral technology for preventing unwanted pregnancy, to be dispensed over the counter like aspirin or Vitamin C, but a vehicle for teaching personal and moral responsibility. This orientation was very clearly reflected in the question put to me by a nursing director with whom I was chatting informally: "Are we teaching responsibility if we call a patient when she misses an appointment?" One may question the consistency of this concern with the clinic's overt objective of providing contraceptive protection, but it is quite consistent with its more covert objective of building moral character.

In a darkened room, four or five black teenagers sit quietly watching an educational film depicting a white girl talking to a white nurse about contraception. The real-life white nurse who will run today's educational session has not yet arrived and the noise of the ancient 16 millimeter movie projector effectively drowns out the soundtrack, limiting the film to a purely visual message. Suddenly lights are switched on, a brisk young woman in blue walks in and takes up her position in front of today's class. Contraceptive education is about to begin.

Although the format varies across clinics, the content of these educational sessions remains the same, following health department guidelines. Included are sexual anatomy and physiology, a review of clinic procedures, and a discussion of alternative contraceptive methods. This content is the medium through which the clinic's message of responsibility, autonomy, and good morals is transmitted.

The first part of the session is over. A poll of the young clients quickly establishes that the pill is their unanimous choice of contraceptive method. The nurse will focus on the pill, going over the other methods as she says, "lightly." Turning to the pill, she begins, "they only work if you take them right. Our job is to make sure that you take them right." Taking them "right" the clients find, imposes conformity to a complex and detailed set of rules and procedures, regulating the most intimate details of conduct. This is how it goes:

> You must start your pills on the Sunday after the first day of your next menstrual period, ("this way," the nurse jokes, "you will never have your period on a weekend," setting off a wave of giggles), you must use foam and condoms with your entire first pack of pills (and it would be better if you don't have sex for the first ten pills); you must use foam and condoms if you miss even one pill; if you miss three, you must use foam and condoms till the end of the pack. You must take the pill at the same time every day. You must always remember the type of pill you've been taking and the date of your last menstrual period. Finally, you must never say, "I got pregnant because I lost my pills."

As this latter comment suggests, the ever-present implication is that failure to conform with the clinic-prescribed regimen will result in pregnancy. The new "good girl" may be "sexually active," but she takes her pills by the book. This shift in the focus of normative attention from chastity to compliance is not lost on clients; they fully expect that conformity to procedural requirements will result in protection against pregnancy, and are correspondingly disturbed when problems arise, as exemplified by the following comments from a young clinic patient: "I've had no period for three months; I did everything by the rule book. Some girls in my high school don't care—they get pregnant. I did everything carefully. It isn't normal that I shouldn't have my period. I do everything right. I'm not a bad girl." By a classic shift in what Joseph W. Schneider and Peter Conrad (1980) call the "paradigm of deviance designation," "sin" has been redefined from having sex outside of marriage to having sex outside the rules for contraceptive protection. The "wages of sin" are still unwanted pregnancy, but the arbiters of "sinful" behavior are no longer theologians but physicians and nurses.[3] This paradigm shift is exactly what President Reagan attacked in the remarks cited earlier.

Changes in designations of deviance carry in their train changes in "reality" as well as rhetoric (Schneider and Conrad, 1980:9). Among the consequences of defining the prevention of unwanted pregnancy as a medical rather than a moral problem are changes in the appropriate agents of social control from moral to medical authorities, changes in the meaning of the behavior in question (from "promiscuity" to "sexual activity"), changes in the arena where deviance is identified (from the home, the courts, or the pulpit to the family planning clinic), and changes in the mode of intervention (from the reform school to the pill). That the health professions have more than a trivial invest-ment in protecting their claim to the management of unwanted pregnancy is indicated by the virtually unanimous opposition with which major national medical and public health organizations have met every effort at encroachment by advocates of traditional morality.

Notwithstanding this evidence of organizational solidarity in the face of ex-ternal threat, ownership of the turf represented by teenage pregnancy creates profound dilemmas for medical professionals, and particularly for physicians and nurses with direct service responsibilities—the front line of unwanted pregnancy control. The personal and professional orientations of family plan-ning nurses cause them to approach the provision of contraceptive services to teenage women with marked ambivalence; this ambivalence is resolved by structuring the encounter between provider and client so as to maximize the client's responsibility for contraceptive decisions and outcomes and to mini-mize that of the provider. I introduce my analysis with a brief description of the background and attitudinal orientations that nurses bring to their clinic work and an even more succinct account of that work itself.

THE NURSE

The average family planning clinic nurse in our study was a 42-year-old mar-ried woman with two or three children, who had worked in the county health department for six years. However, both age and length of service covered a wide range. The oldest nurse with whom we spoke was 71, the youngest, 25; 21 percent of the nurses had been in their county health department jobs for thirteen years or more. About two-thirds of the nurses were Protestant, 27 percent Catholic; only 15 out of 338 professed "no religion." Of more significance, 75 percent stated that religion was at least "moderately" important in their lives; 49 percent that it was "very important." Finally, and most importantly, as a group these women had very traditional attitudes toward premarital sex. Only 24 percent approved of an unmarried girl having sex with a boy with whom she was in love; less than half approved even if marriage was intended. The implications of their sexual conservatism for the structuring of the nurses' family planning clinic role are considered below.

As a basis for understanding the nurse's orientation to her clinic role, it is also important to be aware that few nurses had chosen to work in the family planning clinic. It was simply one aspect of their assignment as county health department staff nurses. Over 90 percent worked in other clinics as well, and indeed, 54 percent preferred to work in other clinics (only 24 percent preferred family planning; the rest stated no preference). The principal work of the clinic nurse was patient interviewing and counseling; nurses also did the blood work that was required for family planning clinic patients, took blood pressures, and were present during the physical examination by the physician. Although the focus of this analysis is on nurses' experiences with teenage women, all but six of the seventy-eight clinics I studied saw women of all age groups combined. As a final note, before proceeding to a broader analysis of the nurse's role, we asked nurses which age group they found easier to work with and which one they preferred to work with. Among the nurses willing to state a preference, only 24 percent found teens easier to work with than older women but, in testimony to their readiness for challenge, 62 percent preferred to work with teens.

THE NURSE'S CLINIC ROLE

The role of the nurse in the family planning clinic is a particularly difficult one. The difficulties are, in part, generic to the role of the professional with a lay clientele, and include problems of obtaining recognition of professional authority and compliance with professional advice (Freidson, 1968). However, these generic problems are compounded in the present case by characteristics peculiar to the "condition" for which "treatment" in the family planning clinic is sought and by the nature of the treatment itself.

Every strategy adopted for the management of sexuality in unmarried young women—from the first state reform school for girls in Lancaster, Massachusetts, to the contemporary birth control clinic—has been structured by its assumptions regarding the location of responsibility for the behavior it sought to control. Attribution of responsibility is a central issue in determining societal responses to deviant behavior. Conditions for which the individual is held responsible tend to be treated punitively while involuntary conditions are managed with permissive treatment or instruction. In the case of sexual unorthodoxy, attributions of responsibility—questions of guilt or innocence, of "deliberate choice" versus "accident, inheritance, infection, or witchcraft"— loom large in part, perhaps, because sexual intercourse is inherently ambiguous with respect to these questions (cf. Freidson, 1972:334). In itself it is neither deviant nor irresponsible. Whether or not intercourse is socially defined as deviant or irresponsible depends entirely on the conditions under which it occurs. And how intercourse is socially defined determines how the "treatment" for intercourse is regarded. Thus, Margaret Sanger in her campaign to sell birth control to medical and social elites was at pains to portray the potential clients for this service as poor, hard-working married women, more often than not the victims of an insatiable husband, consequently neither deviant nor irresponsible (Reed, 1978). By contrast, Reagan, in advocating the parental notification rule, focused entirely on the deviance of the behavior in question: sexual intercourse by unmarried girls was defined in moral terms, as "promiscuity" not "sexual activity," a violation of moral norms, requiring moral as opposed to medical treatment.

In their encounters with teenage clients, family planning nurses found themselves in a most uncomfortable position with respect to these issues of deviance and responsibility. By background and orientation, the nurses I interviewed were conventional women with highly traditional moral values. By virtue of their positions as health department employees they were socially mandated to provide an essentially medical, that is, nonpunitive service directed toward preventing young women from experiencing the consequences of what many nurses regarded as their immoral behavior. Reconciliation of this conflict was accomplished by redefining virtue as contraceptive "responsibility," that is, conformity to a set of detailed rules and procedures for contraceptive use (and for other aspects of client behavior as well), and by heavily emphasizing the pedagogical as opposed to the dispensary functions of the family planning nurse. As one of the nurses commented, "It's very nice to be able to say to parents, 'She's got to go to a group; we don't dispense pills like candy.'" By structuring their role in terms of character building, nurses were able to sustain a satisfying professional self-image despite their profound ambivalence toward the behavior that created the need for their services. There are, nevertheless, certain inherent contradictions in this role if the functions of a family planning clinic are defined as assisting women to prevent unwanted pregnancy rather than as contributing to the development of moral responsibility. These contradictions and the conflicts that they engender may be illustrated by an examination of nurses' conceptions of the desirable, as contrasted with the undesirable, teenage client.

Complementing the nurse's conception of her role as educator and counselor, the most rewarding client was the one who was eager to learn: "knows what you've been talking about and absorbs the instructions, interested in learning something about herself." The girl who was interested, asked questions, and was responsive was, furthermore, the one who was perceived as a potentially good contraceptor. Similarly, the undesirable client was the one who was perceived as disinterested in, or actively rejecting of, the educational/ counseling component of the nurses' role: "the ones who sit and just want the pill and not the advice that goes with it," who say "just give me pills and don't ask a lot of questions." Girls with this orientation were a problem for the nurse on two levels: first, they undermined the very foundations of professional authority by not only prescribing for themselves but attempting to set the terms on which the prescription was received; second, they rejected what was, to the family planning nurse, the most-valued component of her professional role by treating her as an "over-the-counter" pill dispenser. In these circumstances, the weight of the health department bureaucracy was, of course, all on the side of the nurse: Education and counseling (as well as history taking, blood work, and a complete physical examination) were conditions (and 78 percent of the nurses "strongly agreed" that they should be conditions) for receiving a birth control method. Furthermore, nurses believed that young women who did not show interest in the educational sessions were unlikely to be good contraceptors. Whether they were right or wrong, the potential for conflict with clients who had a different service model in mind should be clear.

A second major dimension of client "desirability," conformity to clinic procedures, was a direct consequence of the somewhat formalistic, even ritualistic, content of education and counseling in family planning clinics, and of the inherently bureaucratic nature of the clinics themselves. Earlier, the rules for "correct" pill taking were described. The salience of procedural issues in structuring client-provider interaction is further enhanced by clinic practices of: (1) giving out only three packs of pills at the first visit, and (2) requiring a complete annual physical examination to renew the pill prescription. In addition, fewer than half of the clinics accepted clients without a scheduled appointment even "occasionally" and less than a third held evening or Saturday hours. In these circumstances, opportunities abounded for teenage clients to miss appointments, run out of pills, request emergency visits at unscheduled times, and the like. Between the complexities of the contraceptive regimen and of the clinic's procedures, it is perhaps not surprising that nurses were highly sensitive to the question of who was "at fault" if a pregnancy occurred.

The rewarding client, then, was the one who conformed—who kept her appointments and used her method correctly. The term "responsibility" was constantly on the lips of clinic nurses, and one (among several) of its meanings was conformity to clinic and contraceptive rules. Similarly, the "irresponsible" client was the one who did not follow the rules: she "comes back pregnant because she doesn't bother to follow instructions." She will say, "I only skipped one pill and look what happened," or she will "call and say, 'I'm out of pills'" and want to come in right away instead of at a scheduled clinic time.

Underlying these conceptions of the desirable patient was the nurses' struggle to control the sexual and contraceptive behavior of their teenage clients, a struggle that reflected their ambivalence toward the behavior itself. Control was exercised in two partially contradictory ways: first, through education and counseling, consisting of detailed prescriptions for having "responsible" sex, and second, through clinic procedural requirements. The principal sanction against nonconformity to the former set of rules was the threat of pregnancy: "The pills won't work if you don't take them right." The principal sanction against nonconformity to clinic administrative procedures was the threat of not being able to obtain the pills. Lapses in conformity to either set of rules were attributed to client "irresponsibility." Given that nurses used their position as gatekeepers (their control over access to resources desired by the client) to insist that contraception was obtained on their terms, this conception of the "irresponsible" client seems virtually inevitable. Otherwise, pregnancy could conceivably be blamed on the barriers that prevented the client from getting contraception on her terms. Correct use of oral contraception does require adherence to a scheduled routine, and organizations do need certain rules to facilitate the orderly conduct of their business. However, reliance on a detailed set of rules and procedures also functioned in this case to absolve the nurse of responsibility for "mistakes."

In addition to its meaning as conformity to clinic procedures, "responsibility" was also used by nurses to mean autonomy. The desirable patient, the girl who was perceived to be a potentially good contraceptor, made her decision to attend the clinic free of any external influence: "If mother [or boyfriend or girlfriends] made her come, she won't be a good contraceptor." She made an independent choice of contraceptive method: "We try hard not to be trapped into recommending a method." Finally, she adhered to the method and did not blame the clinic if things went wrong. (There was a striking aversion among clinic staff to "follow-up" of clients after they had left the clinic, an aversion that was justified by reference to the need for inculcating "responsibility" by discouraging dependency; the need, in other words, for building moral character.)

The ideology of client autonomy, like the heavy reliance on procedural details, served, in part, to protect the nurse from feeling responsible if a client "comes back pregnant." The inherently contradictory nature of nurses' expectations for client behavior is, however, readily apparent. The "independent" autonomous client who came to the clinic knowing what she wanted was correspondingly less likely to be uncritically accepting of clinic procedures. The client who was less sure of herself, on the other hand, might have readily accepted what the clinic had to offer, but she might have had great difficulty in making autonomous contraceptive decisions. Clients in the latter mold are potentially the most vulnerable to nurses' preference for character building over pregnancy prevention.

This analysis of the role of the family planning nurse has shown how individuals directly involved in the provision of contraceptive services to a morally suspect set of clients resolve conflicts between their personal moral orientations and their professional responsibilities. They do this in three ways: first, by redefining "sin" from transgression of sexual norms to transgression of medical and bureaucratic norms; second, by structuring their professional role as one of developing personal and moral character; and, third, by absolving themselves, insofar as possible, from responsibility for failure. The latter point deserves brief elaboration. As Carole Joffe points out, "in family planning work, measures of 'success' are far more elusive than those of 'failure'" (1986:73). Feedback on contraceptive successes is rare; failure is all too visible. Furthermore, a teenage client who comes back to the clinic pregnant or after an abortion is a direct reminder of the underlying behavior for which contraception is the remedy. Her transgression of sexual norms is there for all to see; she is "punished" by the presumption of responsibility for transgression of medical norms as well.

THE MEANING OF
CONTRACEPTIVE RESPONSIBILITY

There are several reasons why the issue of responsibility may be particularly salient in the settings I have described. The age of the clientele—in our study ranging from 11 through 19, with a median age of 16—rendered nurses' expectations for an adult level of autonomous contraceptive compliance inherently problematic. "Mistakes" were virtually assured. Attribution of mistakes to client "irresponsibility" arose in part from professional sensitivity to failure. However, at least two additional motives appear to be at work as well. First, in claiming the turf represented by adolescent pregnancy, the health professions risk being held accountable for behavior they cannot fully control. The problematic nature of control, and therefore, the size of the risk, are most apparent to workers in direct contact with clients—"street-level bureaucrats," to use Michael Lipsky's felicitous phrase (1980). Concomitantly, it is at the "street-level" that the need to defend against this risk by stressing client responsibility—or irresponsibility, as the case may be—is most strongly felt. There appears to be little difference in this conception of client responsibility between the lay Planned Parenthood counselors studied by Joffe and the nurses described here. However, and this is my second point, behind the fervor of nurses' condemnation of the irresponsible client lies the additional weight of their underlying disapproval of sexual behavior outside of marriage. By not condemning they may appear to condone not only lapses in contraceptive technique, but lapses in personal morality as well.

Although questions concerning the meaning and locus of responsibility may be unusually prominent in the encounter between the family planning nurse and her teenage client, they are by no means unique to that setting. Attribution of responsibility to the client for following medical direction and corresponding condemnation for noncompliance, (where, in Zola's words, "moral judgements [are] but a pinprick below the surface" [1975:173]) are implicit in the medical model of social control. The assumptions of the medical model are merely highlighted and made more problematic when health professionals attempt to extend their control outside of the consulting room and into the most intimate details of daily life. Problems very similar to those

I have described between nurses and teenage women arise between genetic counselors and their clients (Kessler, 1980; President's Commission, 1983). Clients who, having been given full information about their risks of bearing an affected child, state that they plan no more children but do nothing about initiating effective contraception are a source of frustration to genetic counselors; counselors' feelings closely resemble those of the family planning nurse whose teenage client forgets her pills. From the professional's perspective the client's behavior is irrational; behavior that is perceived as irrational has a high probability of being labeled irresponsible.

One outcome of family planning nurses' conception of responsibility is that—for better or for worse—it places distinct limits on their willingness to intervene in clients' behavior. Thus, nurses' focus on the shaping of responsible moral character appears to preclude certain activities that are logically related to the prevention of unwanted fertility, for example, the provision of active, ongoing support to the novice contraceptive user in order to avoid contraceptive "mistakes." Reluctance to provide this support is justified on the grounds that coddling of clients will promote dependency; a more subtle implication is that individuals who are made to bear the consequences of their mistakes will learn to be more responsible. However, the cost of this lesson in responsibility is high if the consequence is unwanted pregnancy. As Janet Radcliffe Richards has pointed out:

> There are in the nature of things no natural, inevitable consequences of most actions. People make mistakes and suffer setbacks as a result, but what happens in the long run depends not only on the nature of the mistake, but also on the action they take to put matters right afterwards. . . . *The only time when we insist that a particular consequence must follow a particular action . . . is when the consequence is intended as a punishment* (1980:223, emphasis added).

In the moral universe of the family planning clinic, the punishment for young women's contraceptive and bureaucratic mistakes is pregnancy.

Notions of responsibility are as salient in clients' as in nurses' perspectives on contraceptive and reproductive decisions. However, the meanings assigned to this concept by the young women we interviewed are very different and—as Chapter 10 demonstrates—do not invariably result in contraceptive use, even when no pregnancy is intended.

PRIVATE BEHAVIOR AND PERSONAL CONTROL: CONTRACEPTIVE MANAGEMENT STRATEGIES OF ADOLESCENT WOMEN

Chapter 10

UP TO this point I have focused on the social control of young women's private sexual behavior exclusively from the perspective of its anxious adult observers: outsiders who perceive danger and are concerned to prevent it or to minimize its consequences. In this chapter I look through the lens from its other side.[1] I attempt to capture the perspectives of young women themselves: how they construct their own sexual behavior and how they frame the critical questions of reproductive responsibility and control. It should be pointed out that the data I describe were collected in 1984, before AIDS had become the major public health issue it is today. Sex and birth control were evaluated by these young women in the context of protection against pregnancy, not against disease.

A distinguishing characteristic of the birth control methods used by adolescent women is that the decision to use them must be constantly renewed. The design of the project this chapter describes was based on the hypothesis that major obstacles to unmarried young women's management of their sexuality arise out of the ongoing processes by which contraceptive use is constantly renegotiated with partners, parents, peers, and providers. Three premises guided this research: first, that the contraceptive decision principles, or criteria, employed by young women were unknown and must be allowed to emerge from the data; second, that the opinions and advice of people with whom contraceptive problems were discussed would prove to be critical factors in the decision process; third, that in order to learn how contraceptive decisions were made, it was essential to focus on concrete instances of decision making (as opposed to opinions or attitudes divorced from specific circumstances). These premises dictated a design in which our ability to obtain detailed substantive accounts of contraceptive decision-making events took precedence over considerations of representativeness (in the statistical sense) and quantifiability of data. I will describe the interview format we used following a brief account of how we selected the sample of young women to be interviewed and of their social and demographic characteristics.

Respondents for this project were drawn from the larger population of young women interviewed for the study of adolescent women's contraceptive use described in the preceding chapter. This latter population consisted of approximately three thousand women, unmarried and under age 20, who attended one of the seventy-eight county health department family planning clinics included in that study. These young women were interviewed at the time of their clinic visit and at 6- and 12-month intervals subsequent to the visit, to determine patterns of contraceptive use. Three criteria were employed in selecting respondents for the substudy of decision processes described here: first, a history of discontinuity in contraceptive use (since a major objective of this project was to account for discontinuities); second, age and race; and, third, location within approximately fifty miles of the survey office (in order to reduce interviewing costs). Based on these criteria, a stratified pool of eligible respondents was identified; potential respondents were selected randomly from within each stratum until the requisite number had been reached.[2]

It is important to emphasize that the aim of the procedures described above was to include a range of young women with different backgrounds and experience, not to select a random sample. In accomplishing this aim, we were reasonably successful. Interviews were obtained with one hundred girls; of this number, 64 percent had reported some break in contraceptive use at the 6-month follow-up interview. At the time of the present project, these young women's average age was 17. In other respects, respondent characteristics were similar to those of the original study population. These characteristics are described in Table 10.1. This is, of course, a small sample of young women residing in a single state. Nevertheless, there is little reason to think that these young women are unrepresentative of the teenage women who attend public family planning clinics in the United States, or that the birth control problems they experience and the decisions they confront are very different from those of young birth control users elsewhere in this country.

The interview schedule employed for this project was constructed on the principle that young women should be allowed to describe *in their own words* the circumstances surrounding contraceptive events in which decisions were made. However, although our purpose was to lead respondents as little as possible, we did provide a structure within which questions were framed. This structure was based on a conception of "family decision-making" developed by John Scanzoni and Maximiliane Szinovacz (1980). In this conception, the primary focus is on elements of the decision *process,* a process which these authors analogize to the innings of a baseball game, in which interest lies in the ongoing sequence of events rather than on "who wins." In order to get at this process, we developed a contraceptive "event history."

The purposes of the event history were to identify a "critical incident" in the respondent's recent contraceptive experience (discontinuing a method,

TABLE 10.1

SELECTED CHARACTERISTICS OF STUDY SAMPLE AND SUBSAMPLE

Characteristics	Study Sample		Subsample	
	N	%	N	%
CLINIC LOCATION				
Suburban	1011	35	66	66
Rural	1873	65	34	34
	2884	100	100	100
RACE				
White	2120	74	70	70
Black	753	26	30	30
Other	11	0	0	0
	2884	100	100	100
MOTHER'S EDUCATION				
8 years or less	221	8	9	9
9–11 years	814	28	5	5
High school graduate	1178	41	66	66
Some college	228	8	9	9
College graduate or above	189	6	0	0
Unknown	254	9	11	11
	2884	100	100	100
MEDIAN AGE	16.4		15.5	

switching methods, having unprotected intercourse) and then to use this incident as the focus for a series of open-ended questions. These questions were intended to ascertain how a decision process was initiated (referred to henceforth as the "trigger"); whether and under what circumstances other individuals became involved in the decision process; and, of critical importance, how influence processes operate in a concrete contraceptive decision-making situation. Questions centered on the following specific influence dimensions: who is influential; the strength, direction and success of influence attempts (both measured directly and inferred from responses to questions regarding the importance of the issue to the respondent and her satisfaction with the outcome); the bases of influence on respondents' actions (qualities of the relationship and/or the type of strategy employed); and the presence or absence of conflict.

A second purpose of these interviews, in addition to the description of decision-making patterns, was to identify underlying normative principles on the basis of which alternative choices are evaluated. Young women's accounts of specific decisions are, of course, an important source of information about these principles. However, additional information was sought through the employment of "vignettes" describing typical contraceptive decision-making situations: problems are encountered with the method itself or with significant others (boyfriend, mother, girlfriend) in situations affecting contraceptive use. In each situation, the respondent is asked to state what the protagonist *should* do and what she, the respondent, would do, were she confronted with this situation. Further questions asked how the respondent would handle conflicting normative prescriptions from significant others. Intensive probe questions were used to get at the specific normative bases for young women's responses to each vignette. These vignettes formed the second part of the interview schedule.

Once a young woman had been selected for interview she was contacted by telephone to set up an appointment.[3] Interviews took place at a wide variety of sites, ranging from under a tree in the local park to the respondent's home. They lasted anywhere from thirty minutes to one and one-half hours; the majority took about an hour. All interviews were tape-recorded (with the young woman's permission) and subsequently transcribed by the interviewer. Virtually without exception, these young women were extremely cooperative. They were very willing to talk about their contraceptive experiences; they appeared to find the event history format a congenial framework within which to describe them. In evaluating the results of these interviews, it is important to keep in mind certain special characteristics of this study that were extremely helpful in facilitating the interview process. The young women whom we approached were thoroughly familiar with the larger project of which this was a substudy; they had all been personally interviewed in a clinic and twice subsequently by telephone. This prior experience provided a powerful basis for confidence in the thoughtfulness and discretion of our interviewers. Furthermore, the interviewers we employed had all participated in the larger study; they were selected for this smaller project for their interest in and capacity to develop rapport with teenage girls. The result is an extremely rich source of data on the problems young women experience in using contraception and on the solutions they devise.

This project was conceived as exploratory. It was based on the premise that until we know *how* teenage women's contraceptive decisions are made, we will be unable to predict the circumstances under which those decisions will facilitate or impede contraceptive use, much less intervene in those decisions. Consequently, analytic procedures were designed to uncover descriptive regularities in decision processes associated with effective as compared with ineffective contraception. Several approaches to this task were employed; each is briefly described below.

A major analytic objective was to compare decision-making *sequences* leading to different outcomes. In order to compare parallel dimensions across one hundred sometimes very lengthy interviews and, at the same time, to preserve the processual dimension of decision-making, detailed abstracts of each event history were prepared. The young woman's description of "what happened" was summarized under three major categories: "triggers," or what got the decision process started; the process itself, including the girl's own evaluation of the situation plus the positions taken and influence of "significant others";[4] and, finally, the "outcome," and how the girl felt about what had happened. A simple event chronology [e.g., stopped pills (1/82)—restarted pills (3/82)] and space for clarifying comments were also included. Insofar as possible, the girl's own words were used in preparing the abstract. The use of a common format and no more than a single page for each abstract enormously facilitated analysis of decision processes: abstracts were sorted by outcome (favorable or unfavorable to contraceptive use); detailed comparisons were made of decision sequences associated with outcomes of each type.

More traditional coding methods were employed to make possible the quantification of regularities in interpersonal influence processes: the frequency with which different categories of significant others (mother, boyfriend, girlfriend[s], clinic staff) became involved in the respondent's decision, what positions they took, and the respondent's statement of *how much* influence each "involved" individual had on her final decision. In addition to the simple description of influence patterns, these data also allow us to examine variations in patterns associated with differences in event "triggers" and in outcomes. Responses to several of the vignettes were also coded numerically to permit simple frequency counts of alternative decisions (stop pills, stay on pills) and to quantify the effects on respondents' initial responses of hypothetical "contrary" influence attempts from significant others.[5]

A major purpose of these interviews was to discover the normative principles on which respondents' decisions were based. This was accomplished by standard content analysis techniques: interviews were read and reread by two investigators, noting recurrent themes. Once a theme had been identified, instances of its reappearance were recorded, paying careful attention to the context in which particular themes occurred. Thematic content was cross-checked across respondents and circumstances (for example, how regularly and under what conditions is young women's "health" an issue in contraceptive decisions?) and was subjected to intensive discussion between the two analysts. The objectives of these procedures were to arrive at a complete and accurate understanding of the meanings intended by these respondents as they described the reasoning behind their particular decisions and, at the same time, to uncover the regularities in their reasoning patterns.

RISK AND DECISION-MAKING:
ALTERNATIVE PATTERNS
The data in this chapter are based on detailed accounts of real contraceptive decisions. In order to give the reader a feeling for the reality behind my more abstract analyses, I begin the description of results with four representative

decision-making scenarios. Each scenario is a composite of many interview responses, not an individual case history. The purpose of these scenarios is to illustrate the major dimensions of contraceptive decision-making patterns (intra- and interpersonal processes, normative considerations) associated with "successful" (i.e., resulting in contraceptive protection) compared with "unsuccessful" negotiation of a potentially risky contraceptive situation.

In evaluating these scenarios, it is important to remember that *decision-making patterns* are being compared, not personality types. The young woman who successfully negotiates a risky situation is not necessarily a "non–risk-taker" as compared with the unsuccessful "risk-taker." Threats to contraceptive protection are (in the population under study) a frequent occurrence; success on one occasion may not predict subsequent success under changed circumstances. The birth control reality for most teenage women is one of risky *circumstances* and *response patterns* not of risk-taking individuals.

Unsuccessful Negotiation: Alice

Alice is having headaches and "knots" in her stomach; she thinks they are due to the pill, since it is the only "medicine" she is taking. She is afraid the pill is "too strong," and is worried about the long-term effects on her health if she keeps taking it. Alice doesn't like other birth control methods: her girlfriend got pregnant on the diaphragm; condoms make her sore; the IUD causes infections.

When Alice talks to her boyfriend, he tells her to stop taking the pill because of all the discomfort it is giving her; he suggests alternative methods of birth control. Alice believes her boyfriend is really concerned about her well-being; they have a close and mutually supportive relationship. He says he will stick by her if she gets pregnant.

Alice's mother's primary concern is the side effects; she suggests Alice stop the pill and go to the clinic to find out what's going on. Her mother doesn't want Alice to get pregnant, but she is helpful and concerned about the side effects. Alice trusts her mother's advice because her mother is experienced and has "been through it."

Alice reports that when she went to the clinic, the nurse told her headaches were "no reason to stop the pill." Alice doesn't trust the nurse; she thinks the nurse isn't really very interested in her well-being. When Alice goes to her private doctor about the headaches he gives her the devil for having gone to the health department before seeing him. He tells her boyfriend (who accompanied her to see the doctor) that the best thing he (the boyfriend) can do for Alice is get her off the pill.

Alice stops the pill and has unprotected intercourse. She feels better and healthier because the headaches and stomach pains are gone.

Successful Negotiation: Brenda

Brenda is having a lot of symptoms—cramps, headaches, weight gain—which she thinks are due to the pill. She's afraid of long-term effects of the pill on her fertility. Nevertheless, she doesn't want to stop taking the pill because she doesn't want to get pregnant.

Brenda's boyfriend tells her to call the clinic and get the problem checked out. Brenda and her boyfriend talk about birth control: he's concerned about her and wants her to feel comfortable with the method she's using. They plan to marry eventually.

Brenda's mother also thinks she should call the clinic. Brenda trusts her mother's judgment; they are very close.

Brenda goes to the clinic. The nurse agrees that Brenda shouldn't be having so many side effects and advises her to switch to a lower dose pill. Brenda believes in following "professional" advice. She thinks the nurses at the clinic know what they're doing, and she was reassured by her clinic visit.

Unsuccessful Negotiation: Amanda

Amanda frequently forgets to take her pills. She worries about the side effects that might be caused by irregular pill use. She is also concerned that if she got pregnant because of forgetting pills, then taking them could hurt the baby. Besides, Amanda smokes, and she knows it isn't good to take pills if you smoke. Amanda knows about other methods but thinks they don't work very well: you can get pregnant easily on foam; the diaphragm's a lot of trouble; the IUD can slip.

Amanda's boyfriend wants her to stay on the pill, but Amanda thinks that's just because he "doesn't want me to hook him into something." Guys are only interested in one thing anyway, "putting it in and taking it out." The first thing they ask you is, "Are you on the pill?" Since Amanda wasn't serious about this guy anyway, it didn't seem worthwhile to start the pills up again when she forgot. She wouldn't be with him that long. Besides, it's her body; she's the one who's having the problems and will have to suffer the consequences.

Amanda doesn't talk about "personal" things with her mother. Her mother thinks Amanda is "innocent" and would be hurt if she knew that Amanda was having sex. Amanda's mother had children "too young," and Amanda knows her mother doesn't want Amanda to follow her example.

Amanda's sister tells her she is "crazy" to go off the pill, that she is risking pregnancy. Amanda and her sister are "close"; nevertheless, her sister didn't listen to their mother's advice about early pregnancy (she has a baby), and "I don't have to listen to her."

Amanda's visit to the clinic was so rushed that she doesn't clearly remember what the nurses said to do if you missed pills. She doesn't want to go back there. The wait was too long, and when she had a Pap test she didn't think the nurse knew what she was doing.

Amanda has unprotected intercourse and a pregnancy scare; she thinks she probably should have stayed on the pill.

Successful Negotiation: Barbara

Barbara ran out of pills. The weather was bad, and she didn't want to go out to the clinic in bad weather for fear of arousing her parents' suspicions.

TABLE 10.2

DISTRIBUTION OF REPORTED CONTRACEPTIVE EVENTS

Event	N	%
Stopped method	47	57
Started new method after interval of nonuse	12	14
Switched from existing to new method	10	12
Changed pill dosage	10	12
Continued method, no change	4	5
Total	83[a]	100

[a]Seventeen respondents reported no contraceptive event.

Barbara talked to her boyfriend; they agreed not to have sex until she got back on the pill. He didn't say anything about her running out. Barbara says they don't have "that kind of relationship." She makes up her own mind. He doesn't tell her what to do.

Barbara hasn't told her mother she's on the pill. Her mother wouldn't approve of Barbara having sex; she would have said to stay off the pill permanently.

When Barbara talked to the nurse at the clinic, she was told to wait until the next month to restart the pills. Barbara thinks the nurse knows what she is talking about: Barbara wouldn't want to do anything to hurt her body.

THE CONTRACEPTIVE EVENT

The first step in the interview process was to identify a single, specific contraceptive "event" or decision to serve as the focus for subsequent detailed questions. The respondent was asked if, during the past year, she had *started* a birth control method for the first time, *changed* the method she was using, *stopped* using a method, or had *sex without using anything* to prevent pregnancy. If more than one such event was elicited, the interviewer was instructed to determine which event was "the most difficult decision . . . or caused the most conflict with other people." Employing these procedures, eighty-three contraceptive events were identified. The remaining seventeen respondents had no event in any of the categories specified.

The distribution of events by category is given in Table 10.2. Over half of the events reported were discontinuations of contraceptive use. The remainder represented changes in the pattern of use or, in four cases, contemplation of change where none, in fact, was made. I now turn to a detailed analysis of the decision processes that preceded these events.

TRIGGERS: STARTING THE DECISION PROCESS

"Triggers" are what get a decision-making sequence started: the young woman herself may become aware of a "problem"; others may call a problem to her

TABLE 10.3
FREQUENCY OF MAJOR "TRIGGER" CATEGORIES

Trigger Category	N		%	
Method-related problems	56		54.4	
Immediate symptoms attributed to pill		32		31.1
Feared long-term side effects of pill		5		4.8
Forgets pill		15		14.6
Other method problems		4		3.9
Relationship change	24		23.3	
Break in relationship with boyfriend		13		12.6
New boyfriend or back with old boyfriend		11		10.7
Intervention by other "significant others"	7		6.8	
Mother		3		2.9
Father		2		1.9
Sister		1		1.0
Girlfriend		1		1.0
Pregnant or wants pregnancy	7		6.8	
Other	9		8.7	
Total[a]	103		100.0	

[a]Reflects total mentions of triggers.

attention; her personal circumstances may change. Any of these occurrences can be the signal for a reevaluation of the girl's current contraceptive status and for the working out of a new contraceptive "solution."

Method-Related Problems

The frequency with which each of five trigger categories were cited in the interviews is shown in Table 10.3. Over half of the contraceptive "events" recorded in these interviews were precipitated by problems attributed directly to the contraceptive method (oral contraception in over 90 percent of these cases). Under the rubric of method-related problems are included a wide range of immediate physical and mental symptoms, anticipated long-term side effects of the pill, and "forgetting" pills with the "catch-up" problems forgetting entails. The words of the young women themselves clearly convey how these problems are perceived.

IMMEDIATE SYMPTOMS

"The pill gave me migraine headaches and made me nervous."

"I gained twenty pounds, and I love to eat and couldn't stop. Also, my periods weren't regular."

"I just didn't feel like myself. I had headaches and gained weight."

"I'd read each pack of pills they give you. [I smoke] and they tell you that smoking can have a great effect on you. It could give me a blood clot, something like that."

"Another reason I had stopped the pills was because I thought I was pregnant. It could affect the baby during pregnancy, any kind of medication."

FORGETTING

"I couldn't remember to take pills, that was a big problem. I would go out and come home, go to sleep, forget to take them. In the morning I would be rushing to go to school. I would forget to take them. I was always gone on the weekends, and I would forget to take them."

Method-related problems trigger contraceptive reevaluation for at least two reasons. First, and most obviously, they arouse anxiety. How the pill works remains mysterious to most girls: side effects and irregular periods create significant health concerns; weight gain, breast swelling, and late or missed periods are often perceived as symptoms of pregnancy. Second, and equally important, side effects and unexpected or unduly delayed menses threaten to compromise young women's control over the *visibility* and, consequently, the independent management of their sexual activity: "If I was to stay sick for a long time, this would involve my parents." The importance to these young women of establishing and maintaining a sense of personal control will be more fully elaborated later in the chapter.

Relationship Changes

The second largest category of triggers are changes in the young woman's relationship with a boyfriend: the breakup or reactivation of an old relationship or the initiation of a new one. Breakup often precipitates the discontinuation of oral contraceptive use: "I stopped seeing my boyfriend, so I stopped the pill a month later. I just didn't see any sense in taking the pill without seeing anybody."

When the question of continuing or stopping the pills when a relationship breaks up was posed as a hypothetical vignette, 70 percent of the respondents stated that the girl in question *should* continue: she might meet someone else or get back with her old boyfriend. Confronted with the reality of a breakup, however, young women may react less in terms of their fear of pregnancy than of their perceptions of the pill: as potentially dangerous medicine *and* as a statement about the quality of a particular relationship.

DANGER

"I believe you shouldn't be on the pill for a long time. It's safer to take breaks."

"I wasn't having sex, and besides the pills are dangerous. People have to stop early because of side effects."

"I would use foam and condoms until I was serious with a boy, then get the pill."

"I would wait first. If I knew it would be serious . . . then I would start taking [the pill]."

As these remarks indicate, it is misleading to think of birth control methods as simply instrumental devices. Just as these methods have meanings for nurses, they also have meanings for young women that go far beyond obvious considerations of safety and effectiveness.

Other Trigger Categories

Parents, sisters, and friends may also, though less frequently, precipitate changes in contraceptive behavior. "Discovery" by parents can lead to contraceptive interruption: "My father found out I was taking birth control pills and got real upset. He told me to stop because my grandmother died from them. I don't believe him, but he told me to stop so I did." Or, on the other hand, intervention can have positive consequences: "My sister went on the pill. She said, 'Go ahead and do it. Guys like pills better than condoms.'"

While certain triggers, e.g., breakup with a boyfriend, pregnancy or the desire for a pregnancy, are almost invariably associated with contraceptive discontinuation, in the case of method-related problems the ultimate outcome is by no means preordained. Among respondents who reported these latter problems about half stopped using the method; the remainder had their pill prescription changed or switched to a different method. The following section describes the specific decision process dimensions that are associated with these alternative outcomes.

DECISION PRINCIPLES: THE NORMATIVE BASES
OF CONTRACEPTIVE DECISIONS

The decision process consists both of subjective preferences for particular outcomes (variously labeled "tastes, utilities, goals, interests") and of influence processes that emerge in interaction with "significant others" (see, e.g., Fishbein, 1972). These subjective preferences can be thought of as "guiding philosophies" that "decisioning parties carry with them" into their discussions and negotiations (Scanzoni and Szinovacz, 1980). In the present case, young women's "guiding philosophies" decide the terms in which contraceptive choices are structured and provide the bases on which influence attempts from significant others are evaluated. We did not begin this investigation with preconceived ideas as to what decision principles women would employ; indeed, a major aim was the discovery of these principles. In this section, I identify the major guiding principles that emerged from our data.

Information on these principles was extracted from both event histories and vignettes. As they described their personal contraceptive experiences, young women frequently voiced the underlying concerns that led them to respond in particular ways; consistent elements in these concerns are taken to reflect basic decision principles. More direct information on these principles was obtained from the vignettes: A respondent's statement of what the hypothetical protagonist *should* do is used as evidence of the normative principles she applies to particular contraceptive decisions. The three sets of decision principles described below are abstracted from a much more confused reality. In life decisions are based on mixed and overlapping principles. The principles a young woman applies in one situation may conflict with those she uses in another or even with those applied in the same situation when it is posed hypothetically.

Health and Protection: Conflicting Values

"When it comes to something where it concerns my health *or* something else, my health is more important."

The decision to continue or to stop the use of oral contraception is most frequently structured as a conflict between "my health" and the need for contraceptive protection. Health concerns prompt the decision to stop not only as a consequence of side effects but in apparently unrelated circumstances as well, for example, when the breakup of a relationship is seen as a welcome opportunity to take a "breather" from the pill.[6]

A series of examples will show how these concerns are expressed and the range of circumstances in which they arise. Any perceived change in physical or mental health may be attributed to the pill:

"It never happened like this till I went on the pill."

"I was blaming it all on the pill because I don't take no medicine.... That's the only thing I was taking."

Irregular menstrual cycles cause uneasiness both because of the perceived power of the pill to cause such changes and because they set off a chain of pregnancy-related concerns:

"Didn't get my period. Thought it was because I missed a pill or two. Then thought I might be pregnant and didn't take the pill because of danger to the baby."

Girls who experience spotting or multiple monthly periods worry that "something is wrong," their "insides are messed up."

Concern about long-term effects of the pill is clearly reflected in the (frequently expressed) fear of its potentially deleterious effects on an existing pregnancy. Additional concerns include fears of "a blood clot," the possibility that "hormones will be thrown off," and the danger of combining pills with smoking: "smoking and the pill cause cancer." Finally, as noted above, the readiness of young women to "give my body a rest" from the pill when a relationship breaks off is additional evidence for the salience of health concerns.

Not only is "health" a salient concern, but when decisions are structured in terms of "health" versus other values, including protection from pregnancy, health more frequently prevails and is used to legitimize whatever decision is made: "Anything in regards to my health is very important." The pill is perceived as highly effective but (and perhaps for this very reason) as a major potential health threat.[7]

The value Americans attach to health is not, of course, a new observation. In recent years the salience of this concern has been markedly increased by the public attention given to food and environmental hazards, by the publicity that surrounds major health "events": Legionnaire's disease, toxic shock syndrome, AIDS, and the like; and, I would also suggest, by the emphasis in medical writing and public policy on the individual's *personal* responsibility in health matters. "Health" has achieved widespread legitimacy as a basis for both public and private decisions.

Health concerns are further enhanced for these young women by the very nature of effective contraception—"pills" are medicine, and medicine is something you take when you are sick;[8] by fears that nurses may (often unintentionally) instill in their efforts to insure compliance with the contraceptive regimen; and by the rituals of medical history, blood work, pelvic examination, Pap smear, and the like, that accompany contraceptive prescription in a medical setting. Thus, due both to the salience of health as a public concern and to the additional force given to this concern by the social structure of contraceptive use, pill taking is regarded as a serious step, not to be embarked upon, or continued, lightly.

The majority of young women we interviewed are also strongly committed to protecting themselves from an undesired pregnancy. This commitment emerged most clearly in the vignette responses: In hypothetical situations, challenges to contraceptive protection provoked unambiguous normative statements of the need to use birth control and "avoid pregnancy." "Health" was seldom raised as an issue. In the single vignette focused directly on how a hypothetical young woman should respond to "side effects" slightly more than a third of the respondents said the pills should be stopped; however, 77 percent recommended immediate medical consultation, an action they were much less likely to take in actual events involving side effects.

From the perspective of these young women, their personal health is an immediate and highly legitimate source of concern; pregnancy is hypothetical. They would prefer to avoid pregnancy, but not if the immediate costs in terms of competing health risks are considered too high.[9] Birth control methods other than the pill are, in this population, essentially discounted. They are perceived as less effective and at least equally problematic, if for different reasons. Ironically, conviction of its power is what leads young women to use the pill, to stop using it, and to discount alternatives when discontinuation occurs.

Protection and Love: The Meaning of Contraception

"I would wait until the relationship was serious before I took the pill."

"If I wasn't serious with him, I wouldn't want to get pregnant so I use birth control."

"Seriousness" is a major criterion on the basis of which relationships are evaluated and contraceptive decisions are made. And "serious" relationships are what almost all these young women valued and ultimately desired for themselves. However, the ambiguous connection between seriousness and contraception is clearly reflected in the contrasting statements quoted above.

In this population of young women, there is relatively little evidence of the sentiment that contraceptive preparation is unromantic. Indeed, the question (as the first quote suggests), is often not one of romantic love impeding contraceptive use, but of oral contraceptive use being a sufficiently serious commitment so as to require romantic love:

"I think she [vignette protagonist] should wait [to get pills] until she is close with the person. If she's not going to have a strong relationship, then she shouldn't. She'll end up getting hurt."

In the absence of such a relationship, getting pills may be defined in negative moral terms:

"If no boyfriend, don't [get pills]. She doesn't need them, unless she is loose—if she goes to bed with everybody."

"Seriousness" may occasionally be *defined* by sexual intercourse, but this is by no means invariably true, as evidenced by girls' frequent suggestions that other (less "serious") birth control methods be used until a more committed relationship has been established.

Absence of seriousness, however, is also used as an argument *for* contraception. The question of whether "Mary," who is dating a boy but not yet serious about him, should get birth control pills elicited the following response:

"Start taking them because she might get pregnant. He might not want the baby. They are not really into each other. [If it were you?] I would be on birth control pills. I am not ready to make a family with someone I don't really care about or am not involved with."

From the perspective of the young women we interviewed, contraceptive methods are not morally neutral "preventive medicine"; they are statements about the quality of relationships, sometimes about the presence of commitment and sometimes about its absence.[10] Thus, I would argue that it is misleading to discuss teenage women's contraceptive use in the context of their acceptance of or commitment to "sexuality." Women do not commit themselves to sexuality, but to relationships, relationships which may or may not include sexual intercourse, or may include it at some times but not at others: the quality of the relationship is as, if not more, important than the presence or absence of sex, in determining how contraceptive decisions are made.[11]

"I probably should have kept on [the pill], but it was important I make up my own mind."

"It's important to me to know I could make a decision like that [to go off the pill]. It's a big decision because of the pregnancy risk."

Management of reproduction is, in the eyes of these young women, a major source of power, one that they guard vigilantly and share only under narrowly defined circumstances (for example, with a trusted partner). The phrase "management of *reproduction*" is used advisedly because, although the focus of this study was contraceptive management, contraceptive decision-making power is inextricably tied to power over decisions about sexual activity, pregnancy, abortion, and childbirth. In each of these domains alternative courses of action are frequently evaluated for their significance as indicators of decision-making power or for their impact on actual or potential power. In addition, power and *responsibility* are closely linked, as demonstrated in the following quotes:

"It was very important that I get my way. It's my problem and I would have to deal with the consequences."

"Hard for me to decide for myself [whether or not to have an abortion]. I asked for help from my mom the first time to decide, and then I blamed it on her. So I think it's important for me to decide for myself so I can't blame it on anybody else if I felt guilty."

"What really got me very upset about [side effects of pill] was that if I was to stay sick for a long time then this would involve my parents, and I guess I always try to be so grown up, and I'd like to learn how to take care of myself. I'm not saying that I can't talk to my mother about it. I can if I try, but I don't try because I don't want to try. I'm doing this. It's my body."

As the last quote suggests, maintaining control over what is *communicated* to significant others can appear highly important as a means of preserving and/or asserting independent decision-making power. Consequently, decisions not only about what will be *done,* but about what will be revealed and what concealed, are subject to evaluation on these grounds.

"We never really talked about [birth control] much. He asked me once, 'Are you still on the pill or off? What's going on?' And I said, 'None of your business.' That's all he'd ever get out of me. He'd see it in my purse, but he never was sure cause I never would talk to him about it. [Why?] I really never wanted to get that serious with him, so it just never mattered."

Adolescence is, of course, a time of establishing independence and becoming recognized as capable of self-direction; many of the remarks quoted above can be interpreted as reflecting these concerns. However, two further points are important. First, the opportunities for and the burdens of power and responsibility are probably particularly great for adolescent women trying to manage their reproductive capacities. Not only do we, as a society, place a high value on personal control in the area of sexual behavior and contraception; it is one of the few areas of their lives in which teenage women are in a position to exercise personal control. At the same time, the burden imposed by control can be highly problematic for teenage girls: This double-edged quality is evident in the ambivalence expressed about involving mothers in fertility-related decisions. Second, knowledge of young women's *overall* commitment to the values of power and independence does not predict the *particular* reproductive decisions they will make. It is often asserted that teenage women seek pregnancy and childbearing as a way of demonstrating maturity. Our data indicate that the decision *not* to bear a child (to shoulder the responsibilities of contraception, to have an abortion) is equally likely to be seen as an expression of the independent decision-making power that defines maturity in the eyes of these respondents.

INFLUENCE PROCESSES: BOYFRIENDS, MOTHERS, AND OTHERS

Measurement of Influence
The objectives of our techniques for measuring interpersonal influence were to ascertain *who* became involved in the decision process, the *position* taken by each participant (stop current contraceptive method, switch to a different method, consult clinic, continue current method), and the *amount* of influence each participant was perceived as exerting on the respondent's final decision. In addition, a series of questions were designed to get at, first, the types of "supporting actions" or strategies employed by significant others to reinforce their viewpoint and/or persuade the respondent of its correctness and second, the bases of differential influence on the decision outcome (credibility, quality of relationship, structural position).

In describing what led up to the "event" under discussion, respondents often referred spontaneously to other people's involvement. To supplement this information, they were specifically asked: "Who [else] got involved in what was happening? Did you discuss it with anyone else?" All individuals mentioned were listed; this list was the source of information on *who* participated in the decision and provided the framework for subsequent questioning. (If, after this questioning was fully completed, the respondent had made *no* reference to her mother and/or boyfriend, additional questions were asked about these persons and, if involved, they were listed separately.) After participants had been identified, respondents were asked, "What did [your boyfriend, your mother, your sister, etc.] want you to do?" And, at a later point, they were asked to summarize what had happened in the following way: "Let's go down the list of people whom you've mentioned. Could you tell me how much influence each one actually had on your final decision?" Respondents were requested to rate the amount of influence on a scale from 1 (none) to 5 (very great deal).

TABLE 10.4

IDENTITY OF SIGNIFICANT OTHER(S) INVOLVED IN CONTRACEPTIVE EVENT

Significant Other	N	%
Boyfriend	53	32.5
Mother	29	18.0
Clinic staff	30	18.2
Girlfriend	22	13.5
Other relatives (sister, aunt)	24	14.7
Private doctors	5	3.1
Total[a]	163	100.0

[a]Total is larger than 100 because many respondents mentioned more than one person as a significant other.

Responses to these questions were translated into numerical codes and put on computer tape for use in quantitative analyses. Thematic analyses and simple hand tallies were employed to determine the types of persuasion strategies engaged in by significant others and the bases of their influence.

Participants in the Decision Process

Significant others may become involved in the respondent's decision process with or without her invitation, or they may not become involved at all. Of eighty-three respondents who describe a contraceptive event, fourteen (17 percent) made their decision without talking to anyone else; this was most likely to occur when the event was triggered by breakup with a boyfriend. At the other extreme, obvious physical symptoms (rash, excessive weight gain, vomiting) almost always precipitated the involvement of significant others (whether or not the symptoms were attributed to contraceptive use).

Table 10.4 gives the relationship to the respondent of involved significant others across all events described. Boyfriends are the most frequent participants in the decision process (named by close to two-thirds of respondents with an event) followed, but not very closely, by mothers and clinic staff. Looking at these data in another way, of the total participants identified, 61 percent were peers (boyfriend, girlfriend, sister); only 39 percent were adults (parents, other adult relatives, professionals). Finally, while, with the exception of a breakup in the relationship, the involvement of boyfriends was relatively constant across all trigger categories, clinic staff and, to a lesser extent, mothers were relatively much more likely to become involved when the trigger was a problem in method management.

Direction and Strength of Others' Influence

The measure we employed to rate influence *strength* was described above. *Direction* of influence was coded based on a careful reading of the entire event history, since pertinent information was frequently provided in more than one place. The clarity of individuals' positions varied with their particular

TABLE 10.5

DIRECTION OF SIGNIFICANT OTHERS' INFLUENCE ON CONTRACEPTIVE DECISIONS

	Boyfriend		Mother		Clinic Staff		Other	
Direction	N	%	N	%	N	%	N	%
Favorable	30	36.1	22	26.5	28	33.7	30	36.1
Unfavorable	19	23.0	5	6.0	0	0.0	10	12.0
Unclear	4	4.8	2	2.4	2	2.4	11	13.3
Not involved	30	36.1	54	65.1	53	63.9	32	38.6
Total	83	100.0	83	100.0	83	100.0	83	100.0

TABLE 10.6

STRENGTH OF SIGNIFICANT OTHERS' INFLUENCE ON CONTRACEPTIVE DECISIONS

	Boyfriend		Mother		Clinic Staff		Other	
Strength	N	%	N	%	N	%	N	%
Strong	22	26.5	12	14.5	8	9.6	10	12.0
Weak	29	35.0	16	19.2	17	20.5	34	41.0
Unclear	2	2.4	1	1.2	5	6.0	7	8.4
Not involved	30	36.1	54	65.1	53	63.9	32	38.6
Total	83	100.0	83	100.0	83	100.0	83	100.0

role and with their relationship to the respondent: mothers and clinic staff were almost always unambiguous in their support for or (in the case of some mothers) opposition to continuing with contraception; boyfriends' messages, on the other hand, were frequently mixed and some judgment had to be used in deciding direction. As examples, the boy who supports contraception but *also* supports the respondent's desire to go off the pill when symptoms occur is coded as "unfavorable" to contraceptive use, as is the boy who tells the respondent the decision is "up to her," but is unwilling to use a method of contraception himself. Data on the direction and strength of reported influence on the respondent's decision are given in Tables 10.5 and 10.6 respectively. Overall, only about a third of these young women were encouraged by others they consulted to continue with contraceptive use (either by continuing with the same method or by switching to a "better" method). With the exception of boyfriends, relatively few decision-making participants actively discouraged use. However, the impact of individuals other than the boyfriend is reduced by their lesser probability of being involved in the decision process at all. Not only are boyfriends more likely to act in a way that does not support using contraception, but their influence is perceived as stronger than that of other participants, as shown in Table 10.6. Mothers who *do* become involved in the decision process are as likely as boyfriends to be influential (and, as Table 10.5 shows, their influence is more likely to support contraception). Mothers are, however, much less likely than boyfriends to be brought into the decision process.

Given that method-related problems are the principal reason given for discontinuation, we must call attention to the weak reported influence of clinic staff. Although, as would be expected, staff are uniformly perceived as favoring continued contraceptive use, they are no more likely than mothers to be involved in the young woman's decision, and their influence is even less.

The foregoing results are based on respondents' descriptions of actual contraceptive events, and it is instructive to compare these results with significant other influence patterns generated by the hypothetical vignettes. The vignettes, it will be recalled, were intended to get at *normative* decision processes—what respondents believed *should* happen when contraceptive problems arose. In their responses to the vignettes respondents assigned relatively *more* influence to mothers than boyfriends, and showed far more inclination than in real life to involve clinic staff in resolving a method-related problem.

A detailed description of influence processes within each principal relationship category will help to account for the influence patterns I have described.

DECISION PROCESSES: BOYFRIENDS

Dimensions of the Decision Process
Whether or not boyfriends become involved in the contraceptive decision process, how their influence attempts are interpreted by respondents, and the amount of influence attributed to them depend on a complex interplay between the decision *principles* enunciated earlier and the quality of the *relationship* within which a contraceptive issue arises. The first quote is from a girl who experienced a wide array of symptoms she attributed to the pill:

> "[My boyfriend] didn't urge me one way or another; he was concerned with side effects, not pregnancy. He wouldn't mind a baby. He feels like it's my body and my decision, but he has a great deal of influence. We're in this thing together."

By contrast (in response to a hypothetical boyfriend who urges remaining on the pill in the face of side effects):

> "I wouldn't pay any attention to him. He's just worried about her getting pregnant and gettin' stuck with a kid. Of course he wants her to stay on it. It's just one less worry for him. . . . I'd say, 'Tough! This is me you're talking about.'"

I have pointed out that respondents structured their decision alternatives around issues of health, of love, and of power. Boyfriends' responses are evaluated in the same terms. Thus, rather than focusing on pragmatic concerns about pregnancy prevention, contraceptive decisions frequently become vehicles for testing relationships. The boy who values "health" above protection and appears prepared to accept responsibility for a potential pregnancy is perceived as truly concerned for his partner's welfare: His support for stopping the pill is interpreted as evidence of this concern. By the same token, boys who support continuation in the presence of side effects may be seen as primarily concerned with their *own* protection (or pleasure) rather than the protection of their partner (as in the second extract cited above). As a consequence, their advice is discounted.

Young women's response to their boyfriends' influence attempts (and, indeed whether or not he is in a position to influence them at all) depend not only on evaluation in terms of "guiding principles," but also on the quality of the relationship and the strength of respondents' interest in maintaining it.

> "My boyfriend has me wrapped around his finger. I'd do most anything he says. [She wanted pregnancy to 'have some hold on him,' but he took her to the clinic for the pill.] He can make me feel real bad."

> "Didn't listen to [boyfriend who said, stay on pills] because I knew I wouldn't be with him that long. He was going out on me."

Earlier, I observed that relatively less influence was attributed to boyfriends in response to the hypothetical vignettes than they appeared to have in actual fact. The most probable explanation for this difference is that quality of the relationship was not a factor in the vignette responses, leading respondents to adopt the cynical view of boyfriends' suggestions that, in real life, characterized only the coolest of relationships.[12] These quotes also make the point that, although power over one's own body is an important value, it may be compromised or redefined ("we're in this thing together") in the context of a more valued relationship.

Additional evidence that contraceptive decisions, much more than decisions about more conventional "preventive" measures, need to be understood in the context of *relationships* is that the validity of the decision itself is often judged not by its efficacy in prevention but by its effect on the relationship.

> "I feel safer and better now I stopped [the pill]. Our relationship is better, and we don't fight anymore."

> "Our relationship was better after I went on the pill because we were both scared of getting pregnant before."

Direction of Boyfriends' Influence

Our objective in the foregoing discussion has been to identify some dimensions of the decision process that goes on between young women and their sexual partners; our illustrations have been drawn equally from comments supportive of and those that fail to support continued use of contraception. However, we know from the quantitative analyses presented earlier that boyfriends are least likely to provide this support. At least three sets of circumstances can be identified in which boyfriends' actions or attitudes are associated with a high probability of unprotected intercourse.

1. As described earlier, young men may share their girlfriends' health concerns and support stopping the pill. Unless action is taken to obtain another method (and often it is not), the result is unprotected intercourse.
2. The boyfriend may leave the decision up to the girl, but be unwilling to use an alternative method himself: "He didn't want to use anything. It was up to me to decide what to do."
3. The boyfriend may express concern about pregnancy but, at the same time, put pressure on the respondent to have sex: "He'd say, 'I hope you're not pregnant,' and later that night he'd want to fool around. [If I had refused], he would've been mad."

A contraceptive social structure in which protection from the risk of pregnancy is defined as primarily a female responsibility, male acceptance of that risk is defined as a sign of love, and males are expected to take the sexual initiative seems designed to generate a wide variety of circumstances in which boyfriends' actions will be unsupportive of contraceptive use (however supportive of other values) and pregnancy risks will, indeed, be taken.[13]

DECISION PROCESSES: MOTHERS

"[My mother and I] don't talk about that kind of stuff much. . . . She never really discusses much my sex life, my private life. [When she found foam in my room] she said, 'I hope you have enough sense not to get pregnant. What you do is your own business. I know it's a new day and age, but please don't get pregnant. I guess if she had her way, she'd still have me a virgin: 'I'm not bad, mom. Why do you look at me like that? I don't run around.' [But] she figures if I have to do it, she'd rather I be safe."

When faced with a contraceptive problem, two-thirds of these respondents reach a decision without involving their mothers at all. Many believe, as in the foregoing extract, that their mothers would prefer contraception to pregnancy; however, respondents are also afraid of the confrontation with their daughter's sexual activity that raising a contraceptive issue would inevitably entail: "No mother wants to know their child is having sex." Noncommunication is both protective—"my mom thinks I'm the innocent one. I don't want to disappoint her"—and, as indicated earlier, a principal means by which control over decision-making power is preserved.

"Not only would [mother] not want me on the pill, but she wouldn't want me to be having sex or going out at all."

"[Mother's] the one who suggested the pills. I kept telling her I didn't want them, but I had to get them anyway. So I wasn't gonna tell her [that I wasn't taking them]."

Thus, mothers are not consulted to avoid confrontation or interference, one or both of which are very often anticipated. The following quote suggests what can happen when the delicate "balance of silence" breaks down.

"[Mother] said that it would upset her if I was having relations with him, and then I was even afraid to ask her about birth control. So then I got some on my own, and then she found it, and she got really upset; so then I decided not to use any at all, and then I got pregnant."

When mothers do become directly involved in the contraceptive decision process, the messages they convey are relatively straightforward (unlike the mixed signals received from boyfriends).[14] Opposition may stem from concern about the long-term side effects of oral contraception.

"Mother found the pills. My parents had a long talk with me and [boyfriend] about the long-term effects of using birth control pills."

"We read the pamphlet together that tells you all about the problems you can have. Since I smoke, she said I shouldn't be on [the pill]."

However, under circumstances where mothers' involvement is deliberately invited (rather than occurring by "accident") support for contraception is much more likely than opposition:

"She said the best thing was to go on the pill or give up sex."

"She wanted me to go back on [the pill] right away. . . . She knows how it is to have kids and take care of them, the responsibilities and all that. She knows I'm kind of young to be having a baby yet, and she was worried about me getting pregnant."

DECISION PROCESSES: OTHERS

Girlfriends, although they are involved in the contraceptive event almost as frequently as boyfriends, are assigned relatively little influence on the final decision. However, they appear to play an important role as sounding boards and as sources of "information" and advice, based on their own contraceptive experience.

"[My girlfriend] told me if [the pill] was going to cause that many problems I should go off of them. . . . She suggested the diaphragm to me also. [Any influence on your decision?] No, she just was there for me to talk to."

"I just talk to [my girlfriend] about things. I don't take her seriously. She's been on the pill since high school. It's like second nature to her. She says, 'you don't have to take [the pill], so if you don't want to I don't see why you should. It's up to you.'"

"I didn't want to be bothered with the diaphragm. Cause my girlfriend said they can fall out of place, and they're not that reliable."

"[My girlfriend] was the first person I talked to about [leg cramps]. I told her what my problem was, and she told me to call up one of the nurses, and she asked me what kind of pill I was taking. I told her, and I remember that was the same type of pill she used to take. When she used to come on, she used to get real sick."

Female peers (relatives as well as girlfriends) contribute to the decision process by helping respondents to arrive at a "definition of the situation" (e.g., this is a "pill problem") and to structure their alternative options (call the clinic, go off the pill, use another method). In addition, they usually provide evaluations of these options. Although respondents *attribute* relatively little influence to girlfriends, it is important to point out that what influence they do exercise comes at a very early stage in the decision process; girlfriends and other female peers are often the first persons consulted when a problem arises. They may not directly influence the respondent's final decision, but their role in channeling the decision process along particular lines can be substantial.

Like mothers, clinic staff are brought into the decision process infrequently (by about one-third of these young women); however, when they *are* involved (almost always in response to method-management "triggers"), the probability that a contraceptive "event" will entail pregnancy risks is much less. The reasons volunteered by respondents for not consulting clinic staff usually refer to one or more negative aspects of the clinic experience.

> "Little kids running around. Annoying place. So impersonal. Never see same doctor twice. Don't get to ask any questions. Don't like going up there and waiting all that time."

> "Every time I went back they wanted to examine me. They gave me a hard time about giving me my pills. You can't have pills til you have an exam."

> "[I didn't ask nurses about the pill 'catch-up' problem because] I usually just rush in and rush out. There are nurses around, but I usually go right in and come out."

By contrast, when nurses *are* deliberately consulted, their input is described in positive terms.

> "The people who I talk with is the women, you know . . . the nurses. They was talking to me like I was their daughter. They were saying, 'Are you crazy [to go off the pill]?' "

> " 'Don't you know a pill a day keeps the doctor away?' They were explaining things to me in detail, especially this one particular lady who I really know well."

> "Logically, it would have been dumb not to follow [the nurse's] advice. I couldn't lose by going to the clinic. I gained peace of mind by talking to her, going to clinic."

Many contraceptive decisions are structured in such a way as not to "require" medical advice; the young woman who breaks up with her boyfriend and goes off the pill may explain her decision in part on medical grounds, but she feels no need to have the decision medically sanctioned. However, close to half of the contraceptive decisions triggered by method-related problems are also made without medical consultation. The reason for this apparent anomaly becomes clear once it is recognized that even in these latter decisions the real issues are seldom primarily medical. They revolve (as I argued earlier) around questions of love, power, and the meaning of sexual relationships.

BASES OF INFLUENCE

Significant others' influence is derived from their *credibility* (knowledge, experience, trustworthiness), from the *quality of their relationship* with the respondent (closeness, supportiveness, fear), and/or from their *structural position* (relative age, status as parent or physician). A series of examples will illustrate the difference among these influence bases.

Credibility

"The nurse knows something; that's why they are nurses."

"[Mother] doesn't know any more about the pill than I do; she would worry, so I don't tell her I missed a period."

"I usually go by [my mother's] judgment. We trust each other."

"[Mother] knows more because she's probably been through it in her life."

Credibility is judged not only on the basis of knowledge and experience but also, and perhaps of most importance, on the basis of perceptions of others' concern for the *respondent's* welfare as a primary value. I have already noted the loss of credibility suffered by a boyfriend who appears less concerned about side effects than about a potential pregnancy: "He's just worried about her getting pregnant and getting stuck with a kid." Similarly, the mother who is believed to advocate contraception because "she just didn't want me to be like her [and have babies too young]" and the nurse who says a rash is "no reason to go off the pill" lose credibility due to what is perceived as insufficient interest in the respondent's welfare: *Her* concerns are not taken seriously. By contrast, the boyfriend who bases his advice on the respondent's health gains credibility and influence: "He is concerned for my health, and I usually take his advice."

Quality

Closeness, perceived confidence and emotional support as well as fear of emotional reprisal are major components of relationship quality. Earlier, we discussed this dimension in the context of relationships with boyfriends, but it is an important aspect of other relationships as well.

"My mother is proud of me, and I wouldn't want to hurt her."

"[My mother and I are] like sisters."

"The nurse changed my mind completely around. She was really nice to me and talked to me like I was her daughter."

Quality can also be expressed in negative terms:

"I didn't tell my mother. She calls me a slut anyway."

"[Nurses] are nasty. Say, 'You girls all goin' an' gettin' pregnant. You should all have abortions.' "

Emotional reprisals and/or threats, as exemplified by the latter two extracts, are, of course, effective only insofar as the respondent has a stake in maintaining the relationship. Where the costs of breaking it off altogether are too high, respondents still have the alternatives of compliance (more likely if the threatening party is a boyfriend) or resistance combined with avoidance of communication (more likely if the mother-daughter relationship is at stake). Clinic staff have little prospect of commanding compliance on the basis of threats or reprisals since the professional-client relationship can easily be broken off.

Structural Position

Finally, influence varies with structural characteristics of the relationship between young women and their significant others. More influence was attributed to mothers in the hypothetical vignettes than they appeared to have in actual fact. This difference may be explained by the additional influence that accrues to "mother" as a position over and above the influence that particular mothers in particular situations are able to exercise. Other structural bases of influence are relative age—"[My boyfriend's] older than me. I usually follow his advice"—and the provision of economic support—"[My parents and I] cannot afford a baby now."

Our data suggest that some bases of influence are much more effective than others in producing acquiescence and, furthermore, that access to these bases of influence varies substantially among different categories of significant others. Of persons with whom young women discussed their contraceptive problems, family planning clinic nurses were the *most* likely to be described in terms reflecting their credibility (professional, knowledgeable) and the *least* likely to be described in terms referring to the quality of their relationship with the respondent.[15] By contrast, there is a much wider range of variation in respondents' descriptions of their mothers. Both credibility and quality are salient dimensions; however, mothers are almost equally likely to be described as lacking credibility (knowing no more about contraception than the respondent) as possessing it (based on their age and experience), and the mother-daughter relationship is characterized in negative almost as often as in positive terms. Finally, at the other end of the spectrum, boyfriends' influence is based far more frequently on the quality of the relationship than on the boyfriend's credibility as a source of information or advice. In light of the relative importance of boyfriends' influence on respondents' contraceptive decisions, we must conclude that relationship quality is substantially more significant than credibility in determining the amount of influence significant others can command: A warm relationship increases both the probability that contraceptive issues will be discussed and the likelihood that advice proferred will be accepted. A warm relationship does *not* predict what that advice will be, as we have earlier observed. However, the *absence* of discussion characteristic of cooler or more conflicted relationships—with clinic nurses, with mothers, and with less-loved boyfriends—is as effective in precluding advice favorable to contraceptive protection as in screening out unfavorable advice.

CONCLUSION: CONTRACEPTIVE DECISION
PROCESSES AND THE RISK OF PREGNANCY

Whereas much of previous research on adolescent women's use of contraception has focused on their background characteristics, psychological predispositions, and attitudes (Nathanson and Becker, 1983; Whitley and Schofield, 1986; Hofferth, 1987b) the project I have described was based on the proposition that unsuccessful contraception may result from unfavorable *circumstances* rather than from unfavorable individual characteristics. Specifically, attention was centered on contraceptive decision processes *subsequent* to obtaining a medical method of contraception at a health department family planning clinic. As a way of summarizing the results, I offer some tentative answers to two questions: First, what is it about the circumstances of adolescent women's contraceptive use that increases the probability of pregnancy risks? Second, under what circumstances are those risks more or less likely to be successfully negotiated?

There is little question that young women's perceptions of oral contraception—as both powerful, leading to the discounting of alternative methods, and dangerous, leading to a low threshold for discontinuation—were the most important circumstances in conditioning their risk of pregnancy. Other research has documented the problems in obtaining compliance with *any* medical regimen that must be continued indefinitely in the absence of symptoms (Haynes, Taylor, and Sackett, 1979) but less well recognized are the problems that oral contraception, specifically, presents to adolescent women: It has side effects that may be difficult to conceal, thereby compromising independent management of sexuality; and its side effects may mimic pregnancy, generating fear of the very event the pill is designed to prevent. Under these conditions the predictable risks of pregnancy often appear less threatening than the mysterious and unpredictable risks of the pill.

A second circumstance that increases the probability of pregnancy risk is that the decision to use contraception is seldom made with the intention of preventing pregnancy *in the abstract*. Young women make these decisions in the context of *particular relationships,* and it is these relationships that give meaning to their decisions. On the one hand, contraceptive events may be used to test the relationship, and, on the other, changes in the relationship frequently precipitate changes in the pattern of contraception. Both of these occasions are associated with increased risk of pregnancy, and the inherent fragility of adolescent relationships means that they occur with some frequency.

Finally, I must emphasize that contraceptive decisions are made in a larger climate of values where norms against premature parenthood and favorable to alternative roles for women must compete with a host of other considerations. I have called attention to respondents' more immediate concerns about health, about the quality of relationships, and about control over their own sexual and reproductive powers. However, their contraceptive decisions are powerfully influenced, in addition, by a normative climate in which adolescent sexuality still must be concealed, adolescent pregnancy is disapproved, and "babies" are highly valued. We are still (or have become again) a society in which sex is redeemed by motherhood. High rates of adolescent pregnancy and childbearing are attributable, in part, to these conflicting values.

In our data, the single variable most frequently associated with *successful* negotiation of a potential pregnancy risk, particularly a risk associated with contraceptive method-related problems (the largest category of event "triggers," as I have noted), was immediate consultation with family planning clinic staff. (Consultation with a private physician was both much less frequent and less likely to be "successful" in our terms.) Young women who were quick to consult the clinic generally defined their problem in "medical" terms, were concerned about pregnancy, and were strongly advised by boyfriends and others to seek medical advice. However, many respondents who did not turn to the clinic could be similarly described. The principal distinguishing characteristic of the former group are their positive comments about the professionalism and concern for the respondent's welfare of clinic staff. Earlier, I pointed out that clinic nurses were regarded as a highly credible source of information and advice. Our data suggest that, given the opportunity, they can also be highly influential.

To some extent, the same circumstances that promote pregnancy risks simultaneously work against the successful negotiation of risk. *Unsuccessful* negotiation is the product of relationships with boyfriends in which contraception takes on meanings that have little to do with protection from pregnancy and of a value hierarchy in which preventing pregnancy is not the most pressing concern. These meanings and these values are neither pathological nor inexplicable. They reflect a set of priorities that are, however, very different from the priorities of the adult authorities with whose ideas and actions this book has been largely concerned, accounting perhaps for the perception reflected in David T. Ellwood's recent statement that, "ample evidence supports almost any model of teenage behavior (i.e., teenage pregnancy) except a model of pure rational choice" (1989:12).

Judgments of rationality are, of course, heavily dependent on who is the judge. From the perspective of the young women we interviewed, the model within which their sexual and contraceptive decisions are made—a model in which their need for personal control of their bodies and of their fates must constantly be weighed against the values that inhere in their relationships with others—is at least as "rational" as any of the models that I have previously described.

PART FIVE *Conclusion*

SEXUAL SOCIAL CONTROL AND THE MANAGEMENT OF SOCIAL CHANGE

Chapter 11

THIS book is about the ways in which Americans have attempted to define and to cope with that most dangerous period of a woman's life: her transition from childhood to adulthood. It is, on the one hand, about the strategies that have been designed to insure an orderly transition and to manage and contain individual disorder, and, on the other, about the periodic transformation of individual disorder into a menace to the order of society itself. My aim in this final chapter is less to summarize the empirical material I have presented—although I will, of course, refer to it—than to draw together the threads of theoretical argument that have appeared and reappeared throughout the book. My discussion falls into two broad sections, corresponding roughly to the two levels—individual and societal—where dangers from young women's transition have been identified and responses devised.

THE SEXUAL SOCIAL CONTROL
OF ADOLESCENT WOMEN

Among the most poignant accounts of the perils that attend young women's transition from girlhood to womanhood was written over 350 years ago: Juliet's unsanctioned employment of her newly awakened sexuality leads— very quickly, in Shakespeare's narrative—to her death.[1] The dangers in this transition were not a discovery of the nineteenth century. However, changes during the nineteenth century in both social structure and ideology com- bined to increase its seeming perils: shifts in the structure of family and work weakened the institutional supports for a sexually protected transition at the same time that sexuality and its consequences came to be seen as definitive of women's identity and prospects. The specific parameters of a safe passage from puberty to womanhood have changed since the nineteenth century, as has the language in which its perils are expressed; however, it continues to be portrayed as a period of heightened opportunities and dangers, a time when the consequences of a false step today are not easily retrievable tomorrow. Until recently, as I have pointed out, it was her prospects as a wife and mother that the young woman was seen to endanger; now, it is her prospects for a successful career.[2] Nevertheless, whether girls who "consent" are said to lose their chastity and be "ruined" for all but suicide or prostitution, or whether—less colorfully—they are described as risking pregnancy and "severe problems which may impede their opportunities to lead fulfilling adult lives," their futures as adults have a far higher probability than those of their male counterparts of being portrayed as determined by their sexual behavior as adolescents.[3]

The "truth" of this portrayal is, of course, an empirical question. The question is unanswerable—except anecdotally—for most of the period covered by this book; the accuracy of deterministic portrayals as descriptions of current reality is a matter of scholarly disagreement as I described in Chapter 8. There may, indeed, be no single answer; the degree of determinism in the life course—and what, in fact, determines what—varies with time, place, and circumstances (see, e.g., Brinton, 1988; Burton, 1990). Nevertheless, culturally predicted "moral careers"—Erving Goffman's term for the common pathways followed by members of a social category—are more than simply descriptive. Because they influence how others respond to the individuals in question, these career predictions are often self-fulfilling. Prophecies of "ruin" (however defined) simultaneously warn of and prescribe the fate that awaits young women who depart from the path of sexual orthodoxy.

Women's too precocious sexuality "disorders" far more than just their individual lives or the tenets of conventional morality. Male as well as female sexuality in adolescence represents an assertion of adult status—of maturity and independence of parental control—by individuals socially defined as children. However, the sexuality of adolescent women—with its potential for nonmarital pregnancy and birth—violates not only the hierarchy of generations but of genders as well. In patriarchal systems of gender stratification, sexual autonomy is the prerogative not simply of adults but of males. Young women are expected to preserve their sexuality to be bargained in exchange for a man's social protection and economic support—support for themselves and for their children. The sexually unorthodox girl threatens not just her own future, but an entire system of social and economic relationships based on the assumption that each individual woman and her children will be supported by an individual man. And it is in these structurally disruptive possibilities that the dangers of young women's transition to adulthood most particularly lie. Changes in society, economy, and ideology since the Victorian era have put the terms of the traditional patriarchal bargain under enormous strain; yet no generally accepted alternative has emerged to replace it. Until, and unless, another system is developed to insure the support of mothers and children, the sexuality of an adolescent woman will continue to be regarded as a source of danger to her and to others.

Women's transition from childhood to adulthood may always have been seen as a dangerous period. However, the structural and the ideological dimensions of this period have undergone a series of changes since the middle of the nineteenth century, contributing to very different visions both of the danger itself and of how it should be managed and controlled. These changes consist, first, of alterations in the structure of young women's lives: Until sometime in the nineteenth century, the majority of young American women passed the period from puberty to marriage in their own homes as domestic assistants to their mothers. With the movement of domestic production outside the home this became an increasingly less viable role even for young women of the middle class, and work in the home was replaced by work outside the home, either as wageworkers or, increasingly, as students. Thus, the structural conditions for a protected female adolescence disappeared at the same time as the duration of "adolescence"—in the sense of dependence on parental support—grew longer. There have been ideological changes as well. The ideology of the innocent girl—the notion of the unmarried postpubescent girl as intrinsically innocent and without sexual interest—has been supplanted by a recognition of her sexual interests, although that recognition has yet to be integrated into any coherent ideological alternative: Young women's sexuality is recognized but not affirmed. Finally, there has been a change in conceptions of the futures for which young women are being prepared. Until very recently young women's futures continued to be ideologically defined in terms of marriage and motherhood. This conception has by no means disappeared, but now it must compete with an alternative ideology in which priority is given to young women's preparation for work outside the home. Women's adolescence continues to be defined as dangerous; it is the future it endangers that has been changed. The notion of adolescence as a period of struggle with life's basic purposes for girls—as well as boys—is a new one. Much as boy's puberty became of interest in the early twentieth century at a time of expansion both in the range and in the perceived decisiveness of choices made during adolescence, so contemporary interest in female adolescence may in part be explained by parallel developments in the situation of girls.

The questions of precisely how and by whom the dangers of female adolescence should be managed and controlled have been answered in many different ways. In his play, Shakespeare assigns responsibility for resolving the problem of Juliet's dangerous passion for Romeo to her father, her nurse, and her priest, none of whose strategies was, of course, successful. Since the mid-nineteenth century, there has been a continuous, if halting, shift in responsibility for the regulation of young women's sexuality away from parents and the clergy to professional "experts" and the state. In this process, the "problem" represented by the sexually unorthodox girl has been repeatedly redefined, from moral to criminal to medical to economic; however, new designations do not so much supplant the old ones as become their competitors. "Philosophies of moralistic judgement and punitive treatment . . . , of a nonmoralistic and clinical effort to cure disease and protect society, and of a reformative attempt to produce a better adjustment to the community and its standards" struggle today as they did when Paul Tappan wrote these words in 1947, referring to the management of sexually active young women in the juvenile court of Chicago (1947:88). The actions of birth control advocates in the 1970s simply moved this struggle to a larger and far more public arena. Their goals were to have young women's sexuality—under the label of "teenage pregnancy"— designated as a problem in preventive medicine, and for the medical solution to be sponsored by the state. Among the results of this endeavor was the politicization of female adolescence. The state did intervene. The sexual and reproductive behavior of unmarried young women was accorded official recognition as a problem requiring the attention of government. The effect of state intervention, however, was to substantially raise both the philosophical and the programmatic stakes in deciding which of the competing definitions of the problem and which of the competing solutions the government would, in fact, adopt. Suddenly, access to programmatic resources and the success of political agendas appeared to hinge on the meanings attributed to young women's sexuality and its consequences.

Effectively, no single definition of the problem or proposed solution has commanded wholehearted government support—at any level of government. Ironically, birth control is for the time being both the least "officially" popular solution and, relatively speaking, the best funded. This lack of resolution gives old players a stake in keeping the problem of "teenage pregnancy" alive—if only to protect the investment they have already made, and attracts a constant stream of new players with new definitions and new solutions into the game. In recent years, almost no domestic social problem—from education to AIDS to drugs to welfare—has escaped being linked to teenage pregnancy. In part, these actions are a measure of the salience of adolescent pregnancy as a reflection and symbol of change in gender roles and the structure of the family in the United States and the absence of any societal consensus either on the meaning of these changes or on what should be done about them. However, they also reflect intense competition for the extremely limited pool of financial and political resources that are currently available to be expended on the fragile infrastructure of U.S. society, and a willingness to make rhetorical use of whatever symbols appear most likely to hold the public's attention. Sexual disorder has been among the most consistently effective of these symbols.

Over the last century, there has been a constant expansion of medical jurisdiction over the control of deviant behavior. Mental illness, alcoholism, obesity, child abuse, learning problems, and other categories of social deviance have been redefined from moral or criminal to medical problems and been treated by medical means (Conrad and Schneider, 1980). If this overall direction of social change, together with the paths taken by other industrialized countries to cope with adolescent sexuality, are any guide then birth control and abortion will ultimately prevail as the socially as well as the statistically normative responses to premarital sexual activity. It is important, therefore, to reemphasize that medicalization itself incorporates moral judgments of the behavior in question. Designation of adolescent pregnancy as a medical problem does not vindicate sexual unorthodoxy; it "reorganizes how we define and react to it and those who engage in it" (Schneider and Conrad, 1980:4). "Children having children"—phraseology regularly employed by birth control advocates—is not a morally neutral description of adolescent childbearing. It is an affirmation of age- and gender-based sexual and reproductive norms and, at the same time, an appeal to our humane understanding for the plight of the innocent "children" trapped by the consequences of normative violation. Advocates of medical solutions are no more likely than advocates of other solutions to contest fundamental structural norms. Their aim is to reorganize the manner and the threshold of response to normative violations. Regardless of where the normative threshold is placed, departures from these norms are seen as aberrations to be explained. Only the questions have changed: from Why does she have sex? to Why doesn't she use contraception? and, sometimes, Why doesn't she have an abortion?

This underlying moral framework is starkly reflected in the actions and reactions of family planning workers described in Chapter 9. These individuals—almost entirely women—are the missionaries of the new contraceptive morality. Whether their professional identity is as nurses or as counselors, they regard nonuse of contraception not primarily as a technical but as a moral failing, a sign of "personal inadequacy" (Joffe, 1986:67). As health-care workers, they are, nevertheless, required to offer humane "treatment" to a category of clients—teenage women—concerning whose sexual behavior these providers are ambivalent at best, and whose compliance with the treatment regimen can seldom be assured. The strategies workers use to resolve the resulting clash between medical and moral frameworks of evaluation and control are variations on recurrent themes of responsibility and visibility. Nurses cope with potential failure—that of their teenage clients' and, by extension, their own—by attempting to instill in young women a sense of personal contraceptive responsibility, to induce them to behave correctly out of choice and in the absence of surveillance: To convert them, in other words, into moral persons. While this strategy is intended to insure treatment success, it also allows failure—pregnancy or sexually transmitted disease—to be interpreted as a defect of character attributable to the client rather than a technical failure attributable to the nurse. An alternative strategy—more risky for the provider but also, perhaps, more rewarding—is to create a relationship with the client in which she is induced to reveal details of her sexual behavior: Once problematic behavior is made visible it becomes available for correction and control.

Moral conversion and redemption, constructions of innocence and responsibility, and tensions between visibility and concealment are recurrent themes in the practice of managing young women's private sexual behavior. This society's response to the sexually unorthodox girl has consistently depended on whether she was believed to have courted danger voluntarily or to be the victim of forces—external or internal—beyond her control. Attributions of guilt or innocence dominate the rhetoric of sexual social control practitioners; establishment of responsibility is central to the management strategies that have been devised because responsibility determines the probability of redemption. How questions of guilt and innocence are framed has changed over time to correspond with changes in beliefs about the sexual character of young women and in the popularity of one or another paradigm of social control. There is substantial continuity, nonetheless, between the situation of a sexually unorthodox young woman in the nineteenth century ejected from a Florence Crittenton Home for her failure to repent and that of the similarly unorthodox young woman of today whose second pregnancy causes her to be dropped from a program for teenage mothers. Wherever the line between deviance and conformity is drawn, a single crossing may be excused as involuntary; crossings that are repeated or unrepented are likely to be regarded as the outcome of deliberate choice. And whether the choice is characterized as sin or as irresponsibility, the response it evokes is one of punishment rather than treatment and care.

Judgments of personal responsibility have always been important in deciding a society's response to behavior it defines as deviant. However, the peculiar salience of these judgments in the case of the sexually unorthodox girl suggests that more than ordinary considerations of guilt and responsibility are at work. Unlike departures from the norms of physical health from which recovery is possible and expected, departures from sexual norms tend, as I have noted earlier, to be regarded as reflecting intrinsic and unalterable qualities of the individual. The difficulty, and the significance, of judgments about the meaning of these departures are substantially increased when—as in the case of women's adolescence—the intrinsic nature of the individual is already in doubt. Should the sexual "irresponsibility" of an adolescent woman be judged as if she were an innocent, and redeemable, child or a knowing, and unredeemable, adult? It is this second level of uncertainty—the uncertainty created by the transitional state itself—that lends an unusual intensity to the questions of innocence and responsibility that pervade discussion of the sexually unorthodox girl.

An additional recurrent theme is that of visibility and concealment. The importance of sexual privacy in American society goes far beyond considerations of personal modesty. Behavior that is unknown and unseen cannot and, of equal importance, need not be regulated or controlled. The impulse to evade discovery and control is inherent in our conceptions of sexuality as an uncontrollable force and, at the same time, as the supreme means of individual expression. Concealment, however, has a dual meaning. It is associated, on the one hand, with sexual autonomy; on the other, it testifies to the power of the social norms that make concealment necessary. Similarly, visibility signals the lifting of normative constraints—the early twentieth-century "repeal of reticence" on sexual matters has been so interpreted as, of course, has contemporary openness about sex; at the same time, the production of visibility opens up new possibilities for control.

Negotiation of visibility is a central issue in the social control of private sexual behavior. Mothers in the nineteenth century were told how to recognize their daughters' secret masturbation; the daughters were told that masturbation could not be concealed. In the late twentieth century, there has been persistent conflict between those who would reveal young women's sexuality to their parents by various schemes to require parental consent for abortion and contraception and those who regard parental consent requirements as (among other things) a betrayal of sexual secrets. At the same time, revelation of sexual secrets has become a major strategy for professional— and even semiprofessional—management of sexuality. On a national scale, statistics publicizing the sexual activity, pregnancies, and abortions of teenage women are among the most indispensable tools of program advocates. The purposes for which sexual visibility is produced may be benign or repressive. Nevertheless, the fact of knowledge allows—and may even require—a regulatory response. Invisible deviance can be ignored. To ignore visibly deviant behavior runs the risk of appearing to condone it. Decline in private sexual space is, for better or worse, often accompanied by an increase in the public regulation of sexual behavior.[4]

The principal agents of female social control are other women. Since the middle of the nineteenth century, the concerns of largely middle-class, white women with the sexual and/or social exploitation of women by men have led some among them to become advocates for women's greater protection and control and have influenced others to participate in movements for women's empowerment. Although these activities are, in some sense, two sides of the same coin, their impact on status relationships among women and between women and men can be very different. As the activities of protection and control became increasingly bureaucratized, a gender-based division of labor emerged in which the frontline workers in the sexual regulation industry—social workers, nurses, counselors, teachers, members of the semiprofessions—were, and continue to be, almost exclusively female. Estelle Freedman (1981) has described how nineteenth-century middle-class women were drawn into prison reform in part by their identification with women— even women prisoners—as a sexual class, redeemable through their intrinsic moral superiority *as women*. With the establishment of separate women's prisons staffed by women, divergent class and institutional interests overwhelmed common interests based on gender, and control replaced redemption as the dominant philosophy of correction in women's prisons as well as in those for men. Throughout the period of this book, the most likely subjects for protection and control have been very young women, women in "trouble" (where trouble is almost invariably defined in sexual terms), and women whose class, ethnic, or racial backgrounds diverged sharply from those of their would-be protectors. However women are drawn into organized activities regulating the behavior of other women, the gender-based interests they have in common with those whom they have engaged to help must compete with, and are often superceded by divergent interests not only of class, ethnicity, race, and organizational role, but—in the case of teenage women—of generation as well.

As I warned in my introductory chapter, this book has been primarily concerned with the activities and ideologies of the philosophers and practitioners of sexual social control: policy advocates, moral reformers, scholars and judges, religious and social workers, workers in the fields of health and medicine. I have attempted to place those activities and ideologies in the context of change in the circumstances of young women in the aggregate but, with the exception of the material contained in Chapter 10, the voices of young women themselves have been largely absent. However, as that chapter tries to make clear, young women are very far from being passive objects of control. Kathy Peiss (1986) has described how, within the framework of contemporary ideologies and opportunities, working-class young women in New York City at the turn of the century negotiated "heterosocial" occasions and encounters, balancing their own interests against the concerns of their parents and the desires of men. Similarly, young women interviewed in the mid-1980s negotiated with parents, boyfriends, and health workers, attempting both to protect their sexual autonomy and to preserve cherished relationships with their families and their male companions. These goals were often conflicting and are even in some respects contradictory: Young women's sexual autonomy was readily compromised by the demands of their sometimes fragile relationships with boyfriends. Nevertheless, these young women were not victims, either of the social control bureaucracy or of their personal relationships. They were resourceful individuals who used the means available to them—including the services of family planning clinics—in their own fashion and to attain their own ends.

SEXUALITY, SOCIAL DISORDER, AND SOCIAL CHANGE

In the first chapter of this book I called attention to two aspects of societal response to the sexually unorthodox girl: as a target of intervention to bring about the redemption and control of deviant individuals and as a symbol of social disorder and social change.[5] Since the late nineteenth century young women's sexual unorthodoxies have twice become the focus of societywide social movements for sexual control. Earlier, I proposed three sets of conditions to account for the emergence of these movements; I return to the further consideration of those conditions below. However, I first want to address a question raised—but not answered—at the beginning of the book: Why in recent times has the sexuality of unmarried young women become such a powerful vehicle for the personalization and moralization of social change?

This is not an easy question. It has been addressed directly or indirectly by historians as well as sociologists, and in my own answer I try to weave together the different and somewhat disparate threads of their ideas. The notion of sex as each individual's central and most distinguishing characteristic, dividing the population into two incommensurable gender classes, first appeared early in the nineteenth century. Its appearance coincided with major changes in Western social and family structure: the decline of the authoritarian state, the rise of the bourgeoisie, and the emergence of the private family. All of these changes have been associated with the new importance attached to distinctions based on sex and gender.

Thomas Laqueur suggests that "the new biology, with its search for fundamental differences between the sexes and between their desires, emerged at precisely the time when the foundations of the old social order were irremediably shaken," undermined by the egalitarianism of Enlightenment philosophers and apostles of democratic government (1987:16). The old "natural" feudal and theological bases for patriarchal authority were destroyed but the newly discovered "natural" distinctions between the sexes allowed patriarchal authority itself to be retained. A somewhat similar argument was made by Michel Foucault: the nineteenth-century bourgeoisie, he suggests, used distinctions of sex—of "body, vigor, longevity, progeniture, and descent"—in the same way that the aristocracy had employed distinctions of caste, to affirm the self and to mark out differences from other, less-favored, beings (1978:123). The essential point of both these arguments is that sexually defined inequalities became an increasingly important basis of the social order in Western societies as the legitimacy of other bases fell away. Laqueur cites de Tocqueville to suggest that this point applied with particular force to the United States (1987:18).

At the same time, equally profound changes were taking place in the structure of the family. What Carl N. Degler describes as the "modern" American family "emerged first in the years between the American revolution and about 1830" (1980:8). Among the central characteristics of this family was its clear separation of male and female roles.

> The primary role of the wife was the care of children and the maintenance of the home. Furthermore, the wife, as the mistress of the home, was perceived by society and herself as the moral superior of the husband, though his legal and social inferior. The organizational basis for this relationship was that woman's life was physically spent within the home and with the family, while the man's was largely outside the home, at work. The ideological justification of this division of labor and activity [was] "the doctrine of . . . separate spheres" (1980:8–9).

The private family—insulated from the harsh masculine world of work with the mother as its central figure and linchpin—was the structural embodiment of the new "natural" hierarchy of gender on which the stability of the social order was seen to depend. It is not difficult to see that the uncontrolled sexuality of women appeared to threaten this structure at its core: ready availability of women's sexual and other services outside of marriage would compromise one of the principal incentives for men to marry and to remain married. Women, on the other hand, had few alternatives to economic dependence on men; sexual exclusivity in marriage was a principal resource with which they bargained for their economic security. However, uncontrolled female sexuality threatened more than just the "modern" family. In the nineteenth century, when the gender-based structure of the family became identified with the stability of the social order, the sexuality of women was perceived to endanger the very foundations of society itself. It is this latter perception, I believe, that accounts for the continued resonance of young women's nonmarital sexuality as a sign and symbol of social disorder and social change.

The resonance of sexuality as a marker of social and cultural boundaries is a necessary but not a sufficient condition for the coalescence of social movements around sexual issues. Theories of the rise and decline of social movements suggest that their explanation requires careful attention to the specific ideologies and beliefs that these movements embody and to the social structural conditions under which they appear. In Chapter 1, I advanced three hypotheses—one normative and two structural—to account for the emergence of sexual social movements in the nineteenth and twentieth centuries. These hypotheses have guided my examination of turn-of-the-century movements centered around prostitution, the age of consent, and venereal disease and of contemporary movements to control adolescent pregnancy; they will also serve as a framework for comparison between these two sets of movement activities.

I have proposed a two-dimensional conceptualization of sexual social movements: on the one hand, as moral boundary crises—occasions in which the society's moral order is reasserted against the threat of deviant behavior; and, on the other, as classical social movements—collective, organized attempts to bring about, or to resist and reverse, social change. The three conditions necessary for sexual social movements to appear, in the order in which they will be discussed, are: first, the visibility of normative violations; second, the compounding of perceived normative violations by conflict over the legitimacy of the norms themselves; and third, the presence in society of social "entrepreneurs" prepared to exploit normative crises as a means to the advancement of organizational or political objectives.

The Visibility of Normative Violations
The underlying issues at stake in the turn-of-the-century sexual social movements, as well as in contemporary activities surrounding adolescent pregnancy, were and are changes in the roles of women, changes foreshadowed by the behavior of women in adolescence. This assertion is likely to be more controversial in its application to earlier than to the more recent movement activities. However (as I argued in Chapter 7), it is supported by several historians' interpretations of the earlier movements as well as by movement participants' own accounts of their motives; it is also consistent with the theoretical argument identifying adherence to gender-defined social and sexual roles with nineteenth-century conceptions of the social order.

For a variety of reasons—demographic, economic, and social—the visibility of single young women as a social category increased substantially between 1850 and 1900 and, again, in the late 1960s and early 1970s. The visibility of a social phenomenon is not sui generis; it results from a conjunction of objective conditions (which may or may not be "new" conditions) with the desires and capacities of human actors to put these conditions before the public and to define them in particular ways. There is, nevertheless, a striking parallel between these two periods in at least one set of objective conditions affecting young women: The U.S. population at the turn of the century as well as in the recent past was characterized by high proportions of youth relative to adults and by relatively late ages at marriage. Thus, both sexual social movements have been associated with the presence in the population of unusually large numbers of unmarried young women. Both movements were, in addition, preceded and (to varying degrees) accompanied by other social changes— the movement of single young women into the urban labor force in the late nineteenth century, the politicization (and sexualization) of youth in the 1960s, the legalization of abortion in the early 1970s—that called attention to single young women as a social category. These changes were well-documented by contemporary observers; they were made known to a receptive audience; and demand for more data was generated. This is, of course, a circular process wherein cause and effect are virtually impossible to disentangle. The outcome, nonetheless, both at the turn of the century and in the 1970s, was an unprecedented explosion of information bearing on the sexuality of unmarried young women: In each case, sexually unorthodox behavior acquired a level of visibility unknown to the immediately preceding generation.

Normative Violations and Normative Legitimacy
The increased visibility of sexually unorthodox behavior was accompanied by an apparent blurring of moral boundaries between deviant and respectable sexuality. Among the beliefs common to both social movements were that individuals socially defined as respectable were engaging in unrespectable behavior and that behavior traditionally defined as unrespectable was in danger of being sanctioned by the state. Movement participants portrayed the very definition of sexual orthodoxy as at stake and demanded action either to restore the old boundaries or to erect new ones.

Historically, in the United States sexuality has been attributed to categories of persons clearly located outside the margins of respectable society—immigrants, lower-class women, prostitutes, and blacks. In the early 1900s, as I have described, a combination of demographic, economic, social, and ideological changes began to cast doubt on the validity of these attributions, particularly as they applied to unmarried young women. They were openly challenged by well-publicized evidence of sexual interest on the part of mainstream, supposedly "innocent" girls ("nice" girls in "good positions in society," "country girls," and the like). Similarly, in the late 1960s, circumstances again led to the perception of blurred boundaries between deviant sexuality—identified in that period primarily with blacks rather than with immigrants or prostitutes— and the sexuality of white middle-class youth. As the evidence of their publications and testimony to Congress clearly demonstrates, this latter perception was subsequently fostered and, indeed, employed as a major political resource by birth control advocates in their promotion of teenage pregnancy. The emergence of adolescent pregnancy as a public problem in the early 1970s coincided with a shift in public perception of the social location of heterosexual deviance from black to white young women, just as the antiprostitution crusade coincided with a period of intense public concern about *white* slavery. Thus, both sexual social movements were preceded and accompanied by proclamations of a moral boundary crisis, proclamations that were stated in remarkably similar terms. In the 1980s, the designation of "deviant" sexuality and reproduction as predominantly black problems was resurrected, amounting, in effect, to a reassertion of the moral boundaries blurred by the social changes of the late 1960s and by birth control advocates' effective exploitation of these changes.

Rhetorically exaggerated shifts in the social location of sexual unorthodoxy are a relatively minor challenge to traditional moral boundaries compared with the perceived threat that behavior formerly designated as deviant will be legitimized by the state. In the Progressive Era legitimation was represented by government "regulation" of prostitution (the medical inspection of prostitutes and their official confinement to specified sections of the city); in our own time, it has been represented by federally funded birth control services for adolescent women and by school-based clinics offering contraception to female students. The arguments advanced in support of these activities by late nineteenth-century and early twentieth-century regulationists and by contemporary birth control advocates are remarkably similar. The "deviant" sexual behavior *itself* is described as essentially uncontrollable; attention is directed instead to the behavior's consequences. These consequences are defined, in turn, as a public health not a moral problem, as inevitable in the absence of deliberate intervention, and as manageable by rational, scientific means. From the perspective of moral conservatives, on the other hand, state-subsidized birth control for teenage women, like state regulation of prostitution, not only rewards immoral behavior by making it "safe"; it threatens to legitimize sexual activity outside of marriage and without reproductive intent, specifically—in the case of birth control clinics—the sexual activity of *women*. Moral conservatives are far more likely to be galvanized by the possibility of legitimation than by the frequency of normative violations.

Contests over the social location of sexuality and over assignment of responsibility for the management of sexual unorthodoxy reflect a series of underlying concerns: about the challenge of single young women's sexuality to patriarchal and gender-based definitions of the female role; about the threat of penalty-free sexual access to the traditional structure of marriage; and about the status of individuals who espouse traditional conceptions of marriage and the family. They also reflect the value of symbols of sexual danger to groups engaged in what are essentially political struggles to advance particular public policy agendas.

Entrepreneurial Groups

In the language of social movement theory, sexual ideologies and ways of living that express those ideologies can be conceptualized as "collective goods," shared interests from whose realization all those in a given group will benefit and in whose protection they all, correspondingly, have a stake (e.g., Fireman and Gamson, 1979). However, as I have argued earlier, shared ideological interests and a set of social and/or political circumstances that can be defined as threatening to those interests are not sufficient conditions for the emergence of sexual social movements. A further, critical, condition is the existence of reasonably well-organized and powerful groups or individuals to whom the construction and promotion of these definitions appears politically or socially advantageous. Women, physicians, politicians, and a varied catalog of lay social and moral reformers have all, at one time or another, been successful in converting the sexuality of unmarried young women into organizational and political capital.

I identified three major groups of turn-of-the-century sexual social movement participants: women, politicians and businessmen, and physicians. Sexual issues were highly effective tools for the organization and politicization of women in this period, a fact of which movement leaders were well aware. Questions of sexual morality offered women a means of gaining access to the political arena through the exploitation of issues on which they were already held to be authorities by virtue of their sex and which did not threaten the male political establishment—a point that assumed increasing importance in the context of the early twentieth-century suffrage debate. Indeed, several historians have attributed turn-of-the-century sexual social movements primarily to the organizational activities of middle-class married women (e.g., Degler, 1980:279–97). However, although women set the stage, once the organizational and political potential of sexual issues had been demonstrated, other and more powerful groups began to exploit these issues as well. I have described how early twentieth-century politicians, businessmen, and physicians capitalized on public concerns about prostitution and venereal disease to advance their respective political, social, and professional agendas.

The stage in the late twentieth century was set not by groups opposed to the "scientific management" of sexuality, but by those who favored it. And the organizational interest of these groups was less in gaining access to social and political power than in protecting that which they already had. Birth control advocates' discovery of adolescent pregnancy coincided with a period of declining birth rates and of decreasing political support for family planning services directed specifically to older women and/or women publicly defined as poor and black—the very clients on whom the success of the birth control movement in the late 1960s had been built. Survival of the services network developed in earlier prosperous times demanded that a new and politically more acceptable set of clients be found. And, much as in the late nineteenth century, once the stage had been set and the political resonance of sexuality as a public issue demonstrated, other groups with their own organizational and political agendas entered the scene: some to directly contest the "scientific management" position (with, it is important to note, far less success than their turn-of-the-century counterparts), others to enhance their position by claiming special authority and/or expertise in a new and highly visible arena of public policy. Much as in the late nineteenth-century organized women's groups demanded—and were accorded—special expertise on sexual issues by virtue of an ascribed characteristic, sex, so in the late twentieth century organized groups of African-Americans have claimed—and been accorded—special expertise in the area of adolescent pregnancy by virtue of an ascribed characteristic, race. Disproportionate numbers of black young women experience nonmarital pregnancies and births, and many young women and—more recently—young men have benefited from the activities these groups have undertaken in support of family stability and educational attainment. Nevertheless, the cost of this successful claims-making activity—and I believe the cost to be high—has been the reframing of adolescent pregnancy (or sexuality or childbearing) from an issue affecting all Americans to one that is unique to blacks.

Very little has been said in the course of this book about the *constituents* of sexual social movements. Almost by definition, participants in movements for moral reform are drawn from the ranks of would-be reformers rather than from the targets of their reforming zeal.[6] These are quintessentially middle-class movements designed to support and protect middle-class values by changing the values and behavior of others to conform more closely with their own. Adherents of these movements bear some resemblance to what social movement theorists refer to as "conscience constituents," ideologically motivated individuals who have little to gain directly from movement success (e.g., McCarthy and Zald, 1977). However, along with disinterested benevolence there is, I would argue, a powerful admixture of interest in protecting "the long-run wealth and power of the group and the viability of its design for living" (Fireman and Gamson, 1979:24) against what are perceived as alternative moralities highly disruptive to the social order.

Students of status politics have suggested that moral reform movements draw primarily from socially and politically alienated groups attempting to recover the status and prestige they have lost (e.g., Gusfield, 1963; Lipset and Raab, 1970). This perspective is clearly too narrow to encompass the variety of participants in sexual social movements (physicians, suffragists, politicians, Planned Parenthood volunteers, black churchwomen). The work presented in this book, as well as recent historical research, strongly suggests that these movements have been generated less to protect declining social status than as a means of gaining (or keeping) access to social and political power.

CONSPICUOUSLY absent from my account of the groups that became involved in adolescent pregnancy as a public problem, either at the time of its emergence in the 1970s or since, have been representatives of the feminist movement. Women from the movement's organizations do not appear at Congressional hearings on teenage pregnancy nor have their views on this issue been widely reported in the press. In several recent and widely cited reviews of feminist perspectives on sexuality, adolescent women's sexuality is not mentioned (by contrast, at least half of each review is devoted to lesbian sexuality) (Snitow, Stansell, and Thompson, 1983; Vance, 1984; Rich, 1986). Reading the work of the few feminist scholars who have written on this question (the only one who gives it more than passing attention is Rosalind P. Petchesky) suggests that adolescent sexuality, pregnancy and childbearing are, indeed, uncomfortable issues for feminists (e.g., Gordon, 1977; Greer, 1984; Petchesky, 1984). The reasons for this discomfort and the lacunae in feminist policy and scholarship that have resulted from it deserve some attention.

With few exceptions, the first wave of feminists in the late nineteenth century believed that women had relatively little interest in sex and that the sole beneficiaries of sex separated from reproduction would be men.

> Legal, efficient birth control would have increased men's freedom to indulge in extramarital sex without greatly increasing women's freedom to do so. . . . The double standard of the Victorian sexual and family system, which had made men's sexual freedom irresponsible and oppressive to women, left most feminists convinced that increasing, rather than releasing, the taboos against extramarital sex was in their interest and they threw their support behind social purity campaigns (Gordon, 1977:110–11).

Contemporary feminist attitudes toward both sexuality and reproduction are considerably more complicated than those of their nineteenth-century counterparts. Sexual autonomy and reproductive choice are cornerstones of second-wave feminist ideology. At the same time, heterosexual sex in the context of continued inequalities of gender is often ideologically defined (and experienced) as oppressive to women, and reproductive "choice" is almost invariably used to mean the choice not to reproduce. The inconsistencies inherent in these ideological perspectives—women have the right to choose, but some choices are better than others—may be one of the reasons for feminists' silence on the question of adolescent pregnancy.

To interfere in (even to pass judgment on) the sexual and reproductive decisions of adolescent women violates deeply held principles of reproductive autonomy: one woman does not tell another what to do with her body. Interference across lines of status is particularly problematic. Older, white middle-class women (the majority of feminists) may be especially reluctant to risk the appearance of discrimination by questioning the decisions of women who are not only younger, but have been publicly defined as poor and black. Nevertheless, within the feminist canon the "choices" made by adolescent women are inherently suspect. Young women are seen as confronting cultural and social pressures that seriously limit their capacity for autonomous sexual decisions, pressures that may be exacerbated rather than relieved by the ready availability of birth control and abortion. "Even though the technology of birth control in itself contributes to women's sexual independence, it also deprives women of some important weapons," weapons of sexual denial and of pregnancy that may be used as bargaining chips in women's power struggle with men (Gordon, 1977:409). Unwillingness to forgo these weapons was, of course, exactly the reason for nineteenth-century feminists' opposition to birth control. The choices of adolescent women to become mothers are likely to be as suspect as their choices to have sex. It is difficult for middle-class feminist women—many of whom have condemned the mother role as both oppressive to women and as inhibiting their personal development—to conceive of motherhood, particularly "premature" motherhood, as a positive choice (as, indeed, it almost certainly is for many young women who grow up poor; see, e.g., Geronimus, 1987; Burton, 1990). To "choose" motherhood is to be suspected by modern feminists either of being victimized or of copping out. In neither circumstance is the choice ideologically acceptable.

The conflicting ideological perspectives I have described are perhaps a sufficient reason for feminists to stay out of the adolescent pregnancy issue. However, a second and equally important reason is co-optation of this issue first, by the family planning establishment and, second, by moral conservatives aided and abetted by a conservative federal administration. Implicit in feminists' conceptualization of reproductive control as a "woman's right" is opposition to *any* interference in that right, either for or against. "Family planners'" promotion of birth control as a means of stabilizing the family (in the 1940s), of population control (in the 1960s), and of preventing teen pregnancy (in the 1970s) are beside the point—even contrary to the point—if the central issue in reproductive control is defined as empowering women to make their *own* choices. There is a strong vein of antielitism, antiprofessionalism, anti-medicalization in this position: birth control and abortion belong to women, not to doctors or, indeed, to any other "agents of social control" that presume to tell women what is good for them. In this same vein, feminists are, of course, equally opposed to negative interference in reproductive control, and the specter of adolescent pregnancy has been used to promote the restrictive agenda of moral conservatives as well as the protective agenda of birth control advocates. Irrespective of where they stood on adolescent pregnancy, feminists could find themselves in alliances with groups whose company they would prefer to avoid; under these conditions to ignore the issue may appear as the wisest course. I believe, however, that this appearance is deceiving. As a summary label, "adolescent pregnancy" both problematizes and politicizes young women's transition to adulthood. In conceding this territory to mainstream policy analysts, program advocates, and politicians, feminist scholars allow among the most basic parameters of women's lives to be defined by groups and individuals with conceptions of the good society—and of the place of women in it—that are often very different from their own.

REFLECTIONS

There is in the United States a powerful strain toward locating the sources of social conflict and social change in the failings of individuals rather than in the inadequacies of social institutions. Social dislocations that result from large-scale social and economic change are framed as personal problems and their solutions couched in terms of alterations in individual behavior. Since the nineteenth century, when women's adherence to narrowly defined sexual and family roles became identified with the overall stability of the social order, women's departures from these roles have routinely been translated into causes as well as symbols of disorder and change: The burden of transformation not only in sexual mores, but in other dimensions of society as well, has come to be placed upon women (cf. Brandt, 1985:168). By the same token, for order to be restored requires that women's disorderly behavior be controlled. "It was sex not capitalism," as David J. Rothman (1980:56) succinctly puts it, that had to be contained.

Rothman was writing about the Progressive Era. However, I would argue that there is little difference between turn-of-the-century moral reformers who attributed the social problems of a rapidly urbanizing and industrializing society to prostitution and contemporary policy analysts who attribute poverty in the ghettos of America's largest cities to adolescent pregnancy. Both scenarios deflect attention away from underlying social and economic arrangements to the unorthodox sexuality of women; both suggest that the solution to social problems lies in the control of sexuality rather than in more fundamental institutional change. There is, for example, substantial agreement among at least some policy analysts that poverty in American cities is the outcome of profound changes in the larger American economy (Harrington, 1984; National Conference of Catholic Bishops, 1986; Wilson, 1987). However, among the social policy consequences of the individualistic perspective I have described is that responsibility for managing the effects of economic change is assigned not to groups or individuals whose mandate is to examine and propose changes in the economic structures of the United States as a whole but to specialists in the manipulation of individual behavior—medical and social service personnel, public health officials, and educators, together with what have been described as "the least powerful and most poorly organized sectors of the national government" (Weir, Orloff, and Skocpol, 1988:425). This assignment insures that existing relationships of wealth and power and the institutions that embody these relationships will remain undisturbed.

The inventors of "adolescent pregnancy" intended to draw attention to what they believed to be a national health and social problem calling for action on a commensurate scale. They could have foreseen neither the level nor the shape of their success. The campaign launched by birth control advocates in the 1970s had by the mid-1980s moved almost entirely out of its originators' control. In the process a new category of sexually unorthodox woman was created who—like the prostitute, the "wayward girl," and the "woman adrift"—became a ready-made symbol of, and sometimes scapegoat for, the undesired consequences of social and economic change. This transforming process was markedly accelerated in the early 1980s by the reframing of "adolescent pregnancy" from a problem of U.S. society as a whole to a problem of its African-American minority.

The reframing of adolescent pregnancy was an integral part of the conservative political revival that began in the late 1970s; the resulting shift in public perceptions concerning the social location of adolescent sexuality and childbearing had and continues to have serious consequences for the formation of social policy. These consequences include, first, the marginalization of "adolescent pregnancy" as a social issue and, with it, the larger issue of sexuality as a force in American society, and, second, the reinforcement of already well-established tendencies to attribute poverty and other social dislocations to the sexual unorthodoxies of women. There are few more effective strategies for deflecting challenge to the existing institutions and values of a society than to locate the challengers outside not only of that society's traditional moral boundaries but of its traditional social boundaries as well, outside—in current jargon—the "mainstream."

In his book, *The Undeserving Poor*, Michael B. Katz quotes an unnamed talk-show host who told him, "I don't mind paying to help people in need, but I don't want my tax dollars to pay for the sexual pleasure of adolescents who won't use birth control" (1989:215). Apart from its other implications, few comments could have illustrated so clearly the change that had taken place between the 1960s and the 1980s in the moral status of birth control for single adolescent women: from a private option for the wealthy to a public prescription for the poor. The host's comments point, in addition, to the dangers that lie in advocating birth control (or abortion) on grounds other than as a means for enlarging the opportunities of women to gain control of their lives. Advocacy on the grounds that birth control use by adolescent women will solve society's problems of health, poverty, and public spending invites the inference that these problems are a direct result of adolescent childbearing and, by an easy transition, the selective prescription of birth control as their solution—not as an option, but as a demand.

Thus, the "social problems" argument for birth control, as well as the identification of "adolescent pregnancy" with young women who are black, contributes to the deflection of responsibility for social misery away from the institutions and values of society at large and toward the deviant behavior of individual young women. If "adolescent pregnancy" is a black problem, then it cannot logically be attributed to the sexual hypocrisy of the larger American society (see, e.g., Jones et al., 1986). If social problems can be solved by the selective prevention of childbearing, then untimely childbearing—not "institutional relationships that distribute power and wealth inequitably" (National Conference of Catholic Bishops, 1986:420)—must be their cause. These inferences are simplistic, but they are easily made, and they lead to policies that call not for institutional change but for the social control of women.

Notes,
Bibliography,
and
Index

Notes

CHAPTER 1

1. "Teenage" and "adolescent" pregnancy are popularly employed as generic labels for the social problem represented by the sexual activity, pregnancy, and child-bearing of unmarried women between the ages of puberty and marriage or adulthood. This choice of label (the use of one aspect of the problem, and that the most transient, to refer to the whole) is itself a curious phenomenon, and one to which I will return. For ease of exposition, however, from here on I follow popular usage and employ the generic labels "adolescent pregnancy" or, more rarely, "teenage pregnancy" without quotation marks.

2. Among the few critical voices have been Petchesky (1984), Geronimus (1987), Huling (1988), and Vinovskis (1988).

3. "Cultures of resistance" is Weeks's term for that aspect of the history of sexuality that documents "avoidance of, or resistance to, the moral code" (1981:15). Lee's book *The Search for an Abortionist* (1969) vividly describes women's abortion referral networks under conditions of illegal abortion. A more recent example is provided by Cartoof's data on the operation of Massachusetts's parental consent for abortion law. As young women affected by the law become increasingly knowledgeable about and accepting of out-of-state abortion, a larger and larger number "will be influenced by their peers to leave Massachusetts in search of an abortion" (1984:193).

4. Contemporary adolescent pregnancy literature focuses primarily on young women's behavior, as I stated earlier. However, the perspective from which this behavior is examined is that of parents concerned to keep their daughters out of trouble, not, for the most part, that of young women themselves. It is the latter perspective for which evidence is lacking. Among literature on the contemporary adolescent pregnancy scene, Ladner's *Tomorrow's Tomorrow: The Black Woman* (1971) is an important exception. Some examples of recent works that describe aspects of young women's sexual strategies in the nineteenth and early twentieth centuries are Peiss (1983, 1986), Fass (1977), Bailey (1988), and Rothman (1987). I make more detailed reference to these works in later chapters.

5. My summary of approaches to the conceptualization of sexuality is heavily indebted to Weeks's review, published under the title, "Sexuality and the Historian," as chapter 1 of his book, *Sex, Politics and Society: The Regulation of Sexuality Since 1800* (1981).

6. The theoretical questions raised in this paragraph have been addressed by a wide range of scholars with very different perspectives. See, e.g., Collins (1971), Padgug (1979), Eisenstein (1981), Ortner and Whitehead (1981), Laqueur (1987), and Caldwell, Caldwell, and Quiggin (1989).

7. This orientation is exemplified by two somewhat distinct bodies of literature, the more general work on the sociology of social control referred to earlier, and the work of medical sociologists specifically concerned with the medicalization of deviance. Work in the first category is reviewed in Cohen and Scull (1983) and Scull (1988). In the second category, see Zola (1975), Schneider and Conrad (1980), and Conrad and Schneider (1980).

8. The European witchcraze was conceptualized in boundary crisis terms by Ben-Yehuda (1985), the Massachusetts Bay crime waves by Erikson (1966), and the McCarthy witch-hunt by Bergesen (1984).

9. The conditions for sexual social movements that I propose fit both *social movements* for social change and *countermovements* against social change (Mottl, 1980). Thus, although I recognize the distinction, it is not directly relevant to my argument at this point.

10. Ben-Yehuda's resolution of the Durkheimian contradiction is similar in that he calls attention to the importance of specific social and historical circumstances that create conditions for stability or change (1985:20). In his most recent book, *The Politics and Morality of Deviance*, Ben-Yehuda (1990) elaborates a theoretical framework for the analysis of deviance that has many elements in common with that suggested here.

CHAPTER 2

1. Unless specifically noted otherwise, demographic data presented in this section were obtained directly from or calculated from the following sources: National Center for Health Statistics, *Vital Statistics of the United States*, Vol. 1, *Natality*; Robert L. Heuser, *Fertility Tables for Birth Cohorts by Color: United States, 1917–73*, DHEW publication no. (HRA) 76-11152 (Rockville, Md.: National Center for Health Statistics, 1976); National Center for Health Statistics, "Advance Report of Final Natality Statistics, 1987," *Monthly Vital Statistics Report*, Vol. 38, no. 3, supplement (Hyattsville, Md.: Public Health Service, 1989); U.S. Bureau of the Census, *Current Population Reports*, ser. P-25, no. 519, "Estimates of the Population of the United States, by Age, Color, and Sex, April 1, 1960 to July 1, 1973" (Washington, D.C.: U.S. Government Printing Office, 1974); U.S. Bureau of the Census, *Current Population Reports*, ser. P-25, no. 917, "Estimates of the Population of the United States, by Age, Sex, and Race: 1970 to 1981" (Washington, D.C.: U.S. Government Printing Office, 1982); U.S. Bureau of the Census, *Current Population Reports*, ser. P-25, no. 1022, "United States Population Estimates by Age, Sex, and Race: 1980 to 1987" (Washington, D.C.: U.S. Government Printing Office, 1988); Alice M. Hetzel and Marlene Capetta, "Teenagers: Marriages, Divorces, Parenthood, and Mortality," *Vital and Health Statistics*, ser. 21, no. 23, DHEW publication no. (HRA) 74-1901 (Rockville, Md.: National Center for Health Statistics, 1973); Stephanie J. Ventura, "Trends in Teenage Childbearing, United States, 1970–1981," *Vital and Health Statistics*, ser. 21, no. 41, DHHS publication no. (PHS) 84-1919 (Hyattsville, Md.: National Center for Health Statistics, 1984).

2. For a perceptive discussion of youth "as a source of moral anxiety and panic" in Britain during this period, see Weeks (1981:252–56). In England as well as in the United States, "the problems of youth were dominating themes in the sexual debates of the 1960's."

3. Increased attention to adolescent fertility in recent years has been associated with a trend toward finer age distinctions within the larger teenage category and with a more focused concentration of professional concern on the youngest age groups.

4. Calculated from data obtained in national surveys of young women conducted by Zelnik and Kantner in 1971 and 1979. These data and the methods of calculation employed are fully described in Nathanson and Kim (1989).

5. For example, it was not until 1982 that the federal government felt able to include single women who had never born a child as part of the population sample for the National Survey of Family Growth. In previous surveys, it had been considered inappropriate for a federal agency to ask single nonparents questions about sexual intercourse and pregnancy.

6. In circular fashion, increased knowledge has, of course, *led to* increased, and more focused, attention. I return to the role of knowledge in shaping problem definitions and proposed solutions at many points in this book.

7. In addition, by placing his rejection in a framework of conflict between birth control for "minors" and "family relationships" President Nixon set the stage for virtually all of the subsequent controversy that has surrounded this issue.

8. Reflecting the data available at that time, the principal authority Reiss cites for this statement is Kinsey's *Sexual Behavior in the Human Male*, published in 1948 and based on interviews collected between 1938 and 1947 (Kinsey et al., 1948). Scholarly articles on "premarital" sex published prior to 1970 regularly cite not only Kinsey, but Freud, Havelock Ellis, and even Kraft-Ebbing. It is difficult to remember over what a remarkably short time today's explosion of data on the sexual behavior of adolescents has taken place.

9. It is fair to point out that the focus of these scholars on the behavior of college women is hardly surprising, since this population was the one most available to them for research.

10. Parallel data, indicating that college women interviewed in 1968 were, indeed, substantially more likely to report having had sexual intercourse than women interviewed ten years earlier, were presented by Christensen and Gregg (1970). Retrospective confirmation of these findings has recently appeared. Data from the 1982 National Survey of Family Growth show that, over the two and one-half decades between 1955 and 1981, the biggest increase in probability of having had nonmarital intercourse by age 17 occurred between the cohort of women who reached that age from 1965 to 1969 and those who became 17 from 1970 to 1974. Although these data are consistent with reports from earlier studies, there is no suggestion in the NSFG results that the change was confined to "college girls" (Hofferth, Kahn, and Baldwin, 1987).

11. The perception of middle-class college students as the vanguard of social change was among the phenomena of the late 1960s. Siegel quotes the response of *New York Times* columnist Tom Wicker to the confrontation between young people and police at the 1968 Democratic National Convention: "These were *our* children in the streets of Chicago" (1984:197, emphasis added). Interestingly, in testimony before the Presidential Commission on Campus Unrest, youthful alienation was linked to the "hypocritical sex attitudes" of adult society (*New York Times*, July 16, 1970:1:3).

12. In the twentieth century, the arrival of a "sexual revolution" has been repeatedly proclaimed: in the Progressive Era (immediately prior to World War I), in the 1920s, and, most recently, in the 1960s. This cyclical pattern suggests that what has been, in fact, a fairly gradual change is perceived by each new generation as a marked departure from its own well-established norms and values.

13. The sexual behavior of black women did receive attention during this period, as we see below, but in a framework quite different than that employed in the literature on "premarital sex."

14. Petchesky argues that the new *visibility* of teenage sex created by access to legal abortion is responsible for current "hysteria" about teenage pregnancy, including, if I understand her argument correctly, the development of federal programs offering birth control services to teenagers. Although I believe that legal abortion statistics played an important role in activating conservative *opposition* to birth control services, they were used by birth control *advocates* principally as ammunition. The roots of advocacy lie elsewhere, as I will show.

15. This attack was quite unanticipated by sociological observers in the mid-1960s: "The pressures of our system are operating to promote permissiveness, and the likelihood of any reversal is slim indeed" (Reiss, 1966:133). Although the probability of *actual* reversal may be low, by the mid-1980s reversal had become the stated policy of the federal government.

16. "Sexually active" as the label to describe teenagers who have engaged in sexual intercourse is an invention of the 1970s. Prior to that invention, academic terminology uniformly incorporated the norm from which the behavior of interest was a deviation. In addition to "premarital sex" other examples of this practice are "illicit intercourse," "nonvirginity," "promiscuity," and, of course, "unwed," "unmarried," and "illegitimate." All of these terms have been or are gradually being expunged from *academic* vocabularies.

17. Contemporary critiques of the use and misuse of "illegitimacy" statistics can be found in Herzog (1966), Vincent (1966), and Hill and Jaffe (1966). The illegitimacy-welfare relationship was discussed in Rainwater and Yancey (1967), Piven and Cloward (1971), and Placek and Hendershot (1974).

18. Detailed documentation of U.S. physicians' attitudes from the Victorian era through 1960 can be found in the work of Gordon (1977) and Reed (1978, 1979).

19. Remarks on physicians' attitudes in the period from 1960 to 1972 are based on a review of all pertinent articles appearing between those dates in the *Journal of the American Medical Association*, the official organ of the American Medical Association.

20. This presumption was questioned by some physicians even at the time (Nokes, 1958; Aznar and Bennett, 1961; Stearn, 1963; Grant, 1970). It was, nevertheless, widely accepted by medical and public health authorities (e.g., Wallace, 1965). Recent literature shows quite convincingly that medical problems associated with adolescent pregnancy and delivery are due to environmental factors, not biological age (Zuckerman et al., 1983; Strobino, 1987).

21. My discussion of 1960s adolescent pregnancy programs conducted under medical auspices is based on the following references: Day (1965), Sarrel and Davis (1966), Sarrel (1967), Osofsky, Hagen, and Wood (1968), Gordis et al. (1968), Dickens et al. (1973).

22. Reading of Congressional hearings on H.R.1 (the bill proposing these and other amendments to the Social Security Act) as well as the Report of the Committee on Finance on these amendments leaves no doubt as to their underlying objective. See: U.S. Cong., House, Committee on Ways and Means (1969a); U.S. Cong., Senate, Committee on Finance (1972a and 1972b).

23. The American Birth Control Federation (subsequently, the Planned Parenthood Federation of America) began pushing for federal involvement in birth control as early as 1938 with, however, very limited success. The Federation itself, for reasons to be described, opposed dissemination of birth control information to the lay public outside of medical channels. Thus, although birth control has been a topic of active debate during much of the twentieth century, it was not until the mid-1960s that it began to be

openly discussed as an issue of public *policy*. Aspects of the birth control movement in the United States prior to 1960 are described in Kennedy (1970), Gordon (1977), and Reed (1978).

24. Eisenhower subsequently supported the birth control cause and became an officer of Planned Parenthood. Littlewood suggests that Eisenhower was sympathetic to birth control even as president but felt that the subject was a "divisive" one which he—as a non-Catholic—could not afford to confront directly (1977:44).

25. The 1958 New York City case is described in Littlewood (1977:22–23). See also, *The Anatomy of a Victory: A Panel Discussion of a Public Controversy*. New York: Planned Parenthood Federation of America, 1959 (cited in Littlewood, 1977:222).

26. However, as late as 1964, a member of the House of Representatives felt obliged to publicly reject the suggestion of another member that his "antipoverty" bill might allow federal funds to be used for birth control projects (*New York Times*, April 18, 1964:13:1).

27. Detailed documentation of this change in emphasis is contained in Gordon (1977), chapters 10 and 12.

28. The word "complex" is used advisedly. Among the many circumstances creating this "opportunity" were increased concern about population size both in the United States and abroad, the introduction of birth control methods that were acceptable to physicians and marketable on a mass basis, liberalizing changes in the legal status of birth control, the issues of illegitimacy and welfare costs to which I have already alluded, and President Lyndon B. Johnson's War on Poverty, which both called attention to the "problems" of the poor and made funds available to tackle those problems.

29. The role of lay "claims makers" in constructing social problem definitions is nicely described by Schneider and Conrad (1980).

30. My analysis of the birth control movement's "poverty–family planning" campaign is based on the following documents: Harkavy, Jaffe, and Wishik (1967), President's Committee on Population and Family Planning (1968), Campbell (1968), Jaffe (1968), Jaffe and Polgar (1968); Jaffe and Guttmacher (1968); London (1968); Corsa (1968); U.S. Cong., House, Committee on Ways and Means (1969b); U.S. Cong., House, Committee on Interstate and Foreign Commerce, Subcommittee on Public Health and Welfare (1970).

31. The term "birth control" was never used in the advocacy literature I have cited. By means of this rhetorical device ("family planning," instead of "birth control,") contraceptive use was presented in positive terms, identifying it with conventional values of family stability and "rational" planning. By the same token, opponents of uncontrolled contraceptive availability have used the phrase, "birth control," as a way of divesting contraception of these positive connotations. The irony of this turnabout is that the term birth control was invented by Margaret Sanger and accurately reflected her aims; she was strongly opposed to the change that removed "birth control" from the name of "her" organization.

32. Levitan and LaVor point out that the principal "delegate agency" running Office of Economic Opportunity–funded family planning programs was Planned Parenthood "with its experience in running programs." "More than a fifth of the organization's $15 million annual budget comes from OEO" (1969:5). In 1950, according to Reed, Planned Parenthood's annual budget was less than $200,000 (1978:269). By 1981, the Association's total income was approximately $146 million; slightly over 50 percent of this amount came from government grants.

33. See exchanges between Dr. Joseph Beasley and Congressman Burke in U.S.

Cong., House, Committee on Ways and Means (1969b); and between Dr. Alan Gutt-macher and Congressman Kyros, and Rev. Carl Flemister and Congressman Kyros, in U.S. Cong., House, Committee on Interstate and Foreign Commerce (1970). Congress-man Kyros's comments are particularly pertinent, given that the latter set of hearings produced what was, until 1978, the principal legislative authority for family planning services for adolescent women: "Where there is some kind of breakdown [of the family] certainly counseling should be provided. But we cannot indiscriminately provide family planning services to all youngsters from the age of 12 and beyond. I just do not see how anyone could suggest that" (288).

34. As I have tried to make clear, although over the past twenty-five years the medical model of deviant reproduction has become increasingly influential, alterna-tive models—moral, criminal, and social welfare—have by no means been wholly supplanted. I have more to say about these alternatives in Chapter 4.

CHAPTER 3

1. Vinovskis, a staff member of the House Select Committee on Population, states that *11 Million Teenagers* "provided the framework, though often unacknowledged, for most news stories as well as for briefing papers prepared for decision-makers in the Administration and the Congress" concerning the "epidemic" of adolescent pregnancy (1981:222).

2. The classic statement of the "inevitability" thesis was made by Arthur Campbell in 1968: "The girl who has an illegitimate child at the age of 16 suddenly has 90 percent of her life's script written for her" (1968:238).

3. Although these laws were widely ignored, until the mid-1960s the *only* legal ground for contraceptive prescription, irrespective of the woman's age or marital status, was for the prevention or cure of disease. In recent years, the application of this rationale has been limited to adolescents.

4. Recent analyses point to a marked increase, beginning in the late 1960s, in the percentage of teenage women who had had sexual intercourse (Hofferth, Kahn, and Baldwin, 1987).

5. Much of the material in this section is based on personal conversations and/ or written communication with the following individuals: John F. Kantner, professor emeritus in the Department of Population Dynamics, Johns Hopkins University; Melvin Zelnik, professor emeritus in the Department of Population Dynamics, Johns Hopkins University; Jeannie I. Rosoff, president, Alan Guttmacher Institute; Joy Dryfoos, private consultant and director of planning and research for the Alan Guttmacher Institute from 1969 until 1978; Richard Lincoln, now retired, editor of *Family Planning Per-spectives* from its inception in 1969 until 1987. Responsibility for the presentation and interpretation of this material is, of course, entirely my own.

6. In June 1965 Sen. Ernest Gruening of Alaska opened a year-long series of Senate "Population Crisis" hearings with the statement, "Right here in the United States, in our backyard, the population explosion is creating problems" (U.S. Cong., Senate, Commit-tee on Government Operations, 1965:11). Hearing testimony makes clear the perceived need to address our "problems" at home in order to achieve credibility for U.S.-funded family planning programs abroad.

7. I am indebted to John F. Kantner for reminding me of this point. The term, "epi-demic," was not adopted without controversy, but in the end Fred Jaffe's enthusiasm for it prevailed.

8. Comprehensive programs were not, of course, "uncharted territory." They were the reincarnation, in slightly altered form, of the rehabilitative "solution" to illegitimacy, a solution that Jaffe attacked in the late 1960s in almost the same terms (and more successfully). On both occasions, proposals for comprehensive services were attributed to the "myths and biases" of health and social-service professionals at HEW who believed that "contraception alone" would not (in the 1960s) reduce unwanted pregnancy among poor women and would not (in the 1970s) reduce the incidence of teenage pregnancy (see Jaffe and Polgar, 1968).

CHAPTER 4

1. Petchesky argues that the rhetoric employed by the Court reflects a conservative commitment to medical authority and "the interests of the state in population control" rather than a progressive commitment to women's reproductive autonomy (1984:319). I agree with this argument and believe that this rhetoric is ultimately threatening to the very rights it is used to protect. Nevertheless, the effect of the Court's decisions has been to expand reproductive autonomy, and it is clearly as an expansion of women's autonomy that these decisions are perceived and responded to by moral conservatives.

2. Despite the overt focus of the antiabortion movement on the "right to life" of the fetus, I would argue that the fervor of the opposition is due in at least equal measure to the role of abortion in creating the conditions for sex without penalty and, by implication, for women's sexual and reproductive autonomy. The close ideological connection between opposition to abortion and to premarital sex was clearly demonstrated in Granberg and Granberg's analysis of NORC survey data for the period from 1965 to 1980 (1980). Richard Viguerie, a central figure in the New Right movement, has been quoted as stating that "pre-marital sex and adultery, in my view are much more serious threats to our society than homosexuality" (Hunter, 1981:132).

3. The analysis of themes in the adolescent pregnancy debate presented in this chapter is based primarily on a series of Senate hearings on the federal family planning program (see U.S. Cong., Senate, Committee on Labor and Human Resources, 1981a; U.S. Cong., Senate, Subcommittee on Aging, Family and Human Services, 1981b and 1984). During this four-year period—the Reagan administration's first term—the Senate had a Republican majority, allowing conservatives to set the agenda for debate. Additional sources are Schlafly (1977), McGraw (1980), Ford and Schwartz (1979), Schwartz and Ford (1982).

4. Mirroring (and, indeed, making use of) the work of scholars sympathetic to the birth control cause, opponents have produced a small body of "scientific" analyses purporting to show that making birth control accessible to adolescent girls has, in fact, increased their frequency of sexual activity and, consequently, their pregnancy rates (e.g., Ford and Schwartz, 1979; Schwartz and Ford, 1982; Kasun, 1981). The influence, if any, of publicly funded birth control programs themselves on adolescent women's sexual behavior is an empirical question that has not, to my knowledge, been seriously addressed. Correlation is not, of course, evidence for causality. This work (as well as much of the work of birth control advocates) can best be understood as a contribution to what Gusfield calls "the fiction and drama of public reality," rhetorical weapons in the struggle to shape public and political constructions of the adolescent pregnancy issue.

5. Lest this description of conservative rhetoric appear exaggerated, consider the following comments by Sen. Jeremiah Denton at the family planning "oversight" hearings: There is "a distinct correlation between increased sexual freedom and social

decline. The more sexually permissive a society becomes, the less creative energy it exhibits and the slower its movement toward rationality, philosophical speculation, and advanced civilization" (U.S. Cong., Senate, Committee on Labor and Human Resources, 1981a:85).

6. Perspectives on social policy developments in the 1980s similar to the one presented in this section have recently been published by Zinn (1989) and Katz (1989).

7. Ellwood and Bane's results are based on data aggregated to the state level. Data (as opposed to anecdotal evidence) on whether or how individual women's sexual and reproductive decision processes are affected by welfare or the prospect of welfare are rare. One of the few such studies, based on interviews with a randomly selected sample of welfare recipients aged 15 to 44, was reported by Placek and Hendershot. The data were collected in 1972. They found that "pregnancy intervals while on welfare were characterized by: a greater likelihood of using contraception, less likelihood of defin-ing pregnancies which occurred as wanted, and less likelihood of having a subsequent pregnancy" (1974:658). These data are consistent with the aggregate-level findings. It is important to note that the decision whether or not to seek market work or to remain on welfare subsequent to the birth of a child is a quite separate issue from the decision to bear a child in the first place. There is good reason to think that the former deci-sion is influenced by a weighing of the financial and other costs and benefits of each alternative (cf. Bane and Ellwood, 1989).

8. Based on a series of national opinion surveys conducted in the 1960s, Lipset and Raab identify the constituents of economic conservatism as coming from the "ranks of the better educated and more privileged strata" (1970:449). Moral conservativism is based in the "more fundamentalist, provincial, education- and status-deprived elements in the country" (444). The latter finding was replicated in analyses of data collected in the 1970s (Lipset and Raab, 1978; Granberg and Granberg, 1980).

9. In the spring of 1984, "representatives of well over 100 black organizations" attended a Black Family Summit conference sponsored by the National Urban League and the National Association for the Advancement of Colored People. Its purpose was to "devise strategies to place endangered black families on firmer footing" (Jacob, 1985). In January 1986 "The Vanishing Black Family," hosted by Bill Moyers, appeared on national television with Jesse Jackson and Eleanor Holmes Norton as discussants (reviewed in *New York Times*, January 25, 1986:I, 49:3). A few days later, the first in a series of articles titled, "At Risk: Chronicles of Teen-Age Pregnancy," written by a black reporter, Leon Dash, appeared in the *Washington Post*. The series concerns adolescent pregnancy in a black low-income area of Washington, D.C. A much-cited book, *Choice and Circumstance* by Moore, Simms, and Betsey was published in 1986, and was also focused primarily on adolescent sexuality and fertility among blacks. The research on which this book is based was conducted at the Urban Institute and funded by the Ford Foundation. These examples are cited to illustrate the wide recognition and legitimacy as public problems that the "black family" and, with it, "black" teenage pregnancy, had achieved.

CHAPTER 5

1. This summary is drawn from a wide range of sources, referenced more specifi-cally in later sections of this chapter. I found Jones's general history of the United States, *The Limits of Liberty* (1983), especially useful.

2. American historians attribute the origins of this conception of childhood inno-

cence (both as description and as prescription) to Rousseau (see, e.g., Kett, 1977:133ff.; Degler, 1980:67). Aries dates its beginnings earlier: By the end of the seventeenth century "the idea of the innocence of childhood had become a commonplace" (1962:110).

3. There is some disagreement among historians as to whether the ideology of passionlessness was matched by women's actual behavior or even whether the ideology itself was uniformly accepted (see, e.g., Degler, 1980; Freedman, 1982). With respect to the latter question, regardless of what may have been expected of married women, expectations of young single women were clear and unambiguous. Quite obviously, behavior did not always match these expectations. The importance of normative expectations, however, is not as an index of behavior but as a guide to the ideological bases of social control.

4. This imagery as well as the language in which it is couched have been remarkably persistent. "Lectures to Troops" on sexual hygiene given in World War I divided feminine society into "the 'pure' women to whom the war was dedicated . . . and those who would subvert the American war effort by seducing American fighting men." To reinforce their moral control, soldiers were reminded that the girl who loses her chastity is "ruined." " 'Better had she been on the ill-fated *Lusitania* and gone down to the depths of the sea than that this fate had befallen her' " (Brandt, 1985:67).

5. Edward Clarke may have been an extreme exponent of the restrictions in young women's activities required by their reproductive function, but he was by no means alone in his views. Eliza Duffey, a woman and not a physician, although she objected to doctors' notion that menstruation was an illness, nevertheless agreed that "physical and mental stimulation, from whatever cause, is of all things to be most carefully avoided" during the critical period of female adolescence (1873:32). As late as 1905, G. Stanley Hall, in his monumental and profoundly influential treatise on adolescence, explicitly endorsed both Clarke's view of the hazards of adolescent female development and his prescriptions for how it should be managed (1905:chapter 17).

6. The functions for American women of the nineteenth-century ideology of passionlessness have been the topic of considerable discussion among historians (see, e.g., Smith, 1973; Gordon, 1977; Cott, 1978; Degler, 1980; Freedman, 1982). The interpretation most often advanced has been that this ideology increased women's power in their relationships with men: It raised women's bargaining power by making their sexuality into a scarce commodity; it increased women's reproductive control; it increased their power and autonomy within the family. Rothman contends, however, that "passionlessness created more problems than it solved" (1987:138). In addition to the problems in presented for individual couples, this ideology was an integral part of the rationale for an increasingly elaborate apparatus of social control directed at women who were perceived as violating its premises (described in Chapters 6 and 7).

7. Changes over this period in the social class distribution of single young women workers are difficult to determine. In 1900 almost two-thirds of all women workers in nonfarm employment were (in about equal proportions) factory workers or domestic servants. It is unlikely that many of these women were from middle-class families. However, as the overall proportion of employed single women increased and (particularly in the early twentieth century) as women's occupational distribution gradually shifted toward nonmanual occupations, it is likely that young women from relatively advantaged families were drawn into the labor force as well. It was not until the third and fourth decades of the twentieth century that high school and college became numerically important occupations for single young women.

8. This point of view was not limited to the middle class. Cohen (forthcoming)

cites the case of an Italian father in New York City in the early part of the twentieth century who, given that his wife was dead, "viewed work as an *attractive* option for his daughter . . . because school hours were not long enough and she would therefore be at home alone or would wander about the streets." From this perspective, supervised employment was a functional alternative to supervision at home.

9. The U.S. Bureau of the Census documentation of single young women's numbers and behavior clearly played a role in making them socially visible. However, it seems likely that public awareness and concern about these young women may also have pushed census takers to enumerate them. Smuts remarks that "public concern over the moral conditions of women's employment" led in 1887 to an official investigation by the U.S. Bureau of Labor" (1959:89). Hill prefaces his 1929 analysis of census data on women's employment with the statement that "the interest in women's occupations lies . . . in the extent to which their work takes them away from the home" (4).

10. A much more sympathetic, but otherwise rather similar, portrait of young working girls' search for entertainment in New York City in the early 1900s has been drawn by Kathy Peiss. "Women's wage labor and the demands of the working-class household offered daughters few resources for entertainment. At the same time, new commercial amusements offered a tempting world of pleasure and companionship beyond parental control. Within this context, some young women sought to exchange sexual goods for access to that world and its seeming independence, choosing not to defer sexual relations until marriage" (1983:84).

11. In his 1915 portrait of the flapper, Mencken refers to Ellis's work as "on her summer reading list" (cited in May, 1959:339).

12. Ellis's ideas are described by Hale (1971:259–67) and Robinson (1976:1–41).

13. By "single young woman," I refer to a stage in the life course—the period between puberty and marriage—rather than a precise age range or set of age categories. The specific age groups (younger teenagers, older teenagers, young adults) with which commentators and scholars are primarily concerned have shifted over time and vary from one observer to another. Their common focus is on the problems of sexual control presented by what is socially defined as a dangerous period of transition.

14. The concept of a "rating and dating complex" was introduced by Willard Waller in 1937, based on his observations of behavior on college campuses. Dates were chosen, he suggests, based on their rating in a campus status system in which the major criteria were fraternity/sorority membership, athletic prowess, and economic status (for boys), and looks and manners (for girls). Hollingshead (1949) and Coleman (1961) described similar status systems in the high schools they studied. Despite a shift in emphasis from "promiscuous popularity" in the 1930s to "going steady" in the postwar period, the status system itself remained intact (Bailey, 1988:26).

15. It is important to call attention to a major change over time in the sources from which contemporary images of the adolescent girl are drawn. Beginning in the 1920s psychologists and sociologists began to publish the results of research that reflected, in one form or another, the attitudes and experiences of single young (high-school and/or college-age) women. The objectives and methodologies of this research cover a wide range: questionnaires completed by highly-selected groups of current or former college women (e.g., Davenport, 1924; Davis, 1929; Bromley and Britten, 1938; Burgess and Wallin, 1953); community studies in which high school students were included or reported on (e.g., the Lynds's Middletown studies, published in 1929 and 1937; Hollingshead's study of *Elmtown's Youth*, published in 1949); Coleman's comparative study of ten high schools in Illinois (published in 1961 as *The Adolescent Society*); and field surveys of population samples (e.g., Douvan, 1957). In all cases, the researchers' inten-

tions are to shed the light of objective data on some aspect of experience (including but usually not confined to the experience of young women). And these studies are valuable sources of such data. It is nevertheless true (and, I would argue, inevitable) that these data are filtered through, and reflect, the ideologies of female adolescence current at the time they were collected; indeed, a number of the studies reported on these ideologies directly. Research has both documented and contributed to the social construction of female adolescence.

16. Evidence on the sexual activity of unmarried women comes from three sources: questionnaire or interview surveys of their behavior, examination of birth and marriage records to determine the relative frequency of births less than eight months after marriage, and vital statistics records of nonmarital births. None of these sources is unambiguously interpretable (e.g., prior to 1970 almost all of the survey data was from middle- or upper-class women; how births are recorded may be influenced by the stigma attached to illegitimacy). Nevertheless, although the beginning date of twentieth-century (or late nineteenth-century) increases in nonmarital sex is disputed by social and demographic historians (see, e.g., Fass, 1977:449,455; Smith, 1978; Rosenberg, 1982:192–93), there is consistent evidence of relatively little change between the 1920s and the 1940s and of gradually increasing rates thereafter (Smith and Hindus, 1975; Cutright and Smith, 1986; Hofferth, Kahn, and Baldwin, 1987). For contemporary comment on the relative absence of behavioral change in the 1920s and 1930s, see Newcomb (1937). The materials cited refer to change in the frequency of full sexual intercourse. A wide range of evidence indicates that, during the 1920s and 1930s, petting to a point just short of intercourse became firmly established as the pattern of (at least) middle-class sexual behavior, perhaps first among college and then among high school students as well (Lynd and Lynd, 1929, 1937; Folsom, 1934; Bromley and Britten, 1938; Cuber, 1943; Burgess and Wallin, 1953; Fass, 1977).

17. For example, McGovern cites an analysis of the *Reader's Guide to Periodical Literature* showing that articles on "birth control, prostitution, divorce, and sexual morals" were relatively more numerous between 1910 and 1914 than between 1919 and 1928 (1968:316).

18. For documentation of the rapid increase in secondary school and college enrollments during the 1920s and 1930s see U.S. Bureau of the Census (1975), Rothman (1978:166), Walters and O'Connell (1988).

19. This statement is based on a wide range of literature published in the 1920s and early 1930s: discussions by relatively conservative women teachers concerned with the "problems" of the adolescent girl (Eggleston, 1923; Goodsell, 1923; Blanchard, 1924; Davenport, 1924; Gibson, 1927; Smithies, 1933); writings by the more progressive commentators on youth and sex in the 1920s (Coe, 1924; Lindsey, 1925; Calverton, 1928; Lippmann, 1929; Dell, 1930); and the field observations of the Lynds (1929).

20. The average length of this interval is affected both by time spent in school and by age at marriage. Proportions of young women graduating from high school increased steadily over the period under discussion (1920 to 1960), from 20 percent to 65 percent. Median age at marriage for women increased slightly between 1920 and 1940 (from 21.2 to 21.5), then sharply declined to its "baby boom" low of 20.4 in 1950 and 1960. Thus, the interval between school and marriage became shorter over time. The pattern whereby a majority of young women stopped work when they married began to change in the 1940s, but slowly. In 1940, only 17 percent of married women reported participation in the paid labor force; this figure increased to 25 percent in 1950 and 32 percent in 1960 (Weiner, 1985).

21. This conception of the school as a protected environment was specifically, and

critically, articulated by Hollingshead based on his study of Elmtown in the 1940s. The "youth-training institutions provided by the culture [principally the high school]," he stated, "are essentially negative in their objectives, for they segregate adolescents from the real world that adults know and function in. By trying to keep the maturing child ignorant of this world of conflict and contradictions, adults think they are keeping him 'pure'" (1949:149).

22. My account of social scientists' observations of female adolescence and youth in the 1920s and 1930s is based on the following primary sources: Lynd and Lynd (1929, 1937), Carpenter (1932), Burgess (1934), Folsom (1934), Blanchard and Manasses (1937), Newcomb (1937), Waller (1937), and Bromley and Britten (1938). I am also indebted to Fass's analysis of the mores of college students in this period (1977: 260–90).

23. Field studies of high school and college students carried out in the 1940s and 1950s uniformly alluded to the need for young women to protect themselves against loss of "reputation" among their peers (e.g., in addition to Douvan and Adelson, Hollingshead, 1949; Burgess and Wallin, 1953; Reiss, 1960; Coleman, 1961). This work also suggested that the female peer group was most active in upholding standards of sexual orthodoxy; it was, of course, they who stood to lose in bargaining power from an overall debasage of the sexual coinage.

24. The subject of sex in adolescence was so tabooed in Elmtown that data on its prevalence were virtually impossible to obtain except from lower-class individuals, as Hollingshead himself acknowledged (1949:414).

25. Of the authors I have cited, only Rossi demonstrated an awareness that the apparent passivity and orientation toward marriage and children of her young female contemporaries might have institutional causes tied to the gender-based status system of the larger society as well as to aspects of the social and intellectual climate of post-World War II America. Although Coleman's book placed heavy emphasis on the status system of the *schools* he studied, he paid relatively little attention to the relationship of that system to the structure and value premises of the society as a whole.

26. The continued "official" illegitimacy of youthful sexuality was perhaps most clearly reflected in the discreet, not to say devious, research methods these early investigators found it necessary to employ in order to avoid repercussions from college and/or high school authorities and parents. Burgess and Wallin described a case "in the middle twenties" in which two professors at a state university lost their positions when their research on students' "attitudes toward sex" became known (Burgess and Wallin, 1953:33). Later problems are described by Bromley and Britten (1938:29) and Hollingshead (1949:238).

27. The process of clarifying the legal status of birth control in the United States for married, let alone single, women did not begin until 1965, with the case of *Griswold v. Connecticut*. In that case, the U.S. Supreme Court overturned a Connecticut law that banned the use of contraception, holding that contraceptive use by married persons was protected by the constitutional "right of privacy" (Issacs, 1981:51).

28. It is worth pointing out that if the object was to prevent pregnancy the romantic was far more dangerous than the moral perspective. Moral conservatives opposed both nonmarital intercourse and rational contraceptive preparation. A thoroughgoing romantic (like Dell) was made far more uncomfortable by rational preparation than by sexual intercourse in the context of romantic love.

1. My analysis of late nineteenth-century and twentieth-century strategies for the management of nontraditional sexual behavior by unmarried young women is, of necessity, based on writings and reports by or about institutions, groups, or individuals who had self-conscious strategies that they wished to articulate. Thus, while this analysis reflects the mainstream of publicly acknowledged and advocated strategies, it does not do justice to the private strategies employed by many young women, specifically contraception and abortion (as well, of course, as marriage to legitimate a premarital pregnancy). Among a national probability sample of white ever-married women born from 1900 to 1920, 49 percent reported contraceptive use prior to the first pregnancy; data are not given separately for the use of contraception before marriage (Dawson, Meny, and Ridley, 1980). Of 417 premarital conceptions reported to Kinsey by "white nonprison" women born between 1890 and 1929, only 3 percent ended in a live birth outside of marriage (Gebhard et al., 1958:77). Seventy-eight percent were terminated by abortion, and 19 percent were resolved by marriage before the birth. Unfortunately, comparable data are not available for the generations of women born between 1850 and 1890. Nevertheless, these data indicate that, at least among women born after 1900, "private strategies" were, in fact, very widely used.

2. The contraceptive solution falls into the category of protective strategies. However, it significantly departs from other strategies in this category by its protection from loss of sexual status of the girl who is, by definition, not "innocent," but, indeed, unchaste. Not only is she protected from suffering the consequences of her "illicit" behavior; she is absolved from going through the rituals of repentance and restoration. It is this "protection of the guilty" afforded by contraception that moral conservatives find so offensive.

3. Although the emphasis on "broken homes" suggests environmental causality to the modern social scientist, eugenic theories were at the height of their popularity in the 1920s, and the distinction between environmental and hereditary modes of transmission was often blurred or ignored. Broken homes could transmit their negative influences through heredity or environment or both.

4. So much was this reaction expected by Progressive Era juvenile court judges, according to Schlossman and Wallach, that the "wayward" daughter of parents who did not "at least feign shock" increased her chances of being sent to a reformatory rather than placed on probation (1978:75). Absence of parental contrition was taken as evidence of parental culpability.

5. During the early years of the twentieth century physicians did participate directly in movements for sexual reform through "sex education" of (among others) young people and through the control of venereal disease. However, these movements were directed toward the prevention of sexual unorthodoxy on a community- and nationwide scale; they were only incidentally concerned with the management of the individual wayward girl.

6. What I have called "traditional" maternity homes evolved out of rescue homes founded in the nineteenth century for the "reclaiming of abandoned females" who desired to be saved from a life of sin (U.S. Children's Bureau, 1924:13; see also Smith-Rosenberg, 1985). As the historian of the Florence Crittenton Homes, Otto Wilson, observed, "very soon it became evident that the effort and money involved [in redeeming the fallen] were out of all proportion to the tangible results achieved," and homes turned their attention from the "confirmed professional" to the "erring girl"

(1933:8). Beginning in the 1910s, agitation by the U.S. Children's Bureau as well as by increasingly professionalized social workers led to the passage of state laws requiring the licensing of maternity homes and adoption agencies (U.S. Children's Bureau, 1924). Prior to that period (and doubtless continuing for some time thereafter) nonprofit, religiously based maternity homes coexisted with commercial homes whose objectives were financial rather than moral: In return for a fee, they offered concealment to the unmarried mother and disposal of her inconvenient offspring (Mangold, 1921). In 1966, the National Council on Illegitimacy published a directory of 194 nonprofit "maternity homes and residential facilities for unmarried mothers" in the United States. Of these, all but 11 percent were under religious auspices. By the early 1970s, literature on maternity homes was largely devoted to documenting their demise (Wallace et al., 1974; Verner, 1976). These homes have had something of a revival in recent years, however (e.g., Ginsburg, 1989; *New York Times*, Sunday, May 1990:I, 1:2).

7. Citations are from the following sources: Brenzel (1983:166), Mangold (1921:41), Johnson (1926:396). Additional recent discussions of these theories can be found in Freedman (1981) and Hobson (1987).

8. Lindsey's book *The Revolt of Modern Youth* (1925) was a paean to the regenerating force of youthful sexuality. He focused his attention almost exclusively on the sexuality of unmarried young women, whom he regarded as more sexually responsible than young men (having the most to lose from sexual "irresponsibility") and as most heavily penalized by repressive social norms.

9. These quotes are taken from verbatim summaries of papers presented at annual national conferences of the National Florence Crittenton Mission. Speakers at these conferences were often invited "experts" from outside the Florence Crittenton organization; thus, they reflect a variety of different points of view, by no means limited to the evangelical perspective of the organization's founders and of many of its workers. The Mission's annual reports (which ran from 1897 to 1948) gave a clear picture of change over time in theories of the sexually unorthodox girl; they also reflected the continued coexistence of competing theories.

10. The distinction between cultural and psychic causes of illegitimacy has a long history. The author of a monograph on the subject published in 1921 made a sharp distinction between nonmarital sex and illegitimacy that he saw as being determined by "peculiar customs" and therefore "normal" in its social context, and the "abnormal" behavior of his own countrywomen. It was the latter that he perceived as requiring explanation (Mangold, 1921).

11. So-called wayward girls were most frequently brought to correctional authorities by parents who could no longer control their daughters themselves. Brenzel points out that during the period of her research (1856 to 1905) "more than half of the girls . . . were brought to the court by members of their own families" (1980:204). Similarly, Tappan's study of the Wayward Minor Court of New York City, covering the years 1938 and 1942, shows that 85 percent of complaints were brought by parents (1947:126). Case histories cited by Tappan make clear that the central point at issue for both parents and the courts was the girl's sexual independence (see also Schlossman, 1977:163,180; Schlossman and Wallach, 1978:74–75; Lunbeck, 1987).

12. The frequency with which relatively inexperienced girls were convicted and the long sentences imposed was particularly striking by contrast with the more lenient treatment accorded prostitutes by the same judicial system. Tappan suggests that adolescent girls were perceived as more redeemable by institutional means (1947:90).

13. Social class and ethnicity were principal bases on which young women were

sorted into different types of management institutions, as I discuss below. However, the "programs" of these institutions, reflecting their conceptions of what was "wrong" with the unorthodox girl and how the problem should be fixed, were very similar: irrespective of class, girls' futures were expected to be domestic.

14. It is tempting to think of institutional segregation as an extreme form of birth control for unmarried young women. The analogy extends to the fact that the "prescription" of incarceration was (in the Milwaukee juvenile court between 1900 and 1920) preceded by a pelvic examination to determine whether or not the young woman was a virgin (Schlossman and Wallach, 1978:73); pelvic examination is (in the United States) an invariable prelude to the medical prescription of a contraceptive method.

15. During much of the period on which my analysis is focused religious, psychiatric, biological (glands/heredity), and "social" (i.e., broken homes, poverty) theories of the causes of sexual unorthodoxy (and, consequently, of its reformation) coexisted and had varying degrees of influence on *all* of the institutions I have been describing. However, their relative emphasis varied over time and in the different settings. In the mid-1940s, Tappan described the confusion in juvenile court procedures occasioned by these coexisting (and competing) theories (1947:86–122).

16. The New York City Health Department did not begin to collect data on illegitimacy until 1922 (a step that itself reflected change both in the level and in the quality of attention to this issue). Although Reed raised serious questions about the accuracy of these data, it is reasonable to suppose that underreporting would, if it changed at all, have decreased, not increased, over time. In 1922, 1,296 illegitimate births were recorded, as compared with 1,470 in 1930. Based on her analysis of social-agency records, Reed reported a figure of 1,817 such births in 1930. Reed's account suggests that there was, in fact, considerable friction among agencies, each zealously guarding their own cases, a fact which may be accounted for in part by the relatively small number of illegitimate births to go around (1934:65).

17. I am unaware of any systematic research on the contemporary version of maternity homes created by antiabortion activists. However, anecdotal evidence suggests that they more closely resemble the older, evangelical, model in which babies remained with their mothers than the psychiatric model with its emphasis on adoption (e.g., *New York Times*, Sunday, May 13, 1990 I, 1:2). The representativeness of the two homes described by the *New York Times* is unclear. However, a striking difference from the evangelical model, and, indeed, from all earlier models, is the emphasis placed on young women's educational and occupational preparation, that is, on preparation for *nondomestic* as opposed to domestic work.

18. Available evidence indicates that this statement accurately describes traditional maternity homes in the period (sometime in the 1920s) *after* they began to arrange adoptions rather than insisting that mother and baby be kept together; it may not describe them during their earlier, more heavily evangelical, period. Other than the fact that they served an almost entirely white clientele, no socioeconomic data are available for the latter period. Mangold (a highly biased source) stated in 1921 that better-off and smarter girls got abortions so that "the evil of illegitimacy is largely confined to the ignorant and the poor" (82).

CHAPTER 7

1. *Whose* sexuality was at issue in the sexual social movements of the late nineteenth and early twentieth centuries is one of the points upon which historians disagree

(see, e.g., Gorham, 1978; Degler, 1980; Filene, 1986). This question is addressed in detail later in this chapter.

2. Quotations are from Hale (1971:25, 29). See, in addition, Hale (1971:24–46), Degler (1980: chapters 11 and 12), Filene (1986: chapter 2).

3. Between January and November 1895, the popular journal *The Arena* carried an extensive series of articles, including separate state reports, on the "battle" to raise the age of consent. Although the journal, through its reporter, Helen H. Gardener, strongly advocated an increase in the age, statements on the other side of the issue were included as well. Together, these materials provide valuable information on the terms in which this debate was conducted.

4. Reformers believed that the passage of laws against immorality had value as an end in itself, even if the immoral behavior continued: Legislation, although it may not "stamp out all pollution . . . will place the ban of the state upon such practices, which in itself will help create a healthy public sentiment in that direction" (*The Arena*, November 1895:407).

5. My discussion of the nineteenth-century background of these movements is based primarily on the work of Pivar (1973). Additional sources are: Smith-Rosenberg (1985b), Wunsch (1976), Connelly (1980), and Hobson (1987).

6. *The Philanthropist*, published from 1886 to 1909 by the American Purity Alliance, described its objectives as follows: "Published monthly for the promotion of social purity, the better protection of the young, the suppression of vice, and the prevention of its regulation by the state."

7. For a description of the British response to Stead's revelations, see Gorham (1978).

8. As noted earlier, *The Arena*, published in Boston and edited by B. O. Flower, used its pages to conduct an all-out campaign to raise the age of consent. From January through July, this campaign was presented in the form of a "Symposium" consisting of a series of articles by well-known moral reformers of the period (Aaron Powell, Frances Willard, Edward Janney, Emily Blackwell, and others). The second half, in August through November, consisted of a series of state-by-state reports on legislative progress, compiled and presented with commentary by Helen H. Gardener. Names of authors for each state report are provided only on occasion.

9. For example, in the *Congressional Record* account cited, there is *no* reference to men or males. "Assaults upon women" are mentioned in a petition from the WCTU included in the record, but the perpetrators are unidentified (even as to sex).

10. For example, a bill introduced into the Colorado legislature was described as intended "to protect, until they are eighteen years of age, the girl children of [the] state" (*The Arena*, September 1895:1). Existing age-of-consent laws were characterized as allowing "a little child, a baby girl of fourteen, twelve, ten years of age [to be made] the legal and rightful prey of grown men" (*The Arena*, January 1895:196).

11. Reformers were quite blatant in their construction of white slavery so as to strike terror into the heart of the most innocent girl, not to speak of her parents. "The Illinois Vigilance Association posted signs in 'el' cars and other public places reading: WARNING TO GIRLS: In every city there are immoral and criminal men and women some seemingly respectable who make a business of enticing or entrapping girls into 'white slavery' often pretending to befriend them. *Guard against Strangers and False Friends at all Times and in all Places*" (cited in Wunsch, 1976:132).

12. Hobson, who is an exception among the feminist historians I have cited, makes this point very clearly: "For middle-class women the ideology of passionlessness was a source of power to control sexual relations within marriage. But this ideology was a

source of oppression for working class women who violated chastity codes and came under the purview of the state" (1987:114). I am less sure than Hobson that the ideology of passionlessness was invariably a resource even for middle-class women, but it certainly was not for lower-class women.

13. In a recently published analysis of vice campaigns in three late nineteenth-century American cities, Beisel (1990) also emphasizes the need to combine "culture-centered" with more social structural approaches to the origins of moral reform movements. Her attention is focused on the business elites (Rockefellers, Morgans, and the like) who participated in these movements, and she places more emphasis than I do on the class-based as opposed to the political interests of these reformers. In the urban political circumstances of the late nineteenth century, however, I would argue that these two sets of interests were almost inseparable.

14. Gorham's (1978) article on the age-of-consent debate in Great Britain makes this point very clearly.

15. A similar hypothesis to account for these movements, also based on the work of Kai Erikson, has been proposed by Filene (1986:89). My interpretation, however, adds several other conditions to the one of "uncertain boundaries."

16. Gusfield (1967) describes this shift as a "moral passage" and discusses some of its consequences for social movements and countermovements. In an examination of social movements long past it is particularly difficult to determine how "real" the threat of legitimation was at any given time, since calling attention to such threats was a major means by which movement activists rallied their supporters.

17. Progressive Era physicians strongly opposed public clinics or dispensaries as an invasion of their professional turf (see, e.g., Starr, 1982: chapter 5). Many may have found the moral argument against public venereal disease clinics a useful addition to their rhetorical armamentarium.

18. By no means all women in public life adopted the social control perspective. For example, Emma Goldman "thought the white slave agitation a kind of 'toy' to 'amuse the people for a little while ... and [to] create a few more political jobs [for] parasites who stalk about the world as inspectors, investigators, detectives, and so forth.'" She identified the real cause of prostitution as exploitation of female workers (cited in Wunsch, 1976:146).

19. My description and interpretation of businessmen's role in the moral-reform movements of this period is based on the following sources: Wagner (1971), Goulden (1971), Flexner (1940), and Jones (1983).

20. See, e.g., Haller and Haller (1974), Smith-Rosenberg (1972), Smith-Rosenberg and Rosenberg (1973), and Reed (1979).

21. The sources for my description of physicians' organizational and ideological responses to the issues of prostitution and venereal disease in the late nineteenth and early twentieth centuries are: Pivar (1973), Connelly (1980: chapter 4), Brandt (1985: chapter 1).

22. Women physicians, of whom Elizabeth Blackwell was only the most prominent, played major roles in the early antiregulation and moral-education movements. However, in the 1870s and 1880s, Blackwell's conception of health as a product of morality was still "but a strand of medical thinking favored by feminists and purity reformers" (Wunsch, 1976:108).

23. My comments on physicians' antiabortion activities are based on Mohr (1978); for physicians' role in the birth control movement I rely on Gordon (1977) and Reed (1979).

24. For example, James Marion Sims, the founder of American gynecology and

a president of the American Medical Association, shared "the prevailing sexual ideology which viewed all healthy women as willing mothers." He simultaneously ignored contraception and supported the regulation of prostitution, "officially" sanctioning it at the 1874 AMA Convention (see Reed, 1979:112; and Pivar, 1973:88).

25. For example, Rockefeller, the foreman of the grand jury convened to investigate white slavery in New York City following the Turner exposé, was a major financial contributor to medical education and research in the early twentieth century.

CHAPTER 8

1. The "school-based clinic" is a model, currently popular among birth control advocates, for providing comprehensive health care, including contraceptive and reproductive health services, to junior and senior public high school students *on or immediately contiguous to school premises.* Clinics are generally initiated and run by groups and individuals from outside the school system; the majority of the 138 clinics in operation in 1988 were located in low-income neighborhoods (Dryfoos, 1985; Center for Population Options, 1986; Pittman, 1986; Dryfoos, 1988).

2. The role of the male partner has been receiving increased attention in recent years from researchers, policy analysts, and service providers (see, e.g., Vinovskis, 1988, for a recent review). However, the problem to be solved continues to be identified as a female one, "adolescent pregnancy," and management strategies continue to be directed primarily toward young women.

3. The reality and meaning of these struggles to the individuals involved are illustrated in telling fashion by a recent study of adolescent pregnancy politics in the state of Louisiana (Ward, 1990).

4. As noted in Chapter 4, moral conservatives have consistently attributed the rise in sexual activity among teenage women to the increased availability of contraception. The only study to examine the relationship between family planning availability and the initiation of sexual activity, while controlling for other factors, found no evidence for such a relationship (Moore and Caldwell, 1977). Hofferth cautiously concludes that "there is no evidence on the basis of which to accept or reject the hypothesis that the availability of family planning clinics affects the sexual activity of individual women" (1987a:225).

5. Title X is that section of the Public Health Services Act, originally passed by the Congress in 1970, authorizing federally funded "Population Research and Voluntary Family Planning Services."

6. The actual difference is considerably larger since contraceptive services are also provided under Title XIX (Medicaid) and under Social Services and Maternal and Child Health block grants. However, I have excluded these latter funds (a total of $165,039,000) since available data do not permit the separation of federal from state funds employed in these programs.

7. Rather than close their doors, a number of maternity homes have, in fact, simply reorganized their programs to conform with the "comprehensive services" model (see, e.g., Weatherley et al., 1985).

8. The ideological and professional bases of the early twentieth-century sex education movement are described by Brandt (1985:23–31). Other sources include: Strong (1972), Rosow and Persell (1980), and Hale (1971).

9. I am indebted to Margaret McDonald, M.H.S., for conducting much of the bibliographic research on which my comments about the contemporary sex education debate are based.

10. Project Redirection is only one of many examples that could be cited, for example, a Manpower Demonstration Research Corporation review of recent New York State program and policy proposals states that "promotion of self-sufficiency for teen parents is a central theme of the initiative, its importance underscored both in the Governor's pronouncements and the findings of the Task Force on Adolescent Pregnancy" (Guy, 1986:107).

11. Goffman introduced the term "moral career" to describe "such changes over time as are basic and common to the members of a social category" with particular reference to changes in "the person's self and in his framework of imagery for judging himself and others" (1961:127–28).

12. Based on a recent study of adolescent pregnancy in industrialized countries carried out by the Alan Guttmacher Institute, the authors point out that educational and employment opportunities for adolescents in the United States may be better, and are certainly no worse, than in other countries with substantially lower rates of adolescent pregnancy and birth (Jones et al., 1986:226). However, this study does not directly address the question of differential access to these opportunities by adolescents in varying social locations within the United States.

13. As late as 1979, when the overall popularity of marriage as the solution to a nonmarital pregnancy had substantially declined, 52 percent of white higher SES young women responding to the Zelnik and Kantner survey had resorted to this option, compared with only 21 percent of their lower SES counterparts. Race and SES differences in contraceptive use and in abortion based on the latter survey are consistent with the more recent data used in the references for these differences cited in the text.

14. Pregnant students enrolled in the Webster School Project, generally recognized as among the first comprehensive programs for school-aged pregnant girls were 99 percent black; most were "lower middle class" (Howard, 1968). Over 90 percent of the young female clients of the comprehensive programs in New Haven and Hartford, Connecticut, evaluated by Klerman and Jekel (1973) were black; over 70 percent were from families receiving public assistance. The clients of other early programs on which the requisite data were published had much the same characteristics (e.g., Osofsky, 1968; Furstenberg, 1976).

15. High-profile programs like Project Redirection contribute heavily to public perceptions of the social location of adolescent pregnancy. Thus, it is important to be aware of exactly how selective this program was. Out of a national sample of 12,000 males and females aged 14 to 21, in which blacks, Hispanics, and disadvantaged whites were overrepresented, only 175 individuals or 1.4 percent (3 percent of the females) met the eligibility criteria for Project Redirection: age 17 or younger, pregnant or a parent, without a high school diploma, living in a low-income household in which one or more persons was eligible to receive welfare. Yet in the minds of many policy makers it is this tiny and highly selected group who *are* the problem of adolescent pregnancy.

16. In local communities, the principal lobbyists for reproductive health services to adolescent women are community agencies and service professionals highly sensitive to local opinion. Young women themselves are neither in a position to advocate for services nor are they, or their families, likely to be motivated to do so. "While other stigmatized groups, such as welfare recipients, homosexuals, and the handicapped have ... successfully advocated on their own behalf, pregnant teenagers face a combination of constraints that precludes group activism" (Weatherley et al., 1985:216). Thus, in this particular case, the interest group that has the most at stake and is least beholden to the local power structure is powerless to act.

17. Critiques of culture-of-poverty theories as applied to the explanation of single

parenthood among black teenage women in particular have been published by Wilson (1987) and Huling (1988). Wilson accepts the premise that teenage parenthood represents "aberrant behavior," but rejects the culture-of-poverty explanation in favor of an explanation attributing the problem to aspects of American economic organization that simultaneously increase the social isolation of ghetto residents (thereby decreasing the exposure to conventional normative constraints) and reduce the "marriageable pool" of black men. Huling rejects both the culture-of-poverty explanatory model and the construction of black young women's behavior as pathological.

CHAPTER 9

1. Calculations are based on Bachrach (1984) and U.S. Bureau of the Census (1983).

2. Planned Parenthood clinics, which provide about 10 percent of medical contraceptive services to teenagers in this country, are different in some respects—less dominated by the medical model of client-provider interaction—and quite similar in others. For an excellent and instructive analysis of staff perspectives in a Planned Parenthood clinic, see Joffe (1986).

3. This study was conducted before the mid-1980s discovery of the AIDS epidemic and the accompanying explosion of anxiety and concern not only about AIDS but about other sexually transmitted diseases as well. My current research in sexually transmitted disease clinics strongly suggests that a contemporary study of family planning clinics would find "sin" encompassing nonuse or imperfect use not only of pills but of condoms as well, and the "wages of sin" expanded to include disease as well as pregnancy.

CHAPTER 10

1. Ford Foundation support for the project described in this chapter is gratefully acknowledged. I am indebted, in addition, to Marshall H. Becker, professor and associate dean, University of Michigan School of Public Health and to Wende S. Skidmore, The Futures Group, Washington, D.C., for their major contributions to this analysis.

2. Major reasons for failure to interview the first-contacted respondent were problems in scheduling; no respondent refused to be interviewed. If significant problems in scheduling did occur, or the respondent was quite reluctant, interviewers were instructed to move to the next-listed respondent within the designated stratum. Fewer than 10 percent of first-contacted respondents were lost by these procedures.

3. Procedures for recontacting respondents had been arranged at the time of the larger study's 12-month follow-up interview. These procedures were designed to protect the confidentiality of the respondent and were adhered to uniformly.

4. The term "significant others" is used in this report to refer to other individuals (boyfriend, mother, girlfriend(s), clinic nurse) whom the respondent consulted or whose opinions she took into account in arriving at a course of action.

5. Coding reliability was determined by independent recoding of a 10 percent sample of interviews. With the final draft of the code, reliability for both event histories and vignettes was better than 80 percent.

6. We do not intend to imply that all the "side effects" young women attribute to the pill are, indeed, due to the pill. The important point, however, is not the accuracy of these attributions but their effects on behavior.

7. Medical experts often make the point that pregnancy poses more of a threat

to health than the pill (e.g., Klein, 1985). However, pregnancy is perceived by these respondents (and probably by most women) as a normal, comprehensible event. The pill, on the other hand, is perceived to *interfere* with "normal" physiology in ways that are mysterious and unpredictable.

8. Not only do girls often refer to the pills as "medicine" but they also perceive different dosage pills as "stronger" or "weaker" medicine. "Stronger" pills are thought of as more effective, but with potentially greater side effects; "weaker" pills reduce side effects, but are less effective.

9. It is worth speculating that one consequence of antiabortion fervor has been to enhance the social value of babies as ends in themselves, thus substantially reducing the cost of out-of-wedlock pregnancy and birth. This same social climate also helps to legitimize (and to increase the probability of) going off the pill to protect a possible baby.

10. As we shall see in the next section, boyfriends' views on contraception are also perceived as statements about the relationship; how his statements are interpreted is a major factor in determining how much influence the boyfriend will have.

11. It is frequently proposed, and there is some data to support this hypothesis, that effective contraceptive use is more likely in a "serious" relationship (e.g., Inazu, 1987). As should be apparent, we are suggesting a much more complex and subtle connection between relationship quality and contraceptive behavior.

12. The vignette responses make clear that "mother" as an abstraction evokes a more positive response (as an influence source) than "boyfriend" as an abstraction. The reality, however, is precisely the opposite: Boyfriends are far more influential than mothers.

13. It is important to point out that the boyfriend's support for contraceptive use cannot be predicted from the quality of his relationship with the respondent: Support is as likely to be found in cooler as in more intimate relationships. This statement is consistent with quantitative findings based on the larger population from which this subgroup of respondents was drawn.

14. Mothers whose perceived level of anxiety about their daughters' sexuality is sufficiently great to deter any discussion of contraception but who, at the same time, convey their preference for contraception to pregnancy *are* giving mixed messages. However, mothers described in this way are almost never deliberately involved in the decision process (although they may become involved through inadvertence).

15. Absence of comment on quality of the relationship does not, of course, mean that the relationship was poor. It simply means that qualitative aspects of their relationships with clinic nurses (e.g., love, concern, fear) were not salient to these respondents.

CHAPTER 11

1. A perceptive analysis of *Romeo and Juliet* as a study of female adolescence is given in Dalsimer (1986).

2. These are, of course, alternative solutions to the same problem, that of providing economic support to adult women and, incidentally, their children.

3. The foregoing quotations are taken, respectively, from "Lecture to Troops," cited in Brandt (1985:67) and from the report for 1985 of the New York Governor's Task Force on Adolescent Pregnancy.

4. The relationship between visibility and social control in contemporary strategies for the management of crime and mental illness is discussed in Cohen (1985).

5. It should be pointed out that sexuality has been employed as a symbol of social change by those who welcomed as well as by those who deplored the changes they took it to represent. Progressives of the 1920s (among whom were several quite prominent social critics of the time) were "all committed to the virtues of youthful sexuality. Indeed, for most progressives the sexual habits of youth were laying the basis for a new social order" (Fass, 1977:32).

6. Movements for change in the *moral* designation of homosexuality from sin to alternative sexual orientation are an obvious exception. However, there are important differences between homosexuality and the unorthodox sexualities of adolescence. First, adolescence is an inherently transient state (and adolescent pregnancy even more transient) while self-defined homosexuality is thought of as more or less permanent. Second, the participants in homosexual acts occupy the same gender status and (unless there is a wide age difference) share the same stigma; there is no divisive double standard. Third, homosexual adults possess financial and organizational resources largely unavailable to adolescents in this society. These differences facilitate homosexuals' recognition of their common interests as well as their ability to act on these interests.

Bibliography

Addams, Jane. 1912. *A New Conscience and an Ancient Evil*. New York: Macmillan.

Allen, Charlotte Low. 1989. "Special Delivery: Overcoming the Barriers to Adoption." *Policy Review* 49 (Summer):46–53.

Allen, James E. 1974. "The Politics of Maternal Health Care and Family Planning." Paper presented at the Annual Meeting of the American Public Health Association, New Orleans, October 22.

Allen, MaryLee, and Karen Pittman. 1986. "Welfare and Teen Pregnancy: What Do We Know? What Do We Do?" Children's Defense Fund: Adolescent Pregnancy Prevention Clearinghouse.

AMA Committee on Human Reproduction. 1965. "The Control of Fertility." *Journal of the American Medical Association* 194 (October 25):230–38.

Aries, Philippe. 1962. *Centuries of Childhood: A Social History of Family Life*. New York: Vintage Books.

Aznar, Ramon, and Alwyn E. Bennett. 1961. "Pregnancy in the Adolescent Girl." *American Journal of Obstetrics and Gynecology* 81 (May):934–40.

Bachrach, Christine A. 1984. "Contraceptive Practice among American Women, 1973–1982." *Family Planning Perspectives* 16 (November/December):253–59.

Bailey, Beth L. 1988. *From Front Porch to Back Seat: Courtship in Twentieth-Century America*. Baltimore, Md.: Johns Hopkins University Press.

Bane, Mary Jo. 1986. "Household Composition and Poverty." Pp. 209–31 in Sheldon H. Danziger and Daniel H. Weinberg, eds., *Fighting Poverty: What Works and What Doesn't*. Cambridge, Mass.: Harvard University Press.

Bane, Mary Jo, and David T. Ellwood. 1989. "One Fifth of the Nation's Children: Why Are They Poor?" *Science* 245 (September 8):1047–53.

Barker-Benfield, Ben. 1972. "The Spermatic Economy: A Nineteenth-Century View of Sexuality." *Feminist Studies* 1 (Summer):45–74.

Barrett, Kate Waller. 1897. "Motherhood a Means of Regeneration." Pp. 52–62 in *Fourteen Years' Work Among "Erring Girls."* Washington, D.C.: National Florence Crittenton Mission.

Battaglia, Frederick C., Todd M. Frazier, and Andre E. Hellegers. 1963. "Obstetric and Pediatric Complications of Juvenile Pregnancy." *Pediatrics* 32 (November):902–10.

Beard, Mary Ritter. 1916. *Woman's Work in Municipalities*. New York: D. Appleton.

Becker, Howard S. 1963. *Outsiders: Studies in the Sociology of Deviance*. New York: Free Press.

Beisel, Nicola. 1990. "Class, Culture, and Campaigns against Vice in Three American Cities, 1872–1892." *American Sociological Review* 55 (February):44–62.

Bell, Robert R., and Jay B. Chaskes. 1970. "Premarital Sexual Experience among Coeds, 1958 and 1968." *Journal of Marriage and the Family* 32 (February):81–84.

Bennett, William J. 1987. *AIDS and the Education of Our Children: A Guide for Parents and Teachers*. Washington, D.C.: U.S. Department of Education.

Bennett, William J., and C. Everett Koop. 1987. "Statement on AIDS Education." Jointly released on January 30, Washington, D.C.

Ben-Yehuda, Nachman. 1985. *Deviance and Moral Boundaries*. Chicago: University of Chicago Press.

——. 1990. *The Politics and Morality of Deviance: Moral Panics, Drug Abuse, Deviant Science, and Reversed Stigmatization*. Albany: State University of New York Press.

Bergesen, Albert. 1984. "Social Control and Corporate Organization: A Durkheimian Perspective." Pp. 141–70 in Donald Black, ed., *Toward a General Theory of Social Control*. Vol. 2, *Selected Problems*. Orlando, Fla.: Academic Press.

Bianchi, Suzanne M., and Daphne Spain. 1986. *American Women in Transition*. New York: Russell Sage Foundation.

Blake, Judith. 1969a. "Population Policy for Americans: Is the Government Being Misled?" *Science* 164 (May 2):522–29.

——. 1969b. "Family Planning and Public Policy: Who Is Misleading Whom?" *Science* 165 (September 19):1203–4.

Blake, Judith, and Prithwas Das Gupta. 1972. "The Fallacy of the Five Million Women: A Re-estimate." *Demography* 9 (November):569–87.

Blanchard, Phyllis. 1924. *The Adolescent Girl: A Study from the Psychoanalytic Viewpoint*. New York: Dodd Mead.

Blanchard, Phyllis, and Carlyn Manasses. 1930. *New Girls for Old*. New York: Macaulay.

Blau, Peter M. 1955. *The Dynamics of Bureaucracy*. Chicago: University of Chicago Press.

Blumer, Herbert. 1971. "Social Problems as Collective Behavior." *Social Problems* 18 (Winter):298–306.

Boyer, Paul. 1978. *Urban Masses and Moral Order in America, 1820–1920*. Cambridge, Mass.: Harvard University Press.

Brandt, Allan M. 1985. *No Magic Bullet: A Social History of Venereal Disease in the United States since 1880*. New York: Oxford University Press.

——. 1987. "'Plagues and Peoples': The AIDS Epidemic." Pp. 183–204 in Allan Brandt, *No Magic Bullet*. Expanded ed. New York: Oxford University Press.

Bremner, Robert, ed. 1970. *Children and Youth in America: A Documentary History*. Cambridge, Mass.: Harvard University Press.

Brenzel, Barbara. 1980. "Domestication as Reform: A Study of the Socialization of Wayward Girls, 1856–1905." *Harvard Educational Review* 50 (May):196–213.

——. 1983. *Daughters of the State: A Social Portrait of the First Reform School for Girls in North America, 1856–1905*. Cambridge, Mass.: MIT Press.

Brinton, Mary C. 1988. "The Social-Institutional Bases of Gender Stratification: Japan as an Illustrative Case." *American Journal of Sociology* 94 (September):300–34.

Broderick, Carlfred B. 1966. "Sexual Behavior Among Pre-adolescents." *Journal of Social Issues* 22 (April):6–21.

Bromley, Dorothy D., and Florence H. Britten. 1938. *Youth and Sex: A Study of 1300 College Students*. New York: Harper and Brothers.

Brumberg, Joan Jacobs. 1984. "Chlorotic Girls, 1870–1920: A Historical Perspective on Female Adolescence." Pp. 186–95 in Judith Walzer Leavitt, ed., *Women and Health in America*. Madison: University of Wisconsin Press.

——. 1988. *Fasting Girls: The Emergence of Anorexia Nervosa as a Modern Disease*. Cambridge, Mass.: Harvard University Press.

Buechler, Steven M. 1986. *The Transformation of the Woman Suffrage Movement: The*

Case of Illinois, 1850–1920. New Brunswick, N.J.: Rutgers University Press.

Burgess, Ernest W. 1934. "Sociological Aspects of the Sex Life of the Unmarried Adult." Pp. 116–54 in Ira Wile, ed., *The Sex Life of the Unmarried Adult.* New York: Vanguard Press.

Burgess, Ernest W., and Paul Wallin. 1953. *Engagement and Marriage.* Chicago: J. B. Lippincott.

Burt, Martha L., Madeleine H. Kimmich, Jane Goldmuntz, Freya L. Sonnenstein. 1984. *Helping Pregnant Adolescents: Outcomes and Costs of Service Delivery.* Final Report on the Evaluation of Adolescent Pregnancy Programs. Washington, D.C.: Urban Institute.

Burton, Linda M. 1990. "Teenage Childbearing as an Alternative Life-Course Strategy in Multigeneration Black Families." *Human Nature* 1 (2):123–43.

Caldwell, John C., Pat Caldwell, and Pat Quiggin. 1989. "The Social Context of AIDS in Sub-Saharan Africa." *Population and Development Review* 15 (June):185–234.

Calverton, Victor F. 1928. *The Bankruptcy of Marriage.* New York: Macaulay.

Campbell, Arthur A. 1968. "The Role of Family Planning in the Reduction of Poverty." *Journal of Marriage and the Family* 30 (2):236–45.

Cannon, Kenneth L., and Richard Long. 1971. "Premarital Sexual Behavior in the Sixties." *Journal of Marriage and the Family* 33 (February):36–49.

Card, Josefina J., and Lauress L. Wise. 1978. "Teenage Mothers and Teenage Fathers: The Impact of Early Childbearing on the Parents' Personal and Professional Lives." *Family Planning Perspectives* 10 (July/August):199–205.

Carpenter, Niles. 1932. "Courtship Practices and Contemporary Social Change in America." *Annals of the American Academy of Political and Social Science* 160 (March):38–44.

Cartoof, Virginia. 1984. "Massachusetts' Parental Consent Law: Origins, Implementation, and Impact." Ph.D. diss., Brandeis University.

Caute, David. 1988. *The Year of the Barricades: A Journey Through 1968.* New York: Harper and Row.

Center for Population Options. 1986. *School-Based Clinic Policy Initiatives Around the Country, 1985.* Washington, D.C.: Center for Population Options.

Centers for Disease Control. 1974. "Abortions—United States, 1972." *Morbidity and Mortality Weekly Report* (May 4, 1974). DHEW Publication no. (CDC) 74-8017.

Chambers, Clarke A. 1963. *Seedtime of Reform: American Social Service and Social Action, 1918–1933.* Minneapolis: University of Minnesota Press.

Christensen, Harold T., and Christina Gregg. 1970. "Changing Sex Norms in America and Scandinavia." *Journal of Marriage and the Family* 32 (November):616–27.

Clarke, Edward. 1873. *Sex in Education; or, A Fair Chance for the Girls.* Boston: James R. Osgood and Co.

Coe, George A. 1924. *What Ails Our Youth?* New York: Charles Scribner's Sons.

Cohen, Miriam. Forthcoming. *From Workshop to Office: Employment, School, and Family in the Lives of New York Italian Women, 1900–1950.* Urbana: University of Illinois Press.

Cohen, Stanley. 1980. *Folk Devils and Moral Panics.* New York: St. Martin's. Originally published in 1972.

———. 1985. *Visions of Social Control: Crime, Punishment and Classification.* Cambridge, Mass.: Polity Press.

Cohen, Stanley, and Andrew T. Scull, eds. 1983. *Social Control and the State.* New York: St. Martin's.

Coleman, James S. 1961. *The Adolescent Society.* New York: Free Press of Glencoe.

Collier, Jane F., and Sylvia J. Yanagisako. 1987. *Gender and Kinship: Essays Toward a Unified Analysis*. Stanford, Calif.: Stanford University Press.

Collins, Randall. 1971. "A Conflict Theory of Sexual Stratification." *Social Problems* 19 (Summer):3–21.

Commission on Population Growth and the American Future. 1972. *Population and the American Future*. New York: Signet Books. Originally published by U.S. Government Printing Office, Washington, D.C.

Connelly, Mark Thomas. 1980. *The Response to Prostitution in the Progressive Era*. Chapel Hill: University of North Carolina Press.

Conrad, Peter, and Joseph W. Schneider. 1980. *Deviance and Medicalization: From Badness to Sickness*. St. Louis: C. V. Mosby Co.

Corcoran, Mary, Greg J. Duncan, and Martha S. Hill. 1984. "The Economic Fortunes of Women and Children: Lessons from the Panel Study of Income Dynamics." *Signs* 10 (Winter):232–48.

Corsa, Leslie. 1968. "United States: Public Policy and Programs in Family Planning." *Studies in Family Planning*, no. 27 (March):1–4.

Cott, Nancy F. 1975. "Young Women in the Second Great Awakening in New England." *Feminist Studies* 3 (Fall):15–29.

———. 1977. *The Bonds of Womanhood: "Woman's Sphere" in New England, 1780–1835*. New Haven, Conn.: Yale University Press.

———. 1978. "Passionlessness: An Interpretation of Victorian Sexual Ideology, 1790–1850." *Signs* 4 (Winter):219–36.

Crawford, Alan. 1980. *Thunder on the Right: The "New Right" and the Politics of Resentment*. New York: Pantheon.

Cuber, John F. 1943. "Changing Courtship and Marriage Customs." *Annals of the American Academy of Political and Social Science* 229 (September):30–38.

Cutright, Phillips, and Herbert L. Smith. 1986. "Trends in Illegitimacy among Five English-speaking Populations: 1940–1980." *Demography* 23 (November):563–78.

Dalsimer, Katherine. 1986. *Female Adolescence: Psychoanalytic Reflections on Literature*. New Haven, Conn.: Yale University Press.

Davenport, Isabel. 1924. *Salvaging of American Girlhood*. New York: Dutton.

Davis, Katharine Bement. 1929. *Factors in the Sex Life of Twenty-two Hundred Women*. New York: Harper and Brothers.

Davis, Kingsley. 1939. "Illegitimacy and the Social Structure." *American Journal of Sociology* 45 (September):215–33.

———. 1967. "Population Policy: Will Current Programs Succeed?" *Science* 158 (November 10):730.

Dawson, Deborah A., Denise J. Meny, and Jeanne Clare Ridley. 1980. "Fertility Control in the United States before the Contraceptive Revolution." *Family Planning Perspectives* 12 (March/April):76–86.

Day, Grace A. 1965. "A Program for Teen-age Unwed Mothers." *American Journal of Public Health* 55 (July):978–81.

Degler, Carl N. 1980. *At Odds: Women and Family in America from the Revolution to the Present*. New York: Oxford University Press.

Dell, Floyd. 1930. *Love in the Machine Age: A Psychological Study of the Transition from Patriarchal Society*. New York: Farrar and Rinehart.

D'Emilio, John, and Estelle B. Freedman. 1988. *Intimate Matters: A History of Sexuality in America*. New York: Harper and Row.

Demos, John. 1986. "The Rise and Fall of Adolescence." Pp. 92–113 (chapter 5) in *Past,*

Present, and Personal: The Family and the Life Course in American History. New York: Oxford University Press.

Dennett, Mary Ware. 1929. "Sex Enlightenment for Civilized Youth." Pp. 97–108 in Victor F. Calverton and S. D. Schmalhausen, eds. *Sex in Civilization*. New York: Macaulay.

Dickens, Helen O., Emily Hartshorne Mudd, Celso-Ramon Garcia, Karen Tomar, and David Wright. 1973. "One Hundred Pregnant Adolescents: Treatment Approaches in a University Hospital." *American Journal of Public Health* 63 (September):794–800.

Dienes, C. Thomas. 1972. *Law, Politics, and Birth Control*. Urbana: University of Illinois Press.

Djerassi, Carl. 1979. *The Politics of Contraception*. New York: W. W. Norton.

Douglas, Mary. 1966. *Purity and Danger: An Analysis of the Concepts of Pollution and Taboo*. London: Routledge and Kegan Paul.

Douvan, Elizabeth. 1957. Ann Arbor: University of Michigan, Survey Research Center, Institute for Social Research, Monograph no. 27.

Douvan, Elizabeth, and Joseph Adelson. 1966. *The Adolescent Experience*. New York: Wiley.

Dryfoos, Joy G. 1973. "A Formula for the 1970s: Estimating Need for Subsidized Family Planning Services." *Family Planning Perspectives* 5 (Summer):147–60.

———. 1984. "A New Strategy for Preventing Unintended Teenage Childbearing." *Family Planning Perspectives* 16 (July/August):193–95.

———. 1985. "School-based Health Clinics: A New Approach to Preventing Adolescent Pregnancy?" *Family Planning Perspectives* 17 (March/April):70–75.

———. 1988. "School-based Health Clinics: Three Years of Experience." *Family Planning Perspectives* 20 (July/August):193–200.

Duffey, Eliza B. 1873. *What Women Should Know: A Woman's Book About Women*. New York: Arno Press. Reprinted in 1974.

———. 1874. *No Sex in Education, or An Equal Chance for Girls and Boys*. Philadelphia: J. M. Stoddart.

Duncan, Greg J. 1984. *Years of Poverty, Years of Plenty*. Ann Arbor: University of Michigan Press.

Duncan, Greg J., and Saul D. Hoffman. 1990. "Welfare Benefits, Economic Opportunities, and Out-of-Wedlock Births Among Black Teenage Girls." *Demography* 27 (November):519–35.

Dunn, Patricia. 1982. "Reduction of Teenage Pregnancy as a Rationale for Sex Education: A Position Paper." *Journal of School Health* 52 (December):611–13.

Durkheim, Émile. 1933. *The Division of Labor in Society*. Translated by George Simpson. New York: Free Press of Glencoe. Paperback edition, reprinted in 1964.

———. 1938. *The Rules of Sociological Method*. Chicago: University of Chicago Press. Reprint. Glencoe, Ill.: Free Press, 1950, 1958.

Eggleston, Margaret W. 1923. *Womanhood in the Making*. New York: George H. Doran Co.

Ehrenreich, Barbara. 1989. "Mothers Unite." *New Republic* 201 (July 10):30–33.

Ehrmann, Winston. 1959. *Premarital Dating Behavior*. New York: Holt.

Eisenstein, Zillah R. 1981. "Patriarchy, Motherhood, and Public Life." Pp. 14–30 in *The Radical Future of Liberal Feminism*. New York: Longman.

Elder, Glen H., Jr. 1974. *Children of the Great Depression: Social Change in Life Experience*. Chicago: University of Chicago Press.

Ellwood, David T. 1986. "Working Off of Welfare: Prospects and Policies for Self-Sufficiency of Women Heading Families." Madison: University of Wisconsin, Institute for Research on Poverty Discussion Paper no. 803-86.

———. 1988. *Poor Support: Poverty in the American Family*. New York: Basic Books.

———. 1989. "The Origins of 'Dependency': Choices, Confidence, or Culture?" *Focus* 12 (Spring and Summer):6–13.

Erenberg, Lewis A. 1981. *Steppin' Out: New York Night Life and the Transformation of American Culture, 1890–1930*. Westport, Conn.: Greenwood.

Erikson, Kai T. 1966. *Wayward Puritans: A Study in the Sociology of Deviance*. New York: Wiley.

Falconer, Martha P. 1918. "Reformatory Treatment of Women." National Conference of Social Work, *Proceedings*:253–56.

Fass, Paula. 1977. *The Damned and the Beautiful: American Youth in the 1920s*. New York: Oxford University Press.

Fedder, Ruth. 1948. *A Girl Grows Up*. New ed. New York: Whittlesey House.

Filene, Peter G. 1986. *Him/Her/Self: Sex Roles in Modern America*. 2d ed. Baltimore, Md.: Johns Hopkins University Press.

Fireman, Bruce, and William A. Gamson. 1979. "Utilitarian Logic in the Resource Mobilization Perspective." Pp. 8–44 in Mayer N. Zald and John D. McCarthy, eds., *The Dynamics of Social Movements*. Cambridge, Mass.: Winthrop.

Fischer, Claude S., and Glenn R. Carroll. 1988. "Telephone and Automobile Diffusion in the United States, 1902–1937." *American Journal of Sociology* 93 (March):1153–78.

Fishbein, Martin. 1972. "Toward an Understanding of Family Planning Behaviors." *Journal of Applied Social Psychology* 2 (July–September):214–27.

FitzGerald, Frances. 1981. "The Triumphs of the New Right." *New York Review of Books* 28 (November 19):19–26.

Flexner, Abraham. 1940. *I Remember: The Autobiography of Abraham Flexner*. New York: Simon and Schuster.

Folsom, Joseph K. 1934. *The Family: Its Sociology and Social Psychiatry*. New York: Wiley.

Ford, James H., and Michael Schwartz. 1979. "Birth Control for Teenagers: Diagram for Disaster." *Linacre Quarterly* 46 (February):71–81.

Foucault, Michel. 1978. *The History of Sexuality*. Vol. 1, *An Introduction*. New York: Vintage Books. Paperback edition published in 1980.

Freedman, Estelle. 1974. "The New Woman: Changing Views of Women in the 1920s." *Journal of American History* 61 (September):372–93.

———. 1981. *Their Sister's Keepers: Women's Prison Reform in America, 1830–1930*. Ann Arbor: University of Michigan Press.

———. 1982. "Sexuality in Nineteenth-Century America: Behavior, Ideology and Politics." *Reviews in American History* 10 (December):196–215.

Freidson, Eliot. 1968. "The Impurity of Professional Authority." Pp. 25–34 in Howard S. Becker, Blanche Geer, David Riesman, and Robert S. Weiss, eds., *Institutions and the Person: Papers Presented to Everett C. Hughes*. Chicago: Aldine.

———. 1972. "Disability as Social Deviance." Pp. 330–52 in Eliot Freidson and Judith Lorber, eds., *Medical Men and Their Work*. Chicago: Aldine.

Furstenberg, Frank F., Jr. 1976. *Unplanned Parenthood: The Social Consequences of Teenage Childbearing*. New York: Free Press.

———. 1987. "Race Differences in Teenage Sexuality, Pregnancy, and Adolescent Childbearing." *Milbank Quarterly* 65 (Supplement 2):381–403.

Furstenberg, Frank F., Jr., J. Brooks-Gunn, and S. Philip Morgan. 1987. *Adolescent*

Mothers in Later Life. Cambridge, Eng.: Cambridge University Press.

Gagnon, John H., and William Simon. 1973. *Sexual Conduct: The Social Sources of Human Sexuality*. Chicago: Aldine.

Gallagher, Catherine, and Thomas Laqueur, eds. 1987. *The Making of the Modern Body: Sexuality and Society in the Nineteenth Century*. Berkeley: University of California Press.

Gebhard, Paul H., Wardell B. Pomeroy, Clyde E. Martin, and Cornelia V. Christenson. 1958. *Pregnancy, Birth, and Abortion*. New York: Harper and Brothers.

Geronimus, Arline T. 1987. "On Teenage Childbearing and Neonatal Mortality in the United States." *Population and Development Review* 13 (June):245–79.

Gerson, Kathleen. 1985. *Hard Choices: How Women Decide About Work, Career, and Motherhood*. Berkeley: University of California Press.

Gettleman, Marvin E. 1975. "Philanthropy as Social Control in Late 19th Century America: Some Hypotheses and Data on the Rise of Social Work." *Societas* 5 (Winter):49–59.

Gibson, Jessie E. 1927. *On Being a Girl*. New York: Macmillan.

Gilder, George. 1981. *Wealth and Poverty*. New York: Basic Books.

Gillis, John R. 1981. *Youth and History: Tradition and Change in European Age Relations, 1770–Present*. New York: Academic Press.

Gilman, Charlotte Perkins. 1898. *Women and Economics: A Study of the Economic Relations between Men and Women as a Factor in Social Evolution*. Boston: Small, Maynard and Co. Reprint. New York: Harper and Row, 1966.

Ginsburg, Faye D. 1989. *Contested Lives: The Abortion Debate in an American Community*. Berkeley: University of California Press.

Glasco, Laurence A. 1979. "The Life Cycles and Household Structure of American Ethnic Groups: Irish, Germans, and Native-born Whites in Buffalo, New York, 1855." Pp. 268–89 in Nancy F. Cott and Elizabeth H. Pleck, eds., *A Heritage of Her Own: Toward a New Social History of American Women*. New York: Simon and Schuster.

Goffman, Erving. 1961. *Asylums: Essays on the Social Situation of Mental Patients and Other Inmates*. Garden City, N.Y.: Doubleday Anchor Books.

Gold, Rachel Benson, and Sandra Guardado. 1988. "Public Funding of Family Planning, Sterilization and Abortion Services, 1987." *Family Planning Perspectives* 20 (September/October):228–33.

Gold, Rachel Benson, and Barry Nestor. 1985. "Public Funding of Contraceptive, Sterilization and Abortion Services, 1983." *Family Planning Perspectives* 17 (January/February):25–30.

Goodsell, Willystine. 1923. *The Education of Women: Its Social Background and Its Problems*. New York: Macmillan.

Gordis, Leon, Jacqueline D. Fassett, Ruth Finklestein, and Matthew Tayback. 1968. "Adolescent Pregnancy: A Hospital-based Program for Primary Prevention." *American Journal of Public Health* 58 (May):849–58.

Gordon, Linda. 1977. *Woman's Body, Woman's Right: A Social History of Birth Control in America*. New York: Penguin Books. Published originally by Grossman in 1976.

Gordon, Michael. 1971. "From an Unfortunate Necessity to a Cult of Mutual Orgasm: Sex in American Marital Education Literature, 1830–1940." Pp. 53–77 in James M. Henslin, ed., *Studies in the Sociology of Sex*. New York: Appleton-Century-Crofts.

Gorham, Deborah. 1978. "The 'Maiden Tribute of Modern Babylon' Reexamined: Child Prostitution and the Idea of Childhood in Late-Victorian England." *Victorian Studies* 21 (Spring):353–79.

Goulden, Joseph C. 1971. *The Money Givers*. New York: Random House.

Granberg, Donald, and Beth Wellman Granberg. 1980. "Abortion Attitudes, 1965–1980: Trends and Determinants." *Family Planning Perspectives* 12 (September/October):250–61.

Grant, John A. 1970. "Biologic Outcomes of Adolescent Pregnancy: An Administrative Perspective." In *Perspectives in Maternal and Child Health*, Series A, No. 1, July. Baltimore, Md.: Johns Hopkins University.

Greer, Germaine. 1984. *Sex and Destiny: The Politics of Human Fertility*. New York: Harper and Row.

Grow, Lucille J., and Michael J. Smith. 1971. "Adoption Trends: 1969–1970." *Child Welfare* 50 (July):401–7.

Grubb, W. Norton, and Marvin Lazerson. 1982. *Broken Promises: How Americans Fail Their Children*. New York: Basic Books.

Gusfield, Joseph. 1963. *Symbolic Crusade: Status Politics and the American Temperance Movement*. Urbana: University of Illinois Press.

———. 1967. "Moral Passage: The Symbolic Process in Public Designations of Deviance." *Social Problems* 15 (Fall):175–88.

———. 1981. *The Culture of Public Problems: Drinking-Driving and the Symbolic Order*. Chicago: University of Chicago Press.

Guttmacher, Alan F. 1973. "Commentary: Family Planning Need and the Future of the Family Planning Program." *Family Planning Perspectives* 5 (Summer):175–76.

Alan Guttmacher Institute. 1975. *Report for the Period July 1, 1973–December 31, 1974*. New York: Planned Parenthood Federation of America.

———. 1976. *Eleven Million Teenagers: What Can Be Done About the Epidemic of Adolescent Pregnancies in the United States*. New York: Alan Guttmacher Institute.

———. 1988. *State Legislative Record: 1988 Fertility-Related Bills and Laws as of December 31*. Washington, D.C.: Alan Guttmacher Institute.

Guy, Cynthia A., with Lawrence N. Bailis and Kay E. Sherwood. 1986. *The Community Service Projects: A New York State Adolescent Pregnancy Initiative*. New York: Manpower Demonstration Research Corporation.

Haggstrom, Gus W., David E. Kanouse, and Peter A. Morrison. 1986. "Accounting for the Educational Shortfalls of Mothers." *Journal of Marriage and the Family* 48 (February):175–86.

Hale, Nathan G., Jr. 1971. *Freud and the Americans: The Beginnings of Psychoanalysis in the United States, 1876–1917*. New York: Oxford University Press.

Hall, G. Stanley. 1905. "Adolescent Girls and Their Education." Pp. 561–647 (chapter 17) in *Adolescence: Its Psychology and Its Relations to Physiology, Anthropology, Sociology, Sex, Crime, Religion and Education*, vol. 2. New York: Appleton.

Haller, John S., Jr., and Robin M. Haller. 1974. *The Physician and Sexuality in Victorian America*. Urbana: University of Illinois Press.

Hammack, David C. 1982. *Power and Society: Greater New York at the Turn of the Century*. New York: Russell Sage Foundation.

Handler, Joel F. 1972. *Reforming the Poor: Welfare Policy, Federalism, and Morality*. New York: Basic Books.

Harkavy, Oscar, Frederick S. Jaffe, and Samuel M. Wishik. 1967. "Implementing DHEW Policy on Family Planning and Population: A Consultants' Report." New York: Ford Foundation.

———. 1969. "Family Planning and Public Policy: Who Is Misleading Whom?" *Science* 165 (July 25):367–73.

Harrington, Michael. 1984. *The New American Poverty*. New York: Holt, Rinehart and Winston.

Hassan, H. Mohammed, and Frederick E. Falls. 1964. "The Young Primipara: A Clinical Study." *American Journal of Obstetrics and Gynecology* 88 (January 15):256–69.

Havighurst, Robert J. et al. 1962. *Growing Up in River City*. New York: Wiley.

Hayes, Cheryl D., ed. 1987. *Risking the Future: Adolescent Sexuality, Pregnancy, and Childbearing*. Washington, D.C.: National Academy Press.

Haynes, R. Brian, D. Wayne Taylor, and David L. Sackett, eds. 1979. *Compliance in Health Care*. Baltimore, Md.: Johns Hopkins University Press.

Henshaw, Stanley K. 1987. "Characteristics of U.S. Women Having Abortions, 1982–1983." *Family Planning Perspectives* 19 (January/February):5–9.

Henshaw, Stanley K., and Kevin O'Reilly. 1983. "Characteristics of Abortion Patients in the United States, 1979 and 1980." *Family Planning Perspectives* 15 (January/February):5–16.

Herzog, Elizabeth. 1966. "The Chronic Revolution: Births Out of Wedlock." *Clinical Pediatrics* 5 (February):130–35.

Hilgartner, Stephen, and Charles L. Bosk. 1988. "The Rise and Fall of Social Problems: A Public Arenas Model." *American Journal of Sociology* 94 (July):53–78.

Hill, Adelaide C., and Frederick S. Jaffe. 1966. "Negro Fertility and Family Size Preferences: Implications for Programming of Health and Social Services." Pp. 205–24 in Talcott Parsons and Kenneth B. Clark, eds., *The Negro American*. Boston: Houghton Mifflin.

Hill, Joseph A. 1929. *Women in Gainful Occupations, 1870 to 1920*. Census Monograph no. 9. Washington, D.C.: U.S. Government Printing Office.

Hiner, Ray N. 1975. "Adolescence in 18th-Century America." *History of Childhood Quarterly* 3 (Fall):253–80.

Hobson, Barbara Meil. 1987. *Uneasy Virtue: The Politics of Prostitution and the American Reform Tradition*. New York: Basic Books.

Hodgson, Godfrey. 1976. *America in Our Time: From World War II to Nixon. What Happened and Why*. New York: Vintage Books.

Hofferth, Sandra L. 1987a. "The Effects of Programs and Policies on Adolescent Pregnancy and Childbearing." Pp. 207–63 in Sandra L. Hofferth and Cheryl D. Hayes, eds., *Risking the Future: Adolescent Sexuality, Pregnancy, and Childbearing*. Vol. 2, *Working Papers and Statistical Appendices*. Washington, D.C.: National Academy Press.

———. 1987b. "Contraceptive Decision-Making among Adolescents." Pp. 56–77 in Sandra L. Hofferth and Cheryl D. Hayes, eds., *Risking the Future: Adolescent Sexuality, Pregnancy, and Childbearing*. Vol. 2, *Working Papers and Statistical Appendices*. Washington, D.C.: National Academy Press.

Hofferth, Sandra L., and Cheryl Hayes, eds. 1987. *Risking the Future: Adolescent Sexuality, Pregnancy, and Childbearing*. Vol. 2. Washington, D.C.: National Academy Press.

Hofferth, Sandra L., Joan R. Kahn, and Wendy Baldwin. 1987. "Premarital Sexual Activity among U.S. Teenage Women over the Past Three Decades." *Family Planning Perspectives* 19 (March/April):46–53.

Hofstadter, Richard. 1955. *The Age of Reform*. New York: Alfred A. Knopf.

Hogan, Dennis P., Nan Marie Astone, and Evelyn M. Kitagawa. 1985. "Social and Environmental Factors Influencing Contraceptive Use among Black Adolescents." *Family Planning Perspectives* 17 (July/August):165–69.

Hollingshead, August B. 1949. *Elmtown's Youth: The Impact of Social Class on Adolescents*. New York: Wiley.

Hollingworth, Leta S. 1931. *The Psychology of the Adolescent*. New York: D. Appleton-Century.

Hottois, James, and Neal A. Milner. 1975. *The Sex Education Controversy*. Lexington, Mass.: Lexington Books.

Howard, Marion. 1968. *The Webster School: A District of Columbia Program for Pregnant Girls*. Children's Bureau Research Reports. No. 2. Washington, D.C.: U.S. Children's Bureau.

————. 1975. "Bringing about Change: A National Overview with Respect to Early Childbearing and Childrearing." Pp. 241–58 in Jack Zackler and Wayne Brandstadt, eds., *The Teenage Pregnant Girl*. Springfield, Ill.: Charles C. Thomas.

Huling, Tracy. 1988. *Limited Options: Public Policy Trends in Teenage Pregnancy Prevention and Recommendations for New York State*. New York: Center for Public Advocacy Research.

Hunter, Allen. 1981. "In the Wings: New Right Ideology and Organizations." *Radical America* 15 (Spring):113–38.

Inazu, Judith K. 1987. "Partner Involvement and Contraceptive Efficacy in Premarital Sexual Relationships." *Population and Environment* 9 (Winter):225–37.

Issacs, Stephen L. 1981. *Population Law and Policy*. New York: Human Sciences Press.

Jacob, John E. 1985. "An Overview of Black America in 1984." Pp. i–vi in *The State of Black America 1985*. New York: National Urban League.

Jaffe, Frederick S. 1967. "Family Planning, Public Policy and Intervention Strategy." *Journal of Social Issues* 23 (October):145–63.

————. 1968. "Family Planning and the Medical Assistance Program." *Medical Care* 6 (January/February):69–77.

Jaffe, Frederick S., Joy G. Dryfoos, and Marsha Corey. 1973. "Organized Family Planning Programs in the United States: 1968–1972." *Family Planning Perspectives* 5 (Spring):73–79.

Jaffe, Frederick S., and Alan F. Guttmacher. 1968. "Family Planning Programs in the United States." *Demography* 5 (2):910–23.

Jaffe, Frederick S., and Steven Polgar. 1968. "Family Planning and Public Policy: Is the Culture of Poverty the New Cop-Out?" *Journal of Marriage and the Family* 30 (May):228–35.

Jencks, Christopher. 1989. "What Is the Underclass—and Is It Growing?" *Focus* 12 (Spring and Summer):14–26.

Jenkins, J. Craig. 1983. "Resource Mobilization Theory and the Study of Social Movements." *Annual Review of Sociology* 9:527–53.

Joffe, Carole. 1986. *The Regulation of Sexuality: Experiences of Family Planning Workers*. Philadelphia: Temple University Press.

Johnson, Kate Burr. 1926. "Problems of Delinquency among Girls." *Journal of Social Hygiene* 12 (October):385–97.

Jones, Elise F., Jacqueline D. Forrest, Noreen Goldman, Stanley Henshaw, Richard Lincoln, Jeannie I. Rosoff, Charles F. Westoff, and Deirdre Wulf. 1986. *Teenage Pregnancy in Industrialized Countries*. New Haven, Conn.: Yale University Press.

Jones, Maldwyn A. 1983. *The Limits of Liberty: American History, 1607–1980*. Oxford, Eng.: Oxford University Press.

Kasun, Jacqueline R. 1981. Testimony before the Senate Committee on Labor and Human Resources, *Hearings on Examination of the Role of the Federal Govern-*

ment in Birth Control, Abortion Referral, and Sex Education Programs. 97th Cong., 1st sess., March 31: 89–102.

Katz, Michael B. 1975. *The People of Hamilton, Canada West: Family and Class in a Mid-Nineteenth Century City*. Cambridge, Mass.: Harvard University Press.

———. 1989. *The Undeserving Poor: From the War on Poverty to the War on Welfare*. New York: Pantheon.

Kellogg, J. H. 1888. *Plain Facts for Old and Young*. New York: Arno Press. Reprinted in 1974.

Kennedy, David M. 1970. *Birth Control in America*. New Haven, Conn.: Yale University Press.

Kessler, Seymour. 1980. "The Psychological Paradigm Shift in Genetic Counseling." *Social Biology* 27 (Fall):167–85.

Kessler-Harris, Alice. 1982. *Out to Work: A History of Wage-Earning Women in the United States*. New York: Oxford University Press.

Kett, Joseph F. 1971. "Adolescence and Youth in 19th-Century America." *Journal of Interdisciplinary History* 2 (Autumn):283–98.

———. 1977. *Rites of Passage: Adolescence in America 1790 to the Present*. New York: Basic Books.

Kimmich, Madeleine H. 1985. "Addressing the Problem of Adolescent Pregnancy: The State of the Art and Art in the States." Washington, D.C.: National Governor's Association.

Kinsey, Alfred, Wardell B. Pomeroy, and Clyde E. Martin. 1948. *Sexual Behavior in the Human Male*. Philadelphia: W. B. Saunders.

Kinsey, Alfred, Wardell B. Pomeroy, Clyde E. Martin, and Paul H. Gebhard. 1953. *Sexual Behavior in the Human Female*. Philadelphia: W. B. Saunders.

Klein, Luella. 1985. "To Have or Not to Have a Pregnancy." *Obstetrics and Gynecology* 65 (January):1–4.

Klerman, Lorraine V., and James F. Jekel. 1973. *School-Age Mothers: Problems, Programs, and Policy*. Hamden, Conn.: Linnet Books.

Klerman, Lorraine V., James Jekel, and Catherine S. Chilman. 1983. "The Service Needs of Pregnant and Parenting Adolescents." Pp. 180–206 in Catherine S. Chilman, ed., *Adolescent Sexuality in a Changing American Society: Social and Psychological Perspectives for the Human Services Professions*. 2d ed. New York: Wiley.

Kraditor, Aileen. 1965. *The Ideas of the Woman Suffrage Movement, 1890–1920*. New York: Columbia University Press.

Lacan, Jacques. 1978. *The Four Fundamental Concepts of Psychoanalysis*. New York: W. W. Norton. Paperback edition published in 1981.

Ladner, Joyce A. 1971. *Tomorrow's Tomorrow: The Black Woman*. New York: Doubleday.

Laqueur, Thomas. 1987. "Orgasm, Generation, and the Politics of Reproductive Biology." Pp. 1–41 in Catherine Gallagher and Thomas Laqueur, eds. *The Making of the Modern Body: Sexuality and Society in the Nineteenth Century*. Berkeley: University of California Press.

Law, Sylvia A. 1983. "Women, Work, Welfare, and the Preservation of Patriarchy." *University of Pennsylvania Law Review* 131 (May):1249–1339.

Lee, Nancy. 1969. *The Search for an Abortionist*. Chicago: University of Chicago Press.

Levitan, Sar A. 1969. *The Great Society's Poor Law*. Baltimore, Md.: Johns Hopkins University Press.

Levitan, Sar A., and Judith W. LaVor. 1969. "The Reluctance of Uncle Sam's Bureaucrats to Fight Poverty With 'the Pill.' " *Congressional Record* (September 8):24710–12.

Lief, Harold I. 1966. "The Physician and Family Planning." *Journal of the American Medical Association* 197 (August 22):128–32.

Lindsey, Ben. 1925. *The Revolt of Modern Youth*. New York: Boni and Liveright.

Lippmann, Walter. 1929. *A Preface to Morals*. New York: Macmillan.

Lipset, Seymour Martin, and Earl Raab. 1970. *The Politics of Unreason: Right-Wing Extremism in America, 1790–1970*. New York: Harper and Row.

———. 1978. "Epilogue: The 1970s." Pp. 517–49 in *The Politics of Unreason*. 2d ed. Chicago: University of Chicago Press.

Lipsky, Michael. 1980. *Street-Level Bureaucracy: Dilemmas of the Individual in Public Service*. New York: Russell Sage Foundation.

Littlewood, Thomas B. 1977. *The Politics of Population Control*. Notre Dame: University of Notre Dame Press.

Lloyd, Susan M. 1979. *A Singular School: Abbot Academy, 1828–1973*. Andover, Mass.: Phillips Academy. Distributed by the University Press of New England.

London, Gary D. 1968. "Family Planning Programs of the Office of Economic Opportunity: Scope, Operation, and Impact." *Demography* 5 (2):924–30.

Long, Russell B. 1971. "The Welfare Mess: A Scandal of Illegitimacy and Desertion." Address to the U.S. Senate, 92d Cong., 1st sess., December 14.

Lubove, Roy. 1962. "The Progressives and the Prostitute." *The Historian* 24 (May):308–30.

Lunbeck, Elizabeth. 1987. " 'A New Generation of Women': Progressive Psychiatrists and the Hypersexual Female." *Feminist Studies* 13 (Fall):513–43.

Lundberg, Emma O. 1920. "The Child-Mother as a Delinquency Problem." National Conference of Social Work, *Proceedings*:167–68.

———. 1921. "The Illegitimate Mother as a Delinquency Problem." American Sociological Society, *Publications* 16:204–8.

———. 1933. "Unmarried Mothers in the Municipal Court of Philadelphia." Philadelphia: Thomas Skelton Harrison Foundation.

Lynd, Robert S., and Helen M. Lynd. 1929. *Middletown: A Study in Contemporary American Culture*. New York: Harcourt Brace and World.

———. 1937. *Middletown in Transition: A Study in Cultural Conflicts*. New York: Harcourt Brace Jovanovich.

McAnarney, Elizabeth R., ed. 1983. *Premature Adolescent Pregnancy and Parenthood*. New York: Grune and Stratton.

McCarthy, John D., and Mayer N. Zald. 1977. "Resource Mobilization and Social Movements: A Partial Theory." *American Journal of Sociology* 82 (May):1212–41.

MacDonald, Donald Ian. 1987. "An Approach to the Problem of Teenage Pregnancy." *Public Health Reports* 102 (July/August):377–85.

McGhee, James D. 1985. "The Black Family Today and Tomorrow." Pp. 1–20 in *The State of Black America 1985*. New York: National Urban League.

McGovern, James R. 1968. "The American Woman's Pre–World War I Freedom in Manners and Morals." *Journal of American History* 55 (September):315–33.

McGraw, Onalee. 1980. *The Family, Feminism and the Therapeutic State*. Washington, D.C.: Heritage Foundation.

McKinley, Edward H. 1980. *Marching to Glory: The History of the Salvation Army in the United States of America, 1880–1980*. San Francisco: Harper and Row.

McLaughlin, Steven D. 1977. *Consequences of Adolescent Childbearing for the Mother's*

Occupational Attainment. Final Report. Minneapolis: University of Minnesota Press.

Mangold, George B. 1921. *Children Born Out of Wedlock: A Sociological Study with Particular Reference to the United States*. University of Missouri studies. Social science series, vol. 3, no. 3. Columbia, Mo.: University of Missouri.

Mark, Georgia. 1887. "Legal Protection for Purity." *Philanthropist* 2 (January):1–3.

Marks, James S., and Willard Cates. 1986. "Sex Education: How Should It Be Offered?" *Journal of the American Medical Association* 255 (January 3):85–86.

Marsiglio, William, and Frank L. Mott. 1986. "The Impact of Sex Education on Sexual Activity, Contraceptive Use and Premarital Pregnancy among American Teenagers." *Family Planning Perspectives* 18 (July/August):151–62.

Martin, Emily. 1987. *The Woman in the Body: A Cultural Analysis of Reproduction*. Boston: Beacon Press.

Matusow, Allen J. 1984. *The Unravelling of America: A History of Liberalism in the 1960s*. New York: Harper and Row.

May, Henry F. 1959. *The End of American Innocence: A Study of the First Years of Our Own Time, 1912–1917*. New York: Knopf.

Mennel, Robert M. 1973. *Thorns and Thistles: Juvenile Delinquents in the United States, 1825–1940*. Hanover, N.H.: University Press of New England.

Meyerowitz, Joanne J. 1988. *Women Adrift: Independent Wage Earners in Chicago, 1880–1930*. Chicago: University of Chicago Press.

Mitchell, Juliet. 1975. *Psychoanalysis and Feminism: Freud, Reich, Laing and Women*. New York: Vintage Books.

Mohr, James C. 1978. *Abortion in America*. New York: Oxford University Press.

Moore, Kristin A. 1981. "Government Policies Related to Teenage Family Formation and Functioning: An Inventory." Pp. 165–212 in Theodora Ooms, ed., *Teenage Pregnancy in a Family Context*. Philadelphia: Temple University Press.

Moore, Kristin A., and Martha R. Burt. 1982. *Private Crisis, Public Cost: Policy Perspectives on Teenage Childbearing*. Washington, D.C.: Urban Institute.

Moore, Kristin A., and Steven B. Caldwell. 1977. "The Effect of Government Policies on Out-of-Wedlock Sex and Pregnancy." *Family Planning Perspectives* 9 (July/August):164–69.

Moore, Kristin A., Margaret C. Simms, and Charles L. Betsey. 1986. *Choice and Circumstance: Racial Differences in Adolescent Sexuality and Fertility*. New Brunswick, N.J.: Transaction Publishers.

Moore, Kristin A., Linda J. Waite, Steven B. Caldwell, and Sandra L. Hofferth. 1978. *The Consequences of Age at First Childbirth: Educational Attainment. Final Report*. Washington, D.C.: Urban Institute.

Moore, Kristin A., and Richard F. Wertheimer. 1984. "Teenage Childbearing and Welfare: Preventive and Ameliorative Strategies." *Family Planning Perspectives* 16 (November/December):285–89.

Morlock, Maud, and Hilary Campbell. 1946. *Maternity Homes for Unmarried Mothers: A Community Service*. Washington, D.C.: U.S. Children's Bureau.

Mosher, William D., and Christine A. Bachrach. 1987. "First Premarital Contraceptive Use: United States, 1960–1982." *Studies in Family Planning* 18 (March/April):83–95.

Mott, Frank L., and Lois B. Shaw. 1978. "Work and Family in the School Leaving Years: A Comparison of Female High School Graduates and Dropouts." Unpublished manuscript. Columbus: Ohio State University.

Mottl, Tahi L. 1980. "The Analysis of Countermovements." *Social Problems* 27 (June):620–35.

Moynihan, Daniel P. 1965. *The Negro Family: The Case for National Action.* Washington, D.C.: Department of Labor, Office of Policy Planning and Research.

――――. 1973. *The Politics of a Guaranteed Income: The Nixon Administration and the Family Assistance Plan.* New York: Random House.

――――. 1986. *Family and Nation.* New York: Harcourt Brace Jovanovich.

Muraskin, Lana D. 1986. "Sex Education Mandates: Are They the Answer?" *Family Planning Perspectives* 18 (July/August):171–74.

Murray, Charles. 1984. *Losing Ground: American Social Policy 1950–1980.* New York: Basic Books.

Nash, Margaret A., and Margaret Dunkle. 1989. *The Need for a Warming Trend: A Survey of the School Climate for Pregnant and Parenting Teens.* Washington, D.C.: Equality Center.

Nathanson, Constance A., and Marshall H. Becker. 1983. "Contraceptive Behavior among Unmarried Young Women: A Theoretical Framework for Research." *Population and Environment* 6 (Spring):39–59.

Nathanson, Constance A., and Young J. Kim. 1989. "Components of Change in Adolescent Fertility, 1971–1979." *Demography* 26 (February):85–98.

National Conference of Catholic Bishops. 1986. "Economic Justice for All: Catholic Social Teaching and the U.S. Economy." *Origins: NC Documentary Service* 16 (November 27):409–455.

National Education Association. 1975. *Kanawha County, West Virginia: A Textbook Study in Cultural Conflict.* Washington, D.C.: National Education Association.

National Florence Crittenton Mission. 1928. 45th Annual Report for the Year, 1927. Minutes of the 45th Annual Conference of Florence Crittenton Homes, Indianapolis, Ind., June 3, 4, 5, 1928.

――――. 1938. 55th Annual Report for the Year, 1937. *The Florence Crittenton Bulletin* 13 (May):1–11.

――――. 1948. 65th Annual Report for the Year, 1947. *The Florence Crittenton Bulletin* 23 (August):1–53.

National Urban League. 1985. "Conclusion and Recommendations." Pp. 185–89 in *The State of Black America 1985.* New York: National Urban League.

――――. 1986. "Conclusion and Recommendations." Pp. 175–81 in *The State of Black America 1986.* New York: National Urban League.

Newcomb, Theodore. 1937. "Recent Changes in Attitudes toward Sex and Marriage." *American Sociological Review* 2 (October):659–67.

New York Governor's Task Force on Adolescent Pregnancy. 1985. *Setting Directions.* Initial Report. Albany: New York State Council on Children and Families.

――――. 1986. *Moving Forward: Next Steps.* Second Report. Albany: New York State Council on Children and Families.

――――. 1987. *Benchmarks and Challenges.* Third Report. Albany: New York State Council on Children and Families.

New York State Temporary Commission. 1983. *Teenage Motherhood and Public Dependency: New York State's Response to the Issue of Adolescent Pregnancy.* Study Report no. 10. Albany: New York State Temporary Commission to Revise the Social Services Law.

Nokes, John M. 1958. "Discussion." *American Journal of Obstetrics and Gynecology* 76 (October):751.

Norton, Eleanor Holmes. 1985. "Restoring the Traditional Black Family." *New York Times Magazine*, June 2:VI, 43:1.

O'Hare, William P. 1985. "Poverty in America: Trends and New Patterns." *Population Bulletin* 40 (June):1–44.

Oppenheimer, Valerie Kincade. 1970. *The Female Labor Force in the United States: Demographic and Economic Factors Governing its Growth and Changing Composition*. Population Monograph Series, no. 5. Berkeley: University of California.

Orr, Margaret Terry. 1982. "Sex Education and Contraceptive Education in U.S. Public High Schools." *Family Planning Perspectives* 14 (November/December):304–13.

Ortner, Sherry B., and Harriet Whitehead. 1981. "Introduction: Accounting for Sexual Meanings." Pp. 1–27 in Sherry B. Ortner and Harriet Whitehead, eds., *Sexual Meanings: The Cultural Construction of Gender and Sexuality*. Cambridge, Eng.: Cambridge University Press.

Osofsky, Howard J. 1968. *The Pregnant Teenager: A Medical, Educational and Social Analysis*. Springfield, Ill.: Charles C. Thomas.

Osofsky, Howard J., John H. Hagen, and Peggy W. Wood. 1968. "A Program for Pregnant Schoolgirls: Some Early Results." *American Journal of Obstetrics and Gynecology* 100 (April 1):1020–27.

Padgug, Robert. 1979. "Sexual Matters: On Conceptualizing Sexuality in History." *The Radical History Review* 20 (Spring/Summer):3–23.

Parsons, Talcott. 1951. *The Social System*. Glencoe, Ill.: Free Press.

Peiss, Kathy. 1983. " 'Charity Girls' and City Pleasures: Historical Notes on Working-Class Sexuality, 1880–1920." Pp. 74–87 in Ann Snitow, Christine Stansell, and Sharon Thompson, eds., *Powers of Desire: The Politics of Sexuality*. New York: Monthly Review Press.

————. 1986. *Cheap Amusements: Working Women and Leisure in Turn-of-the-Century New York*. Philadelphia: Temple University Press.

Perlman, Sylvia B. 1984. "Nobody's Baby: The Politics of Adolescent Pregnancy." Ph.D. diss., Brandeis University.

Person, Ethel Spector. 1980. "Sexuality as the Mainstay of Identity: Psychoanalytic Perspectives." *Signs* 5 (Summer):605–30.

Petchesky, Rosalind P. 1981. " 'Reproductive Choice' in the Contemporary United States: A Social Analysis of Female Sterilization." Pp. 50–88 in Karen L. Michaelson, ed., *And the Poor Get Children*. New York: Monthly Review Press.

————. 1984. *Abortion and Woman's Choice: The State, Sexuality and Reproductive Freedom*. Boston: Northeastern University Press.

Pilpel, Harriet F., and Nancy F. Wechsler. 1969. "Birth Control, Teenagers and the Law." *Family Planning Perspectives* 1 (Spring):29–36.

Piotrow, Phyllis T. 1973. *World Population Crisis: The United States Response*. New York: Praeger.

Pittman, Karen. 1986. "Preventing Adolescent Pregnancy: What Schools Can Do." Washington, D.C.: Children's Defense Fund. A publication of the Adolescent Pregnancy Prevention Clearinghouse.

Pivar, David J. 1973. *Purity Crusade: Sexual Morality and Social Control, 1868–1900*. Westport, Conn.: Greenwood.

Piven, Frances Fox, and Richard A. Cloward. 1971. *Regulating the Poor: The Functions of Public Welfare*. New York: Random House (Vintage Books).

Placek, Paul J., and Gerry E. Hendershot. 1974. "Public Welfare and Family Planning: An Empirical Study of the 'Brood Sow' Myth." *Social Problems* 21 (June):658–73.

Platt, Anthony M. 1977. *The Child Savers: The Invention of Delinquency*. 2d ed. Chicago: University of Chicago Press.

Plummer, Kenneth. 1975. *Sexual Stigma: An Interactionist Account*. London: Routledge and Kegan Paul.

Poliakoff, Samuel R. 1958. "Pregnancy in the Young Primigravida." *American Journal of Obstetrics and Gynecology* 76 (October):746–53.

Polit, Denise F., Janet Kahn, and David Stevens. 1985. *Final Impacts from Project Redirection*. New York: Manpower Demonstration Research Corporation.

Polit, Denise F., Janet C. Quint, and James A. Riccio. 1988. *The Challenge of Serving Teenage Mothers: Lessons from Project Redirection*. New York: Manpower Demonstration Research Corporation.

Powell-Griner, Eve, and Katherine Trent. 1987. "Sociodemographic Determinants of Abortion in the United States." *Demography* 24 (November):553–61.

President's Commission for the Study of Ethical Problems in Medicine and Biomedical and Behavioral Research. 1983. *Screening and Counseling for Genetic Conditions*. Washington, D.C.: U.S. Government Printing Office.

President's Committee on Population and Family Planning. 1968. *Population and Family Planning: The Transition from Concern to Action*. Washington, D.C.: U.S. Department of Health, Education, and Welfare.

Preston, Samuel H. 1984. "Children and the Elderly: Divergent Paths for America's Dependents." *Demography* 21 (November):435–57.

Prindle, Mother. 1897. "How Shall We Reach the Street Girl?" Pp. 37–44 in *Fourteen Years' Work Among "Erring Girls."* Washington, D.C.: National Florence Crittenton Mission.

Rafter, Nicole Hahn. 1983. "Chastizing the Unchaste: Social Control Functions of a Women's Reformatory, 1894–1931." Pp. 288–311 in Stanley Cohen and Andrew T. Scull, eds., *Social Control and the State*. New York: St. Martin's.

Rains, Prudence Mors. 1970. "Moral Reinstatement: The Characteristics of Maternity Homes." *American Behavioral Scientist* 14 (November/December):219–35.

——. 1971. *Becoming an Unwed Mother*. Chicago: Aldine-Atherton.

Rainwater, Lee, and William L. Yancey. 1967. *The Moynihan Report and the Politics of Controversy*. Cambridge, Mass.: MIT Press.

Reckless, Walter. 1933. *Vice in Chicago*. Chicago: University of Chicago Press.

Reed, James. 1978. *From Private Vice to Public Virtue: The Birth Control Movement and American Society Since 1830*. New York: Basic Books.

——. 1979. "Doctors, Birth Control, and Social Values, 1830–1970." Pp. 109–33 in Morris J. Vogel and Charles E. Rosenberg, eds., *The Therapeutic Revolution: Essays in the Social History of American Medicine*. Philadelphia: University of Pennsylvania Press.

Reed, Ruth. 1934. *The Illegitimate Family in New York City: Its Treatment by Social and Health Agencies*. New York: Columbia University Press. Reprint. 1971, Westport, Conn.: Negro Universities Press.

Reiss, Ira L. 1960. *Premarital Sexual Standards in America*. Glencoe, Ill.: Free Press.

——. 1966. "The Sexual Renaissance: A Summary and Analysis." *Journal of Social Issues* 22 (April):123–37.

——. 1967. *The Social Context of Premarital Sexual Permissiveness*. New York: Holt, Rinehart, and Winston.

Rich, B. Ruby. 1986. "Feminism and Sexuality in the 1980s." *Feminist Studies* 12 (Fall):525–61.

Richards, Janet Radcliffe. 1980. *The Sceptical Feminist*. London: Routledge and Kegan Paul.

Richardson, John G., and Julie E. Cranston. 1981. "Social Change, Parental Values, and the Salience of Sex Education." *Journal of Marriage and the Family* 43 (August):547–58.

Rindfuss, Ronald R., Larry Bumpass, and Craig St. John. 1980. "Education and Fertility: Implications for the Roles Women Occupy." *American Sociological Review* 45 (June):431–37.

Rindfuss, Ronald R., S. Philip Morgan, and C. Gray Swicegood. 1988. *First Births in America: Changes in the Timing of Parenthood*. Berkeley: University of California Press.

Rindfuss, Ronald R., and Craig St. John. 1983. "Social Determinants of Age at First Birth." *Journal of Marriage and the Family* 45 (August):553–65.

Rindfuss, Ronald R., C. Gray Swicegood, and Rachel A. Rosenfeld. 1987. "Disorder in the Life Course: How Common and Does It Matter?" *American Sociological Review* 52 (December):785–801.

Roberts, Robert W. 1966. "A Theoretical Overview of the Unwed Mother." Pp. 11–22 in Robert W. Roberts, ed., *The Unwed Mother*. New York: Harper and Row.

Robinson, Paul. 1976. *The Modernization of Sex*. New York: Harper and Row.

Rosenberg, Charles E. 1973. "Sexuality, Class and Role in 19th-Century America." *American Quarterly* 25 (May):131–53.

Rosenberg, Rosalind. 1982. *Beyond Separate Spheres: Intellectual Roots of Modern Feminism*. New Haven, Conn.: Yale University Press.

Rosoff, Jeannie I. 1973. "The Future of Federal Support for Family Planning Services and Population Research." *Family Planning Perspectives* 5 (Winter):7–18.

———. 1986. "Teenage Pregnancy: The Evolution of an Issue." Pp. 3–8 in *Annual Report 1985*. New York: Alan Guttmacher Institute.

Rosow, Kenneth, and Caroline Hodges Persell. 1980. "Sex Education from 1900 to 1920: A Study of Ideological Social Control." *Qualitative Sociology* 3 (Fall):186–203.

Ross, Jane. 1970. "The Pill Hearings: Major Side Effects." *Family Planning Perspectives* 2 (March):6–7, 51–52.

Rossi, Alice S. 1964. "Equality Between the Sexes: An Immodest Proposal." *Daedalus* 93 (Spring):607–52.

Roszak, Theodore. 1969. *The Making of a Counter-Culture: Reflections on the Technocratic Society and Its Youthful Opposition*. Garden City, N.Y.: Doubleday.

Rothman, David J. 1980. *Conscience and Convenience: The Asylum and Its Alternatives in Progressive America*. Boston: Little, Brown.

Rothman, Ellen K. 1987. *Hands and Hearts: A History of Courtship in America*. Cambridge, Mass.: Harvard University Press.

Rothman, Sheila M. 1978. *Woman's Proper Place: A History of Changing Ideals and Practices, 1870 to the Present*. New York: Basic Books.

Ryder, Norman B. 1974. "The Demography of Youth." Pp. 45–64 in James S. Coleman, ed., *Youth: Transition to Adulthood*. Chicago: University of Chicago Press.

Sarrel, Philip M. 1967. "The University Hospital and the Teenage Unwed Mother." *American Journal of Public Health* 57 (August):1308–13.

Sarrel, Philip M., and Clarence D. Davis. 1966. "The Young Unwed Primipara." *American Journal of Obstetrics and Gynecology* 95 (July 1):722–25.

Scales, Peter. 1980. "Barriers to Sex Education." *Journal of School Health* 50 (August):337–41.

————. 1981. "The New Opposition to Sex Education: A Powerful Threat to a Democratic Society." *Journal of School Health* 51 (April):300–304.

————. 1986. "The Changing Context of Sexuality Education: Paradigms and Challenges for Alternative Futures." *Family Relations* 35 (April):265–74.

Scanzoni, John, and Maximiliane Szinovacz. 1980. *Family Decision-Making: A Developmental Sex Role Model*. Beverly Hills, Calif.: Sage.

Schlafly, Phyllis. 1977. *The Power of the Positive Woman*. New Rochelle, N.Y.: Arlington House.

Schlossman, Steven L. 1977. *Love and the American Delinquent*. Chicago: University of Chicago Press.

Schlossman, Steven, and Stephanie Wallach. 1978. "The Crime of Precocious Sexuality: Female Juvenile Delinquency in the Progressive Era." *Harvard Educational Review* 48 (February):65–93.

Schneider, Joseph W., and Peter Conrad. 1980. "The Medical Control of Deviance: Contests and Consequences." Pp. 1-53 in Julius S. Roth, ed., *Research in the Sociology of Health Care*, vol. 1. Greenwich, Conn.: JAI Press.

Schwartz, Michael, and James H. Ford. 1982. "Family Planning Clinics: Cure or Cause of Teenage Pregnancy?" *Linacre Quarterly* 49 (May):143–64.

Scull, Andrew T. 1988. "Deviance and Social Control." Pp. 667–93 in Neil J. Smelser, ed., *Handbook of Sociology*. Beverly Hills, Calif.: Sage.

Seagrave, Mabel. 1926. "Causes Underlying Sex Delinquency in Young Girls." *Journal of Social Hygiene* 12 (December):523–29.

Semmens, James P. 1965. "Implications of Teen-Age Pregnancy." *Obstetrics and Gynecology* 26 (July):77–85.

Shulman, Alix Kates. 1980. "Sex and Power: Sexual Bases of Radical Feminism." *Signs* 5 (Summer):590–604.

Siegel, Frederick F. 1984. *Troubled Journey: From Pearl Harbor to Ronald Reagan*. New York: Hill and Wang.

Simmons, Christina. 1982. "Marriage in the Modern Manner: Sexual Radicalism and Reform in America, 1914–1941." Ph.D. diss., Brown University.

Smigel, Erwin O., and Rita Seiden. 1968. "The Decline and Fall of the Double Standard." *Annals of the American Academy of Political and Social Science* 376 (March):6–17.

Smith, Daniel Scott. 1973. "Family Limitation, Sexual Control, and Domestic Feminism in Victorian America." *Feminist Studies* 1 (Winter-Spring):40–57.

————. 1978. "The Dating of the American Sexual Revolution: Evidence and Interpretation." Pp. 426–38 in Michael Gordon, ed., *The American Family in Social-Historical Perspective*. 2d ed. New York: St. Martin's.

Smith, Daniel Scott, and Michael Hindus. 1975. "Premarital Pregnancy in America 1640–1971: An Overview and Interpretation." *Journal of Interdisciplinary History* 5 (Spring):537–70.

Smithies, Elsie M. 1933. *Case Studies of Normal Adolescent Girls*. New York: D. Appleton.

Smith-Rosenberg, Carroll. 1972. "The Hysterical Woman: Sex Roles and Role Conflict in 19th-Century America," *Social Research* 39 (Winter):652–78.

————. 1985a. *Disorderly Conduct: Visions of Gender in Victorian America*. New York: Alfred A. Knopf.

————. 1985b. "Beauty, the Beast, and the Militant Woman: A Case Study in Sex Roles and Social Stress in Jacksonian American." Pp. 109–28 in *Disorderly Conduct: Visions of Gender in Victorian America*. New York: Alfred A. Knopf.

Smith-Rosenberg, Carroll, and Charles Rosenberg. 1973. "The Female Animal: Medical and Biological Views of Woman and Her Role in Nineteenth-Century America," *The Journal of American History* 60 (September):332–56.

Smuts, Robert W. 1959. *Women and Work in America*. New York: Columbia University Press.

Snitow, Ann, Christine Stansell, and Sharon Thompson, eds. 1983. *Powers of Desire: The Politics of Sexuality*. New York: Monthly Review Press.

Sonenstein, Freya L., and Karen J. Pittman. 1984. "The Availability of Sex Education in Large City School Districts." *Family Planning Perspectives* 16 (January/February):19–25.

Spector, Malcolm, and John I. Kitsuse. 1977. *Constructing Social Problems*. Menlo Park, Calif.: Cummings.

Spivack, Sydney S. 1964. "The Doctor's Role in Family Planning." *Journal of the American Medical Association* 188 (April 13):144–56.

Starr, Paul. 1982. *The Social Transformation of American Medicine*. New York: Basic Books.

Stearn, R. H. 1963. "The Adolescent Primigravida." *The Lancet* 2 (November 23):1083–85.

Steiner, Gilbert Y. 1981. *The Futility of Family Policy*. Washington, D.C.: Brookings Institution.

Strobino, Donna M. 1987. "The Health and Medical Consequences of Adolescent Sexuality and Pregnancy: A Review of the Literature." Pp. 93–122 in Sandra L. Hofferth and Cheryl D. Hayes, eds., *Risking the Future: Adolescent Sexuality, Pregnancy, and Childbearing*, vol. 2. Washington, D.C.: National Academy Press.

Strong, Bryan. 1972. "Ideas of the Early Sex Education Movement in America, 1890–1920." *History of Education Quarterly* 12 (Summer):129–61.

Stuart, Irving R., and Carl F. Wells, eds. 1982. *Pregnancy in Adolescence: Needs, Problems, and Management*. New York: Van Nostrand Reinhold.

Taeuber, Irene B., and Conrad Taeuber. 1971. *People of the United States in the Twentieth Century* (Census Monograph). Washington, D.C.: U. S. Government Printing Office.

Tappan, Paul. 1947. *Delinquent Girls in Court*. New York: Columbia University Press. Reprint. 1969. Montclair, N.J.: Patterson Smith.

Thomas, William I. 1923. *The Unadjusted Girl*. Boston: Little, Brown, and Co. Reprint. 1967. New York: Harper and Row.

Thornton, Arland, and Deborah Freedman. 1983. "The Changing American Family." *Population Bulletin* 38 (October):1–43.

Tietze, Christopher, and Sarah Lewit. 1971. "Legal Abortions: Early Medical Complications." *Family Planning Perspectives* 3 (October):6–14.

Tilly, Charles, Louise Tilly, and Richard Tilly. 1975. *The Rebellious Century, 1830–1930*. Cambridge, Mass.: Harvard University Press.

Torres, Aida, and Jacqueline D. Forrest. 1985. "Family Planning Clinic Services in the United States, 1983." *Family Planning Perspectives* 15 (January/February):30–35.

Torres, Aida, Jacqueline D. Forrest, and Susan Eisman. 1981. "Family Planning Services in the United States, 1978–1979." *Family Planning Perspectives* 13 (May/June):132–41.

Trattner, Walter I. 1974. *From Poor Law to Welfare State: A History of Social Welfare in America*. New York: Free Press.

Trimberger, Ellen Kay. 1983. "Feminism, Men, and Modern Love: Greenwich Village, 1900–1925." Pp. 131–52 in Ann Snitow, Christine Stansell, and Sharon Thompson, eds., *Powers of Desire: The Politics of Sexuality*. New York: Monthly Review Press.

Trussell, James. 1988. "Teenage Pregnancy in the United States." *Family Planning Perspectives* 20 (November/December):262–72.

U.S. Bureau of the Census. 1975. *Historical Statistics of the United States: Colonial Times to 1970, Bicentennial Edition, Part 1*. Washington, D.C.: U. S. Government Printing Office.

————. 1983. "Marital Status and Living Arrangements: March, 1982." *Current Population Reports*, Series P-20, No. 380.

U.S. Children's Bureau. 1920. *Illegitimacy as a Child-Welfare Problem. Part 1: A Brief Treatment of the Prevalence and Significance of Birth Out of Wedlock, the Child's Status, and the State's Responsibility for Care and Protection*. Bureau Publication no. 66. Washington, D.C.: U. S. Government Printing Office.

————. 1921. *Illegitimacy as a Child-Welfare Problem. Part 2: A Study of Original Records in the City of Boston and in the State of Massachusetts*. Bureau Publication no. 75. Washington, D.C.: U. S. Government Printing Office.

————. 1924. *Illegitimacy as a Child-Welfare Problem. Part 3: Methods of Care in Selected Urban and Rural Communities*. Bureau Publication no. 128. Washington, D.C.: U. S. Government Printing Office.

————. 1946. *Guiding the Adolescent*. Publication 225. Washington, D.C.: Federal Security Agency, Social Security Administration.

U.S. Congress, House of Representatives. 1888. *Congressional Record*. 50th Cong., 1st sess. (February 23):1432.

————. 1910a. *Congressional Record*. 61st Cong., 2d sess. (January 19):811–23.

————. 1910b. *White Slave Traffic*. 61st Cong., 2d sess., Report no. 886.

————, Committee on Interstate and Foreign Commerce, Subcommittee on Public Health and Welfare. 1970. *Hearings on Family Planning Services*. 91st Cong., 2d sess., August 3, 4, 7.

————, Committee on Ways and Means. 1969a. *Hearings on Social Security and Welfare Proposals*. 91st Cong., 1st sess., October 22, 23, 24, 27.

————, Committee on Ways and Means. 1969b. *Hearings on Social Security and Welfare Proposals*. 91st Cong., 1st sess., October 24. Statements by Joseph D. Beasley and Frederick S. Jaffe. 921–26.

————, Select Committee on Children, Youth, and Families. 1985. *Teen Pregnancy: What Is Being Done? A State-by-State Look*. 99th Cong., 1st sess.

————, Select Committee on Population. 1978. *Fertility and Contraception in America: Adolescent and Pre-Adolescent Pregnancy*. Vol. 2, *Hearings before the Select Committee on Population*. 95th Cong., 2d sess., February 28, March 1, 2. Statement by Frank F. Furstenberg, Jr., pp. 166–70; statement by Frederick S. Jaffe, pp. 170–77.

U.S. Congress, Senate. 1888. *Congressional Record*, 50th Cong., 1st sess. (February 20):1326.

————, Committee on Finance. 1972a. *Hearings on Social Security Amendments of 1971*. 92nd Cong., 1st and 2d sess.

————, Committee on Finance. 1972b. *Social Security Amendments of 1972*. Committee Report.

————, Committee on Government Operations, Subcommittee on Foreign Aid Expenditures. 1965. *Population Crisis. Hearings on S. 1676*. 89th Cong., 1st sess., Part 1-5, June 22–23.

————, Committee on Labor and Human Resources. 1981a. *Oversight of Family Planning Programs*. 97th Cong., 1st sess., March 31.

————, Committee on Labor and Human Resources, Subcommittee on Aging, Family and Human Services. 1981b. *Oversight of Family Planning Programs Under Title X of the Public Health Service Act*. 97th Cong., 1st sess., June 23, September 28.

————, Committee on Labor and Human Resources, Subcommittee on Family and Human Services. 1984. *Oversight of Family Planning Programs Under Title X of the Public Health Service Act*. 98th Cong., 2d sess., April 5, May 1.

————, Committee on Labor and Public Welfare. 1971. *Report of the Secretary of Health, Education, and Welfare Submitting Five-Year Plan for Family Planning Services and Population Research Programs*. 92nd Cong., 1st sess.

————, Committee on Labor and Public Welfare. 1972. *Progress Report on the Five-Year Plan for Family Planning Services and Population Research Programs*. 92nd Cong., 2d sess.

U.S. Office of Population Affairs. 1986. *The Adolescent Family Life Demonstration Projects: Program and Evaluation Summaries*. Washington, D.C.: Office of Population Affairs.

————. 1987. *The Adolescent Family Life Demonstration Projects: Program and Evaluation Summaries, 1987 Update*. Washington, D.C.: Office of Population Affairs.

Upchurch, Dawn M., and James McCarthy. 1990. "The Timing of First Birth and High School Completion." *American Sociological Review* 55 (April):224–34.

Usilton, Linda J., and Newell W. Edson. 1929. "Status of Sex Education in the Senior High Schools of the United States in 1927." Washington, D.C.: U. S. Government Printing Office.

Vance, Carol S. 1984. "Pleasure and Danger: Toward a Politics of Sexuality." Pp. 1–27 in Carol S. Vance, ed., *Pleasure and Danger: Exploring Female Sexuality*. Boston: Routledge and Kegan Paul.

Ventura, Stephanie J. 1984. "Trends in Teenage Childbearing, United States, 1970–1981." *Vital and Health Statistics*, series 21, no. 41. DHHS Publication no. (PHS) 84-1919.

Verner, Mary E. 1976. Analysis of Decreased Utilization of Salvation Army Maternity Homes and Hospitals 1967–1975 and Contributing Factors. A thesis prepared for the Committee on Credentials of the American College of Hospital Administrators.

Vicinus, Martha. 1982. "Sexuality and Power: A Review of Current Work in the History of Sexuality." *Feminist Studies* 8 (Spring):133–56.

Vincent, Clark E. 1961. *Unmarried Mothers*. Glencoe, Ill.: Free Press.

————. 1966. "Teen-Age Unwed Mothers in American Society." *Journal of Social Issues* 22 (April):22–33.

Vinovskis, Maris A. 1981. "An 'Epidemic' of Adolescent Pregnancy? Some Historical Considerations." *Journal of Family History* 6 (Summer):205–30.

————. 1988. *An "Epidemic" of Adolescent Pregnancy? Some Historical and Policy Considerations*. New York: Oxford University Press.

Wagner, Roland Richard. 1971. "Virtue Against Vice: A Study of Moral Reformers and Prostitution in the Progressive Era." Ph.D. diss., University of Wisconsin.

Wallace, Helen M. 1965. "Teen-Age Pregnancy." *American Journal of Obstetrics and Gynecology* 92 (August 15):1125–31.

Wallace, Helen M., Edwin M. Gold, and Samuel Dooley. 1969. "Relationships Between Family Planning and Maternal and Child Health." *American Journal of Public Health* 59 (August):1355–60.

Wallace, Helen M., Hyman Goldstein, Edwin M. Gold, and Allan C. Oglesby. 1974. "The Maternity Home: Present Services and Future Roles." *American Journal of Public Health* 64 (June):568–75.

Waller, Willard. 1936. "Social Problems and the Mores." *American Sociological Review* 1 (December):922–33.

———. 1937. "The Rating and Dating Complex." *American Sociological Review* 2 (October):727–34.

Walsh, Edward J., and Rex H. Warland. 1983. "Social Movement Involvement in the Wake of a Nuclear Accident: Activists and Free Riders in the TMI Area." *American Sociological Review* 48 (December):764–80.

Walters, Pamela Barnhouse, and Philip J. O'Connell. 1988. "The Family Economy, Work, and Educational Participation in the United States, 1890–1940." *American Journal of Sociology* 93 (March):1116–52.

Ward, Martha C. 1990. "The Politics of Adolescent Pregnancy: Turf and Teens in Louisiana." Pp. 147–64 in W. Penn Handwerker, ed., *Births and Power: Social Change and the Politics of Reproduction*. Boulder, Colo.: Westview Press.

Weatherley, Richard A., Sylvia B. Perlman, Michael Levine, and Lorraine V. Klerman. 1985. *Patchwork Programs: Comprehensive Services for Pregnant and Parenting Adolescents*. Seattle, Wash.: Center for Social Welfare Research, School of Social Work, University of Washington.

Weeks, Jeffrey. 1981. *Sex, Politics, and Society: The Regulation of Sexuality Since 1800*. New York: Longman.

Wein, Roberta. 1974. "Women's Colleges and Domesticity, 1875–1918." *History of Education Quarterly* 14 (Spring):31–47.

Weiner, Lynn Y. 1985. *From Working Girl to Working Mother*. Chapel Hill: University of North Carolina Press.

Weir, Margaret, Ann Shola Orloff, and Theda Skocpol, eds. 1988. *The Politics of Social Policy in the United States*. Princeton, N.J.: Princeton University Press.

Welter, Barbara. 1978. "The Cult of True Womanhood: 1820–1860." Pp. 313–33 in Michael Gordon, ed., *The American Family in Social-Historical Perspective*. 2d ed. New York: St. Martin's.

West, B. June. 1955. "The 'New Woman.'" *Twentieth Century Literature* 1 (July):55–68.

Westoff, Charles F. 1978. "Marriage and Fertility in the Developed Countries." *Scientific American* 239 (December):51–57.

White, Theodore H. 1982. *America in Search of Itself: The Making of the President, 1956–1980*. New York: Warner Books.

Whitley, Bernard E., Jr., and Janet Ward Schofield. 1986. "A Meta-analysis of Research on Adolescent Contraceptive Use." *Population and Environment* 8 (Fall/Winter):173–203.

Wiebe, Robert. 1967. *The Search for Order, 1877–1920*. New York: Hill and Wang.

Willard, Frances. 1895. "Arousing the Public Conscience." *The Arena* 11 (January):198–202.

Wilson, Otto. 1933. *Fifty Years' Work with Girls, 1883–1933: A Story of the Florence Crittenton Homes*. Alexandria, Va.: National Florence Crittenton Mission. Reprinted in 1974 by Arno Press.

Wilson, William Julius. 1980. *The Declining Significance of Race: Blacks and Changing American Institutions*. 2d ed. Chicago: University of Chicago Press.

———. 1987. *The Truly Disadvantaged: The Inner City, the Underclass, and Public Policy*. Chicago: University of Chicago Press.

Wilson, William Julius, and Robert Aponte. 1987. "Urban Poverty: A State-of-the-Art Review of the Literature." Pp. 165–87 in William Julius Wilson, *The Truly Disadvantaged: The Inner City, the Underclass, and Public Policy*. Chicago: University of Chicago Press.

Wilson, William Julius, and Kathryn M. Neckerman. 1986. "Poverty and Family Structure: The Widening Gap between Evidence and Public Policy Issues." Pp. 232–59 in Sheldon H. Danziger and Daniel H. Weinberg, eds., *Fighting Poverty: What Works and What Doesn't*. Cambridge, Mass.: Harvard University Press.

Wootton, Barbara. 1959. *Social Science and Social Pathology*. London: George Allen and Unwin.

Wunsch, James. 1976. "Prostitution and Public Policy: From Regulation to Suppression, 1858–1920," Ph.D. diss., University of Chicago.

Yanagisako, Sylvia J., and Jane F. Collier. 1987. "Toward a Unified Analysis of Gender and Kinship." Pp. 14–50 in Jane F. Collier and Sylvia J. Yanagisako, eds., *Gender and Kinship: Essays Toward a Unified Analysis*. Stanford, Calif.: Stanford University Press.

Yarros, Rachelle S. 1920. "The Prostitute as a Health and Social Problem." National Conference of Social Work, *Proceedings*:220–24.

Young, Leontine R. 1954. *Out-of-Wedlock*. New York: McGraw-Hill.

Zelizer, Viviana A. 1985. *Pricing the Priceless Child: The Changing Social Value of Children*. New York: Basic Books.

Zellman, Gail L. 1981. *The Response of the Schools to Teenage Pregnancy and Parenthood*. Prepared for the National Institute of Education. Santa Monica, Calif.: Rand Corporation.

Zelnik, Melvin, and John F. Kantner. 1978. "First Pregnancies to Women Aged 15–19: 1976 and 1971." *Family Planning Perspectives* 10 (January/February):11–20.

———. 1980. "Sexual Activity, Contraceptive Use and Pregnancy among Metropolitan-Area Teenagers: 1971–1979." *Family Planning Perspectives* 12 (September/October):230–37.

Zelnik, Melvin, John F. Kantner, and Kathleen Ford. 1981. *Sex and Pregnancy in Adolescence*. Beverly Hills, Calif.: Sage.

Zimring, Franklin E. 1982. *The Changing Legal World of Adolescence*. New York: Free Press.

Zinn, Maxine Baca. 1989. "Family, Race, and Poverty in the Eighties." *Signs* 14 (Summer):856–74.

Zola, Irving K. 1975. "Medicine as an Institution of Social Control." Pp. 170–85 in Caroline Cox and Adrianne Mead, eds., *A Sociology of Medical Practice*. London: Collier-Macmillan.

Zube, Margaret J. 1972. "Changing Concepts of Morality: 1948–69." *Social Forces* 50 (March):385–93.

Zuckerman, Barry, Joel J. Alpert, Elizabeth Dooling, Ralph Hingson, Herbert Kayne, Suzette Morelock, and Edgar Oppenheimer. 1983. "Neonatal Outcome: Is Adolescent Pregnancy a Risk Factor?" *Pediatrics* 71 (April):489–93.

Zurcher, Louis A. and David A. Snow. 1981. "Collective Behavior: Social Movements." Pp. 447–82 in Morris Rosenberg and Ralph H. Turner, eds., *Social Psychology: Sociological Perspectives*. New York: Basic Books.

Index

Abortion: legalization of, 3, 30, 59, 233n.1; as management strategy for adolescent pregnancy, 50–51, 150–56; parental consent for, 227n.3; political sensitivity of, 50, 163; physicians' role in, 139–40; race and socio-economic status and, 162, 239n.1, 245n.13; underground information exchange about, 5; visibility of adolescent sexuality and, 230n.14. *See also* Antiabortion movement

Abstinence, as management strategy, 3

"Abstinence education," versus sex education, 155–56

Addams, Jane, 121, 124, 130, 135

Adolescence, male versus female, 79–80, 111, 208–9

Adolescent, invention of, 79–80

"Adolescent Family Life Demonstration Projects," 148, 150–51

Adolescent fertility. *See* Fertility rates, of adolescents

"Adolescent Health, Services, and Pregnancy Prevention and Care Act of 1978," 24–25, 57

Adolescent pregnancy: causal models of, 164–66; demographic background of, 24–31; emergence as social problem, 3–4, 31; medicalization of, 38–39, 48–50, 70–72; terminology of, 227n.1

Adolescents: historical background on, 75–102; "innocence" of girls, 106–10, 131–32; as political force, 26–27; population, relative to adults, in U.S., 26, 84–85

Adolescent sexuality: adult reactions to, 5, 227n.4; consequences of, 48–50, 70–72; demography of, 50–51, 232n.4; historical context of, 75–102; innocence of, 14,

108–10, 240n.8; legitimation of, 99–100, 132–33, 238n.26, 243n.16; management versus repression of, 6–7, 155–56, 207–24; romanticization of, 93–94; social control policies and, 3–19; social disorder and social change, 214–20, 248n.5; visibility of, 32–34, 108–9, 230n.14. *See also* Women, sexual autonomy of

Adolescent women: defined as children, 4, 109, 123, 125, 131, 166, 208, 211, 242n.10; family planning services for, 56–58; high school and college enrollment of, 93; historical aspects of, 77–78; labor force participation and, 87–88, 235n.8; management strategies for, 70–72, 115–18, 241n.18; nineteenth-century ideology and, 83–84; nonmarital birth rate, 29–30; unorthodox sexuality in, 239n.1; value systems and, 158–59

Adoption: agency licensing requirements, 240n.6; as management strategy, 27, 30, 113–16, 241n.18

Age-grade norms, adolescent sexuality as violation of, 63, 208

Age of consent: defined, 119–20; historical changes in, 75

Age-of-consent legislation, 122–23, 242nn.8–10; campaigns for, 15–16; as protective management strategy, 110; sexual social movements and, 119–21, 242n.3

Age of reformers, 213, 221

AIDS epidemic: legitimation of chastity and, 155; moral conservative movement and, 64–65; sexual social movements and, 15

Aid to Families with Dependent Children (AFDC): adolescent pregnancy linked to, 66; male employment incentives and, 68; management strategies for adolescent pregnancy and, 148–49

Alan Guttmacher Institute: adolescent pregnancy in industrialized countries and, 245n.12; funding strategies of, 54–55; origins, 52–53; social construction of adolescent pregnancy and, 47–50

Ameliorative solutions, to adolescent pregnancy, 148–56. See also Rehabilitative solutions

American Birth Control Federation. See Planned Parenthood Federation of America (PPFA)

American Medical Association, birth control policies and, 36–39

American Purity Alliance, 139, 242n.6

American Social Hygiene Association, 139

American Society for Sanitary and Moral Prophylaxis, 139

American Vigilance Association, 138–39

Antiabortion movement: maternity homes and, 241n.17; social value of babies and, 247n.9; women's sexual autonomy and, 233n.2

Aponte, Robert, 66

Arena, The, 122–23, 130, 242nn.3, 8

Aries, Philippe, 78, 234n.2

Beard, Mary, 135

Becker, Howard S., 9

Bell, Robert R., 32

Bennett, William J., 65, 150

Ben-Yehuda, 228n.10

Biological age, impact of, on adolescent pregnancy risks, 38–39, 157, 230n.20

Biologization of bodies, 7–9

Birth control services: access to, for adolescents, 3, 57–58; adolescent birth rates and, 60; attribution of responsibility for, 176–77; causal models of adolescent pregnancy and, 164–66; client-provider interaction and,

174–76; comprehensive service programs and, 57–58, 153–54, 233n.8; conservative opposition to, 61–65, 69–70, 230n.14; decision-making patterns and, 185; desexualization of, 41; eugenic implications of, 55–56; legal status of, 101, 238n.27; as management strategy, 46–47, 150–56, 239n.2; medicalization of, 13–14, 36–39, 49–50, 139–40, 167–77, 232n.3, 243n.24; moral status of, 62–65, 221–22, 233n.4; politicization of, 39–44; as preventive device, 35–36, 146–56; privacy and control issues about, 178–204, 211–13; public debate on, 31, 229n.7; public health agencies' distribution of, 170–77; race and socioeconomic status and, 162–63, 245n.13; sexual segregation as, 241n.14; underground information exchange about, 5. See also Contraceptive decisions, normative bases of; Oral contraception

Birth rates: of adolescents, in United States, 24–25; decline of, in nineteenth and twentieth centuries, 86; versus pregnancy rates, 146–47

Black adolescents: behavior of ignored by researchers, 33, 229n.13; causal models of adolescent pregnancy and, 164–66, 246n.17; nonmarital birth rate, 29–30; pregnancy linked with welfare for, 66–68; sexual activity, pregnancy and birth rates for, 159–61; sexual revolution and, 34–36; sexual social control and, 218. See also Race

Black community, opposition to birth control from, 43; underclass designation and, 68

Black families, Moynihan report on decay of, 65–68

Black Family Summit conference, 234n.9

Blackwell, Elizabeth (Dr.), 243n.22

Blackwell, Emily, 242n.8

Blair, Senator, 122

Blanchard, Phyllis, 96

Blau, Peter M., 55

Block grants for family planning, 54, 244n.6

Boarding houses, for single women, 89

Brandt, Allan M., 65, 124–25, 154

Cultural aspects: of adolescent pregnancy, 164–66; of illegitimacy, 240n.10; of sexuality, 8–10

Culture of poverty, 164–65, 245n.17

"Cultures of resistance," 5–6, 227n.3

"Daughters of the Poor, The," 124

Davenport, Isabel, 93

Davis, Kingsley, 104

Decision-making patterns: "contraceptive event," 185; normative bases for, 188–93; peer influence and, 193–98; risk of pregnancy and, 182–85; sexual and reproductive, of adolescent women, 178–202; "trigger" categories for, 185–88

Degler, Carl N., 215

Dell, Floyd, 94

Demographic context of sexual social movements, 127–29. See also Population

Denton, Jeremiah (Sen.), 64, 233n.5

De Tocqueville, Alexis, 79, 215

Deviance: categorization of, 9; masturbation as, 81; medicalization of, 13

Deviance, adolescent sexuality as: attribution of responsibility and, 61–63, 172–76; birth control services and, 168–71; history and, 6–7; medicalization of, 44–45, 70–72, 232n.34; social control and, 10–11

Deviance and social control, theories of, 12–13, 17, 228nn.7, 10, 247n.4

Dienes, C. Thomas, 40

Disease threat as moral sanction, 134, 246n.3

Dix, Dorothy, 89

Domestic education, as management strategy, 113, 152

Domestic service, labor-force participation by women and, 86–88

Duffey, Eliza, 82–83, 96, 235n.5

Durkheim, Émile, 17–18, 228n.10

Economic conservatism, 67, 234n.8

Economic independence: as management strategy, 147, 149, 152–53, 156–59; sexual emancipation and, 94–96

Education, prolongation of, as protective device, 95–96, 237n.21. See also College enrollment; Schools

Eisenhower, Dwight D., 40, 231n.24

Elder, Glen H., 101–2

11 Million Teenagers, 47–48, 57, 232n.1

Ellis, Havelock, 90, 107–8, 134, 236n.12

Ellwood, David T., 159, 204

Emancipation of women (1920s), 91–102

Employment-related services, 152–53

Entrepreneurship: in birth control services, 42–44; management of adolescent pregnancy and, 69–70, 147–48; sexual social control and, 16, 219–20

Environmental factors, risks of adolescent pregnancy and, 38–39, 105, 157, 230n.20, 239n.3

"Epidemic" imagery, of adolescent pregnancy, 56–58, 232n.7

Equal-opportunity ideology, management strategies and, 158–59

Equal Suffrage movement, 135

Erikson, Kai T.: on deviant behavior, 17; and "immorality" of adolescent pregnancy, 5; and moral boundaries, 130

"Essentialist" view of sexuality, 7–8

Ethnicity: historical data on female adolescence and, 77–78; population data and, 85–88; sexual and reproductive management strategies and, 89, 240n.13; structure of women's adolescence and, 86–88

Eugenics, birth control services and, 38, 55–56; "broken home" metaphor and, 239n.3

Family: birth control and, 38; "breakdown" of, for American blacks, 65–68; labor-force participation by women and, 88–89; male-female hierarchy in, 215–16; moral conservatives' embrace of, 63–65

Family planning clinics, health department: atmosphere and physical setting of, 169–71; birth control services in, 167–77; role of nurse in, 172–76

Family Planning Perspectives, 52–53; attacks

Nixon's family planning funding cuts, 54; birth control for adolescents, 46–47

Family planning services: federal funding for, 42–44, 151, 231n.32, 244n.5–6; impact of abortion on, 51; politicization of, 39–42; right-wing extremism and, 60–65; role of Planned Parenthood in, 39–41; sexual social control and, 220. *See also* Birth control services

Family Planning Services Act (Title X), 57–58, 151, 244n.5

Fass, Paula, 96

Federally funded adolescent pregnancy programs, 23–24, 150–51

"Feeble-mindedness" and sexual unorthodoxy, 111

Female delinquency, connotations of sexuality, 107

Feminist movements, and sexual social control, 122, 220–22

Feminist perspectives: on adolescent pregnancy, 158–59, 220–22; on turn-of-the-century moral reform movements, 127

Fertility rates, of adolescents: construction of, as public problem, 46–50; description of, 24–31, 50–51, 160–63; family planning services and, 51–53; international comparisons, 26; medical perspective on, 38–39

Filene, Peter G., 124

Five Million Women, 42

"Flapper," autonomous sexuality of, 89–91

Florence Crittenton Mission. *See* National Florence Crittenton Mission

Flower, B. O., 242n.8

Folk Devils and Moral Panics, 5

Food and Drug Administration (FDA), 37

Foucault, Michel: approach to sexuality, 7–10; semantics of "adolescent pregnancy," 31; on sexual social controls, 3–4, 71–72, 215

Freedman, Estelle B., 135

Freud, Sigmund, 90, 100–101, 107–8, 134

Gardener, Helen H., 130, 242n.3

Garrison, William Lloyd, 122

Gender hierarchies, categorization of sexuality and, 9–10

Gender interests served by moral reform, 135

Gender norms, female adolescent sexuality as violation of, 63, 70, 208, 214–16, 218, 238n.25

Gender of reformers, 134–36, 165–66, 213, 221, 243n.18

Gesell, Gerhard (Judge), 56

Gilder, George, 67

Glasco, Laurence A., 86

Goffman, Erving, 208

"Going steady," adolescent sexuality and, 98

Goldman, Emma, 90–91, 243n.18

Gorham, Deborah, 123, 165–66

Griswold v. Connecticut, 238n.27

Grubb, W. Norton, 53

Gruening, Ernest, 232n.6

"Guiding the Adolescent," 98, 101

Gusfield, Joseph R.: attributions of responsibility, 11–12; on countermovements, 59; legitimation of sexuality and, 243n.16; ownership issues in adolescent pregnancy and, 145–46; public problem definition, 11

Hale, Nathan G., 90

Hall, G. Stanley, 157, 235n.5

Haller, John S., 81

Haller, Robin M., 81

Harvard Medical School, 149

Helms, Jesse, 64

Heredity, as cause of sexual unorthodoxy, 105, 239n.3

High school: dropout rates, pregnancy prevention and, 159; enrollment, increase in sexual activity linked with, 93; mandatory enrollment in, 95

Hill, Adelaide C., 34

Hobson, Barbara Meil, 132–33, 242n.12

Hofstadter, Richard, 129–30

Hollingworth, Leta S., 96

House of Representatives: federal birth control services, 231n.26; Select Committee on Children, Youth, and Families, 146; Select Committee on Population, 47

Huling, Tracy, 158

Ideology of passionlessness, 80–84, 90–91, 127, 209, 235nn.3, 6, 242n.12
Ideology of the innocent girl, 80–84, 107–8, 110, 121, 125, 165, 209, 234n.2. *See also* Sexuality
Illegitimacy. *See* Nonmarital births
Illinois Vigilance Association, 242n.11
Immigration: adolescent sexuality and, 76; labor force participation by women and, 86–88; sexual social movements and, 127–29
Individualist perspective: on causes of sexual unorthodoxy, 166; on social change movements, 221–22
Industrialization: business elites and, 137–38; sexual social movements and, 127–29
Industrial school for girls (Lancaster, Mass.), 112
"Inevitability thesis" of adolescent pregnancy, 49–50, 155, 232n.2
Infant mortality, adolescent pregnancy and, 157
Innocence: in adolescent girls, 12, 78–84, 107–9, 234n.2; sex education as threat to, 155; social class gradations of, 116–18; white slave trade and, 124–26. *See also* Adolescent sexuality; Ideology of the innocent girl
Institutional management strategies: reformation and retribution goals of, 110–11; for sexual unorthodoxy, 103–18

Jackson, Jesse, 234n.9
Jaffe, Frederick S., 34, 52
Janney, O. Edward (Dr.), 126, 242n.8
Jekel, James F., 166
Journal of Social Issues, 32

Kantner, John F., 51
Katz, Michael B., 86, 224
Kellogg, J. H., 80, 89

Kelly, Howard (Dr.), 133
Kessler-Harris, Alice, 128
Kett, Joseph R., 77
Kimmich, Madeleine, 151
Kinsey Report, 229n.8
Klerman, Lorraine V., 166
Knowledge, role of in problem construction, 4, 50–51, 71–72, 129, 217, 229n.6, 233n.4
Koop, C. Everett, 65
Kyros, Congressman, 232n.33

Labor-force participation of women: duration of, 95, 237n.20; entry into labor market, 85–91; sexual social movements and, 128–29; social class and, 235n.7
Ladner, Joyce A., 70
Laqueur, Thomas, 215
Lazerson, Marvin, 53
Legislative response to adolescent pregnancy, 23–24
Legitimation: of sex education, 155; of sexual unorthodoxy, 132–33, 243n.16
Liberal policy analysis, management strategies and, 158–59
Lindsey, Ben, 94–95, 108, 240n.8
Lipset, Seymour Martin, 60
Lipsky, Michael, 176
Livermore, Mary, 84
Lobbying activities, management of adolescent pregnancy and, 245n.16
Local community, adolescent pregnancy programs in, 23
Long, Russell B., 34, 39
Losing Ground, 67
Lundberg, Emma, 108
Lynd, Helen M., 96
Lynd, Robert S., 96

McCarthy, John D., 130
McClure, S. S., 136
McClure's Magazine, 136
McGraw, Onalee, 64
Male partners: absence of, in management strategies, 115–16, 148, 244n.2; age-of-

consent legislation and, 123, 242n.9; decision-making patterns and, 193–98

Management strategies, sexual and reproductive, 109–16; of adolescent women, 6, 178–204, 214, 240n.13; conceptions of the "sexually unorthodox girl" and, 106–9; contemporary, 147–56; ethnicity and, 89, 240n.13; fiscal conservatism and, 156–59; problem constructions and, 145–47; race and, 23, 39, 53–54, 89, 160–63, 241n.18, 245nn.12, 14–15; social class and, 23, 37–39, 42–43, 53–54, 131, 160–63, 240n.13, 241n.18, 245nn.12, 14–15

Management strategy for sexual and reproductive control: adoption as, 113–16; age-of-consent legislation as, 110; domestic education as, 113, 152; moral reformation as, 104, 106–8, 112–13, 115, 117–18, 211–12, 239n.2; retribution as, 115–16; sexually segregated institutions as, 110–12

Manasses, Carlyn, 96

Mangold, G. B., 111

Mann Act. *See* White Slave Traffic Act

Manpower Demonstration Research Corporation, 245n.10

Marital status: interests served by moral reform and, 127; sexual activity and, 237n.16; sexual danger and, 124, 131

Marriage: adolescent pregnancy and, 29–30; age of women at, 85–91, 237n.20; eligibility for birth control services and, 43–44; nineteenth-century adolescent sexuality and, 82–83; sex as preparation for, 96–97

Marsiglio, William, 154

Maryland State Health Department Family Planning Division, 169

Mast, Coleen, 155

Masturbation: as deviant behavior, 81; sexual social control and, 212–13

Maternity homes: antiabortion movement and, 241n.17; comprehensive services approach of, 152, 244n.7; evolution of, 239n.6; licensing requirements for, 240n.6; protective philosophy of, 109–11; sexual segregation principles of, 110–11

Matusow, Allen J., 53

Medicalization of management strategies: for adolescent pregnancy, 13–14, 48–50, 60–61, 149–52; conflict with moral and economic strategies, 150–56, 209–11; impact of, on birth control services, 36–41; and moral reform, 167–77; as sexual social control, 7, 12–13, 70–72, 138–40, 210–11, 243n.22; school-based clinics and, 146–47, 244n.1; versus social work management strategy, 105, 239n.5; women as physicians, 243n.22

Medicalization of reproductive deviance, 232n.34; of sexuality, 101, theoretical perspectives on, 171, 228n.7

Menstruation, 81–82, 235n.5

Mental health, sexual revolution and, 34

Minimum-wage legislation, 89, 135

Minneapolis Vice Commission, 89

Moore, Kristin A., 159

Moral boundaries of sexual behavior, 80–81; challenges to, 16–18, 92, 104, 131, 217–18, 243n.15; redefinition of, 94, 132; reinforcement of, 110–11, 117–18, 130, 132, 224

Moral boundary crises: defined, 15; sexual social movements as, 216, 218

"Moral career" concept, 208, 245n.11

Moral conservatism: economic conservatism and, 67, 234n.8; medicalization of social control and, 70–72; view of contraception as "protection of the guilty," 239n.2

Moral conversion, role of, sexual social control, 105–6, 111–12, 211–12

Morality: adolescent sexuality and, 5, 9, 48–50, 63–64, 81–84; labor-force participation by women and, 88–89; sexual revolution and, 34; status politics of, 220

"Moral panic," sexual social movements and, 15–16, 119

Morrow, Prince, 129, 139

Motherhood: denigration of, in contemporary management strategies, 158–59; redemptive benefits of, 112–13

Mothers: adolescent sexuality and, 83–84, 110; daughter's decision-making patterns and, 193–99, 247nn.12, 14

Mott, Frank L., 154

Mottl, Tahi L., 63
Moyers, Bill, 234n.9
Moynihan, Daniel P., 65–68
Murray, Charles, 66, 67

National Academy of Sciences, 149–50, 160, 164
National Association of Evangelicals, 61, 168
National Committee for Adoption, 30
National Council on Illegitimacy, 240n.6
National Fertility Surveys, 51–52
National Florence Crittenton Mission, 103–4; changing philosophies of, 113–14; occupational therapy program, 113; origins of, 106–7, 239n.6; psychogenic theories of adolescent sexuality and, 108; regeneration and reformation principles of, 112; selection criteria of, 117–18; sexual segregation principles of, 110
National Governor's Association, 147–48, 151
National Institute of Child Health and Development, Center for Population Research, 53
National Institutes of Health, 51
National Survey of Family Growth, 229nn.5, 10
Negro Family, The, 34
Nelson, Gaylord (Sen.), 55
New Conscience and an Ancient Evil, A, 124, 130–31
New Right, historical impetus for, 59–60
New York City Health Department, 241n.16
New York County Medical Society, 139
New York Female Moral Reform Society, 121
New York Governor's Task Force on Adolescent Pregnancy, 158
New York Times, 46–48, 115, 128
Nineteenth Amendment, 136
Nixon, Richard, 31, 229n.7; family planning programs and, 23, 53–54; rejection of birth control services policies, 52
Nonmarital births: abortion rates and, 60; birth control services and, 44; as child welfare concern, 103; cultural and psychic causes of, 240n.10; increases in, 27, 29–30; sexual revolution and, 34; social agency

proliferation and, 113–14, 241n.16; welfare costs and, 34–36
Norton, Eleanor Holmes, 234n.9
Nurses: clinic role of, 172–76; as educator and counselor, 173–74; management of birth control services by, 167–77, 197–202

Occupational attainment, management of adolescent pregnancy and, 156–59
Office of Adolescent Pregnancy Programs, 148, 162, 164
Office of Economic Opportunity, 54
Older women, family planning services for, 55–56
Oral contraception: client-provider interaction and, 174–76; compliance with, 171; education about, 170–71; hazards of, 55–56; health versus protection conflicts and, 189–90, 246–47n.7, 247nn.8–9; long-term effects of, 182–85; medical control of, 37–41, 167–77; method-related problems with, 186–87; patient compliance patterns and, 182–85; protection and love conflicts around, 191; relationship changes and, 187–88, 191; risk of pregnancy and, 182–85, 203–4
Orr, Margaret Terry, 154
Ownership issues: in adolescent pregnancy, 69–70; responsibility attributions, 11–12; role of state in, 145–47

Paradigm of deviance designation, 171
Parental responsibility: for adolescent sexuality, 100, 104–5; contraceptive behavior and, 193–96; notification policies and, 62; oral contraceptive use and, 188
Passionlessness, ideology of, 80–84, 90–91, 127, 235nn.3, 6, 242n.12
Passivity, desirability of, for adolescent females, 98–99, 238n.25
Patriarchal norms, female adolescent sexuality as violation of, 63, 70, 208, 218
Peer pressures on adolescent girls, 96–98

Peiss, Kathy, 236n.10

Pelvic examinations, as requirement for contraceptive prescription, 241n.14

Petchesky, Rosalind P., 41, 221, 230n.14

Petting, 97–98, 100–101

Philadelphia Refuge, 104

Philanthropist, The, 242n.6

Philanthropy, management of female delinquency through, 103

Pilpel, Harriet F., 48

Pittmann, Karen J., 154

Pivar, David J., 121–22, 134

Piven, Frances Fox, 34

Planned Parenthood Federation of America (PPFA): birth control services and, 39–42, 230n.23, 231n.32; Center for Family Planning Program Development, 52; clinics operated by, 246n.2; as target of conservative right, 63–64

Planned Parenthood of New York, 46

Political activities: of business elites, 136–38; family planning programs and, 53–58; ownership issues, 11–12, 61–62; sexual social movements and, 129–40

Politicization of women's adolescence, 69, 210, 222

Politics and Morality of Deviance, The, 228n.10

Population: medicalization of birth control and, 37–41; ratio of youth to adults in, 26, 76, 84–91; single women as proportion of total, 128–29

Population and the American Future, 23

Population Commission, 31, 229n.7

"Population panic," and birth control movement, 54–55, 232n.6

Poverty: adolescent pregnancy and, 48–50; family planning services and, 39–44, 55–58, 231n.28; female-headed households and, 67–68

Poverty and sexual and reproductive management strategies. *See* Management strategies, sexual and reproductive; Social class

"Poverty family planning" campaign of birth control advocates, 42–43, 54–56, 231n.30

Powell, Aaron, 242n.8

Power, contraceptive behavior and, 192–93

Premarital sexual activity: historical context of concern about, 75; "sexual revolution" and, 32–34, 229n.10; terminology for, 230n.16

Presidential Commission on Campus Unrest, 229n.11

President's Commission on Population Growth and the American Future, 23. *See also* Population Commission

Preventive solutions. *See* Birth control services

Princeton University Office of Population Research, 51

Private behavior, control over, 68–72, 178–82

Problem definition: models of sexual and reproductive control and, 146–47; role of knowledge in, 31–32, 58, 229n.6; social class and, 35

Professionalization: of sexual and reproductive control, 14, 113–16, 171; of sexual social movements, 126, 140

Progressive Era: management of sexually unorthodox girls during, 105–6, 239n.4; "repeal of reticence" in, 90–91; sexual social movements and, 121; vice crusades of, 136–38; white slave trade issue and, 124–25; women's movements in, 135

Project Redirection, 152–53, 156, 245nn.10, 15

Prostitution: business elites' crusade against, 136; frequency of, 128–29; labor-force participation by women and concern about, 89–91, 128–29, 236n.10, 243n.18; physician's role in regulation of, 140; Progressive Era campaigns against, 90–91; regulation of, by state, 13–14, 120, 122–26, 132–34; as women's issue, 135

Protective strategies for management of women's adolescence, 104–5, 123, 239n.2

Protestant revival movement, 121–22

Psychiatric approach to unorthodox sexuality, 107–8, 117–18

Public clinics, Progressive Era opposition to, 133–34, 243n.17

Public policy-making: adolescent pregnancy as public problem and, 3–4; birth control services and, 39–41, 230n.23; legitimation of chastity and, 155–56; poor women and, 42–44; welfare construction of adolescent pregnancy and, 156–59

Public problem: adolescent pregnancy as, 31–32, 46–50, 58, 218; adolescent sexuality as, 76; private behavior recognized by state as, 109

Public problems: construction of, 49–50; structure of, 11–12, 24

Punitive solutions, to adolescent pregnancy, 35–36

Puritans, 75

Purity, imagery of, 78–84, 235n.4

Raab, Earl, 60

Race: births to single women and, 27–30; causal models of single parenthood and, 245n.17; eugenic implications of birth control and, 55–56; historical data and, 77–78; management strategies and, 23, 39, 53–54, 89, 160–63, 241n.18, 245nn. 12, 14–15; population data by, 85–88; reformers and, 40, 53, 68, 213; sexual behavior and, 229n.13, 245n.13; structure of women's adolescence and, 86–88, 166

Racial crises of 1960s, 60

Rains, Prudence Mors, 112

"Rating and dating complex," 91, 97–98, 236n.14

Readers' Guide, 126

Reagan, Ronald, 168; conservative right and, 61; "deviance" of adolescent sexuality and, 173; management strategies for adolescent pregnancy and, 150–51

Reckless, Walter, 128

Reed, James, 36

Reed, Ruth, 241n.16

Rehabilitative solutions, to adolescent pregnancy, 35–36

Reiss, Ira L., 32

Relationship quality and contraceptive use, 187–88, 191, 196–98, 201–2, 247nn.11–14

Reproduction: government role in, 39–44; medical model of, 232n.34; women defined by role in, 8–9; women's control of, 59, 130, 235n.6; women's strategies for management of, 55–56, 239n.1

Reproduction, women's role in: conflict with education and work, 94–96, 156–59, 208–9, 221–22; feminist attitudes toward, 221–22; redemptive value of, 113; "sexual revolution" (1960s) and, 33–34; as source of power for adolescent women, 192–93; women's sexuality in conflict with, 9, 81–82

Reproductive health services, lobbying activities for, 163, 245n.16

Research methodology: of book, 19; changes in adolescent sexuality and, 236n.15, 237n.16, 238n.26; institutional management of female delinquency, 239n.1; private behavior and personal control issues, 178–82, 246nn.2–5; sampling techniques, 179–82

Resource mobilization, by social movements, 16

Responsibility, attributions of: adolescent pregnancy and, 11–12, 61–62, 147; causal models of sexual and reproductive behavior and, 164–66, 174–77; family planning clinic policies and, 170–76; of girls versus boys, 240n.8; management strategies and, 75, 82, 98, 106–8, 125–26, 151–52, 192–93, 211–12

Revolt of Modern Youth, The, 240n.8

Richards, Janet Radcliffe, 177

Risk of pregnancy: contraceptive behavior and decision-making patterns, 182–85; environmental factors in, 105, 239n.3

Rockefeller, John D., 137, 244n.25

Romanticization of adolescent sexuality, 93–94, 238n.28

Roosevelt, Theodore, 137–38

Rosenberg, Charles F., 79

Rosenberg, Rosalind, 90

Rosoff, Jeannie I., 52

Rossi, Alice S., 99, 238n.25

Rothman, David J., 223
Rothman, Ellen, 83
Rousseau, Jean-Jacques, 235n.2
Ryder, Norman B., 26

St. Leger Eberle, Abastensia, 125
Salvarsan, 133–34
Salvation Army "Rescue Home for Fallen and
  Homeless Girls," 103
Sanger, Margaret, 41, 173
Scanzoni, John, 179
Schlossman, Steven L., 105, 113
Schneider, Joseph W., 13, 171
Schools: attendance, as management strategy,
  95, 237n.21; clinics based in, 146–47,
  244n.1; programs for pregnant adolescents
  in, 152; segregation of pregnant students
  in, 162
Scientific management of sexuality, 149–51,
  219–20
Scientific theories, of sexuality, 107–8
Scull, Andrew T., 12
Seagrave, Mabel, 116
Search for an Abortionist, The, 227n.3
Senate (U.S.), 60, 233n.3
Sex and the College Student, 33, 35
Sex education, 100–101, 154–56; abstinence
  as theme of, 155–56; physician participation
  in, 105, 138–39, 239n.5, 243n.22
"Sex Respect" curriculum, 155
Sexual Behavior in the Human Male, 229n.8
Sexuality: beliefs about women's, 12, 90–91,
  99, 104, 107–8; domestication of women's
  (1920–1960), 91–102, 132; of unmarried
  women, as symbol of social disorder or
  social change, 14–16, 70, 91–92, 97–99,
  131, 214–16, 223–24; women's control of,
  as source of power, 130, 235n.6; women's
  public assertion of, 92–96. *See also* Adolescent sexuality; Ideology of the innocent
  girl; Unorthodox sexuality
Sexual opportunity structure, change in,
  93, 97
"Sexual revolution": cyclical pattern in per-

ception of, 229n.12; impact of, on perception of sexuality, 32–34; psychological
  consequences of, 33–34
Sexual segregation, as management strategy,
  110
Sexual social control, 3–19; birth control services and, 36–39, 62–63; business elites'
  role in, 136–38; conceptions of adolescent
  sexuality and, 93–94; defined, 10; depoliticization of, 93–94; deterministic implications
  of, 18; increased pervasiveness of, 13–14;
  medical profession and, 70–72, 138–40,
  243n.22; as public policy issue, 10–18, 126–
  41, 207–24; rise and decline of, 119–26;
  role of women, 134–36; social change and,
  207–24
Sexual social movement constituents, 220;
  adolescent women as, 5, 245n.16, 248n.6
Sexual social movements, 10, 14–15; conditions for, 15–16, 126–41, 217–20; turn-of-
  the-century, 119–41
Sexual status, loss of, with nonmarital pregnancy, 104–5
Sexual symbols as political resource, 16–18,
  39–45, 70, 134–40, 148, 218–20
Sherman Antitrust Act, 137
Sims, James Marion, 243n.24
Single women: age 15–24, as proportion of
  adult population, 26–27, 84–86, 127–28,
  217; birth rate increases to, 27–30, 50–51;
  inclusion of, in government population surveys, 84–85, 229n.5; "single young woman"
  as life-course stage, 236n.13
Social change, sexuality and, 89–90, 129–34,
  207, 224
Social class: courtship behavior and, 83;
  domestic ideology and, 159; history of
  female adolescence and, 77–78; interests
  served by moral reform and, 127, 135,
  242n.12; reformers and, 40, 53, 58, 92,
  128, 129–30, 134–36, 165–66, 213, 220,
  221; sexual and reproductive management
  strategies and, 23, 37, 38–39, 42–43, 53–
  54, 131, 160–63, 240n.13, 241n.18, 245nn.12,
  14–15; sexual danger and, 165–66; sexual

Unwed motherhood: contemporary consequences of, 148; welfare costs linked with,
34–36
Urbanization: adolescent sexuality and, 76–78;
sexual social movements and, 127–29
U.S. Children's Bureau, 107–9; actions of, 103;
maternity home monitoring by, 240n.6

"Vanishing Black Family, The," 234n.9
Venereal disease, 123–26; frequency of, 128–
29; government control of prostitution and,
133–34; physicians' campaign against, 139–
40; Progressive Era campaigns against, 90
Verplanck, 78–79
Vice crusades: business elites' participation in,
136–38; political implications of, 129–34,
243n.13
Vincent, Clarke E., 35
Vinovskis, Maris, 57
Visibility, of adolescents' pregnancies and
births, 35, 60, 176; of adolescent women as
a social category, 12, 26, 69, 84–88, 216–17,
236n.9; of adolescent women's sexuality,
33, 62, 81, 106, 117–18, 211–13, 230n.14;
of programs for pregnant and parenting
students, 163; social control and, 247n.4;
women's management of sexuality and,
93, 101

Wagner, Roland Richard, 136
Wallach, Stephanie, 105, 113
Waller, Willard, 97–98
Wall Street Journal, 160
War on Poverty: birth control services, 41–42,
231n.28; family planning programs and, 53
"Wayward" girls: adolescent sexuality and,
80–84; parental relations with, 109, 240n.11;
rescue workers' management of, 103
Wayward Minor Court of New York, 110,
114–15, 240n.11
Wayward Puritans, 17
Weatherley, Richard A., 153, 162

Webster School Project, 245n.14
Wechsler, Nancy F., 48
Weeks, Jeffrey, 7, 58
Welfare: adolescent pregnancy linked with,
65–68, 156–59; breakdown of black family
and, 65–68; unwed motherhood and, 34–
36, 234n.7; work requirements linked with,
158–59
"Welfare Mess: A Scandal of Illegitimacy and
Desertion, The," 34
Wertheimer, Richard F., 159
What Shall We Do with Our Daughters? 84
White, Theodore, 26
White adolescents. *See* Ethnicity; Race;
Social class
White Slave, The (sculpture), 125
White slave trade, 123–26, 242n.11
White Slave Traffic Act, 120, 124–26
Wicker, Tom, 229n.11
Wiebe, Robert, 129
Willard, Frances, 122, 134, 242n.8
Wilson, Otto, 239n.6
Wilson, William Julius, 65–68
Women: autonomy of: 59; organization and
politicization of, 134–36; reproductive func-
tion as essence of, 8–9; role of, in sexual
social control, 213–14
Women, sexual autonomy of, 18, 39, 91–92,
96, 98–99, 102, 208, 212, 240n.11; abortion
and, 233n.2; age-of-consent legislation and,
123; birth control movement and, 40–41;
feminists and, 221–22; government and, 68,
233n.1; as "original sin," 106, 109; sexual
social movements (turn-of-the-century)
and, 130–31, 241n.1; White Slave Traffic Act
and, 126
Women, sexual bargaining power of, 235n.6,
238n.23
Women, transition to adulthood: beliefs
about, 157–58, 166, 208; dangers of, 81–82,
207–9, 236n.13; patterns of, 132, 148, 165;
venue for, 95
Women's adult roles, conceptions of: contemporary uncertainty about, 147; management
of adolescence and, 83–84, 96–97, 109,

Women's adult roles (*cont.*)
112–13, 115, 156–59; sexuality in adolescence and, 208
Women's Christian Temperance Union
(WCTU), 122, 134–35, 139
Women's Rights movement, 135
Wootton, Barbara, 41
"Working Girls of Boston, The," 88
Wright, Carroll D., 88

Wunsch, James, 125–26, 136

Youth and Sex, 101

Zald, Mayer N., 130
Zellman, Gail L., 162
Zelnik, Melvin, 51